Waiting for Spring 7

Anashin

Waiting
for Spring
vol.7

Presented by
Anashin

CONTENTS

WAITING FOR SPRING
Harumatsu Bokura

Character & Story

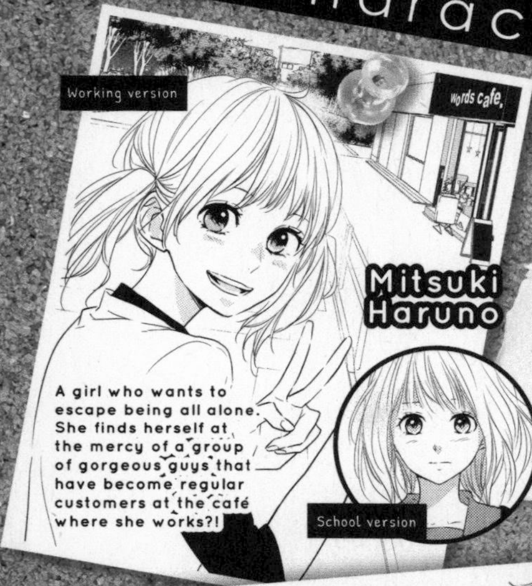

words cafe.

Working version

Mitsuki Haruno

A girl who wants to escape being all alone. She finds herself at the mercy of a group of gorgeous guys that have become regular customers at the café where she works?!

School version

To be like her role model Aya-chan, Mitsuki is determined to make some real friends in high school. One day, the school celebrities—the Elite Four Hotties of the basketball team—appear at the café where she works! Before she knows it, Mitsuki gets caught up in their silly hijinks, but as she gets to know the four of them, she manages to make new friends, and begins to crush hard on her classmate Towa. When she goes to a practice game, she is reunited with Aya-chan and is stunned to learn that her childhood best friend was actually a boy! What's more, he really wants to date her! Over their first summer break, Towa realizes how he feels about Mitsuki... When the second term begins, Mitsuki agrees to be a part of the school festival committee. She does the best she can, but she pushes herself too hard and faints...

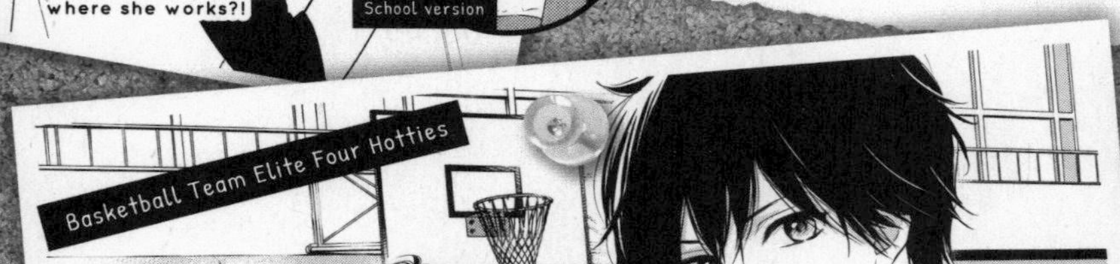

Basketball Team Elite Four Hotties

Ryūji Tada

A second-year. Comes off as a bad boy but is rather naïve. He's crushing on the Boss's daughter Nanase-san.

Kyōsuke Wakamiya

A second-year in high school. Mysterious and always cool-headed, he's like a big brother to everyone.

Rui Miyamoto

A first-year in high school. His innocent smile is adorable, but it hides a wicked heart?!

Towa Asakura

Mitsuki's classmate. He's quiet and a bit spacey, but he's always there to help her.

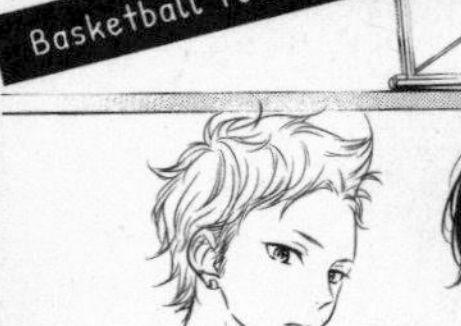

Aya-chan

Mitsuki's best friend from elementary school. When they finally meet again, she discovers he was a boy!

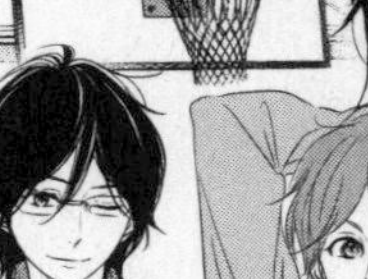

Reina Yamada

Mitsuki's first friend from her class. She has somewhat eccentric tastes?!

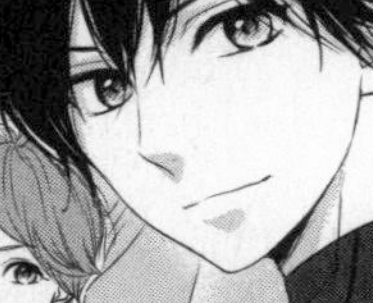

Maki-chan

A first-year on the girls' basketball team who gets along with Mitsuki. Apparently she has a crush on Towa?!

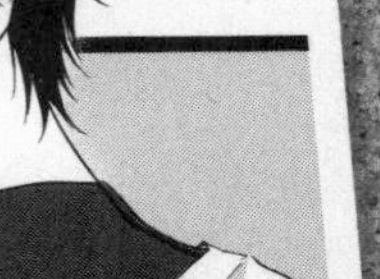

Nana-san

The Boss's daughter. Straightforward and resolute, she is a reliable, big-sister type.

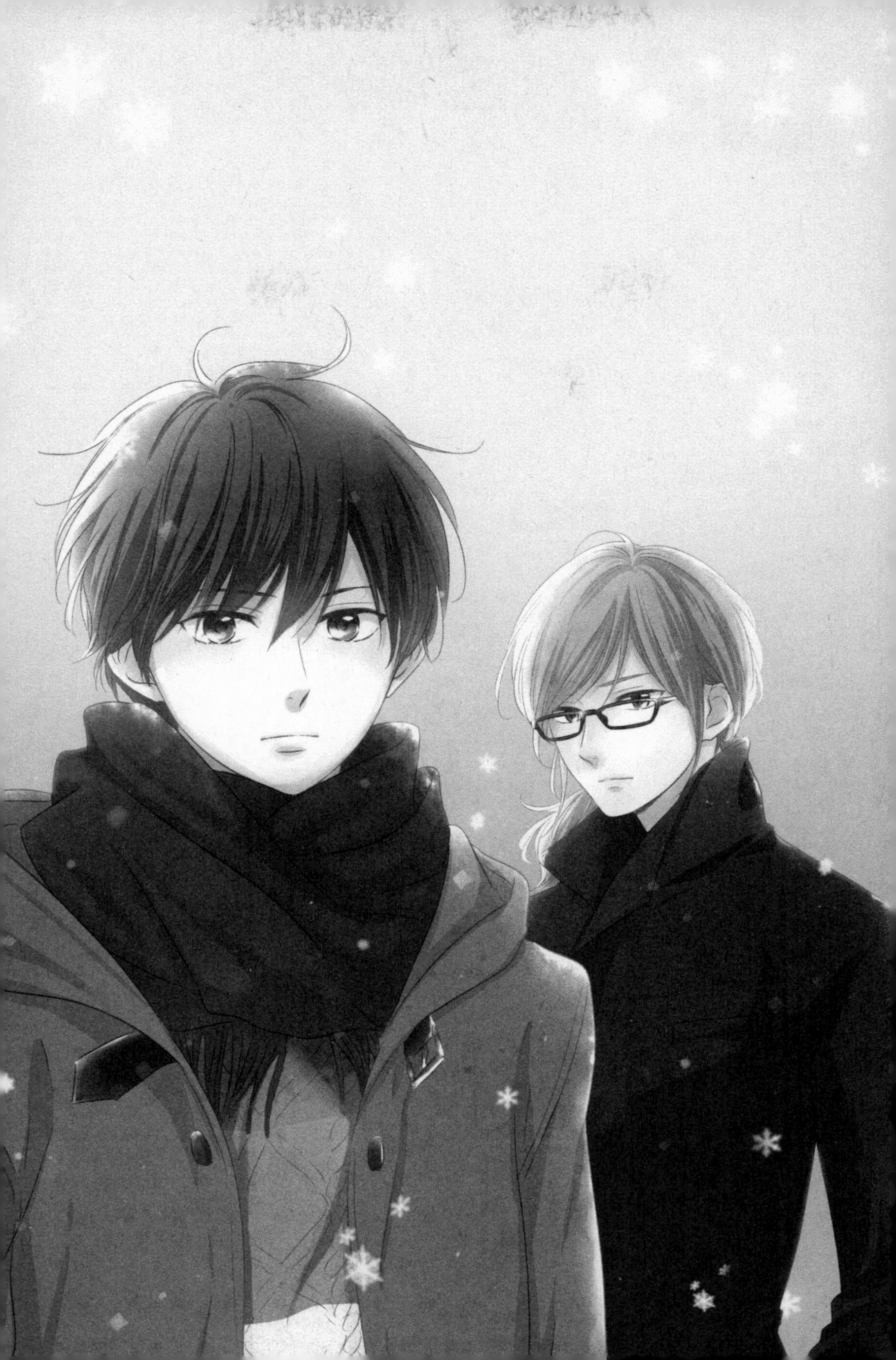

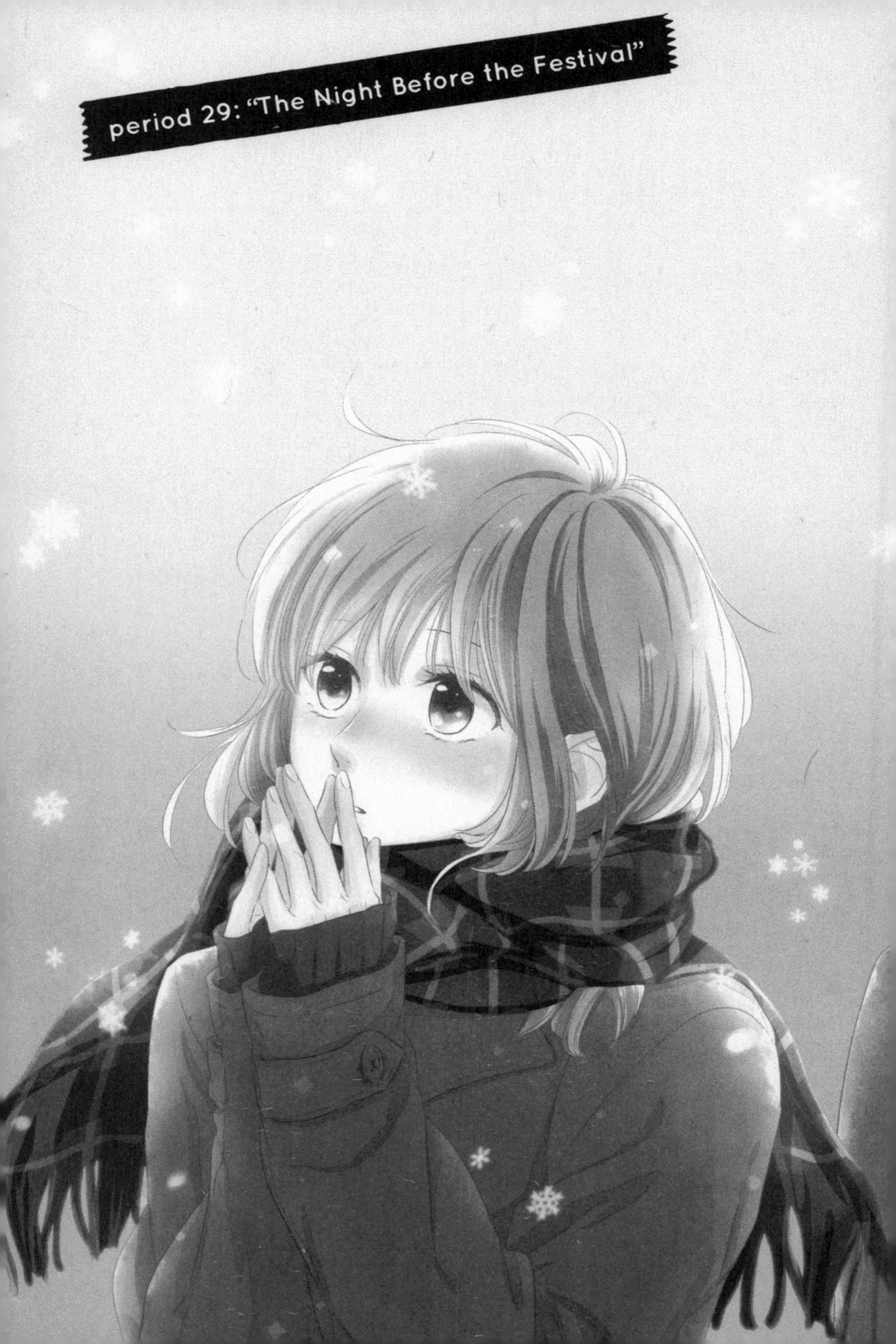
period 29: "The Night Before the Festival"

Hello! Anashin here.

Thank you so much for picking up Volume 6!

From this volume on, I'm going to have two people on the cover, and I kind of figured I could keep pushing myself with a fresh new perspective.

Based on the order last time, the next one will probably be
Rui & Mitsuki...

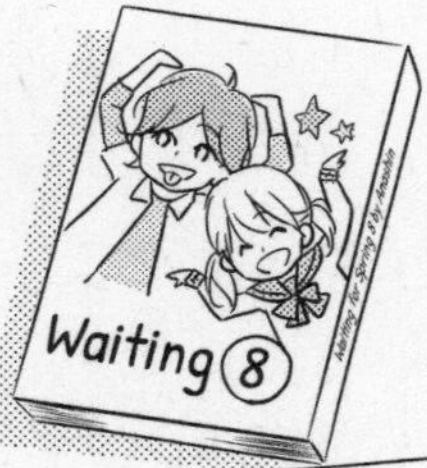
Waiting 8

But it could also be
Aya & Mitsuki...

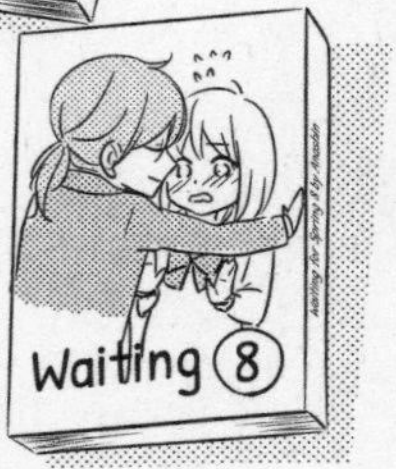
Waiting 8

Or maybe I'll fake you all out with
Reina & Mitsuki?!

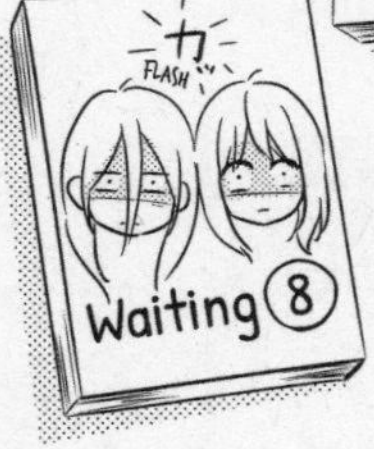
FLASH
Waiting 8

What will it be? (ha ha)

I hope you look forward to Volume 8, too!

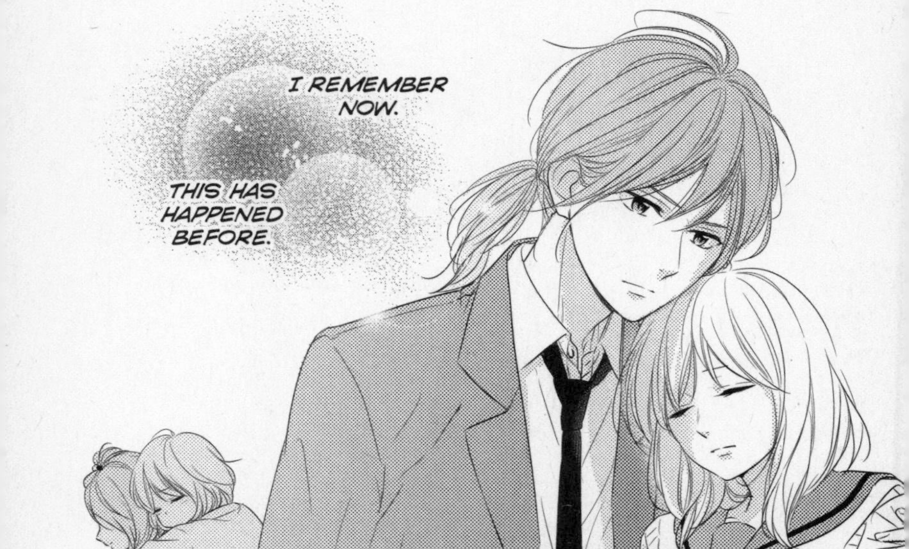
I REMEMBER NOW.
THIS HAS HAPPENED BEFORE.

I thought I'd start using these spaces to write more in depth about each of the characters. ...Little behind-the-scenes tidbits, family information, etc. I'll go in order of what I can talk about the most without disrupting the main story.

☆ In this volume, I'll talk about these two →

I refuse to give up on the Silhouette Pop Quiz (ha ha)

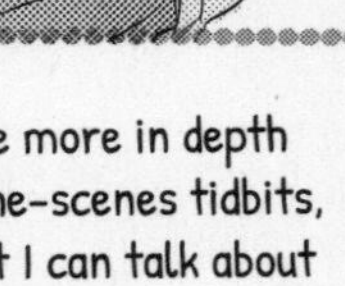

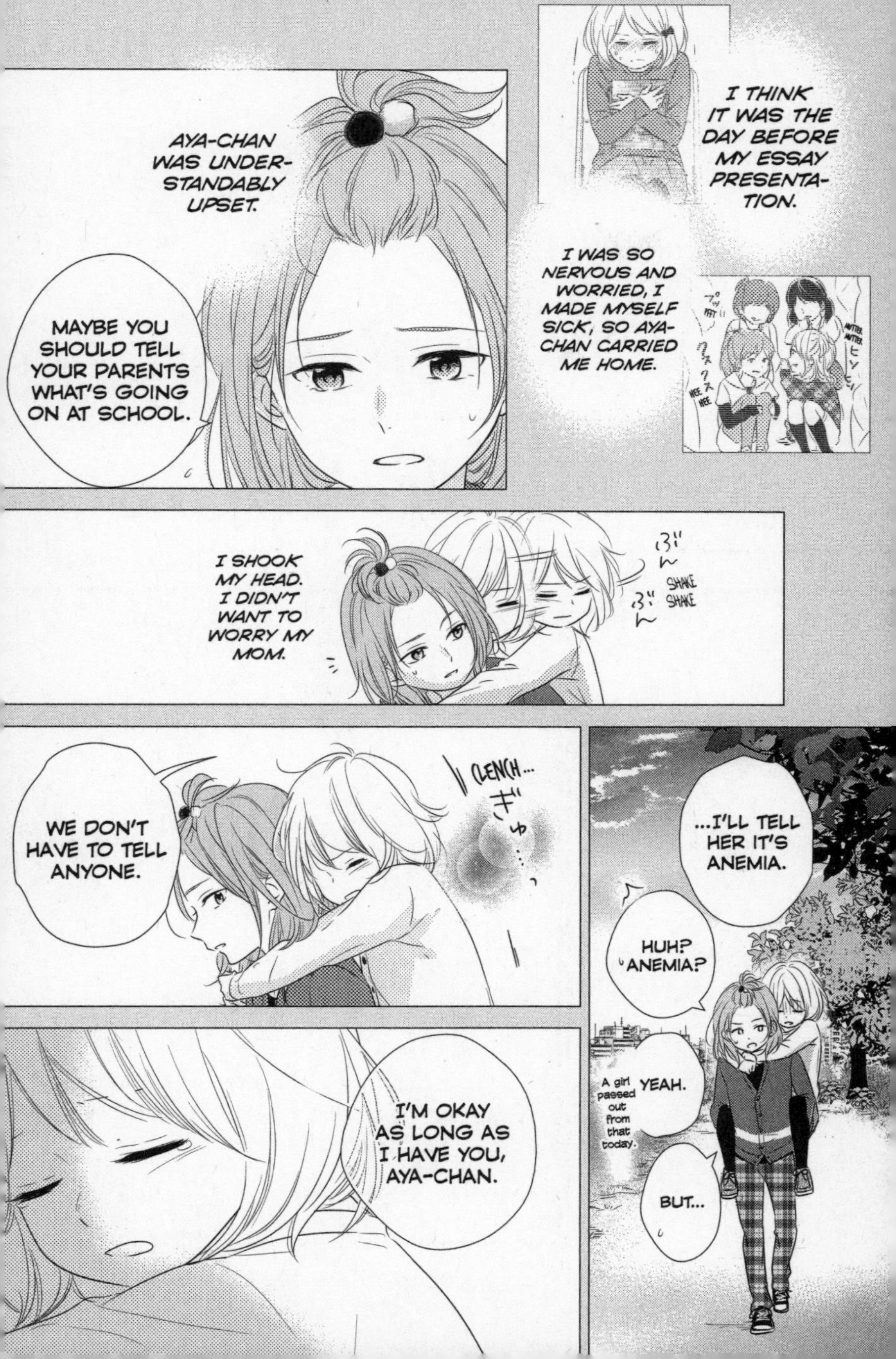
I THINK IT WAS THE DAY BEFORE MY ESSAY PRESENTATION.
I WAS SO NERVOUS AND WORRIED, I MADE MYSELF SICK, SO AYA-CHAN CARRIED ME HOME.
PFFT
MUTTER MUTTER
HEE HEE
AYA-CHAN WAS UNDERSTANDABLY UPSET.
MAYBE YOU SHOULD TELL YOUR PARENTS WHAT'S GOING ON AT SCHOOL.
SHAKE SHAKE
I SHOOK MY HEAD. I DIDN'T WANT TO WORRY MY MOM.
...I'LL TELL HER IT'S ANEMIA.
HUH? ANEMIA?
YEAH.
A girl passed out from that today.
BUT...
CLENCH...
WE DON'T HAVE TO TELL ANYONE.
I'M OKAY AS LONG AS I HAVE YOU, AYA-CHAN.

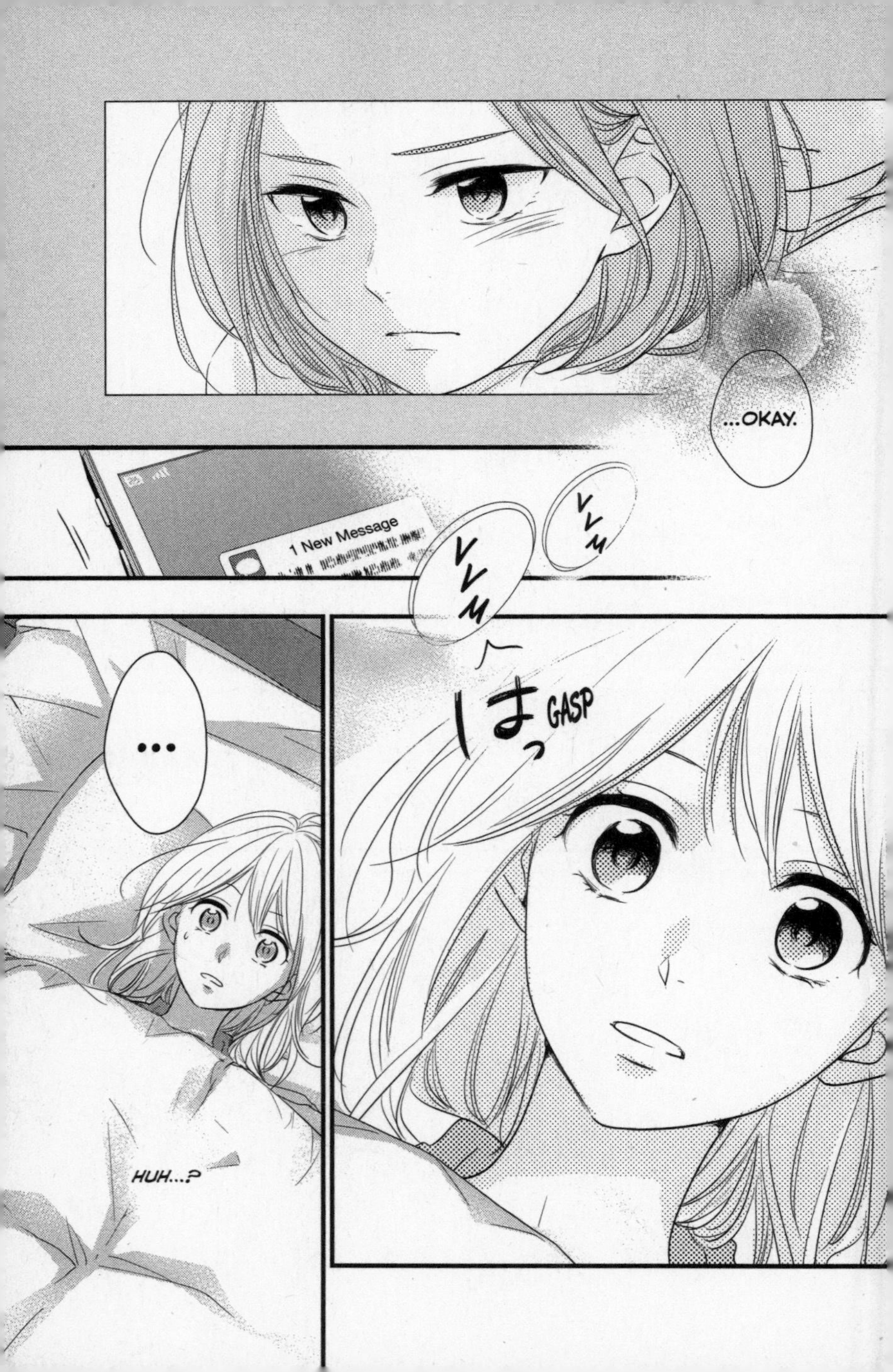
...OKAY.
VVM
VVVM
1 New Message
はっ GASP
...
HUH...?

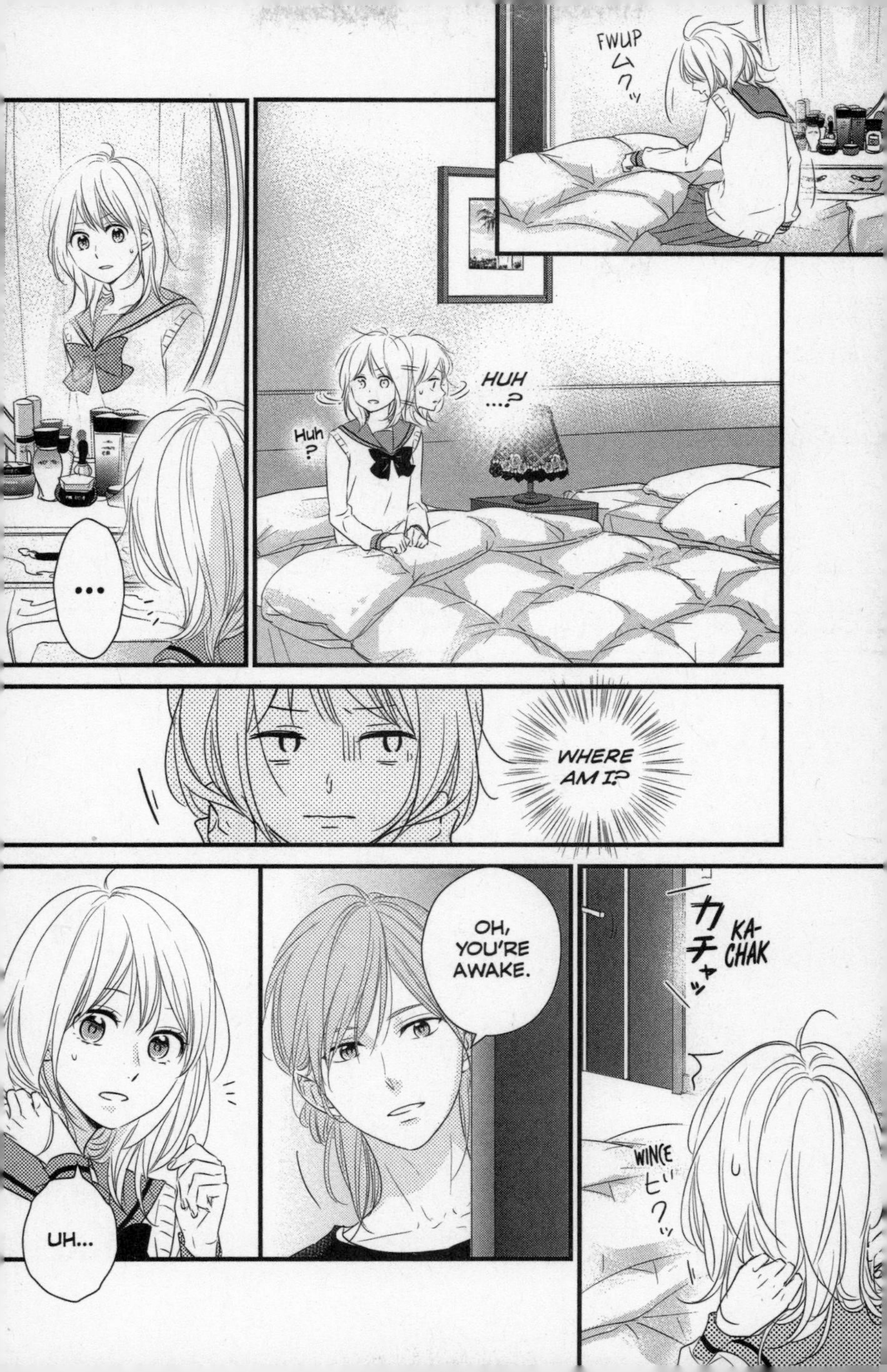
FWUP
ムクッ
HUH ...?
Huh ?
...
WHERE AM I?
KA-CHAK
カチャッ
WINCE
ビクッ
OH, YOU'RE AWAKE.
UH...

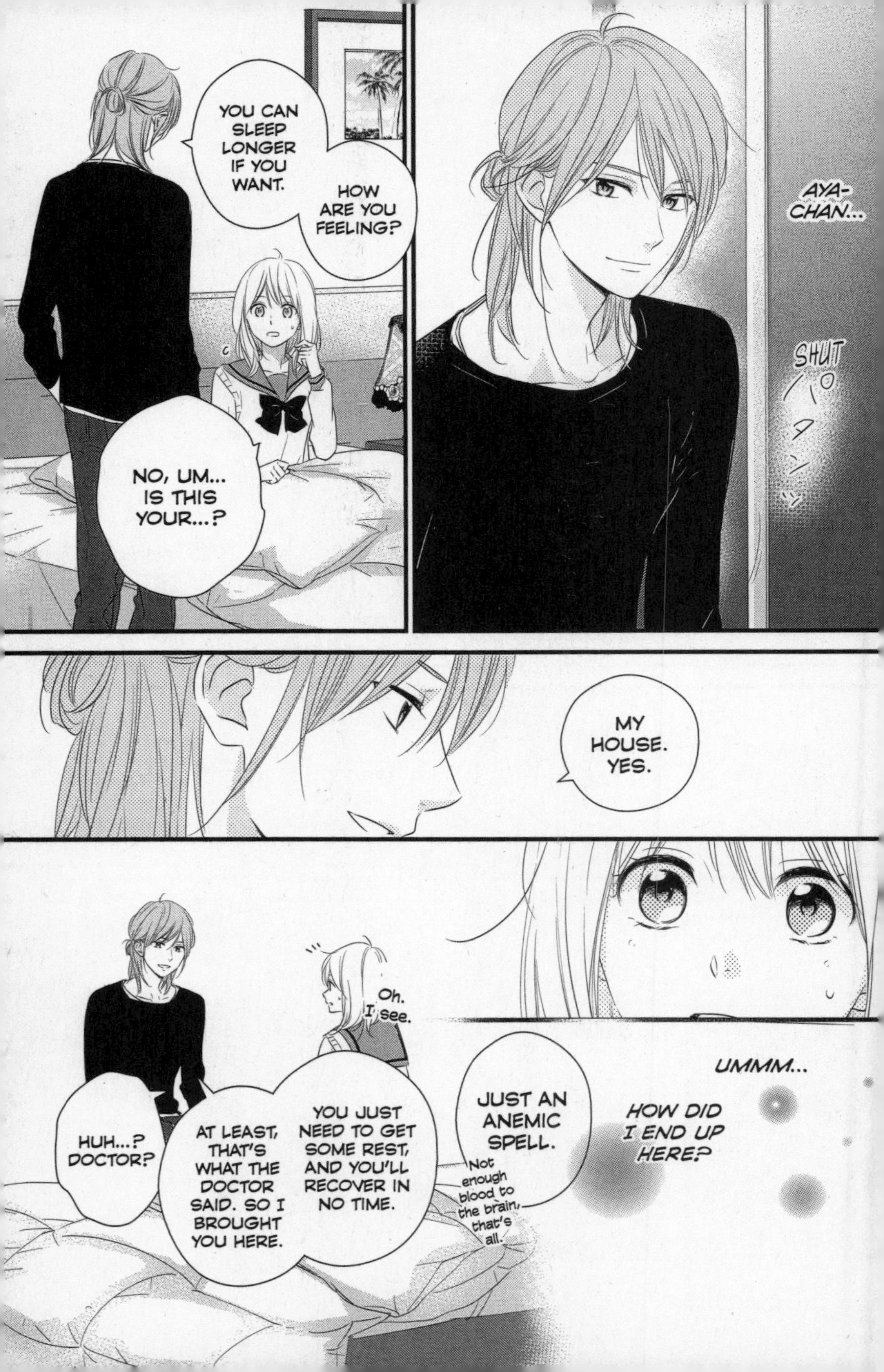
AYA-CHAN...
SHUT パタン
YOU CAN SLEEP LONGER IF YOU WANT.
HOW ARE YOU FEELING?
NO, UM... IS THIS YOUR...?
MY HOUSE. YES.
UMMM...
HOW DID I END UP HERE?
Oh. I see.
JUST AN ANEMIC SPELL.
Not enough blood to the brain, that's all.
YOU JUST NEED TO GET SOME REST, AND YOU'LL RECOVER IN NO TIME.
AT LEAST, THAT'S WHAT THE DOCTOR SAID. SO I BROUGHT YOU HERE.
HUH...? DOCTOR?

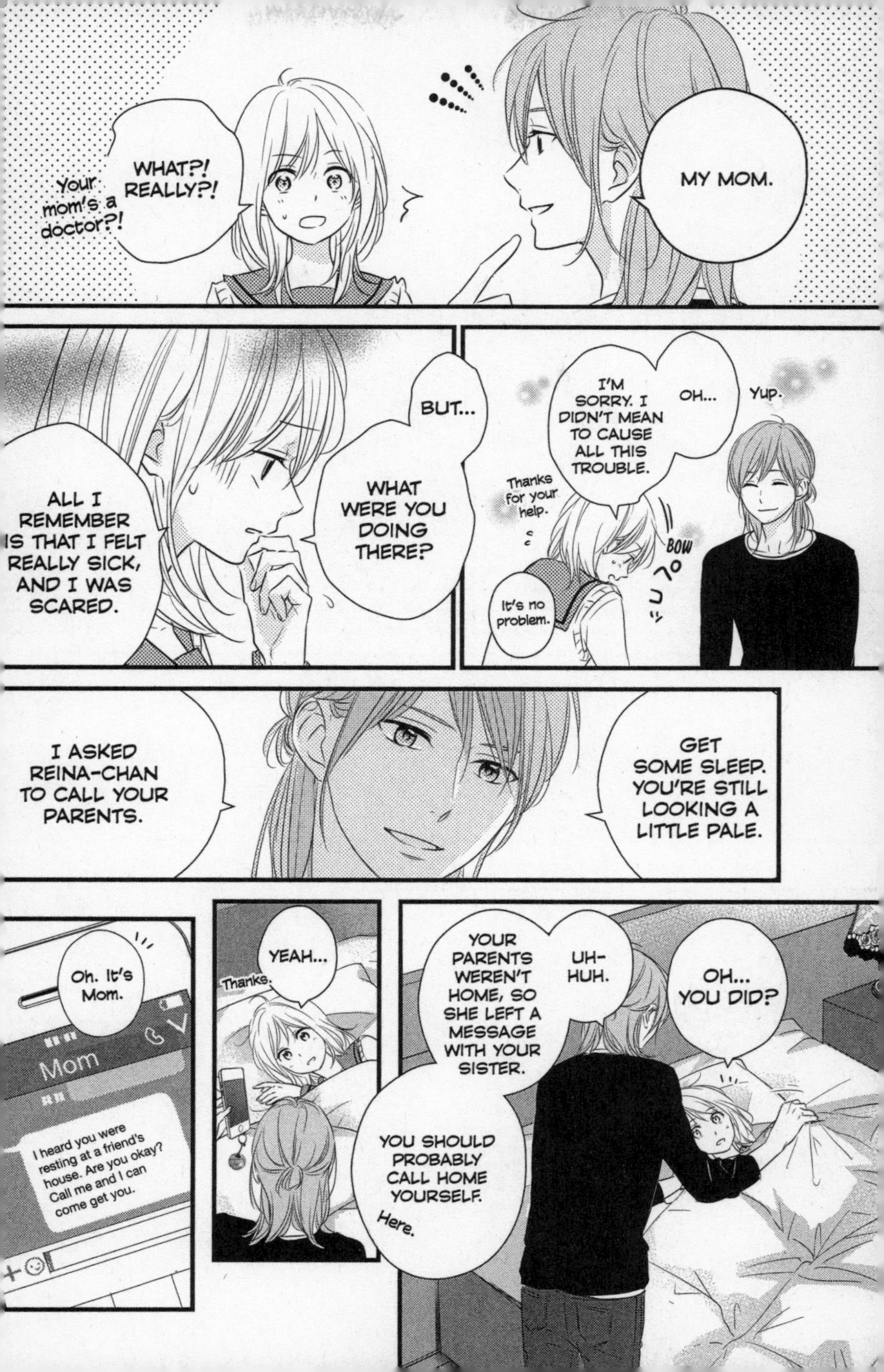
MY MOM.
WHAT?! REALLY?!
Your mom's a doctor?!
Yup.
OH...
I'M SORRY. I DIDN'T MEAN TO CAUSE ALL THIS TROUBLE.
Thanks for your help.
BOW
It's no problem.
BUT...
WHAT WERE YOU DOING THERE?
ALL I REMEMBER IS THAT I FELT REALLY SICK, AND I WAS SCARED.
GET SOME SLEEP. YOU'RE STILL LOOKING A LITTLE PALE.
I ASKED REINA-CHAN TO CALL YOUR PARENTS.
OH... YOU DID?
UH-HUH.
YOUR PARENTS WEREN'T HOME, SO SHE LEFT A MESSAGE WITH YOUR SISTER.
YOU SHOULD PROBABLY CALL HOME YOURSELF.
Here.
YEAH...
Thanks.
Oh. It's Mom.
Mom
I heard you were resting at a friend's house. Are you okay? Call me and I can come get you.

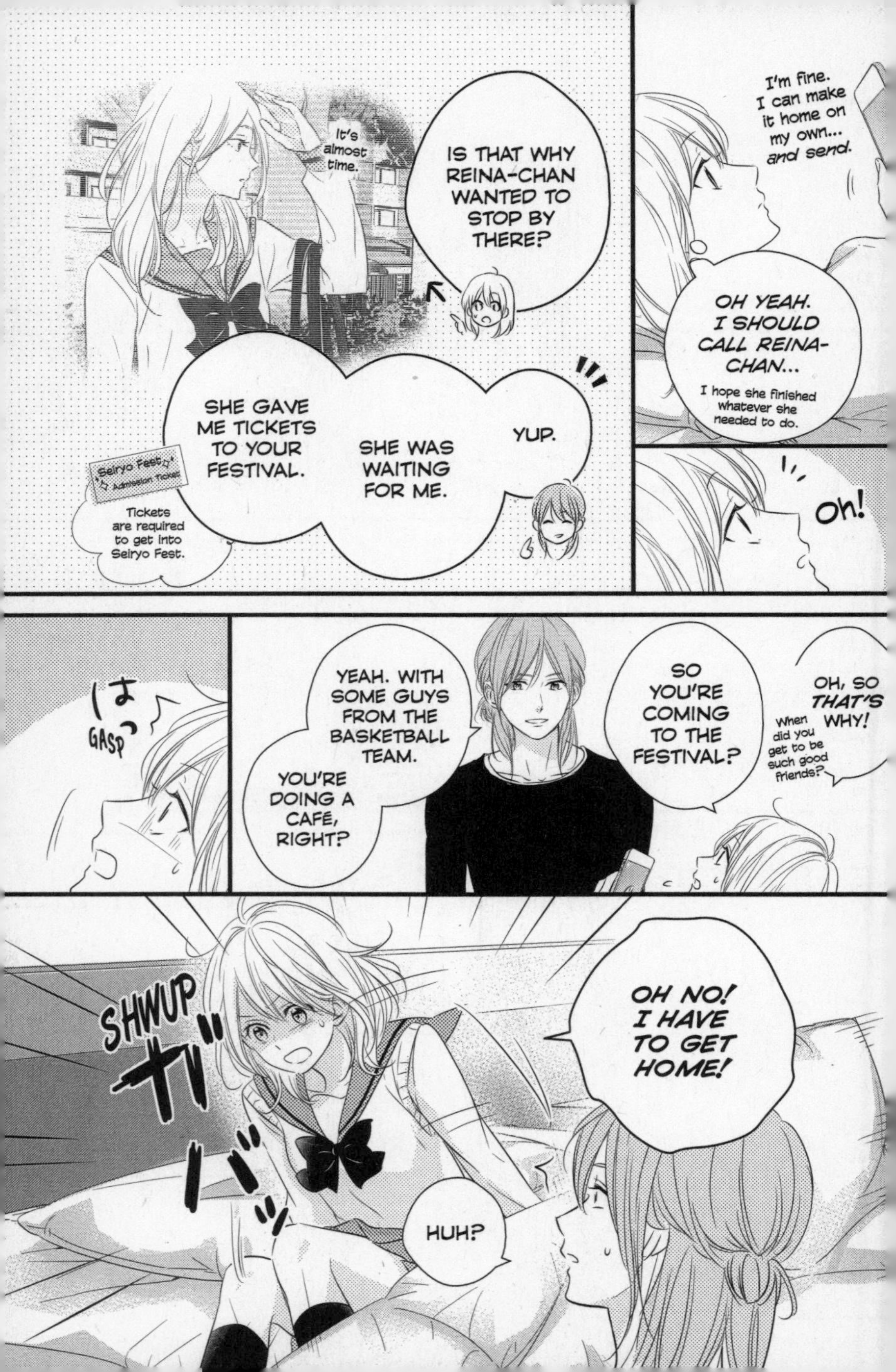
I'm fine. I can make it home on my own... *and send.*
OH YEAH. I SHOULD CALL REINA-CHAN...
I hope she finished whatever she needed to do.
Oh!
IS THAT WHY REINA-CHAN WANTED TO STOP BY THERE?
It's almost time.
YUP.
SHE WAS WAITING FOR ME.
SHE GAVE ME TICKETS TO YOUR FESTIVAL.
Seiryo Fest Admission Ticket
Tickets are required to get into Seiryo Fest.
OH, SO *THAT'S* WHY!
When did you get to be such good friends?
SO YOU'RE COMING TO THE FESTIVAL?
YEAH. WITH SOME GUYS FROM THE BASKETBALL TEAM.
YOU'RE DOING A CAFÉ, RIGHT?
はっ
GASP
OH NO! I HAVE TO GET HOME!
SHWUP
ガバッ
HUH?

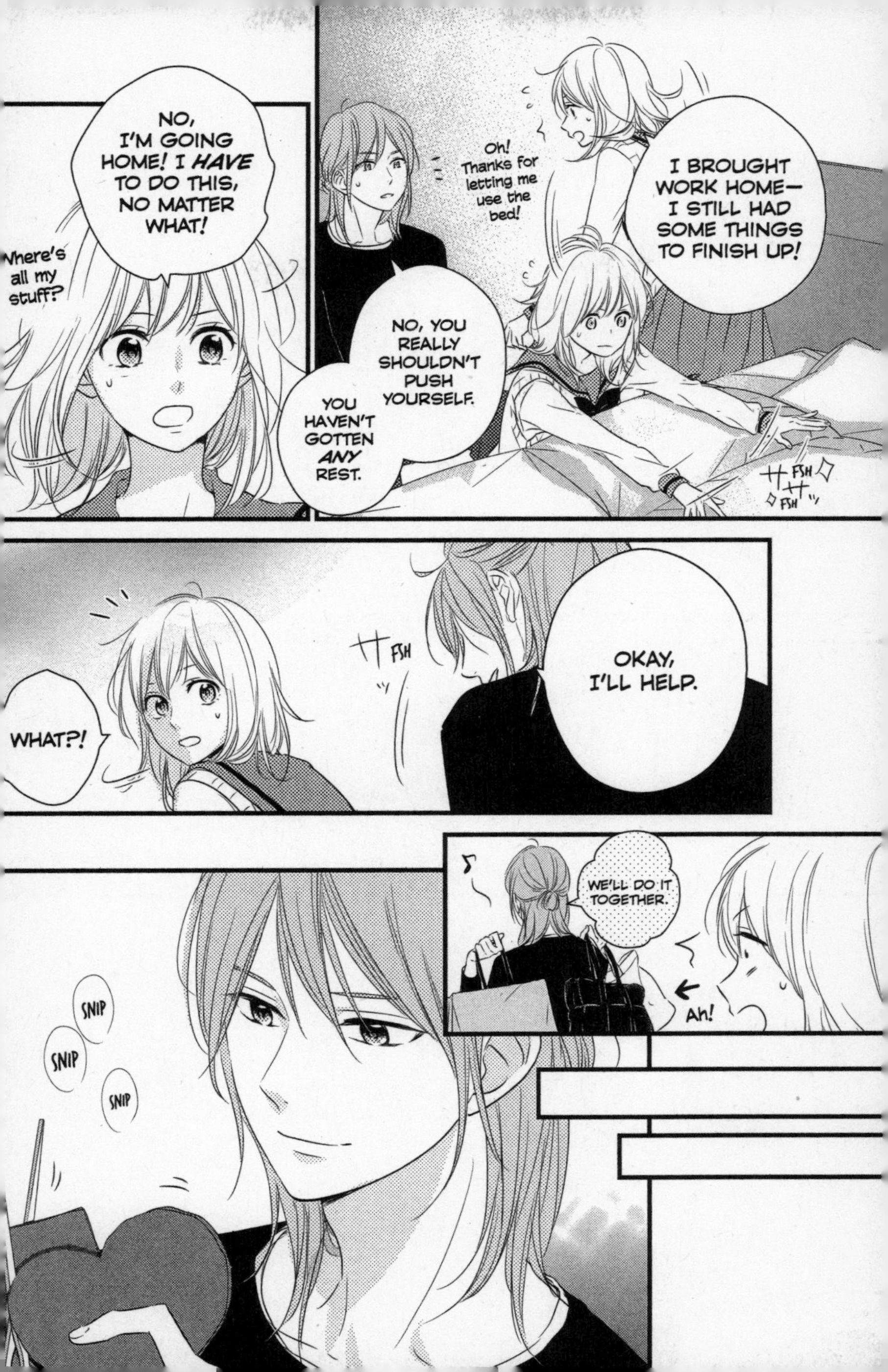

Oh! Thanks for letting me use the bed!
I BROUGHT WORK HOME— I STILL HAD SOME THINGS TO FINISH UP!
NO, YOU REALLY SHOULDN'T PUSH YOURSELF.
YOU HAVEN'T GOTTEN ANY REST.
FSH FSH
NO, I'M GOING HOME! I HAVE TO DO THIS, NO MATTER WHAT!
Where's all my stuff?
OKAY, I'LL HELP.
FSH
WHAT?!
Ah!
WE'LL DO IT TOGETHER.
SNIP
SNIP
SNIP

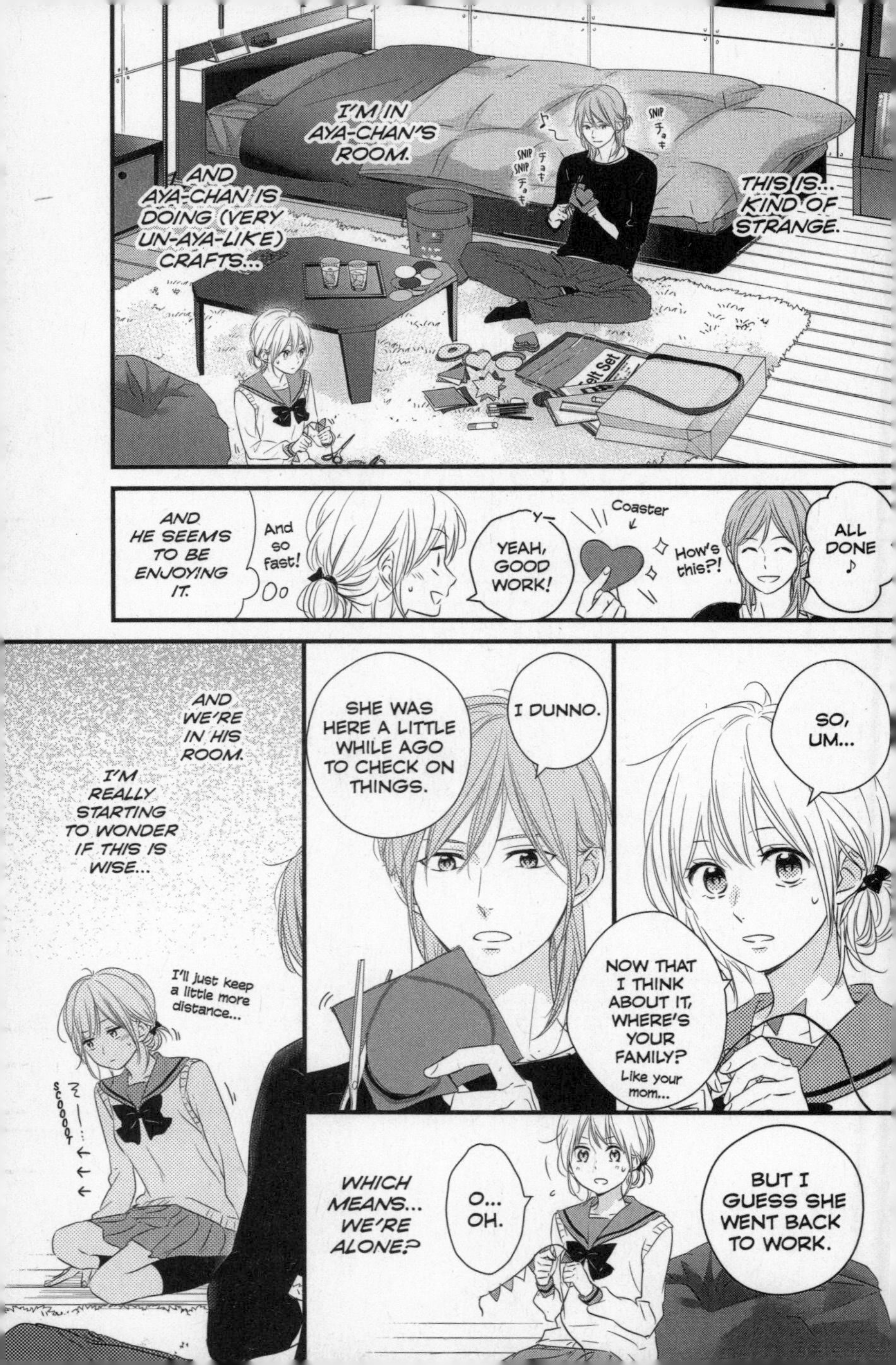
I'M IN AYA-CHAN'S ROOM.
AND AYA-CHAN IS DOING (VERY UN-AYA-LIKE) CRAFTS...
SNIP チョキ
SNIP SNIP チョキ チョキ
THIS IS... KIND OF STRANGE.
ALL DONE ♪
How's this?!
Coaster
YEAH, GOOD WORK!
Y—
And so fast!
AND HE SEEMS TO BE ENJOYING IT.
Oo
SO, UM...
NOW THAT I THINK ABOUT IT, WHERE'S YOUR FAMILY? Like your mom...
I DUNNO.
SHE WAS HERE A LITTLE WHILE AGO TO CHECK ON THINGS.
BUT I GUESS SHE WENT BACK TO WORK.
O... OH.
WHICH MEANS... WE'RE ALONE?
AND WE'RE IN HIS ROOM.
I'M REALLY STARTING TO WONDER IF THIS IS WISE...
I'll just keep a little more distance...
SCOOOOT

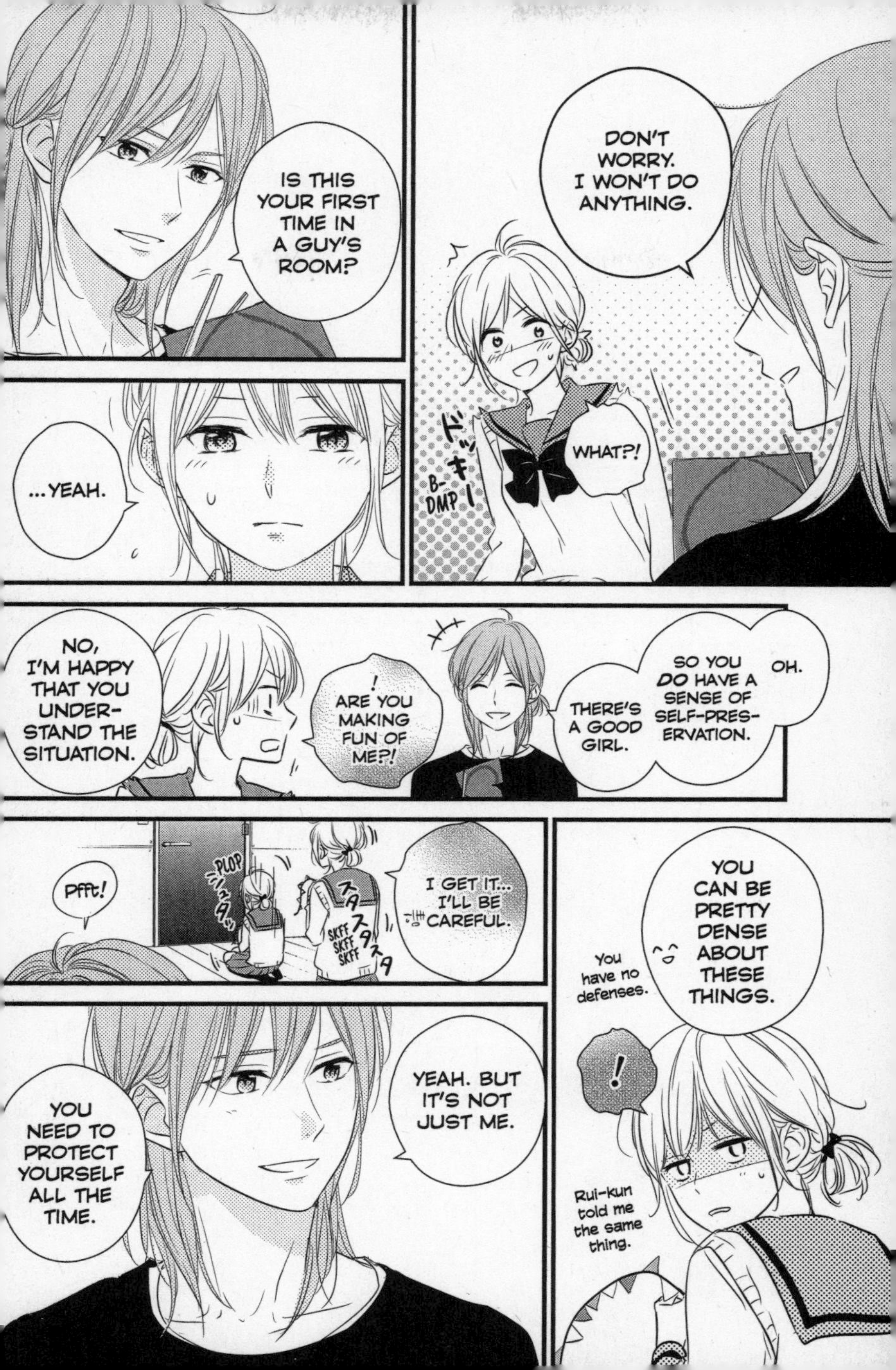
DON'T WORRY. I WON'T DO ANYTHING.
WHAT?!
ドッキー
B-DMP
IS THIS YOUR FIRST TIME IN A GUY'S ROOM?
...YEAH.
OH.
SO YOU DO HAVE A SENSE OF SELF-PRESERVATION.
THERE'S A GOOD GIRL.
! ARE YOU MAKING FUN OF ME?!
NO, I'M HAPPY THAT YOU UNDERSTAND THE SITUATION.
YOU CAN BE PRETTY DENSE ABOUT THESE THINGS.
You have no defenses.
!
Rui-kun told me the same thing.
I GET IT... I'LL BE CAREFUL.
SKFF SKFF SKFF
PLOP
Pfft!
YEAH. BUT IT'S NOT JUST ME.
YOU NEED TO PROTECT YOURSELF ALL THE TIME.

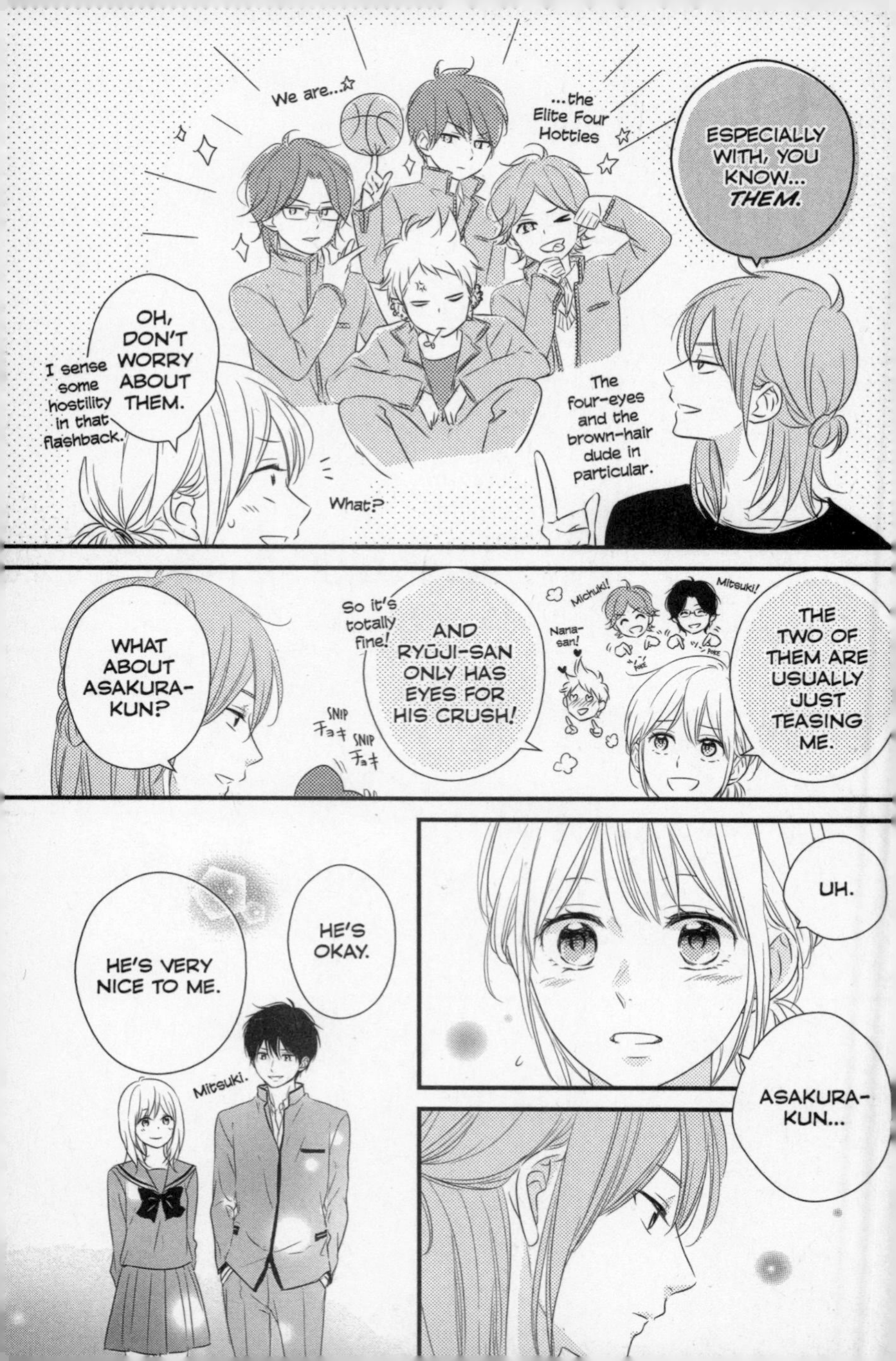
ESPECIALLY WITH, YOU KNOW... *THEM.*
We are...☆
...the Elite Four Hotties
The four-eyes and the brown-hair dude in particular.
OH, DON'T WORRY ABOUT THEM.
I sense some hostility in that flashback.
What?
THE TWO OF THEM ARE USUALLY JUST TEASING ME.
Mitsuki!
Michuki!
Nana-san!
POKE
POKE
AND RYŪJI-SAN ONLY HAS EYES FOR HIS CRUSH!
So it's totally fine!
SNIP チョキ
SNIP チョキ
WHAT ABOUT ASAKURA-KUN?
UH.
ASAKURA-KUN...
HE'S OKAY.
HE'S VERY NICE TO ME.
Mitsuki.

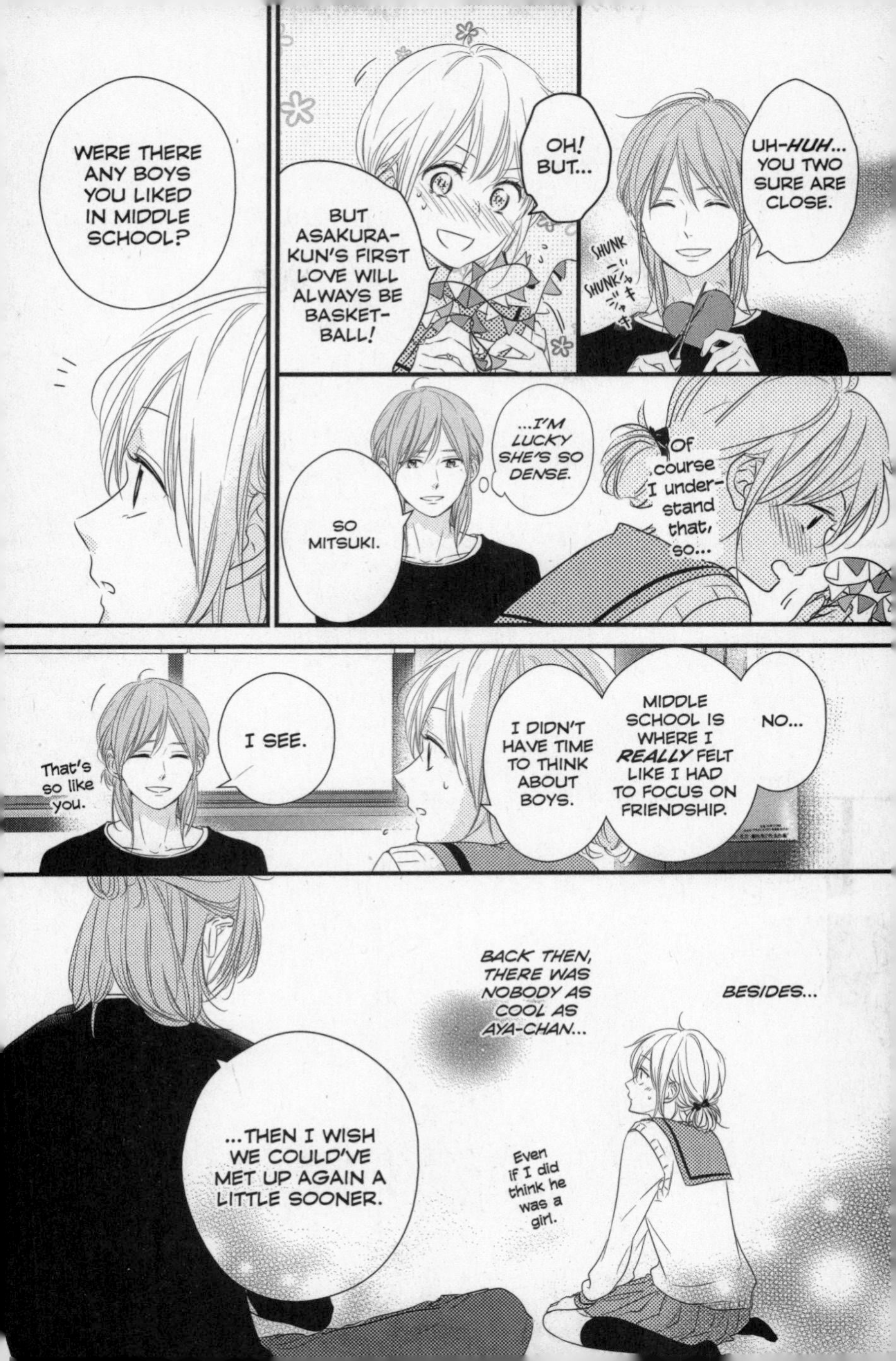
UH-*HUH*... YOU TWO SURE ARE CLOSE.
SHUNK
SHUNK
OH! BUT...
BUT ASAKURA-KUN'S FIRST LOVE WILL ALWAYS BE BASKET-BALL!
Of course I under-stand that, so...
...*I'M LUCKY SHE'S SO DENSE.*
SO MITSUKI.
WERE THERE ANY BOYS YOU LIKED IN MIDDLE SCHOOL?
NO...
MIDDLE SCHOOL IS WHERE I *REALLY* FELT LIKE I HAD TO FOCUS ON FRIENDSHIP.
I DIDN'T HAVE TIME TO THINK ABOUT BOYS.
I SEE.
That's so like you.
BESIDES...
BACK THEN, THERE WAS NOBODY AS COOL AS AYA-CHAN...
Even if I did think he was a girl.
...THEN I WISH WE COULD'VE MET UP AGAIN A LITTLE SOONER.

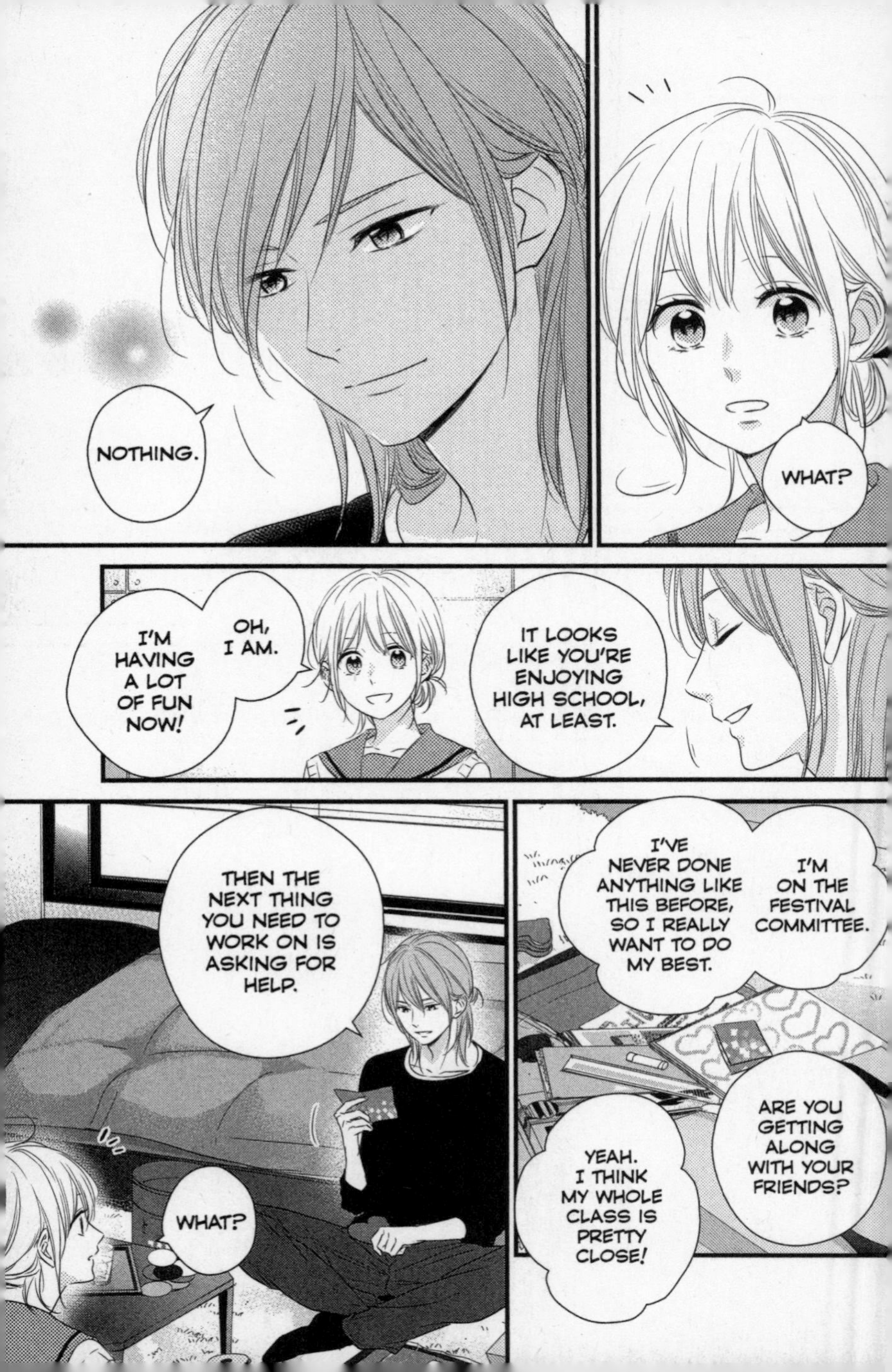
WHAT?
NOTHING.
IT LOOKS LIKE YOU'RE ENJOYING HIGH SCHOOL, AT LEAST.
OH, I AM.
I'M HAVING A LOT OF FUN NOW!
I'M ON THE FESTIVAL COMMITTEE.
I'VE NEVER DONE ANYTHING LIKE THIS BEFORE, SO I REALLY WANT TO DO MY BEST.
ARE YOU GETTING ALONG WITH YOUR FRIENDS?
YEAH. I THINK MY WHOLE CLASS IS PRETTY CLOSE!
THEN THE NEXT THING YOU NEED TO WORK ON IS ASKING FOR HELP.
WHAT?

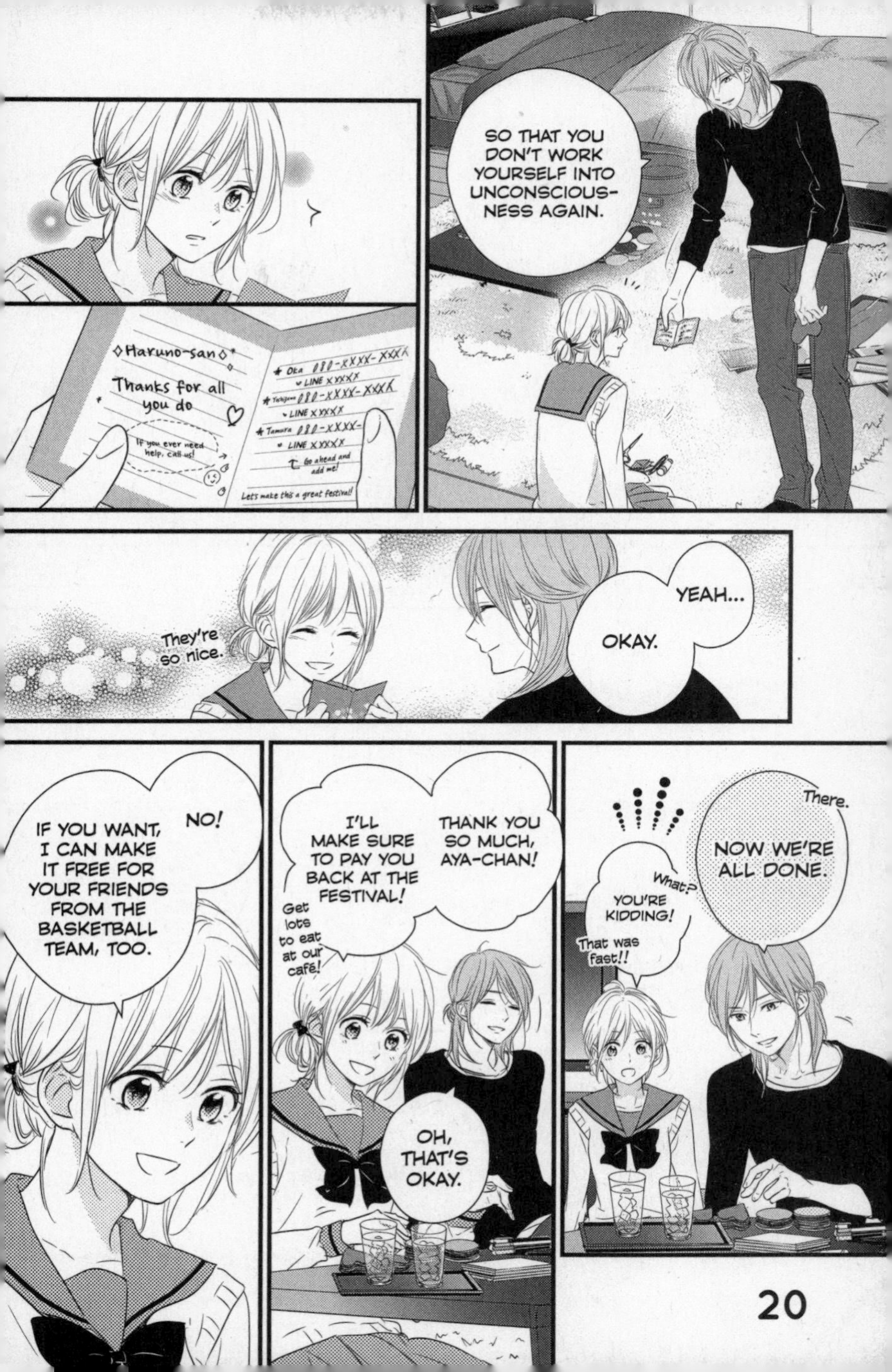
SO THAT YOU DON'T WORK YOURSELF INTO UNCONSCIOUS-NESS AGAIN.
◇Haruno-san◇
Thanks for all you do
If you ever need help, call us!
Oka 080-XXXX-XXXX
LINE XXXXX
080-XXXX-XXXX
LINE XXXXX
Tamura 080-XXXX-
LINE XXXXX
Go ahead and add me!
Let's make this a great festival!
YEAH...
OKAY.
They're so nice.
There.
NOW WE'RE ALL DONE.
What?
YOU'RE KIDDING!
That was fast!!
THANK YOU SO MUCH, AYA-CHAN!
I'LL MAKE SURE TO PAY YOU BACK AT THE FESTIVAL!
Get lots to eat at our café!
OH, THAT'S OKAY.
NO!
IF YOU WANT, I CAN MAKE IT FREE FOR YOUR FRIENDS FROM THE BASKETBALL TEAM, TOO.

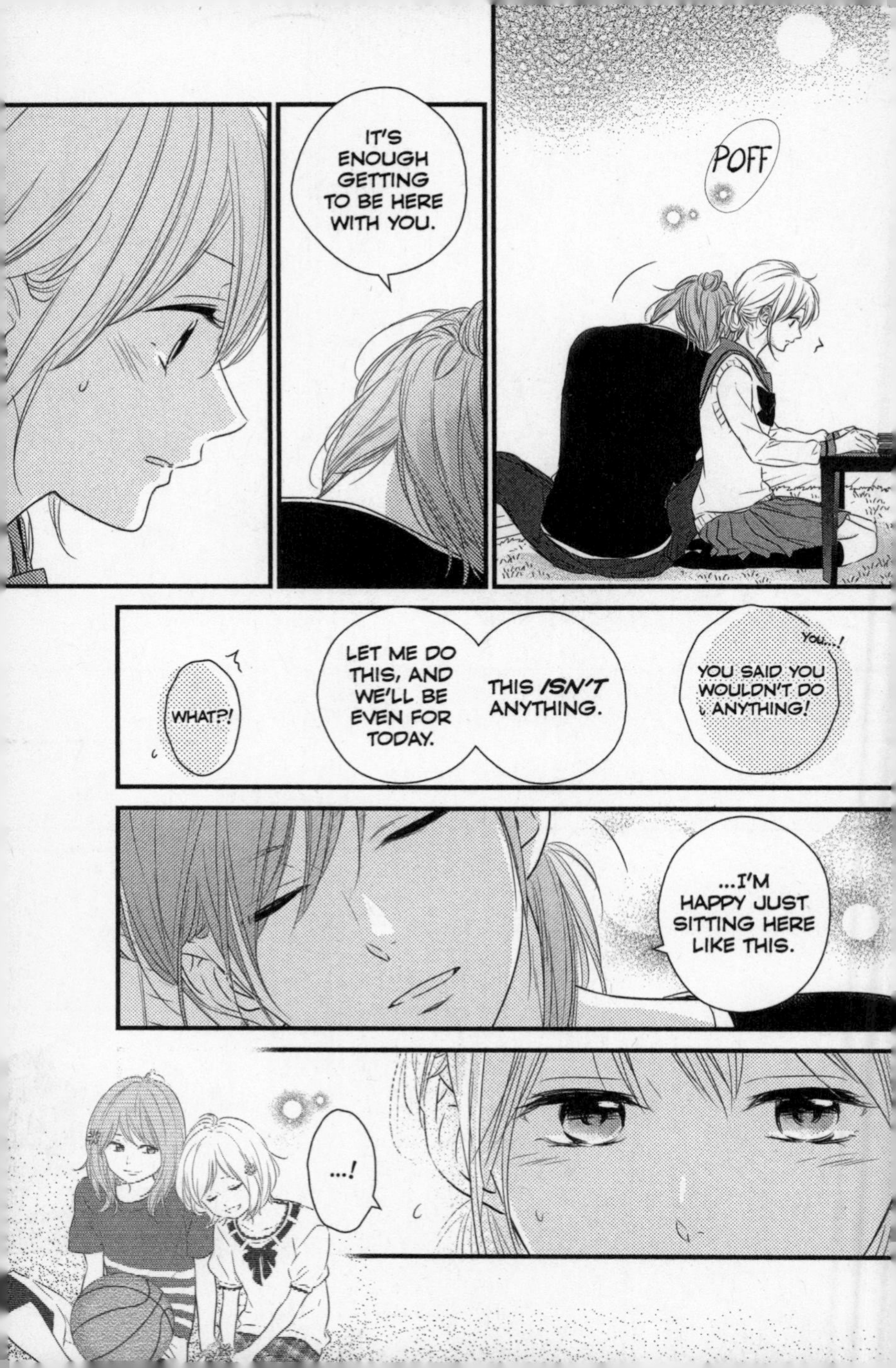
POFF
IT'S ENOUGH GETTING TO BE HERE WITH YOU.
YOU...!
YOU SAID YOU WOULDN'T DO ANYTHING!
THIS *ISN'T* ANYTHING.
LET ME DO THIS, AND WE'LL BE EVEN FOR TODAY.
WHAT?!
...I'M HAPPY JUST SITTING HERE LIKE THIS.
...!

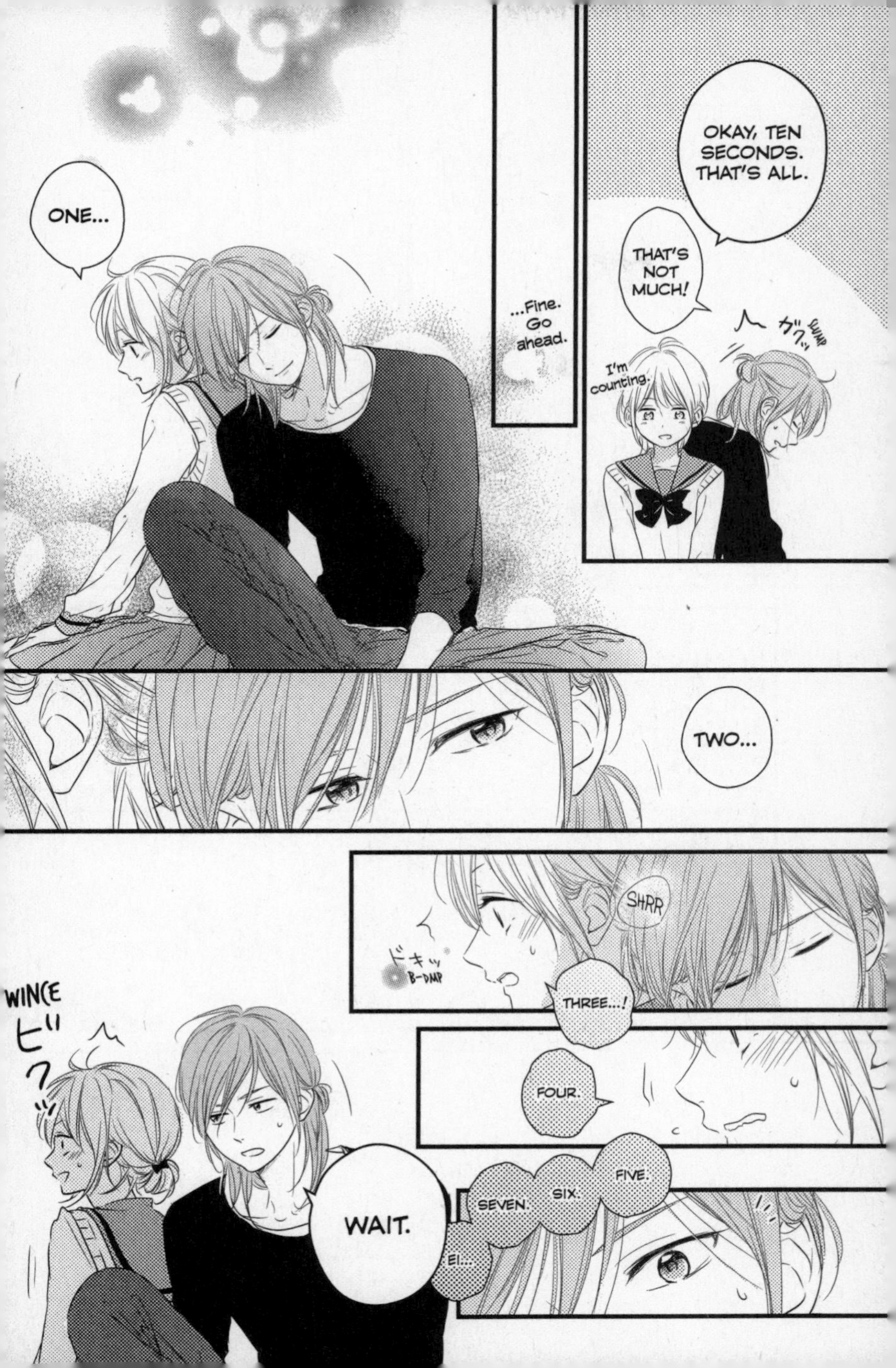
OKAY, TEN SECONDS. THAT'S ALL.
THAT'S NOT MUCH!
ガクッ SLUMP
I'm counting.
...Fine. Go ahead.
ONE...
TWO...
SHRR
ドキッ B-DMP
THREE...!
FOUR.
FIVE.
SIX.
SEVEN.
EI...
WINCE ビクッ
WAIT.

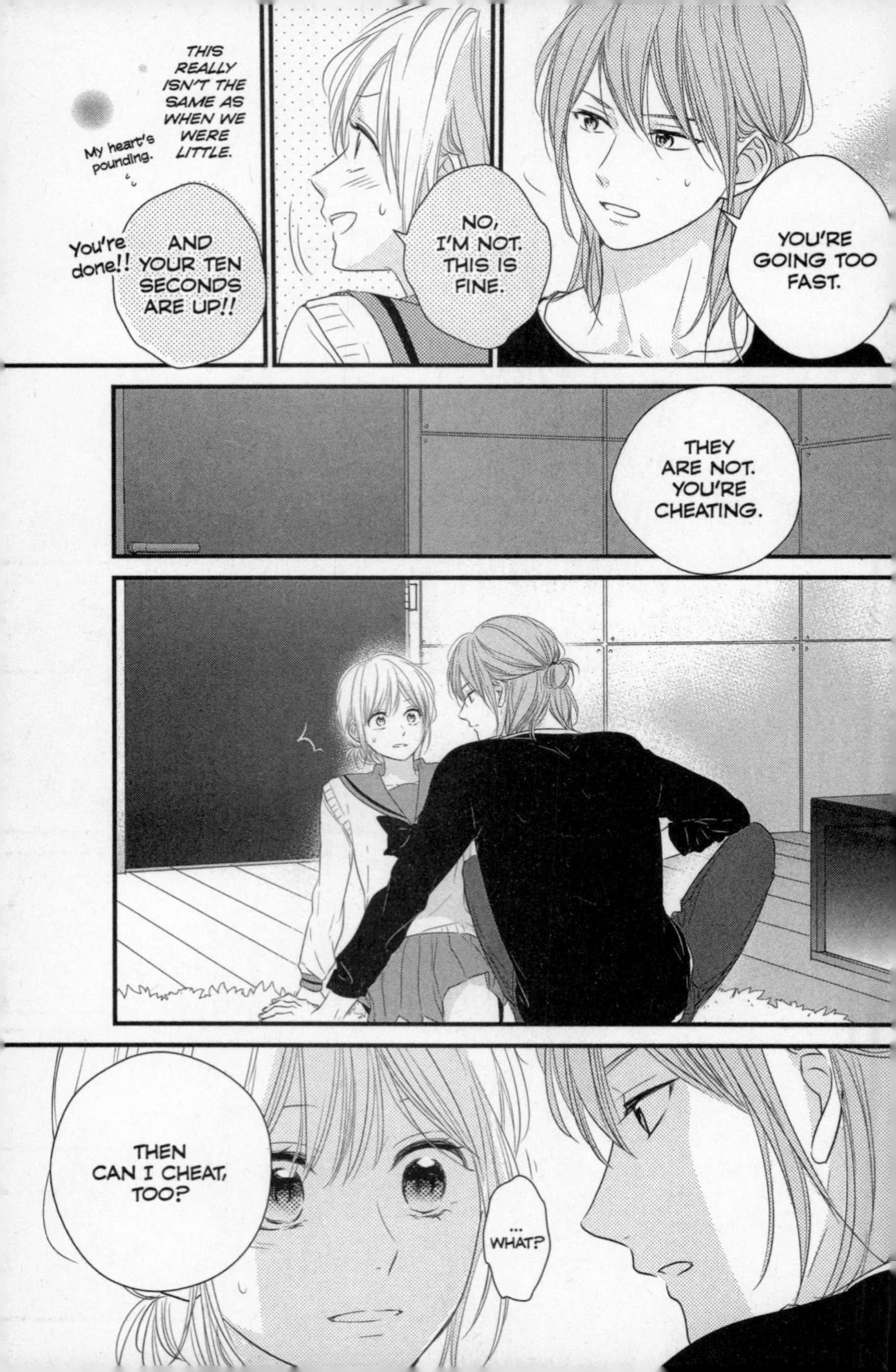
YOU'RE GOING TOO FAST.
NO, I'M NOT. THIS IS FINE.
THIS REALLY ISN'T THE SAME AS WHEN WE WERE LITTLE.
My heart's pounding.
AND YOUR TEN SECONDS ARE UP!!
You're done!!
THEY ARE NOT. YOU'RE CHEATING.
THEN CAN I CHEAT, TOO?
... WHAT?

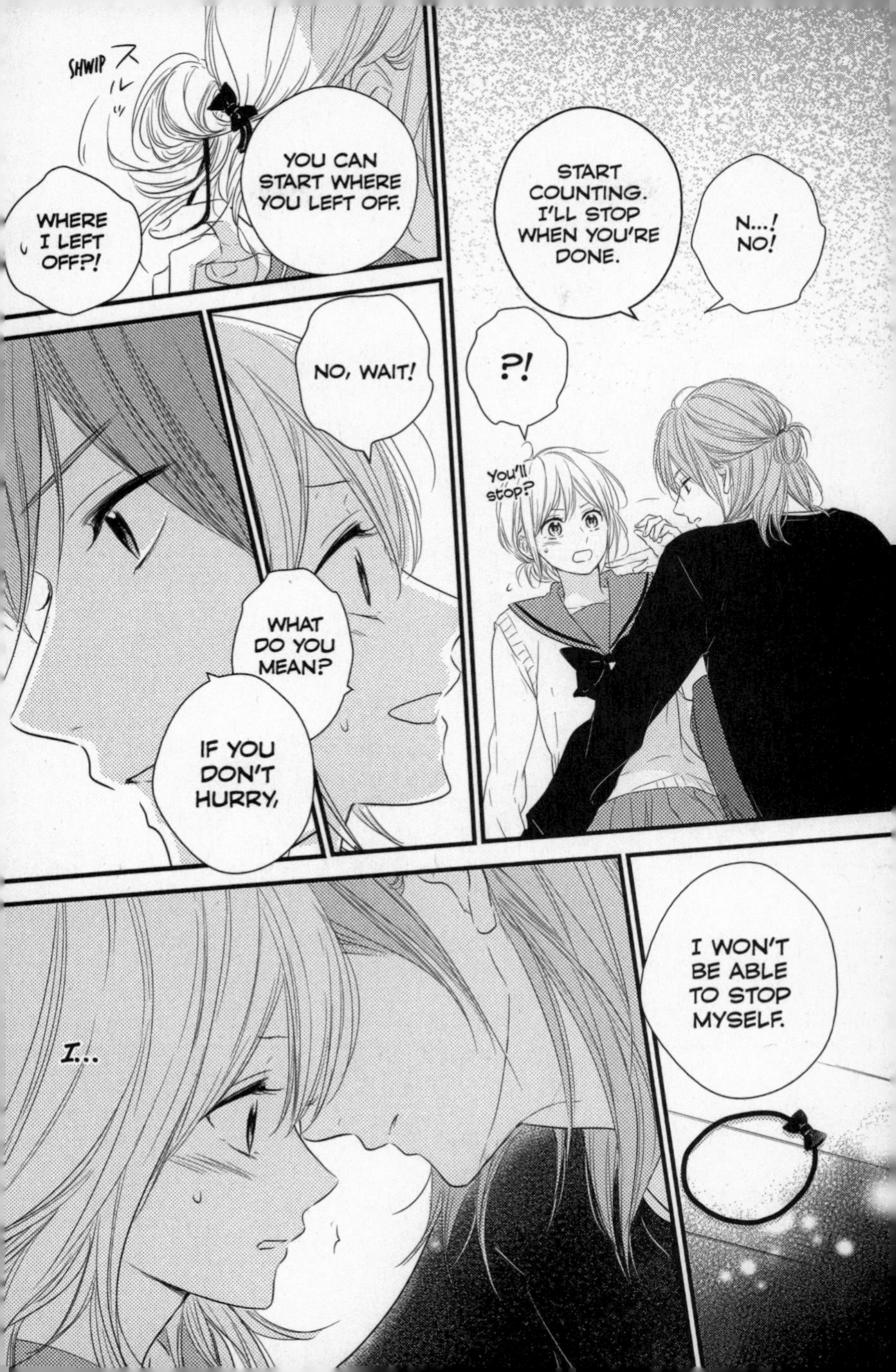
N...! NO!
START COUNTING. I'LL STOP WHEN YOU'RE DONE.
?!
You'll stop?
SHWIP スルッ
YOU CAN START WHERE YOU LEFT OFF.
WHERE I LEFT OFF?!
NO, WAIT!
WHAT DO YOU MEAN?
IF YOU DON'T HURRY,
I WON'T BE ABLE TO STOP MYSELF.
I...

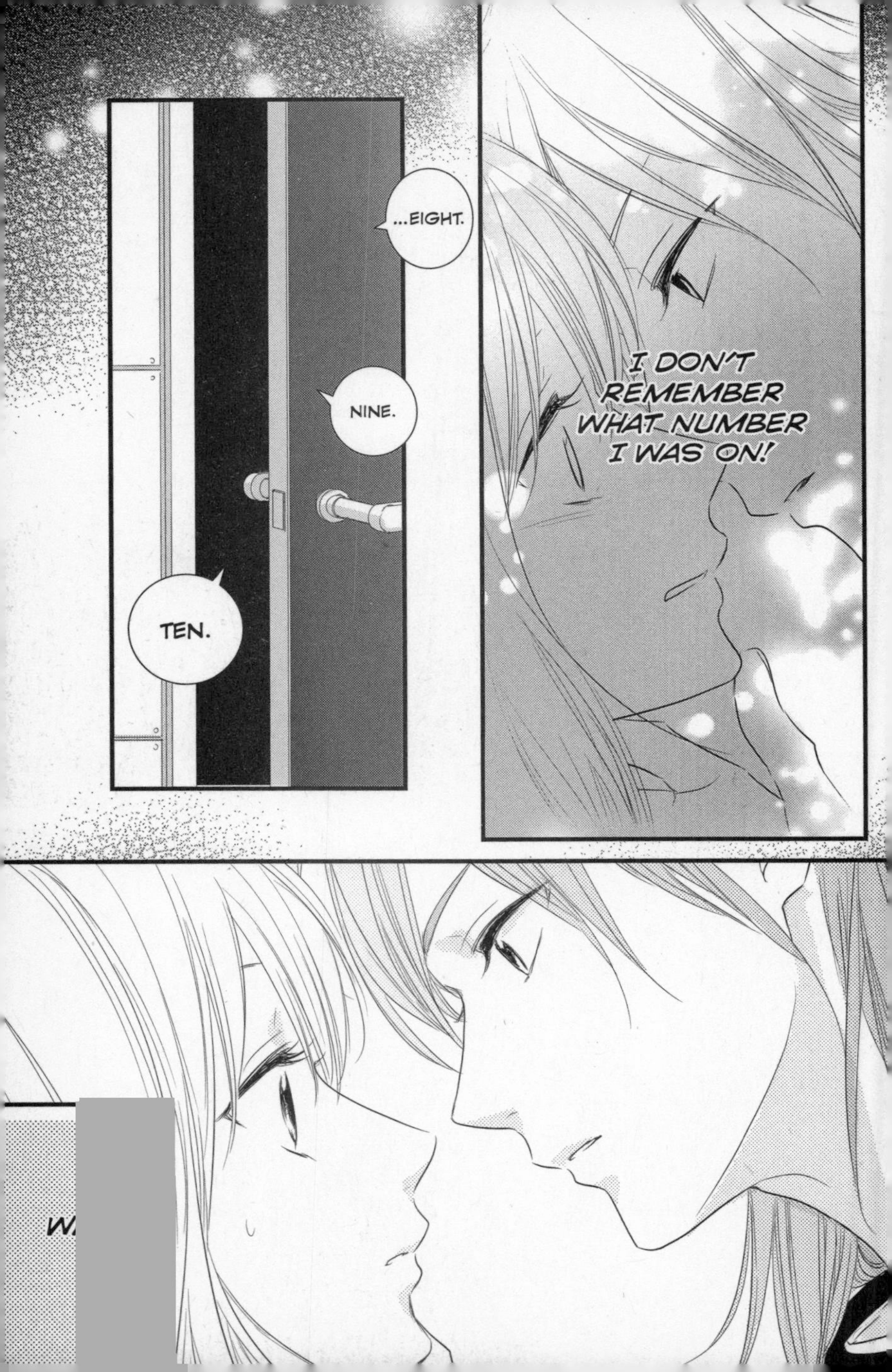
I DON'T REMEMBER WHAT NUMBER I WAS ON!
...EIGHT.
NINE.
TEN.

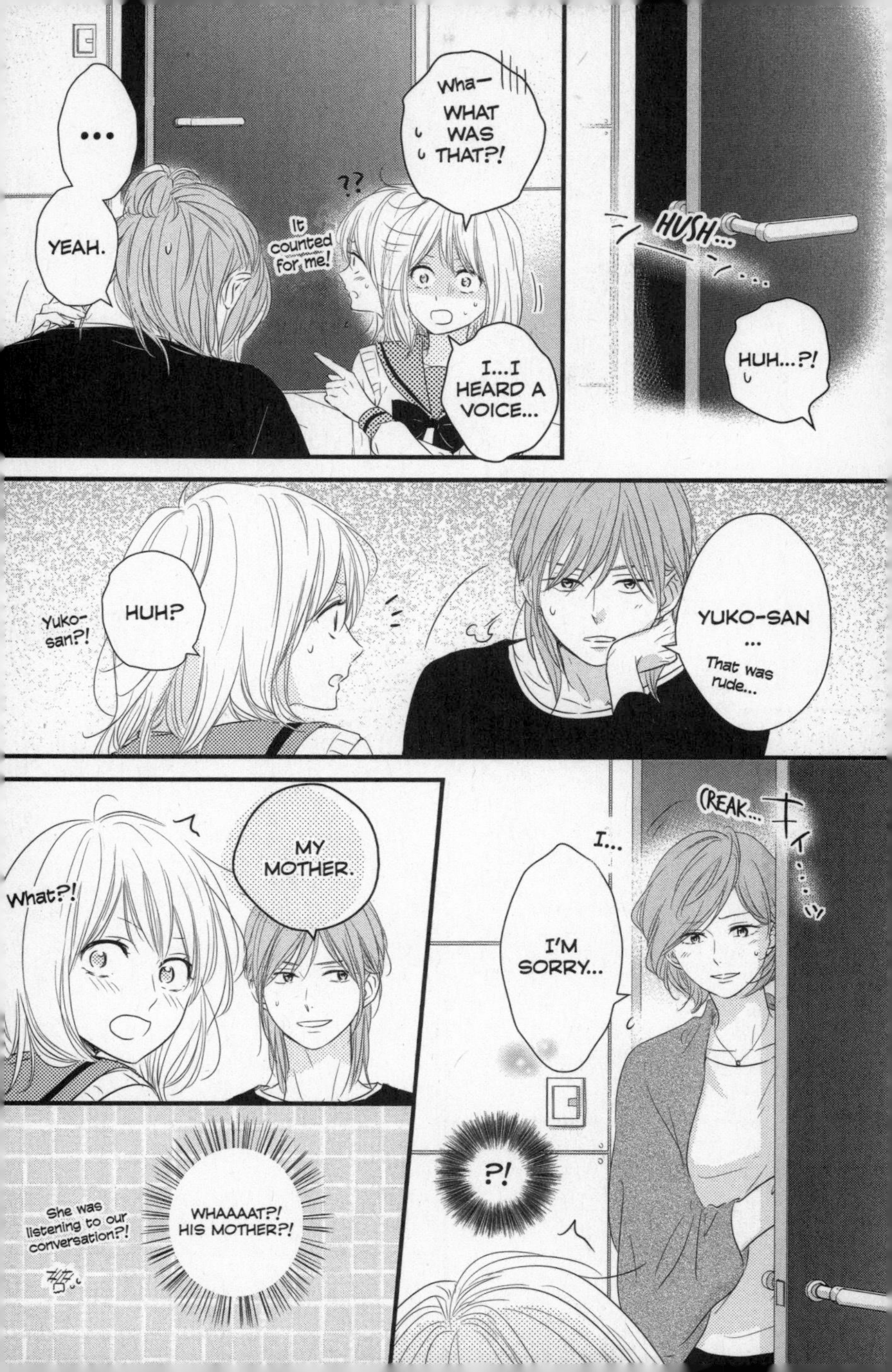
HUSH...
HUH...?!
Wha— WHAT WAS THAT?!
I...I HEARD A VOICE...
...
It counted for me!
YEAH.
YUKO-SAN ... That was rude...
HUH?
Yuko-san?!
CREAK...
I... I'M SORRY...
?!
MY MOTHER.
What?!
WHAAAAT?! HIS MOTHER?!
She was listening to our conversation?!

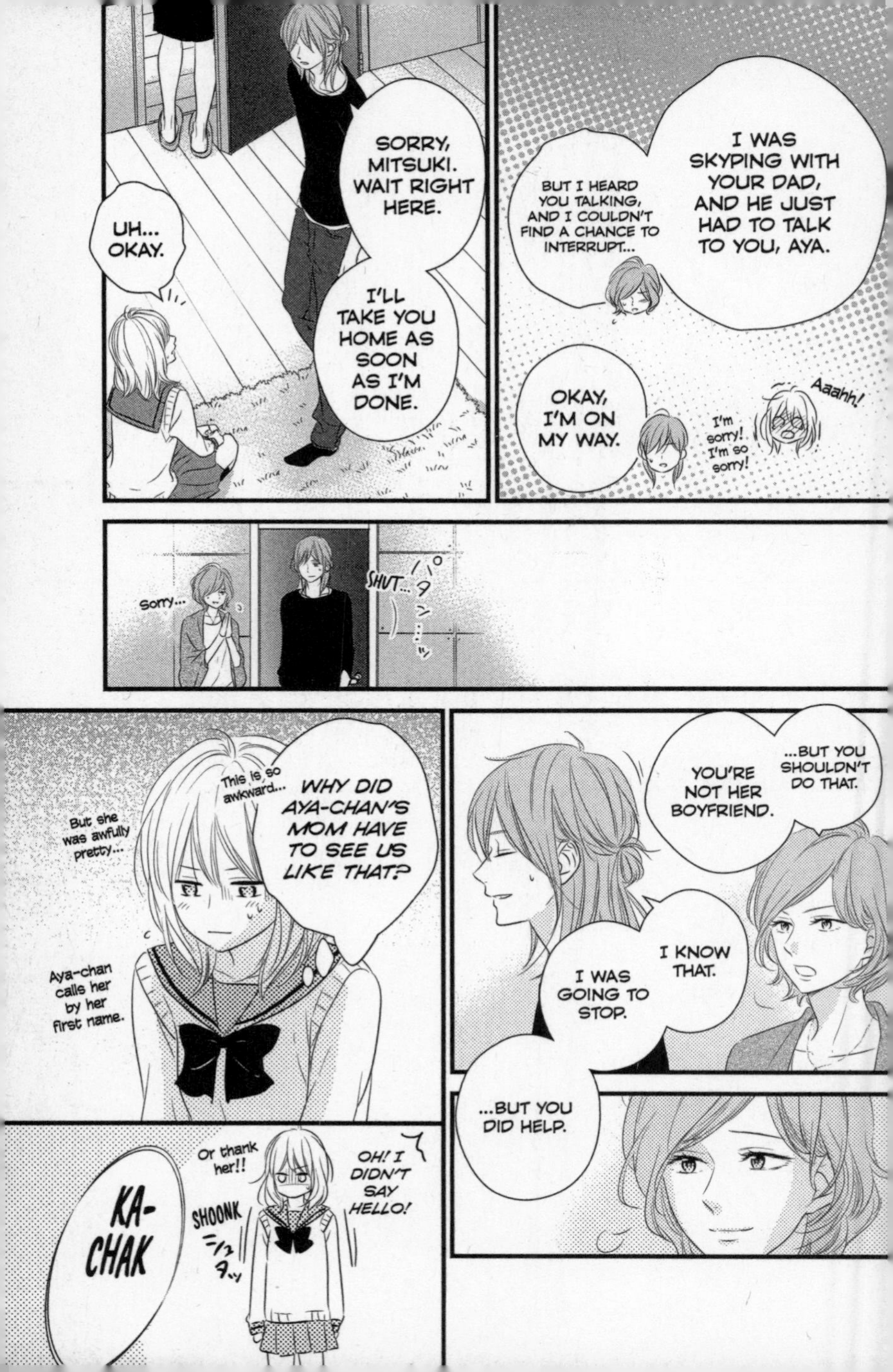
I WAS SKYPING WITH YOUR DAD, AND HE JUST HAD TO TALK TO YOU, AYA.
BUT I HEARD YOU TALKING, AND I COULDN'T FIND A CHANCE TO INTERRUPT...
Aaahh!
I'm sorry! I'm so sorry!
OKAY, I'M ON MY WAY.
SORRY, MITSUKI. WAIT RIGHT HERE.
I'LL TAKE YOU HOME AS SOON AS I'M DONE.
UH... OKAY.
SHUT...
Sorry...
...BUT YOU SHOULDN'T DO THAT.
YOU'RE NOT HER BOYFRIEND.
I KNOW THAT.
I WAS GOING TO STOP.
...BUT YOU DID HELP.
WHY DID AYA-CHAN'S MOM HAVE TO SEE US LIKE THAT?
This is so awkward...
But she was awfully pretty...
Aya-chan calls her by her first name.
OH! I DIDN'T SAY HELLO!
Or thank her!!
SHOONK
KA-CHAK

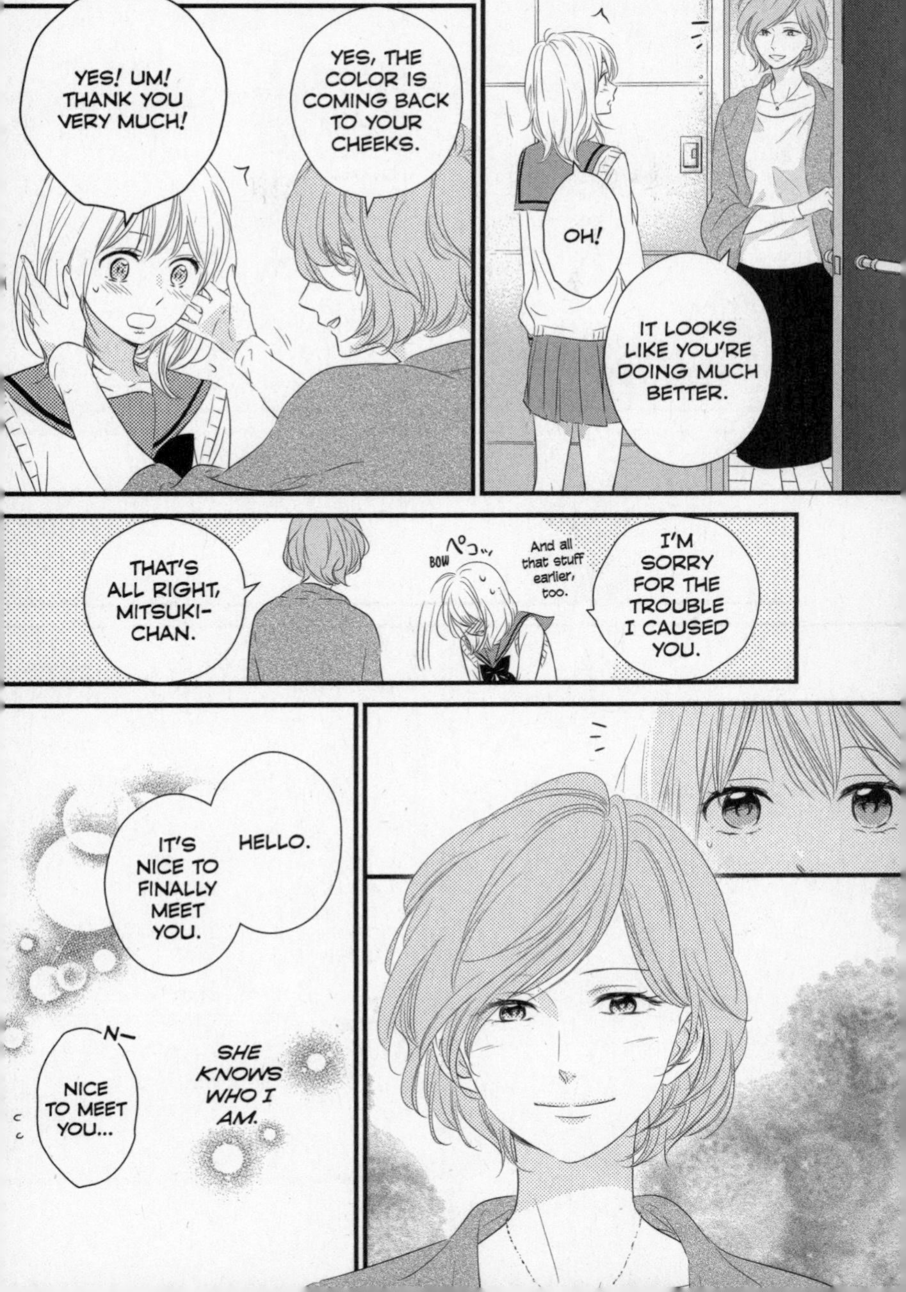
OH!
IT LOOKS LIKE YOU'RE DOING MUCH BETTER.
YES, THE COLOR IS COMING BACK TO YOUR CHEEKS.
YES! UM! THANK YOU VERY MUCH!
I'M SORRY FOR THE TROUBLE I CAUSED YOU.
And all that stuff earlier, too.
BOW
THAT'S ALL RIGHT, MITSUKI-CHAN.
HELLO.
IT'S NICE TO FINALLY MEET YOU.
SHE KNOWS WHO I AM.
N— NICE TO MEET YOU...

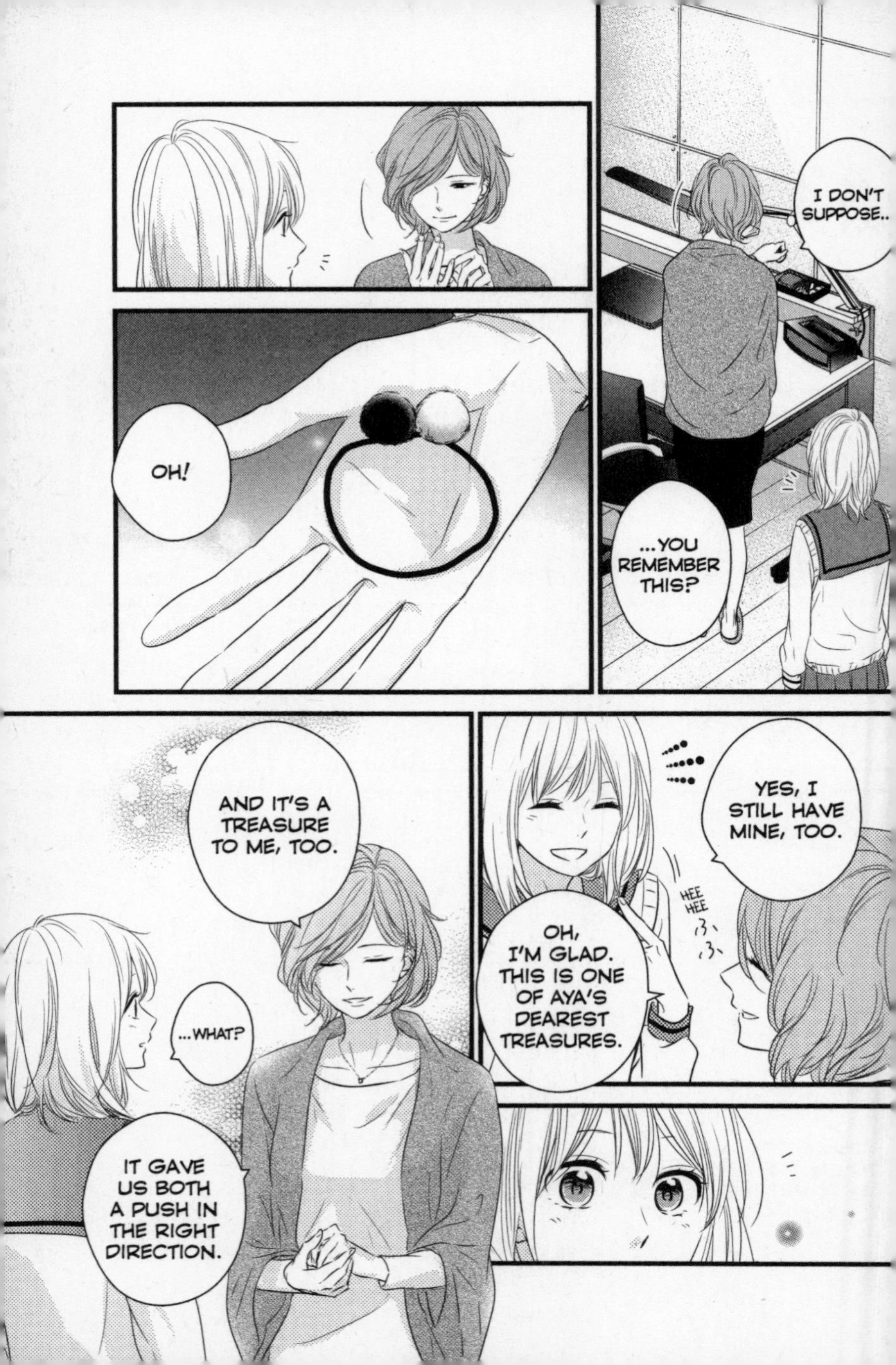
I DON'T SUPPOSE..
...YOU REMEMBER THIS?
OH!
YES, I STILL HAVE MINE, TOO.
HEE HEE ふふ
OH, I'M GLAD. THIS IS ONE OF AYA'S DEAREST TREASURES.
AND IT'S A TREASURE TO ME, TOO.
...WHAT?
IT GAVE US BOTH A PUSH IN THE RIGHT DIRECTION.

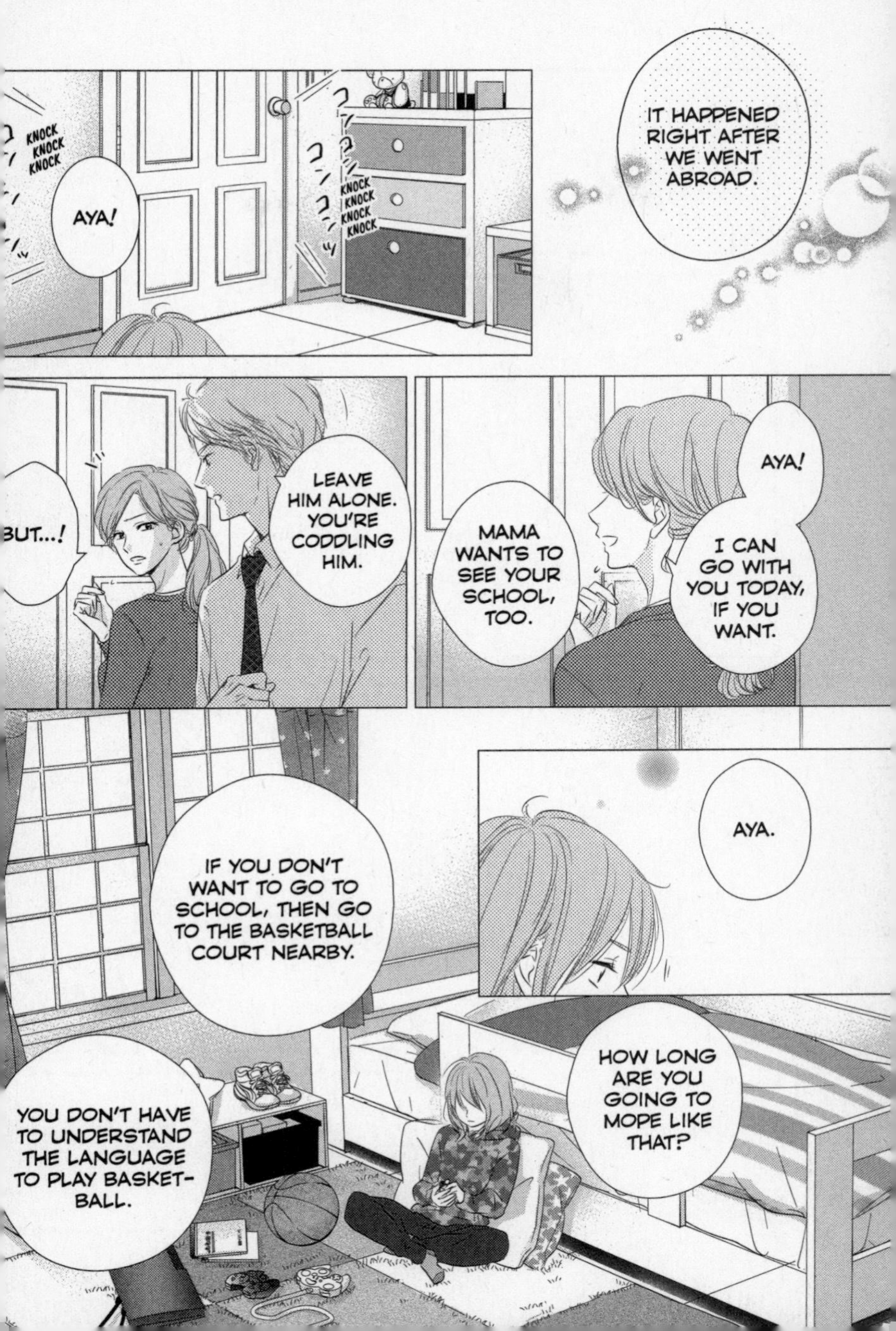
IT HAPPENED RIGHT AFTER WE WENT ABROAD.
KNOCK KNOCK KNOCK KNOCK
KNOCK KNOCK KNOCK
AYA!
AYA!
I CAN GO WITH YOU TODAY, IF YOU WANT.
MAMA WANTS TO SEE YOUR SCHOOL, TOO.
LEAVE HIM ALONE. YOU'RE CODDLING HIM.
BUT...!
AYA.
HOW LONG ARE YOU GOING TO MOPE LIKE THAT?
IF YOU DON'T WANT TO GO TO SCHOOL, THEN GO TO THE BASKETBALL COURT NEARBY.
YOU DON'T HAVE TO UNDERSTAND THE LANGUAGE TO PLAY BASKET-BALL.

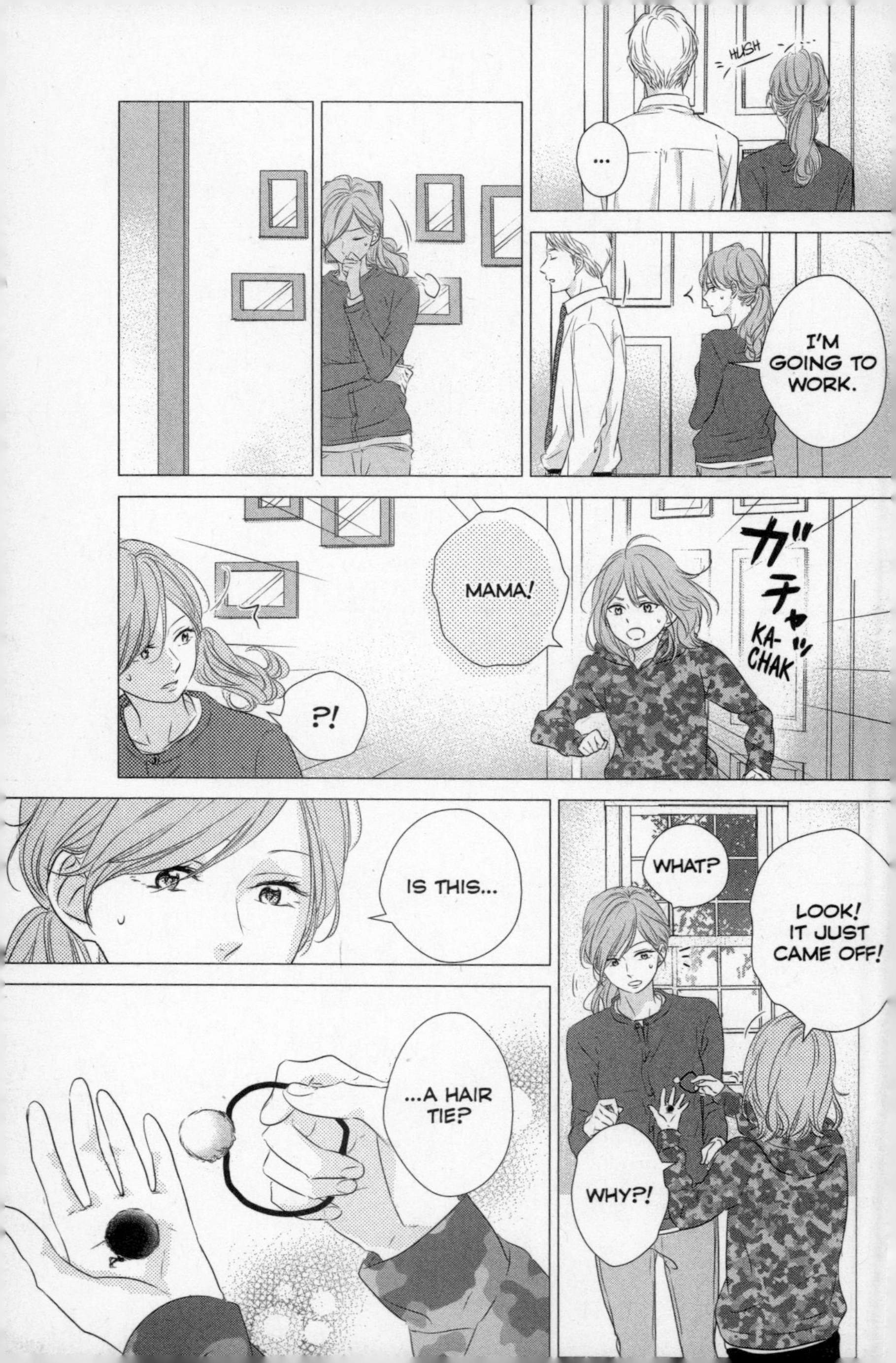
HUSH
...
I'M GOING TO WORK.
ガチャッ
KA-CHAK
MAMA!
?!
LOOK! IT JUST CAME OFF!
WHAT?
WHY?!
IS THIS...
...A HAIR TIE?

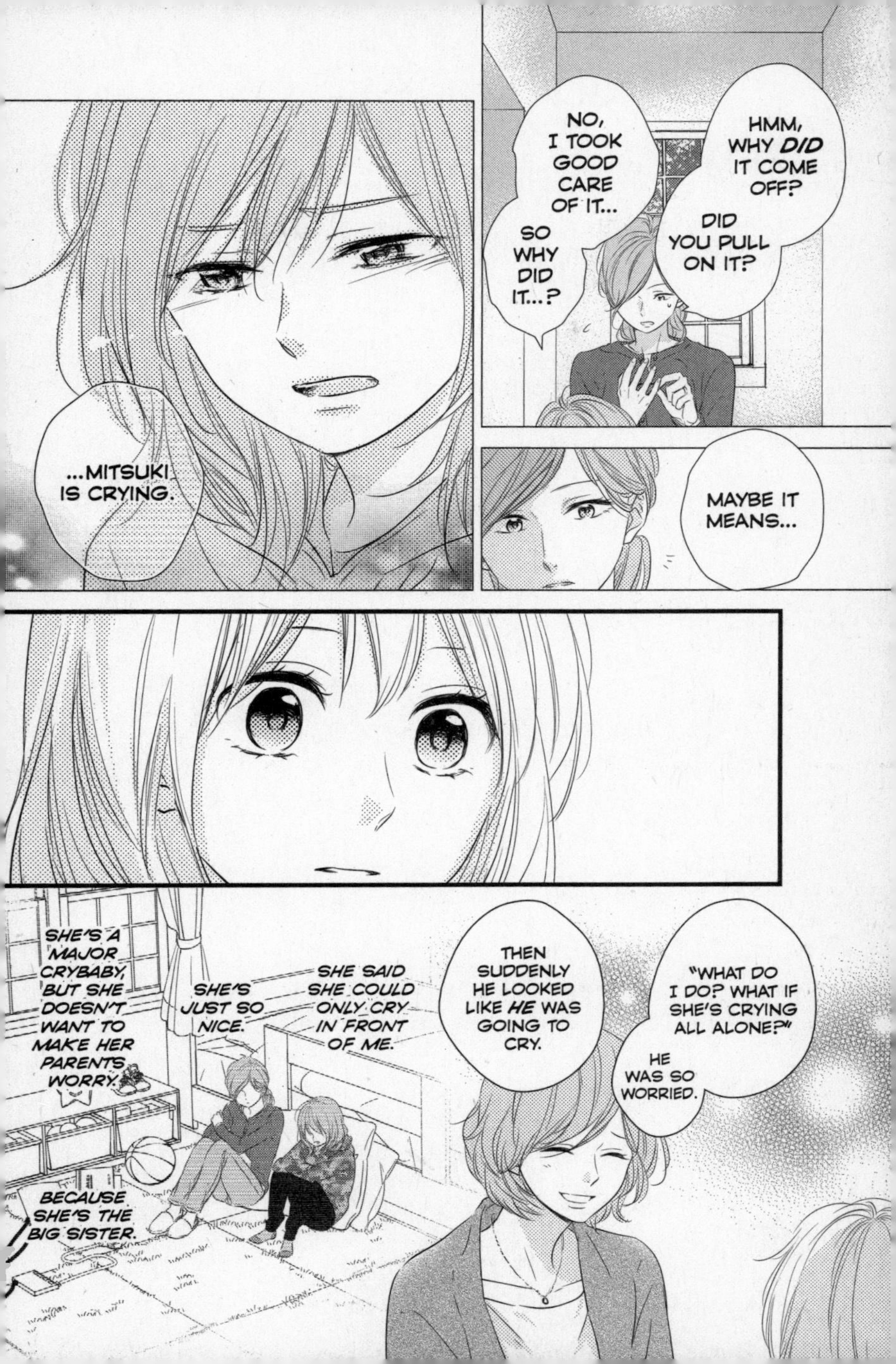
HMM, WHY DID IT COME OFF?
DID YOU PULL ON IT?
NO, I TOOK GOOD CARE OF IT...
SO WHY DID IT...?
MAYBE IT MEANS...
...MITSUKI IS CRYING.
"WHAT DO I DO? WHAT IF SHE'S CRYING ALL ALONE?"
HE WAS SO WORRIED.
THEN SUDDENLY HE LOOKED LIKE HE WAS GOING TO CRY.
SHE SAID SHE COULD ONLY CRY IN FRONT OF ME.
SHE'S JUST SO NICE.
SHE'S A MAJOR CRYBABY, BUT SHE DOESN'T WANT TO MAKE HER PARENTS WORRY.
BECAUSE SHE'S THE BIG SISTER.

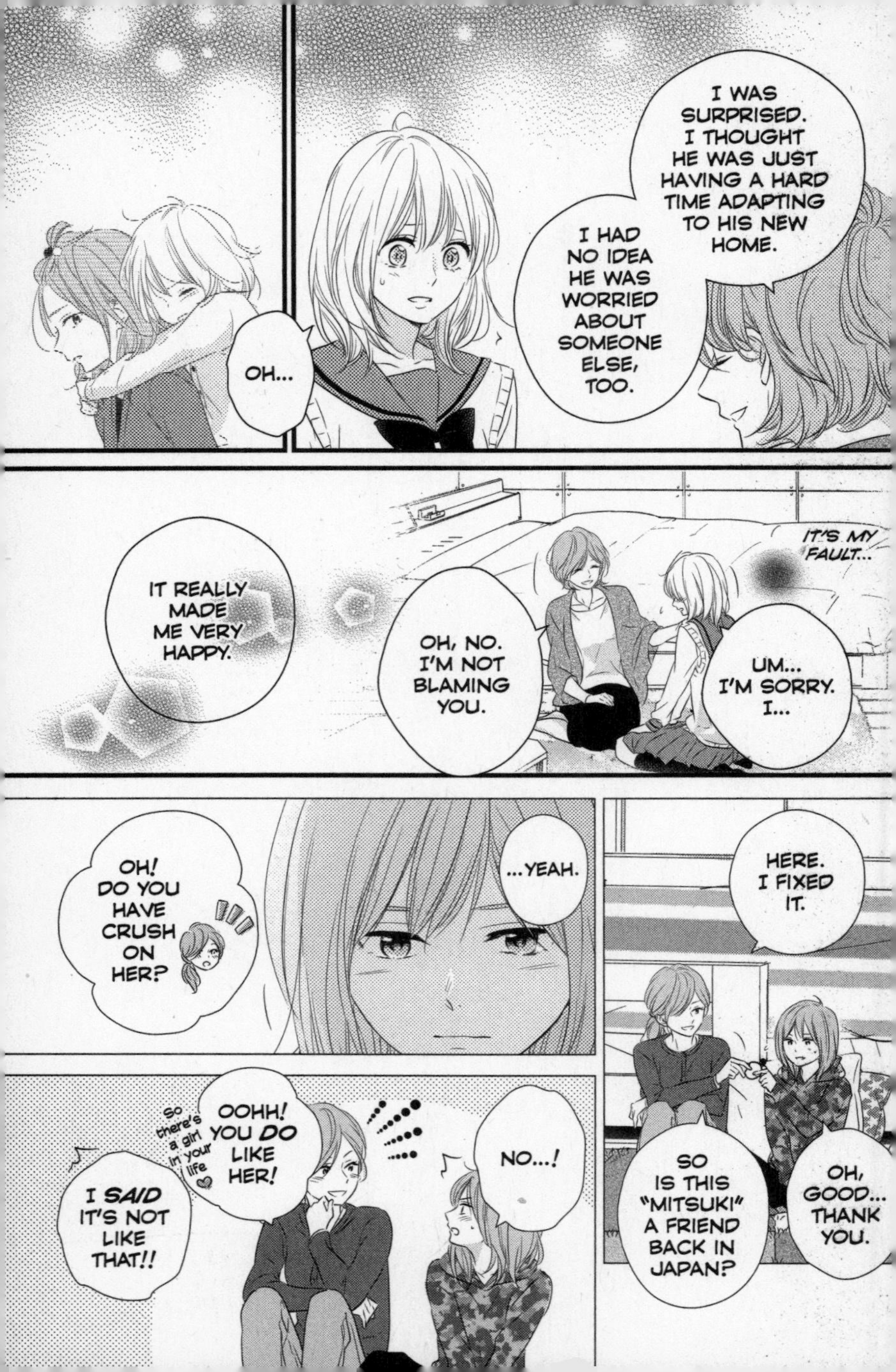
I WAS SURPRISED. I THOUGHT HE WAS JUST HAVING A HARD TIME ADAPTING TO HIS NEW HOME.
I HAD NO IDEA HE WAS WORRIED ABOUT SOMEONE ELSE, TOO.
OH...
IT'S MY FAULT...
UM... I'M SORRY. I...
OH, NO. I'M NOT BLAMING YOU.
IT REALLY MADE ME VERY HAPPY.
HERE. I FIXED IT.
OH, GOOD... THANK YOU.
SO IS THIS "MITSUKI" A FRIEND BACK IN JAPAN?
...YEAH.
OH! DO YOU HAVE CRUSH ON HER?
NO...!
OOHH! YOU *DO* LIKE HER!
So there's a girl in your life
I *SAID* IT'S NOT LIKE THAT!!

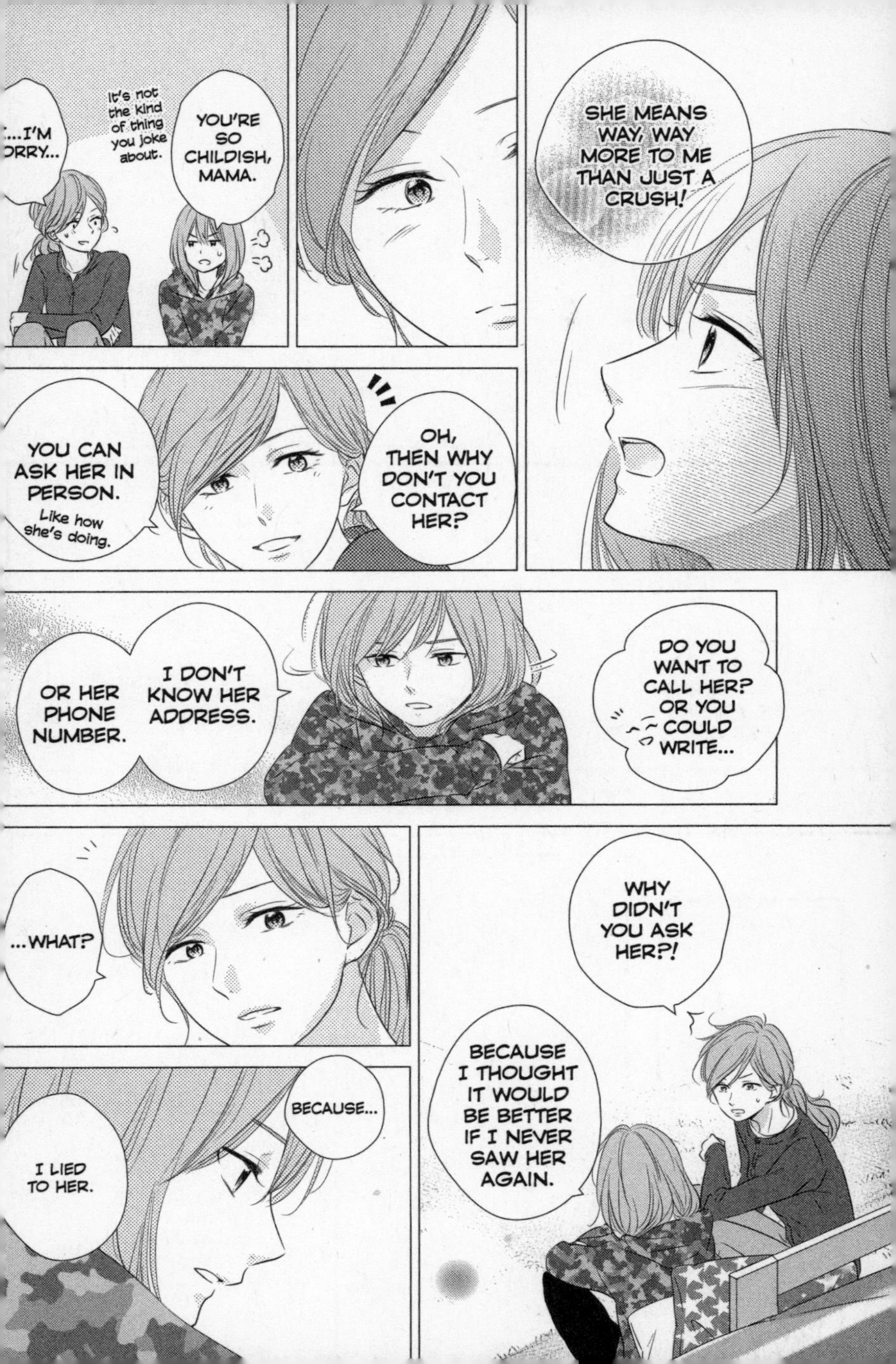

SHE MEANS WAY, WAY MORE TO ME THAN JUST A CRUSH!
YOU'RE SO CHILDISH, MAMA.
It's not the kind of thing you joke about.
...I'M ORRY...
OH, THEN WHY DON'T YOU CONTACT HER?
YOU CAN ASK HER IN PERSON.
Like how she's doing.
DO YOU WANT TO CALL HER? OR YOU COULD WRITE...
I DON'T KNOW HER ADDRESS.
OR HER PHONE NUMBER.
WHY DIDN'T YOU ASK HER?!
BECAUSE I THOUGHT IT WOULD BE BETTER IF I NEVER SAW HER AGAIN.
...WHAT?
BECAUSE...
I LIED TO HER.

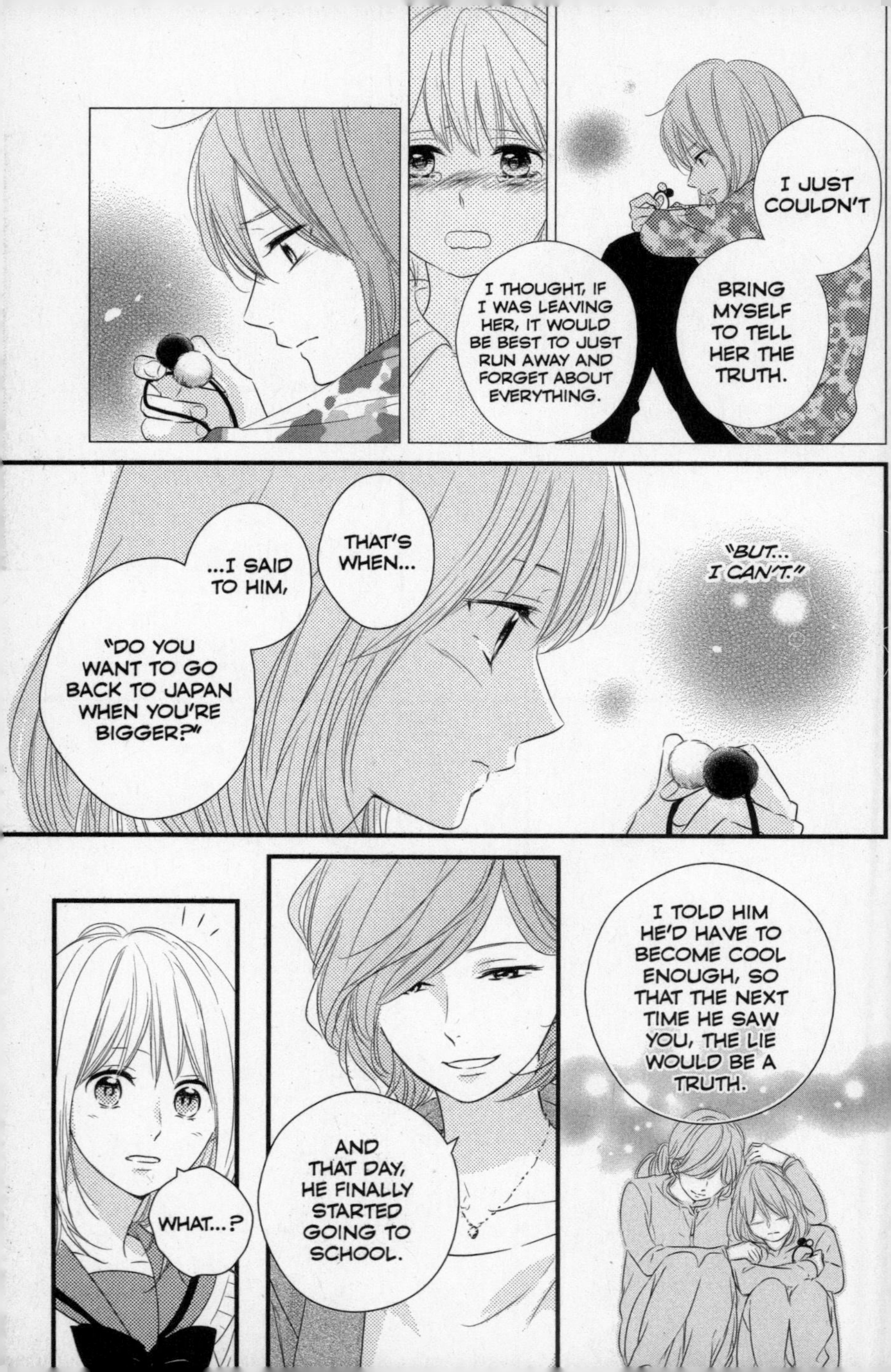
I JUST COULDN'T
BRING MYSELF TO TELL HER THE TRUTH.
I THOUGHT, IF I WAS LEAVING HER, IT WOULD BE BEST TO JUST RUN AWAY AND FORGET ABOUT EVERYTHING.
"BUT... I CAN'T."
THAT'S WHEN...
...I SAID TO HIM,
"DO YOU WANT TO GO BACK TO JAPAN WHEN YOU'RE BIGGER?"
I TOLD HIM HE'D HAVE TO BECOME COOL ENOUGH, SO THAT THE NEXT TIME HE SAW YOU, THE LIE WOULD BE A TRUTH.
AND THAT DAY, HE FINALLY STARTED GOING TO SCHOOL.
WHAT...?

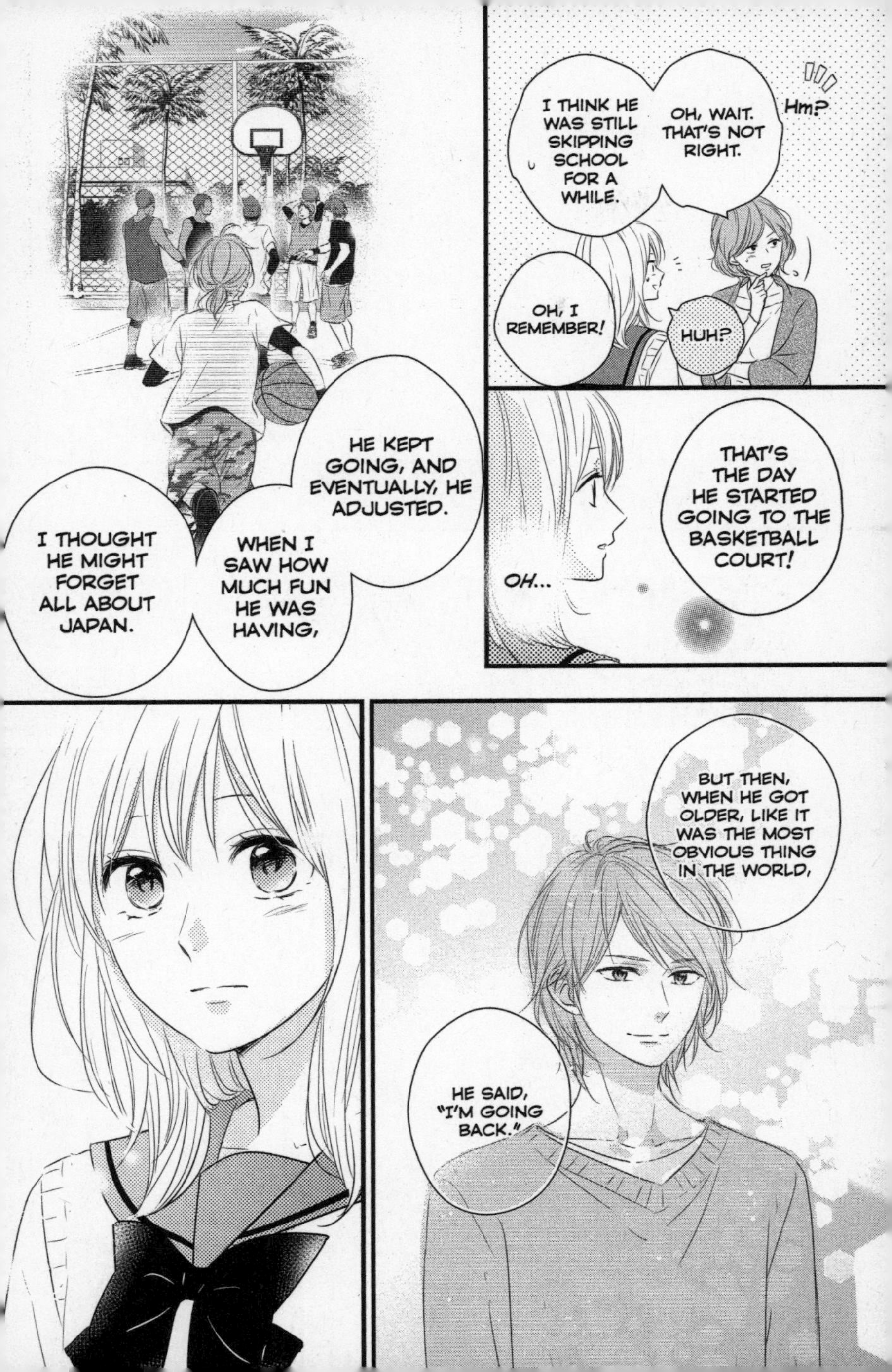
Hm?
OH, WAIT. THAT'S NOT RIGHT.
I THINK HE WAS STILL SKIPPING SCHOOL FOR A WHILE.
HUH?
OH, I REMEMBER!
THAT'S THE DAY HE STARTED GOING TO THE BASKETBALL COURT!
OH...
HE KEPT GOING, AND EVENTUALLY, HE ADJUSTED.
WHEN I SAW HOW MUCH FUN HE WAS HAVING,
I THOUGHT HE MIGHT FORGET ALL ABOUT JAPAN.
BUT THEN, WHEN HE GOT OLDER, LIKE IT WAS THE MOST OBVIOUS THING IN THE WORLD,
HE SAID, "I'M GOING BACK."

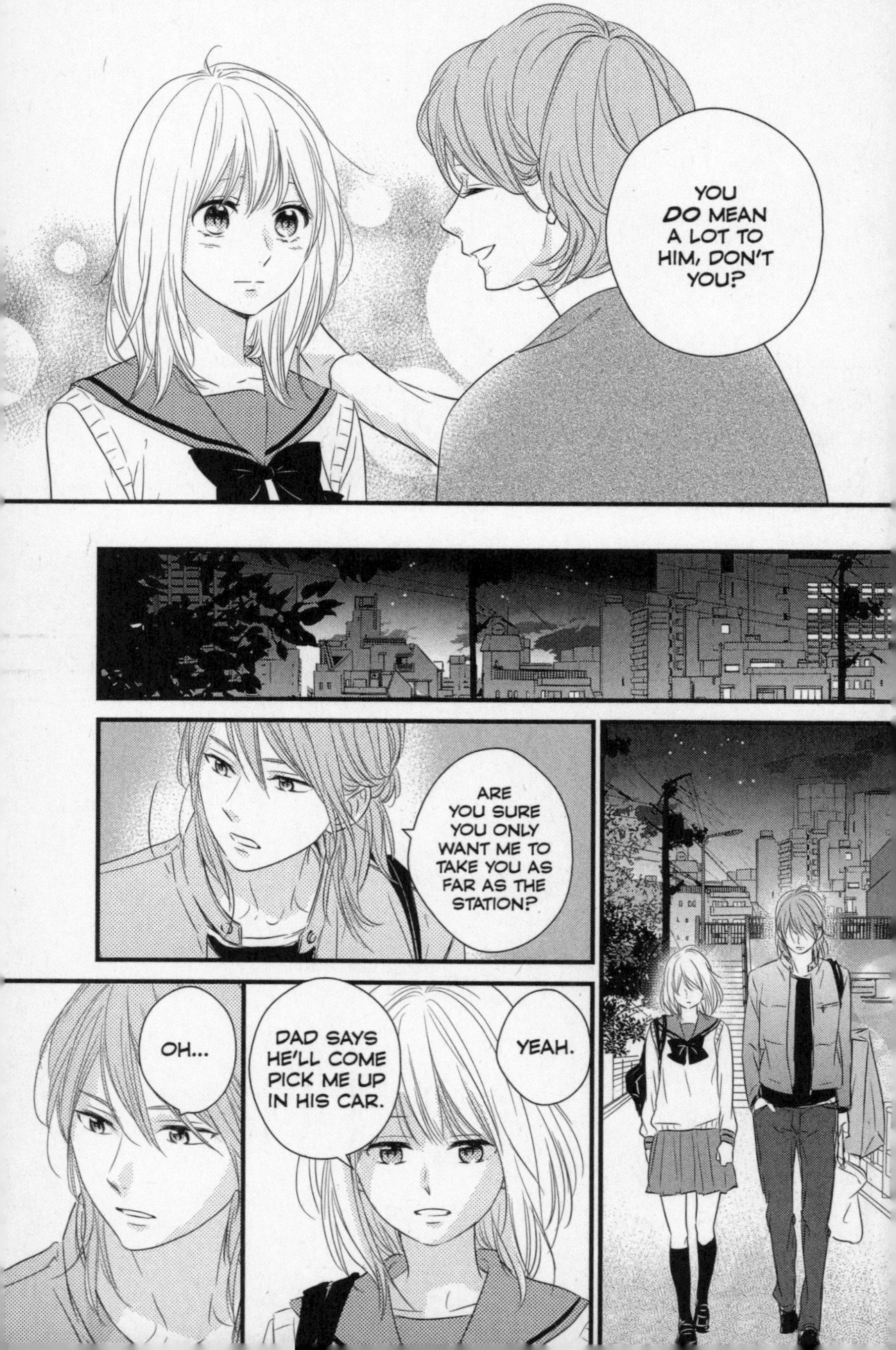
YOU DO MEAN A LOT TO HIM, DON'T YOU?
ARE YOU SURE YOU ONLY WANT ME TO TAKE YOU AS FAR AS THE STATION?
YEAH.
DAD SAYS HE'LL COME PICK ME UP IN HIS CAR.
OH...

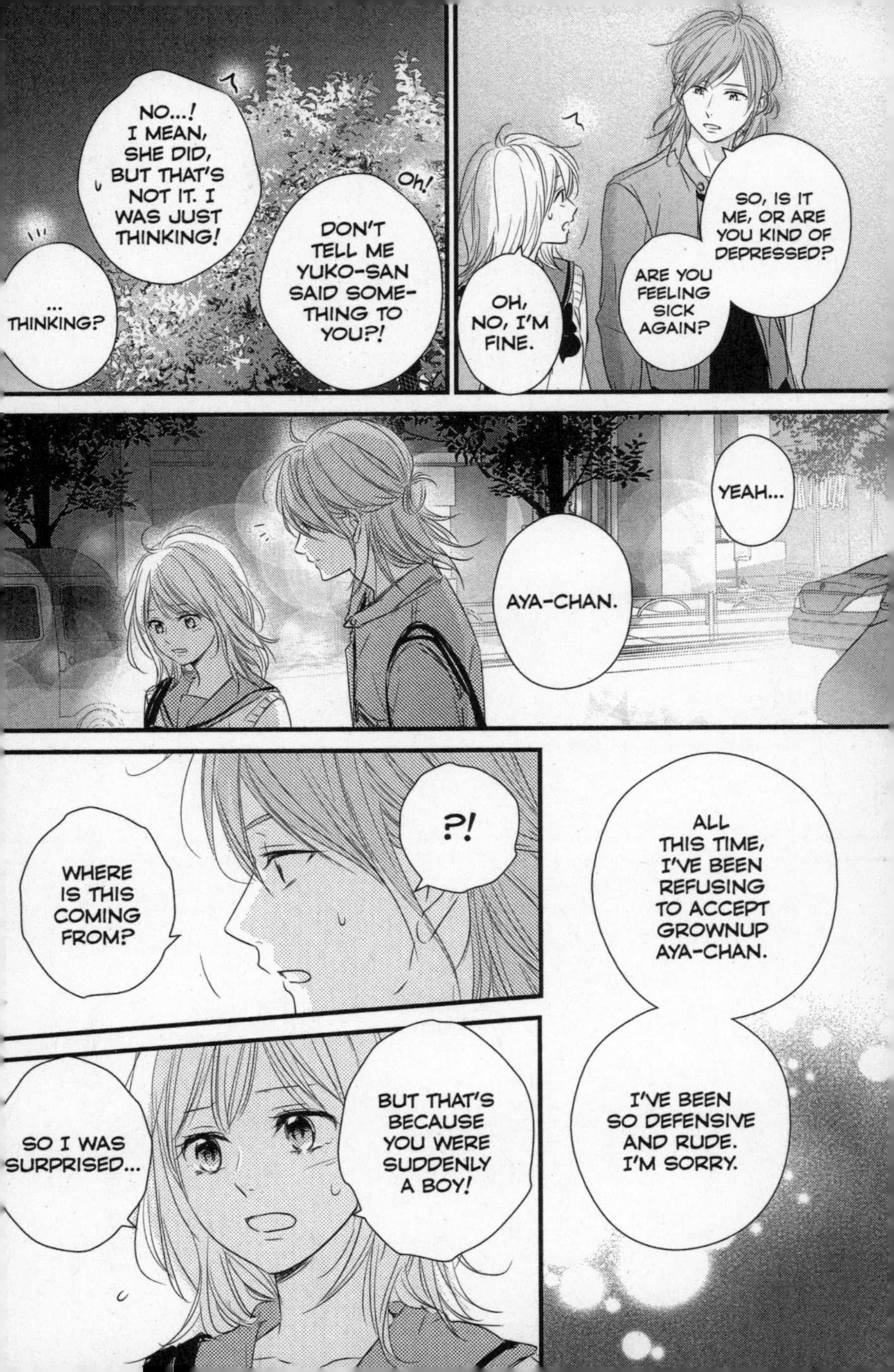
SO, IS IT ME, OR ARE YOU KIND OF DEPRESSED?
ARE YOU FEELING SICK AGAIN?
OH, NO, I'M FINE.
Oh!
DON'T TELL ME YUKO-SAN SAID SOME-THING TO YOU?!
NO...! I MEAN, SHE DID, BUT THAT'S NOT IT. I WAS JUST THINKING!
...THINKING?
YEAH...
AYA-CHAN.
ALL THIS TIME, I'VE BEEN REFUSING TO ACCEPT GROWNUP AYA-CHAN.
I'VE BEEN SO DEFENSIVE AND RUDE. I'M SORRY.
?!
WHERE IS THIS COMING FROM?
BUT THAT'S BECAUSE YOU WERE SUDDENLY A BOY!
SO I WAS SURPRISED...

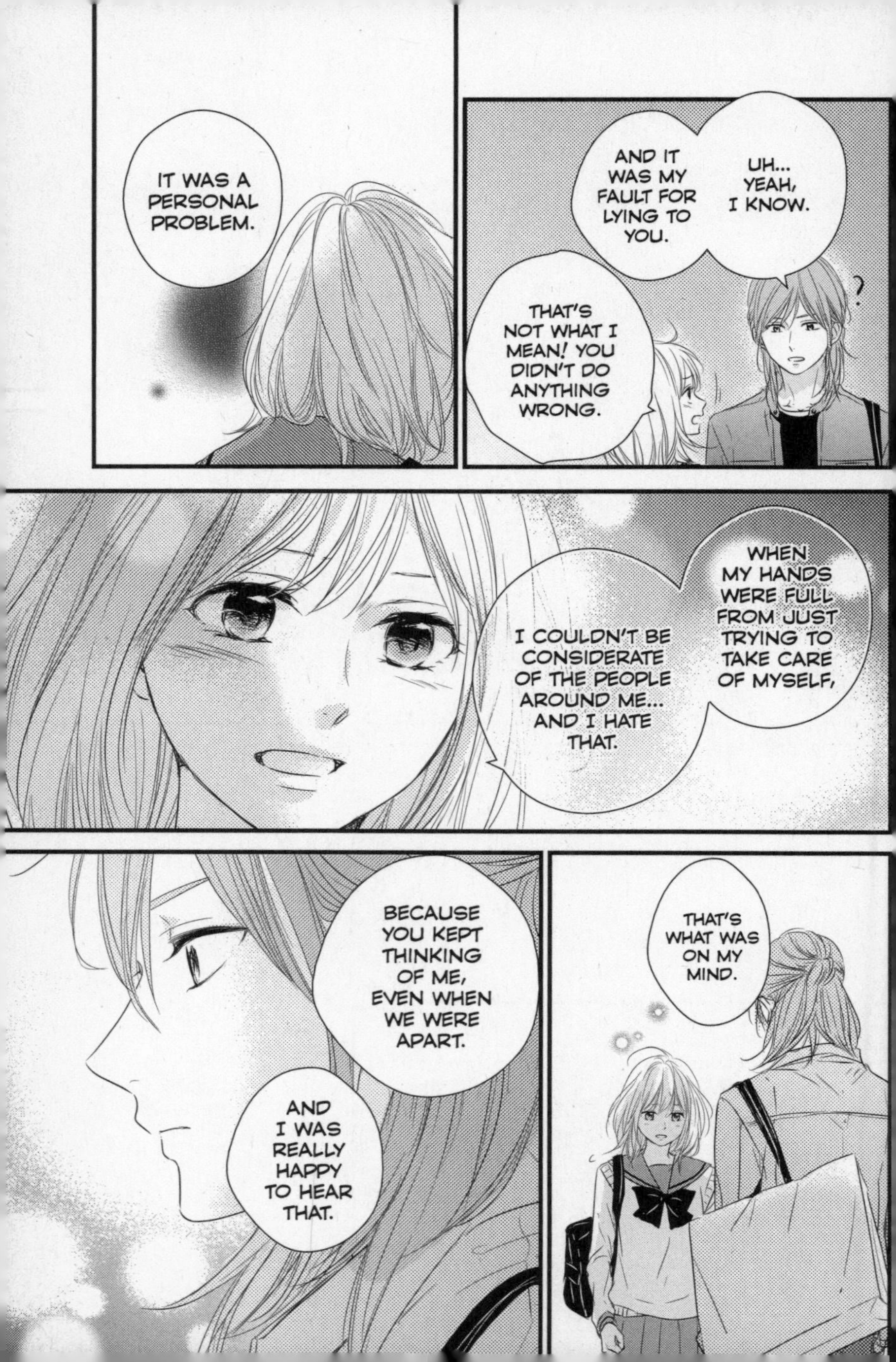
UH... YEAH, I KNOW.
AND IT WAS MY FAULT FOR LYING TO YOU.
THAT'S NOT WHAT I MEAN! YOU DIDN'T DO ANYTHING WRONG.
IT WAS A PERSONAL PROBLEM.
WHEN MY HANDS WERE FULL FROM JUST TRYING TO TAKE CARE OF MYSELF,
I COULDN'T BE CONSIDERATE OF THE PEOPLE AROUND ME... AND I HATE THAT.
THAT'S WHAT WAS ON MY MIND.
BECAUSE YOU KEPT THINKING OF ME, EVEN WHEN WE WERE APART.
AND I WAS REALLY HAPPY TO HEAR THAT.

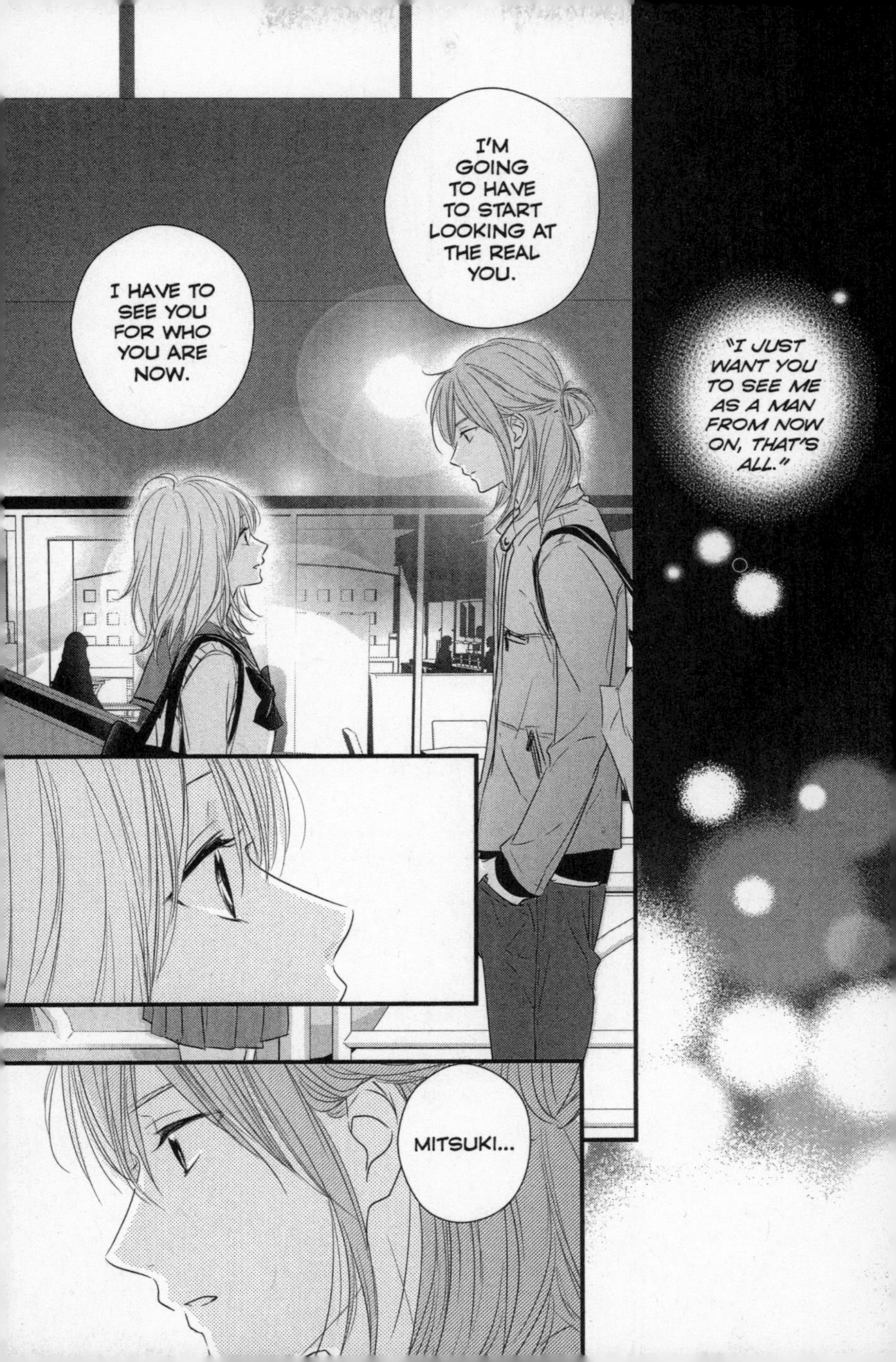
"I JUST WANT YOU TO SEE ME AS A MAN FROM NOW ON, THAT'S ALL."
I'M GOING TO HAVE TO START LOOKING AT THE REAL YOU.
I HAVE TO SEE YOU FOR WHO YOU ARE NOW.
MITSUKI...

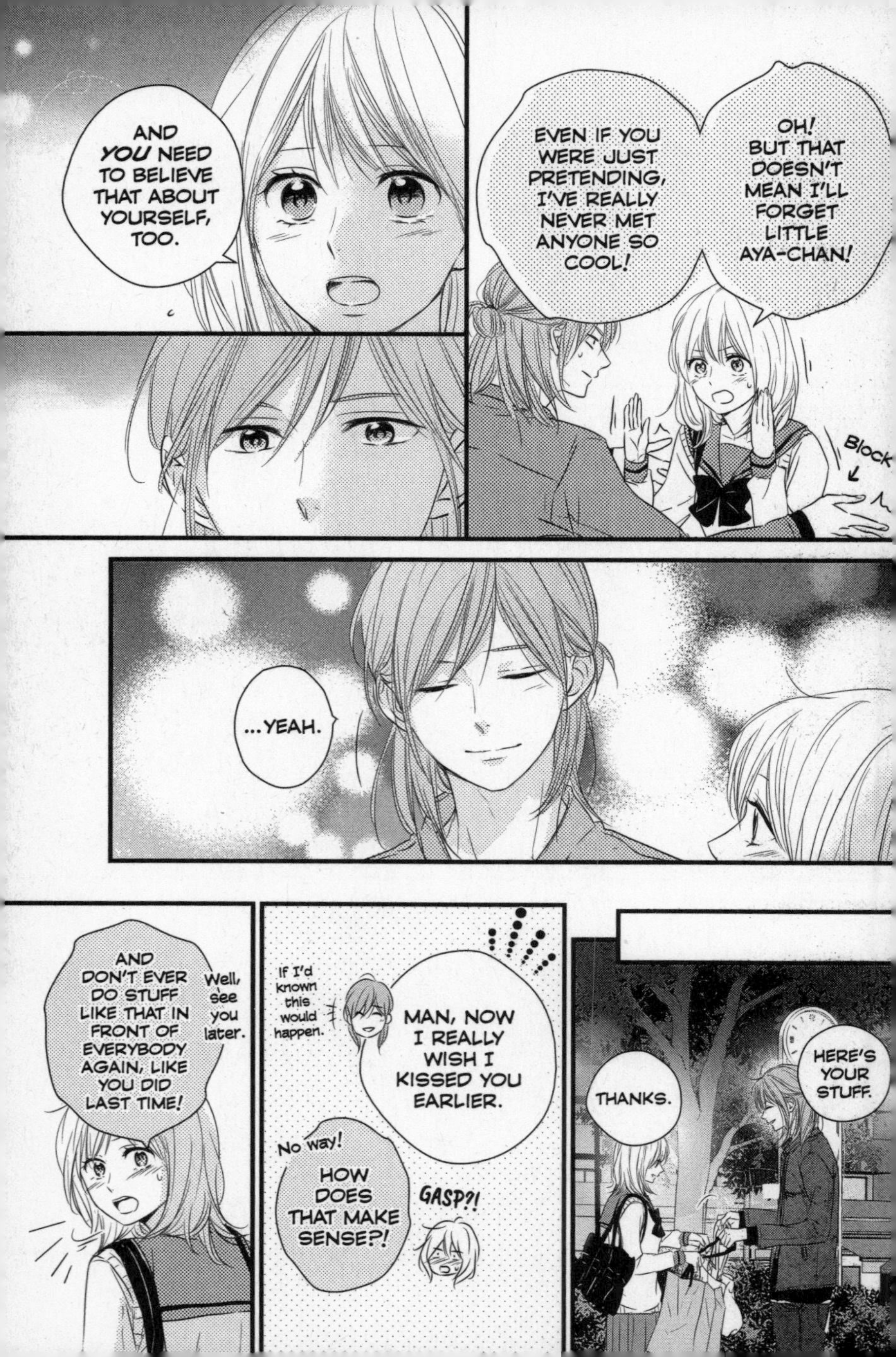
OH! BUT THAT DOESN'T MEAN I'LL FORGET LITTLE AYA-CHAN!
EVEN IF YOU WERE JUST PRETENDING, I'VE REALLY NEVER MET ANYONE SO COOL!
Block
AND *YOU* NEED TO BELIEVE THAT ABOUT YOURSELF, TOO.
...YEAH.
HERE'S YOUR STUFF.
THANKS.
MAN, NOW I REALLY WISH I KISSED YOU EARLIER.
If I'd known this would happen.
No way!
HOW DOES THAT MAKE SENSE?!
GASP?!
Well, see you later.
AND DON'T EVER DO STUFF LIKE THAT IN FRONT OF EVERYBODY AGAIN, LIKE YOU DID LAST TIME!

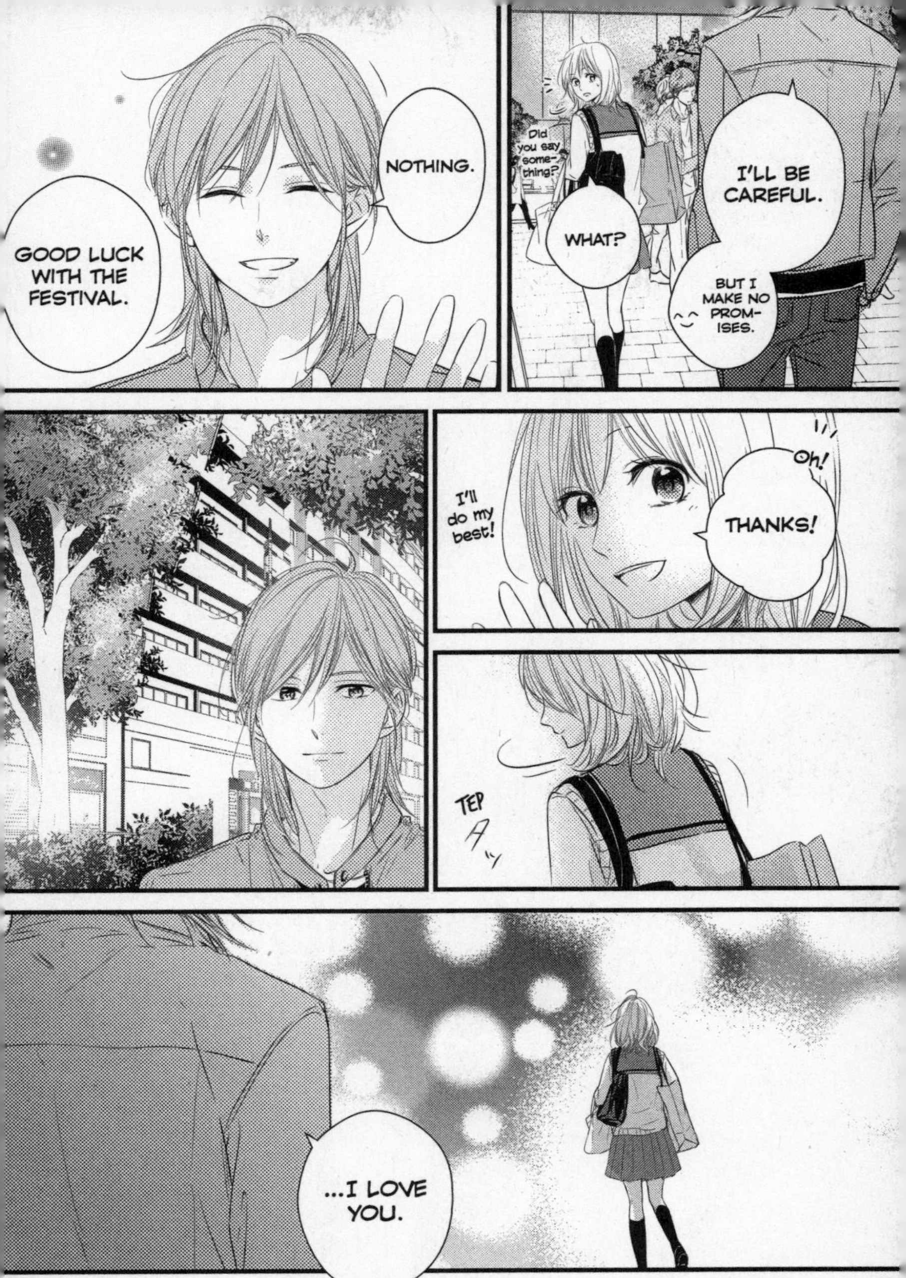
I'LL BE CAREFUL.
BUT I MAKE NO PROMISES.
Did you say something?
WHAT?
NOTHING.
GOOD LUCK WITH THE FESTIVAL.
Oh!
THANKS!
I'll do my best!
TEP
...I LOVE YOU.

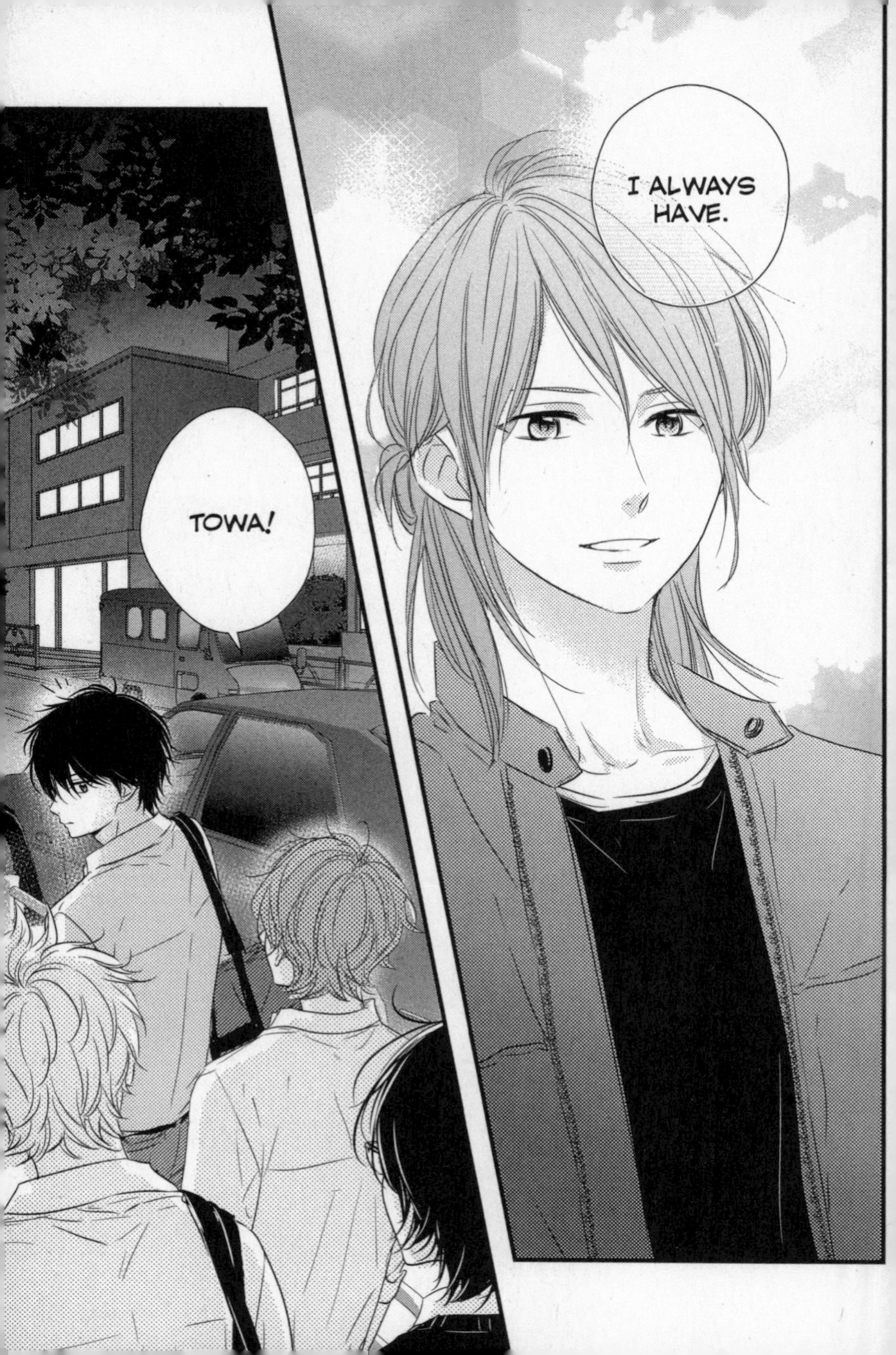
I ALWAYS HAVE.
TOWA!

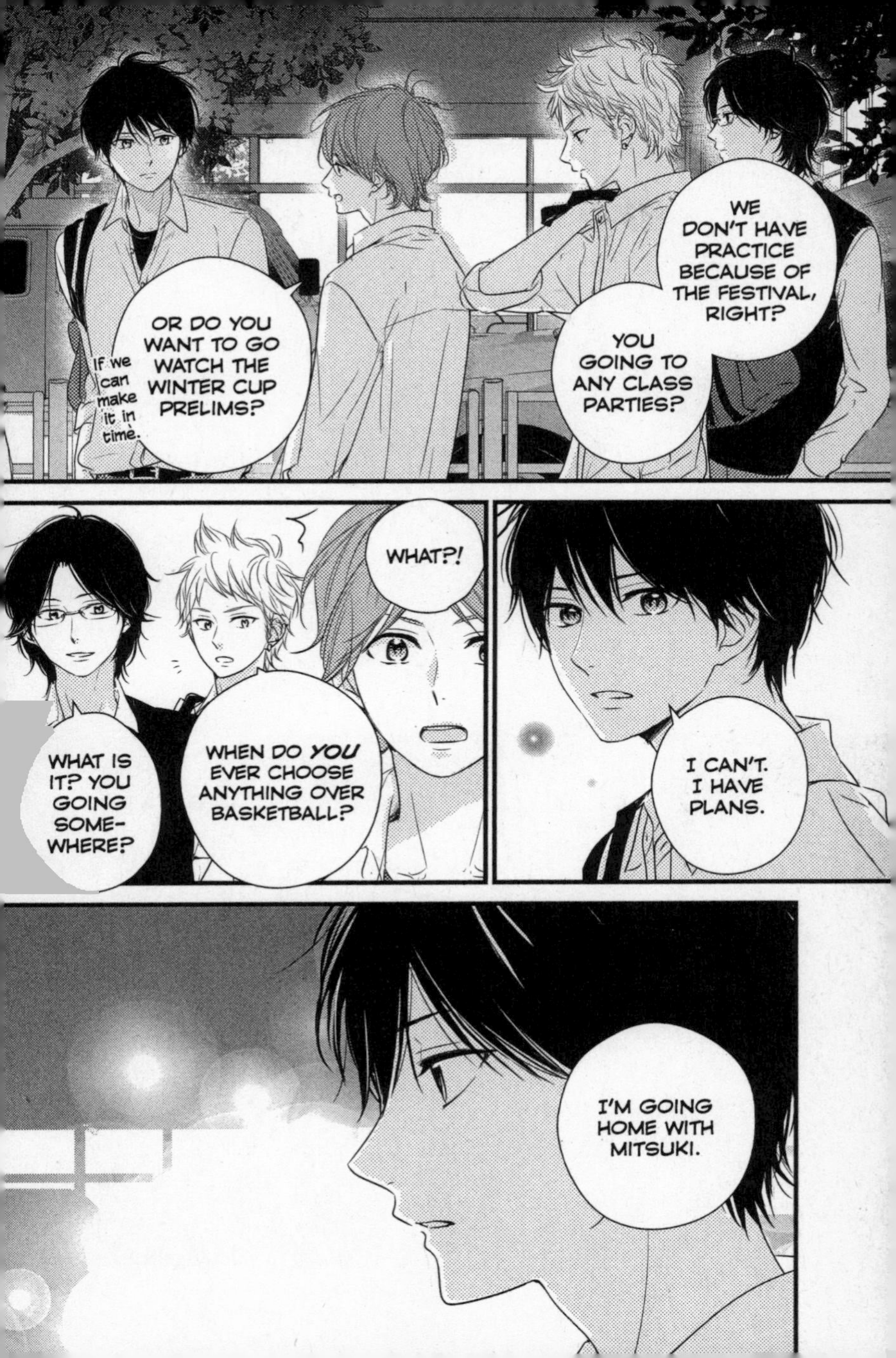
WE DON'T HAVE PRACTICE BECAUSE OF THE FESTIVAL, RIGHT?
YOU GOING TO ANY CLASS PARTIES?
OR DO YOU WANT TO GO WATCH THE WINTER CUP PRELIMS?
If we can make it in time.
I CAN'T. I HAVE PLANS.
WHAT?!
WHEN DO *YOU* EVER CHOOSE ANYTHING OVER BASKETBALL?
WHAT IS IT? YOU GOING SOME-WHERE?
I'M GOING HOME WITH MITSUKI.

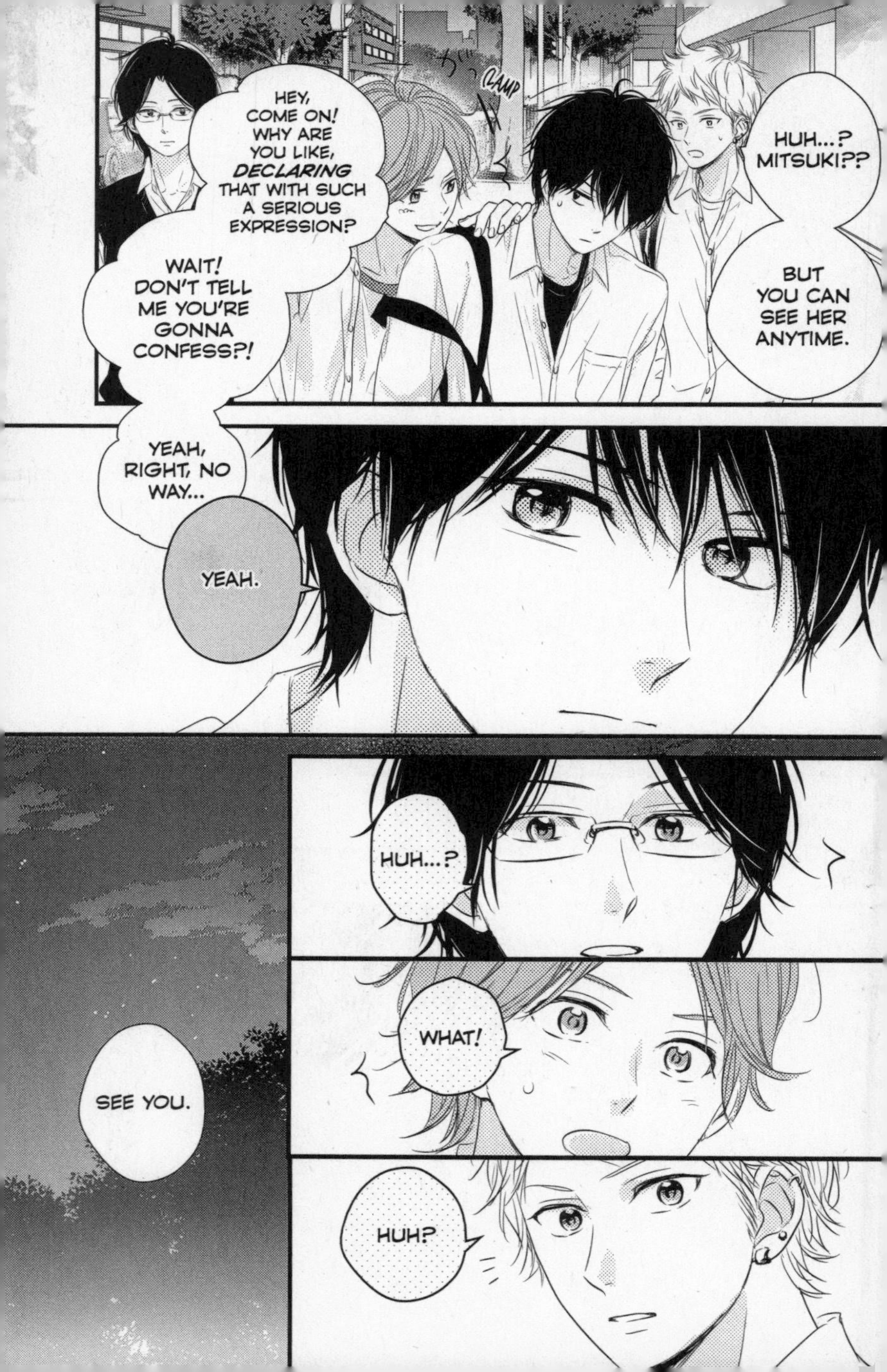
HUH...? MITSUKI??
BUT YOU CAN SEE HER ANYTIME.
HEY, COME ON! WHY ARE YOU LIKE, *DECLARING* THAT WITH SUCH A SERIOUS EXPRESSION?
WAIT! DON'T TELL ME YOU'RE GONNA CONFESS?!
YEAH, RIGHT, NO WAY...
YEAH.
HUH...?
WHAT!
HUH?
SEE YOU.

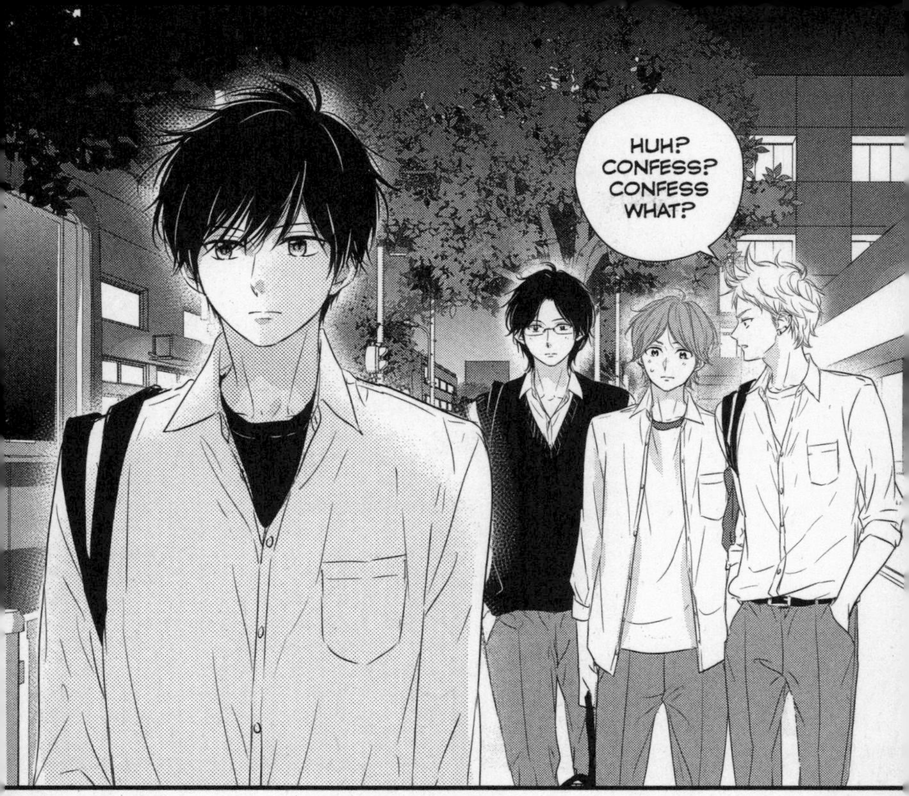
HUH? CONFESS? CONFESS WHAT?

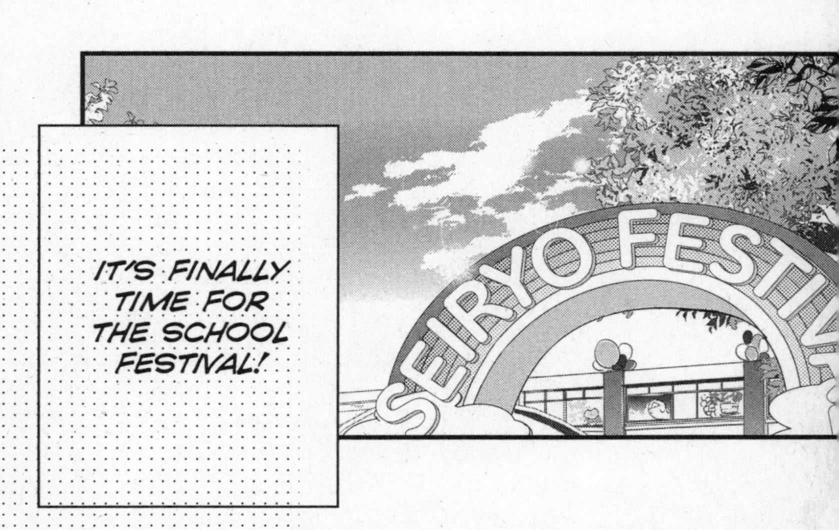
SEIRYO FESTIV
IT'S FINALLY TIME FOR THE SCHOOL FESTIVAL!

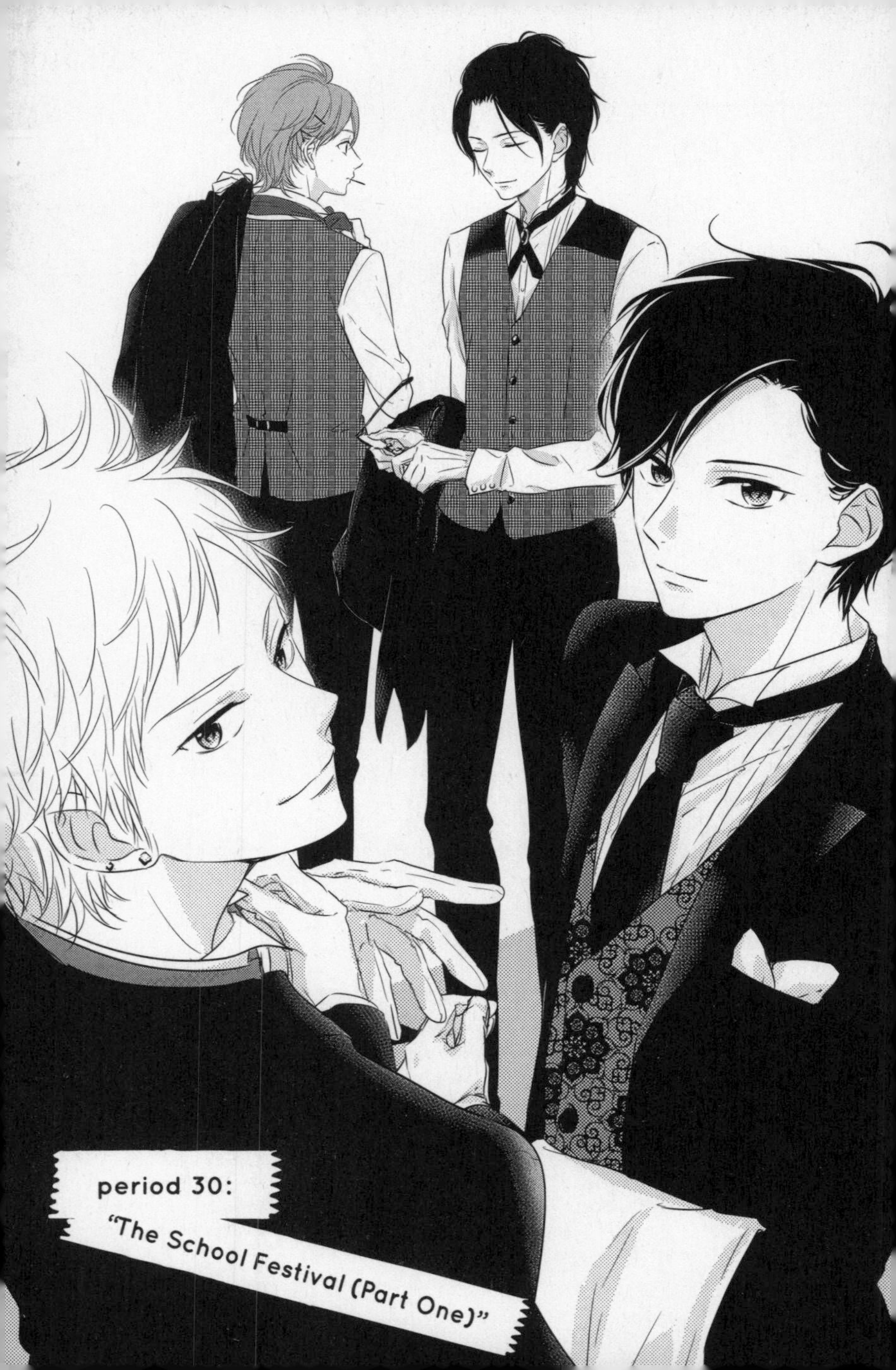
period 30:
"The School Festival (Part One)"

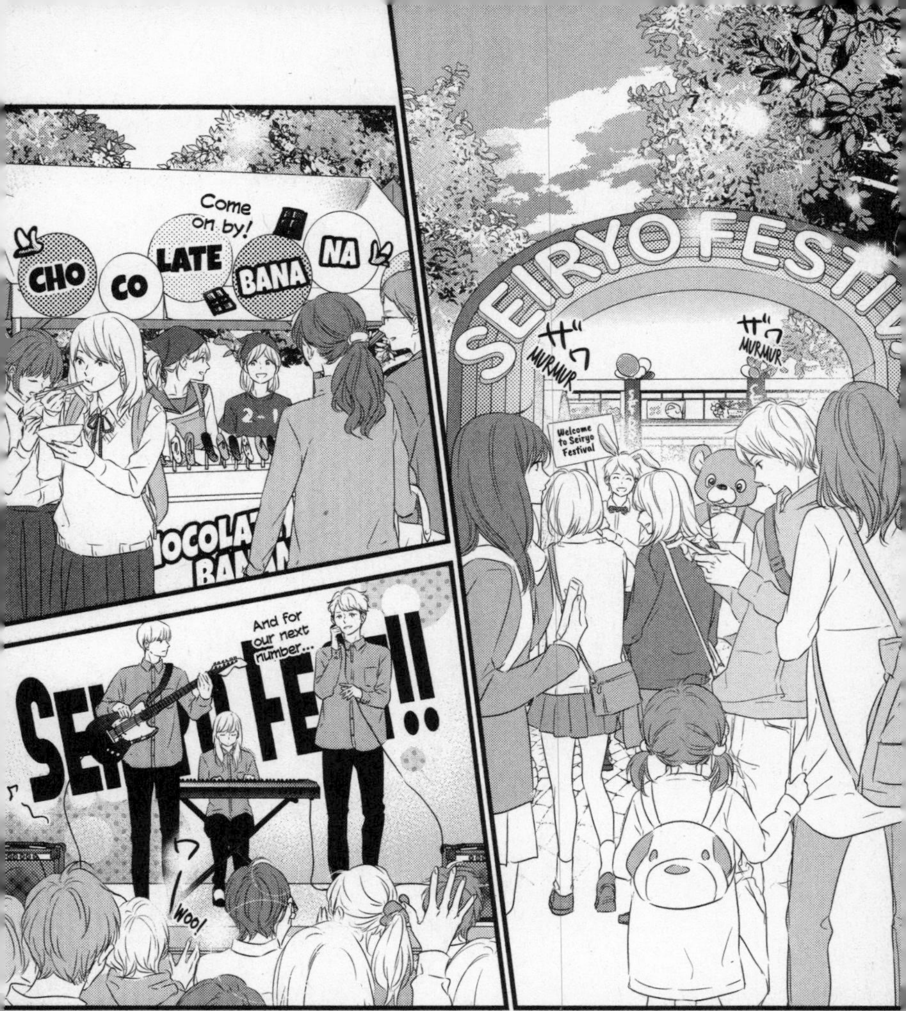
SEIRYO FESTIV
ザワ MURMUR
ザワ MURMUR
Welcome to Seiryo Festival
Come on by!
CHO CO LATE BANA NA
And for our next number...
WOO!

We'll start with Aya-chan.

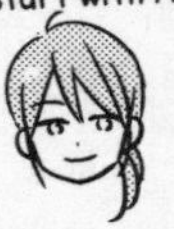

Family: Father, Mother, Aya
His father is currently in America, while he and his mother live in Japan.

Design from before the series started

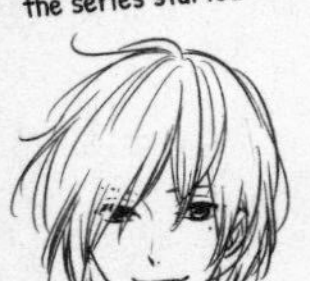

The all-talented Aya-chan is the most unrealistic of all the characters, but actually, his thought process is the closest to mine, which makes him easy to draw. At first, he didn't have long hair, and it wasn't colored with tone, either... He got to his current design in phase two of the planning process. He even had a mole (ha ha). He had other names, too, like Kaoru-chan and Yui-chan.

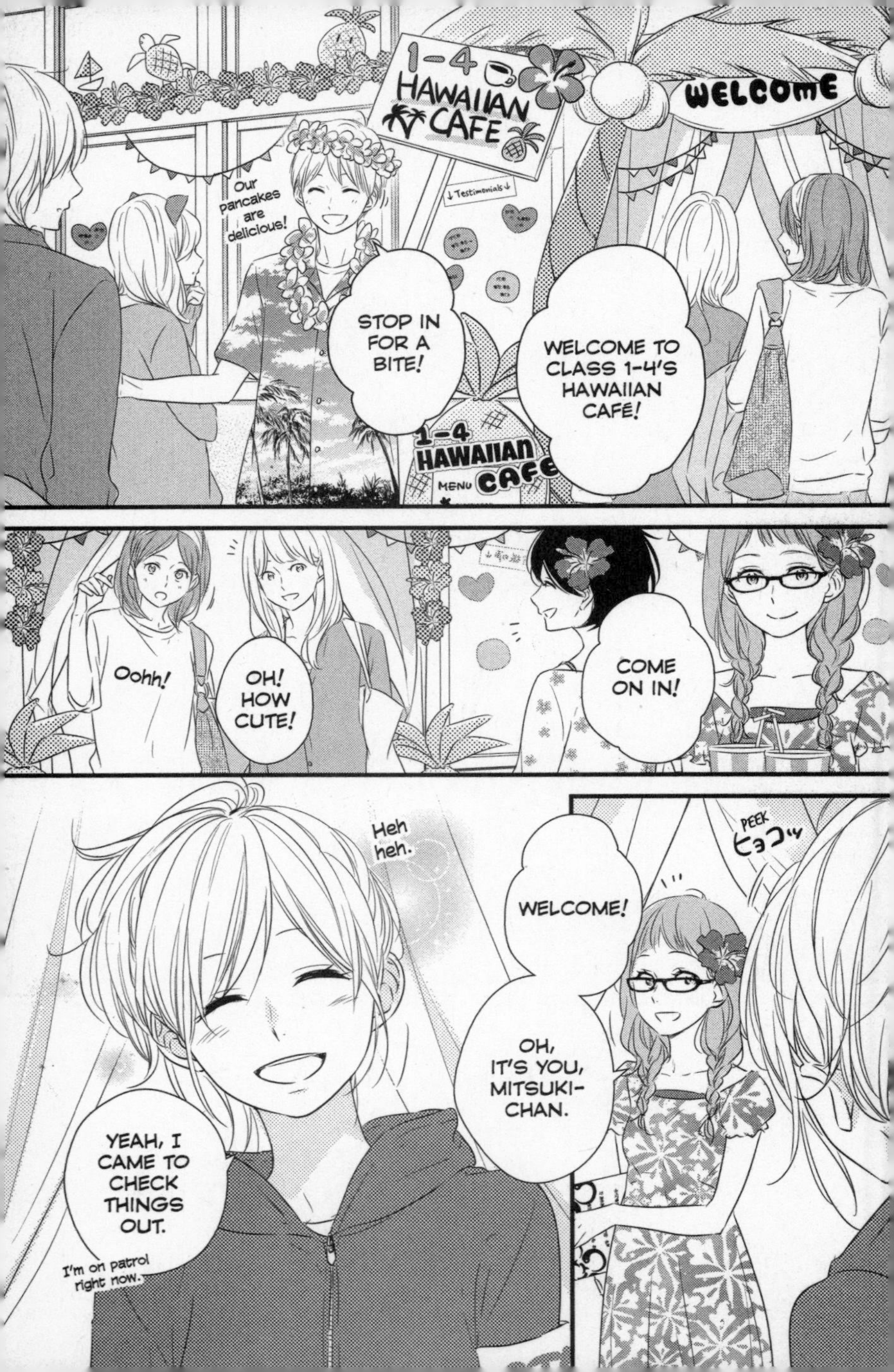
WELCOME
1-4 HAWAIIAN CAFE
WELCOME TO CLASS 1-4'S HAWAIIAN CAFÉ!
↓ Testimonials ↓
STOP IN FOR A BITE!
Our pancakes are delicious!
1-4 HAWAIIAN CAFE MENU
COME ON IN!
OH! HOW CUTE!
Oohh!
PEEK
ヒョコッ
WELCOME!
OH, IT'S YOU, MITSUKI-CHAN.
Heh heh.
YEAH, I CAME TO CHECK THINGS OUT.
I'm on patrol right now.

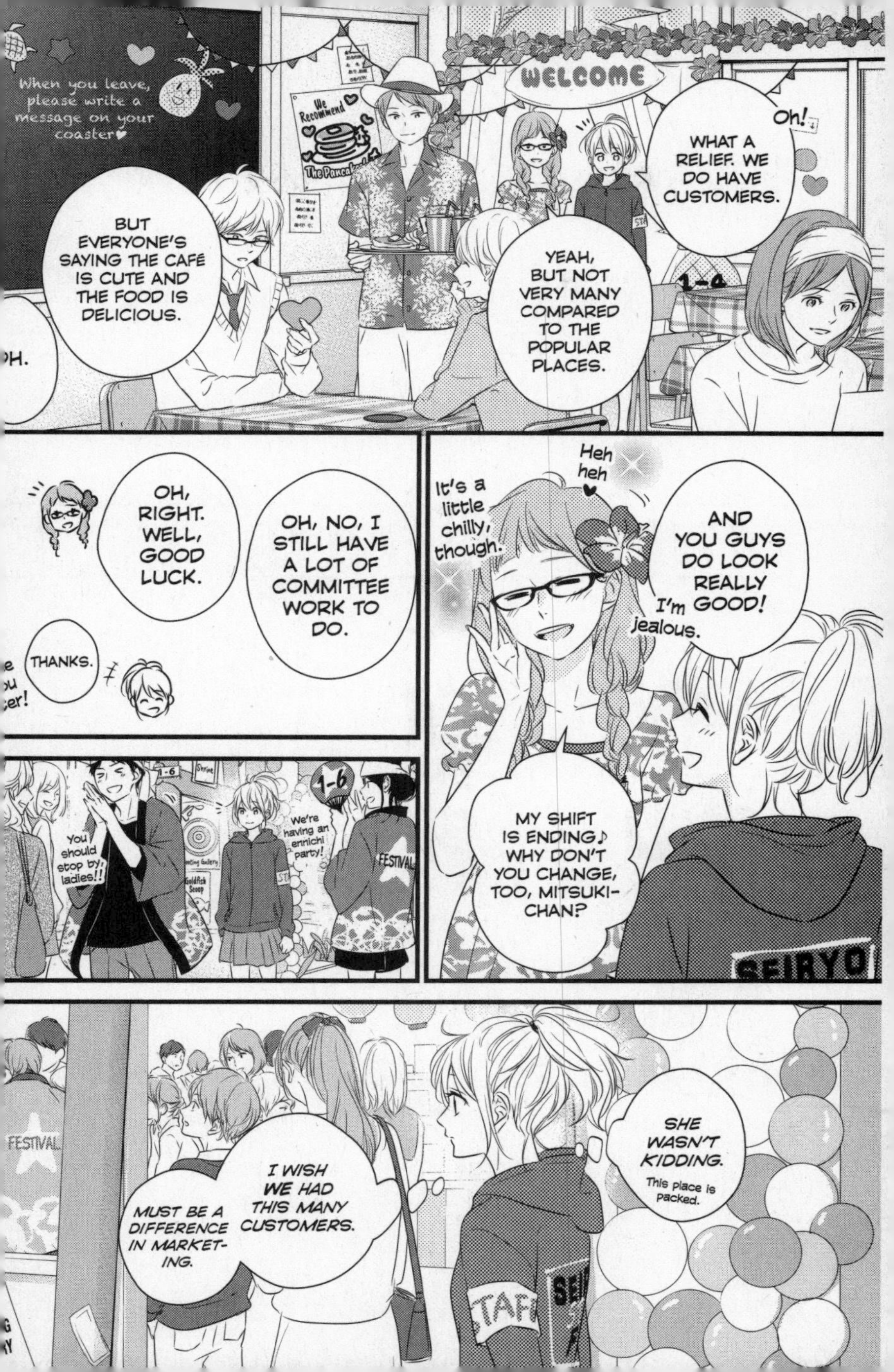
WELCOME
Oh!
WHAT A RELIEF. WE DO HAVE CUSTOMERS.
YEAH, BUT NOT VERY MANY COMPARED TO THE POPULAR PLACES.
1-4
We Recommend
BUT EVERYONE'S SAYING THE CAFÉ IS CUTE AND THE FOOD IS DELICIOUS.
When you leave, please write a message on your coaster♥
Heh heh
AND YOU GUYS DO LOOK REALLY GOOD!
I'm jealous.
It's a little chilly, though.
MY SHIFT IS ENDING♪ WHY DON'T YOU CHANGE, TOO, MITSUKI-CHAN?
SEIRYO
OH, NO, I STILL HAVE A LOT OF COMMITTEE WORK TO DO.
OH, RIGHT. WELL, GOOD LUCK.
THANKS.
1-6
We're having an ennichi party!
FESTIVAL
Shrine
Goldfish Scoop
You should stop by, ladies!!
SHE WASN'T KIDDING.
This place is packed.
I WISH WE HAD THIS MANY CUSTOMERS.
MUST BE A DIFFERENCE IN MARKETING.
FESTIVAL

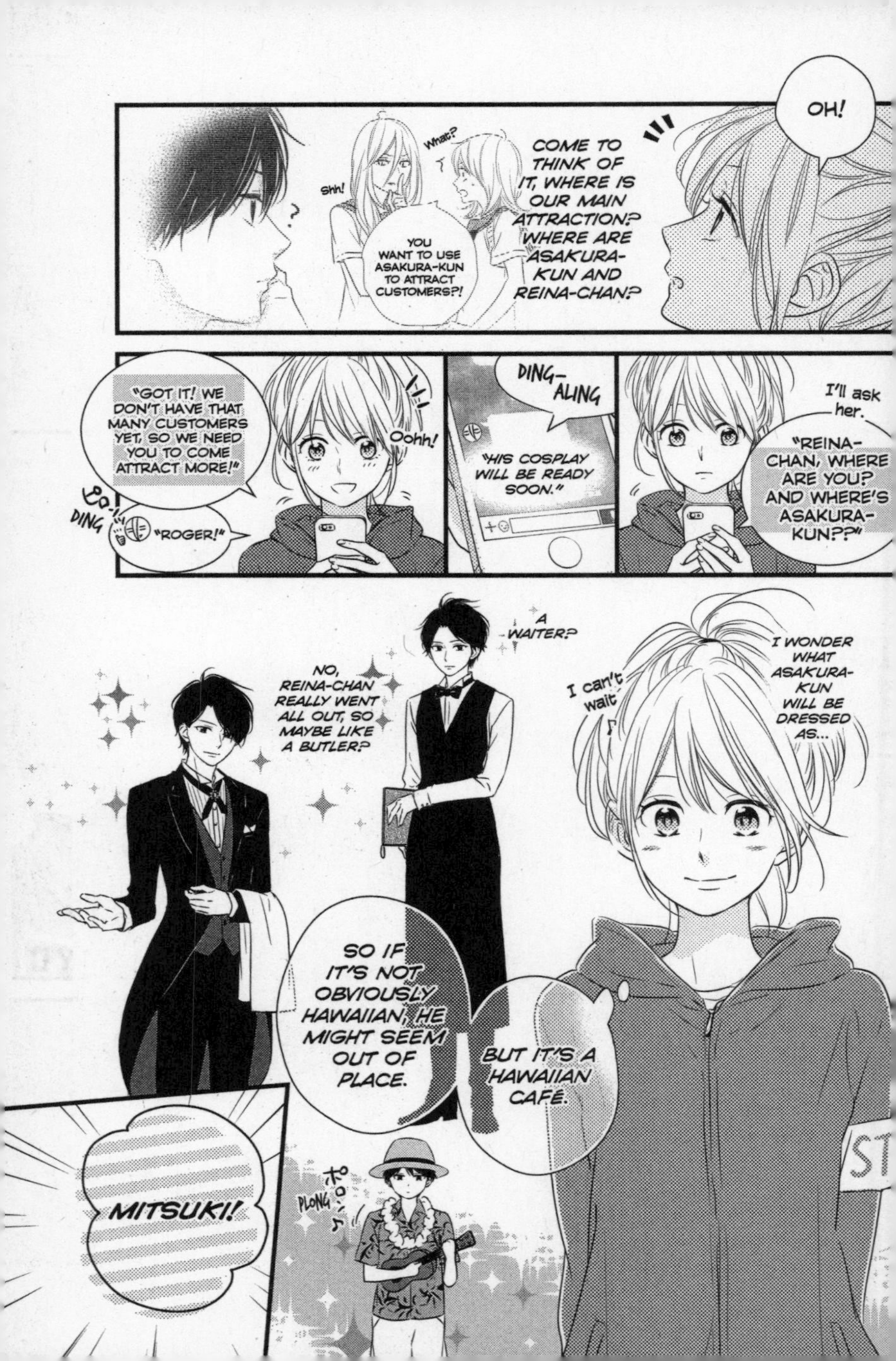

OH!
COME TO THINK OF IT, WHERE IS OUR MAIN ATTRACTION? WHERE ARE ASAKURA-KUN AND REINA-CHAN?
What?
Shh!
YOU WANT TO USE ASAKURA-KUN TO ATTRACT CUSTOMERS?!
I'll ask her.
"REINA-CHAN, WHERE ARE YOU? AND WHERE'S ASAKURA-KUN??"
DING-ALING
"HIS COSPLAY WILL BE READY SOON."
Oohh!
"GOT IT! WE DON'T HAVE THAT MANY CUSTOMERS YET, SO WE NEED YOU TO COME ATTRACT MORE!"
DING
"ROGER!"
I WONDER WHAT ASAKURA-KUN WILL BE DRESSED AS...
I can't wait
A WAITER?
NO, REINA-CHAN REALLY WENT ALL OUT, SO MAYBE LIKE A BUTLER?
BUT IT'S A HAWAIIAN CAFÉ.
SO IF IT'S NOT OBVIOUSLY HAWAIIAN, HE MIGHT SEEM OUT OF PLACE.
PLONG
MITSUKI!

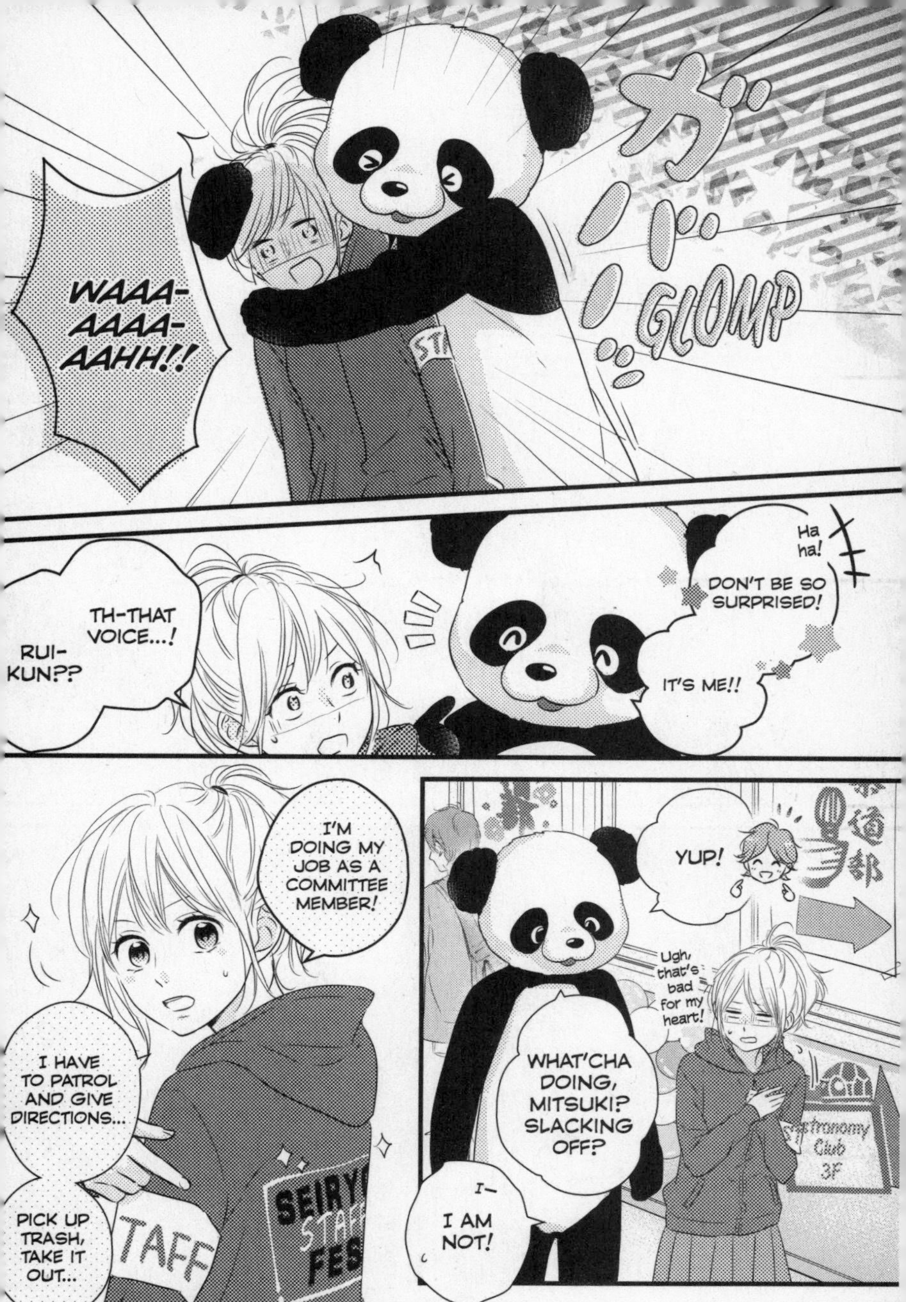
GLOMP
WAAA-AAAA-AAHH!!
Ha ha!
DON'T BE SO SURPRISED!
IT'S ME!!
TH-THAT VOICE...!
RUI-KUN??
YUP!
WHAT'CHA DOING, MITSUKI? SLACKING OFF?
Ugh, that's bad for my heart!
stronomy Club 3F
I— I AM NOT!
I'M DOING MY JOB AS A COMMITTEE MEMBER!
I HAVE TO PATROL AND GIVE DIRECTIONS...
PICK UP TRASH, TAKE IT OUT...
SEIRYO STAFF FES
TAFF

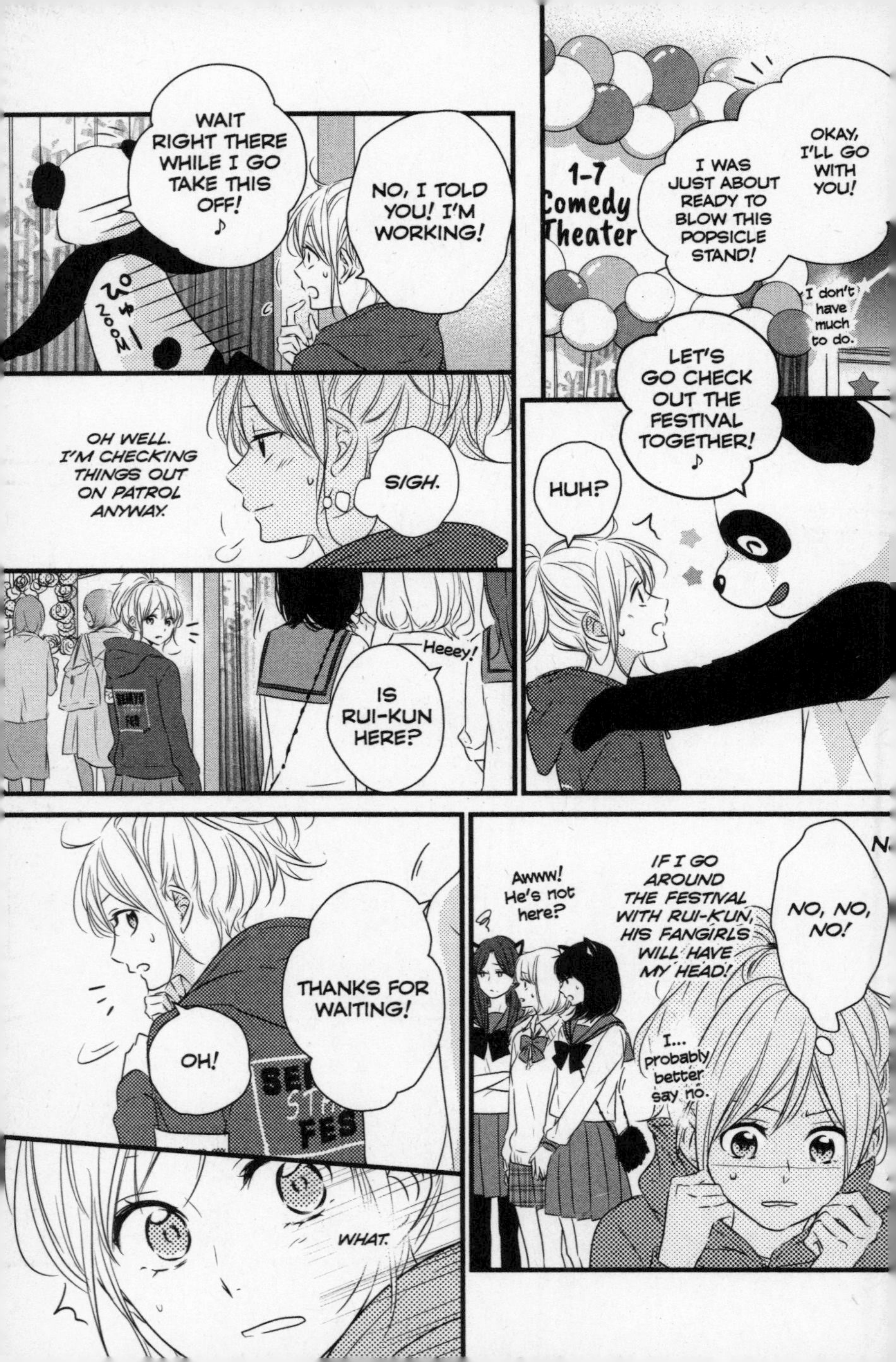
1-7 Comedy Theater
OKAY, I'LL GO WITH YOU!
I WAS JUST ABOUT READY TO BLOW THIS POPSICLE STAND!
I don't have much to do.
LET'S GO CHECK OUT THE FESTIVAL TOGETHER! ♪
HUH?
NO, I TOLD YOU! I'M WORKING!
WAIT RIGHT THERE WHILE I GO TAKE THIS OFF! ♪
SIGH.
OH WELL. I'M CHECKING THINGS OUT ON PATROL ANYWAY.
Heeey!
IS RUI-KUN HERE?
NO, NO, NO!
IF I GO AROUND THE FESTIVAL WITH RUI-KUN, HIS FANGIRLS WILL HAVE MY HEAD!
I... probably better say no.
Awww! He's not here?
THANKS FOR WAITING!
OH!
WHAT.

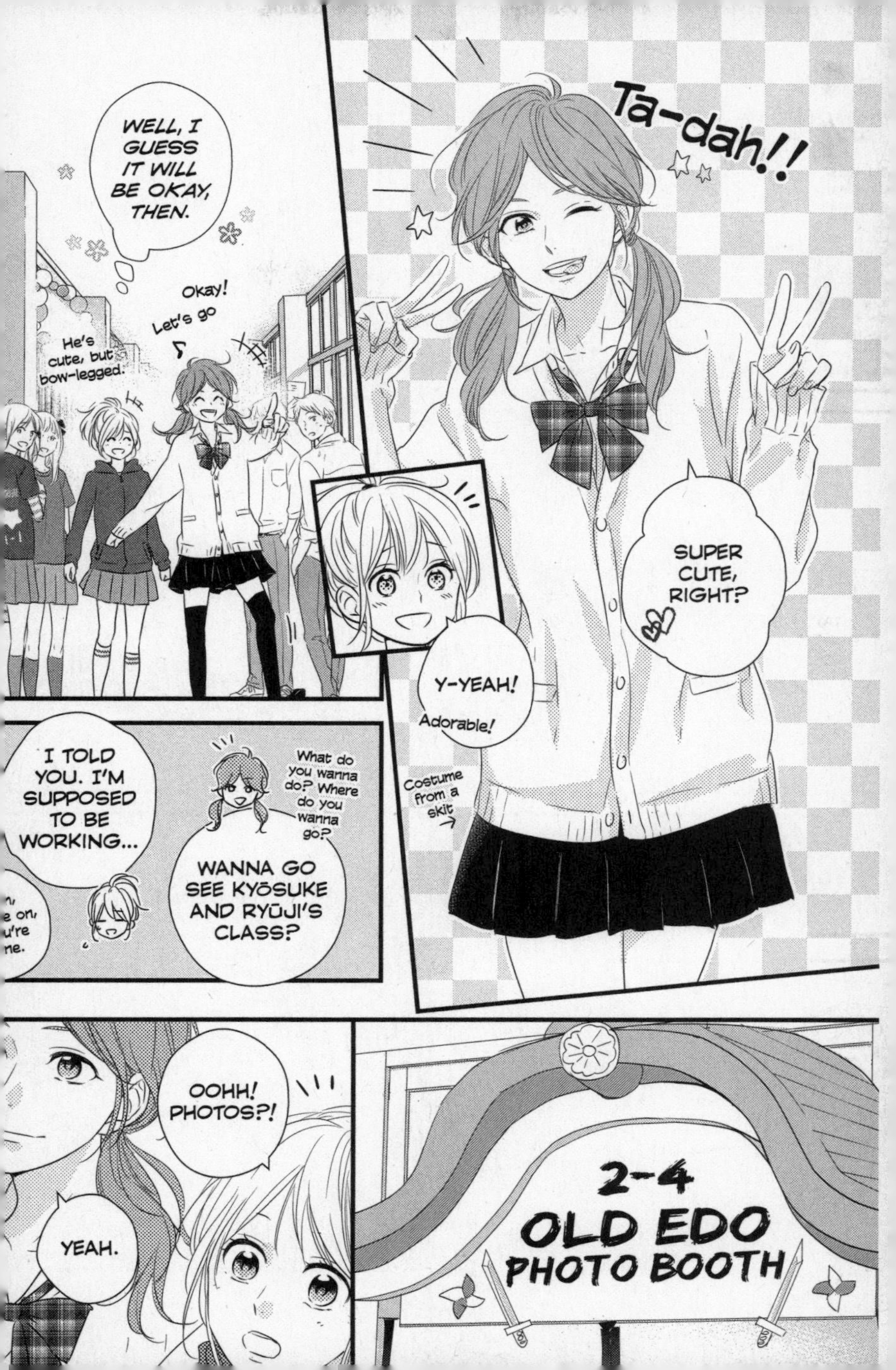

Ta-dah!!
SUPER CUTE, RIGHT?
Y-YEAH!
Adorable!
Costume from a skit
WELL, I GUESS IT WILL BE OKAY, THEN.
Okay! Let's go ♪
He's cute, but bow-legged.
What do you wanna do? Where do you wanna go?
WANNA GO SEE KYŌSUKE AND RYŪJI'S CLASS?
I TOLD YOU. I'M SUPPOSED TO BE WORKING...
2-4 OLD EDO PHOTO BOOTH
OOHH! PHOTOS?!
YEAH.

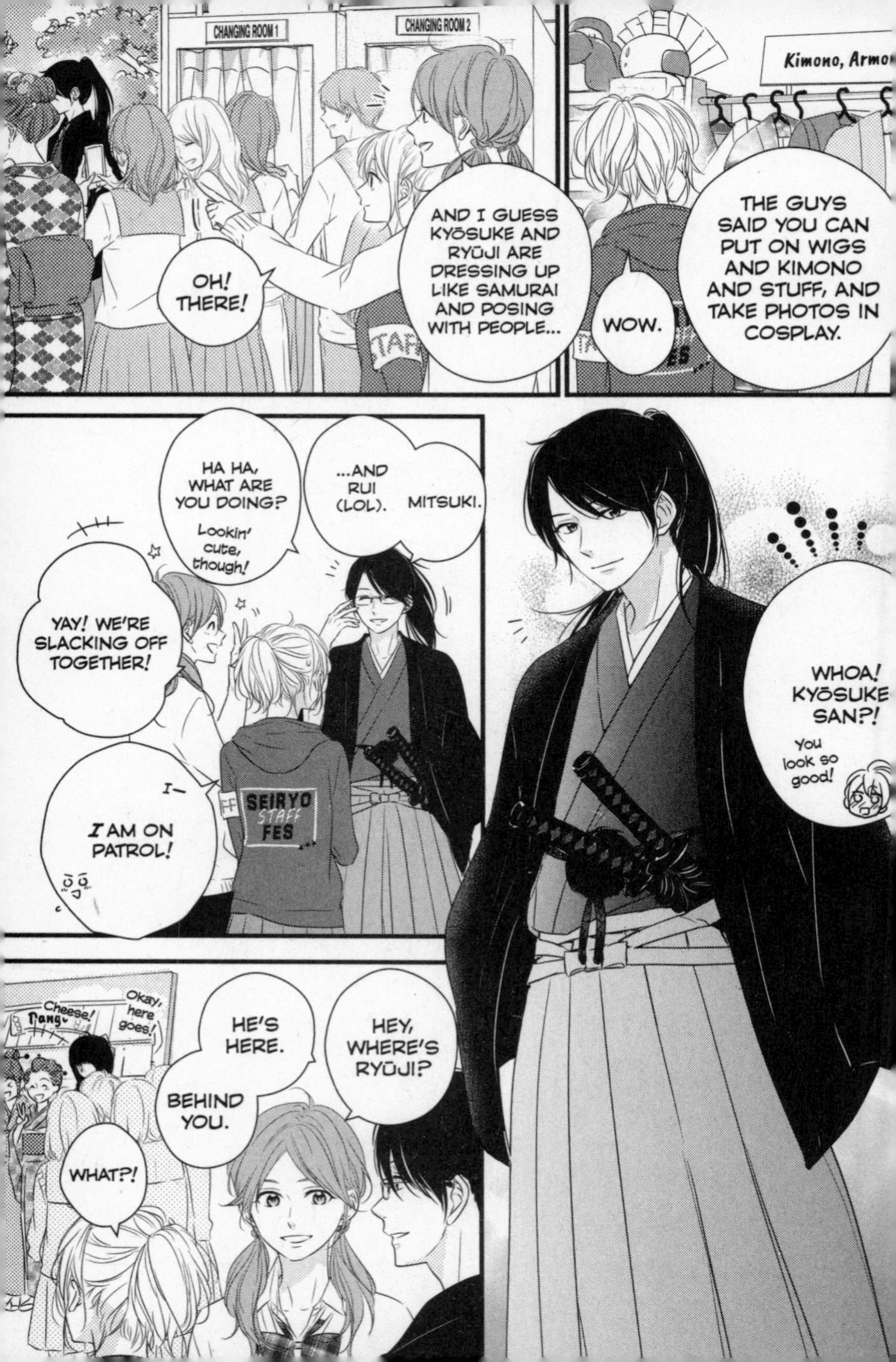

Kimono, Armor
THE GUYS SAID YOU CAN PUT ON WIGS AND KIMONO AND STUFF, AND TAKE PHOTOS IN COSPLAY.
WOW.
CHANGING ROOM 2
CHANGING ROOM 1
AND I GUESS KYŌSUKE AND RYŪJI ARE DRESSING UP LIKE SAMURAI AND POSING WITH PEOPLE...
OH! THERE!
WHOA! KYŌSUKE SAN?!
You look so good!
MITSUKI.
...AND RUI (LOL).
HA HA, WHAT ARE YOU DOING?
Lookin' cute, though!
YAY! WE'RE SLACKING OFF TOGETHER!
SEIRYO STAFF FES
I— I AM ON PATROL!
HEY, WHERE'S RYŪJI?
HE'S HERE.
BEHIND YOU.
Okay, here goes!
Cheese!
WHAT?!

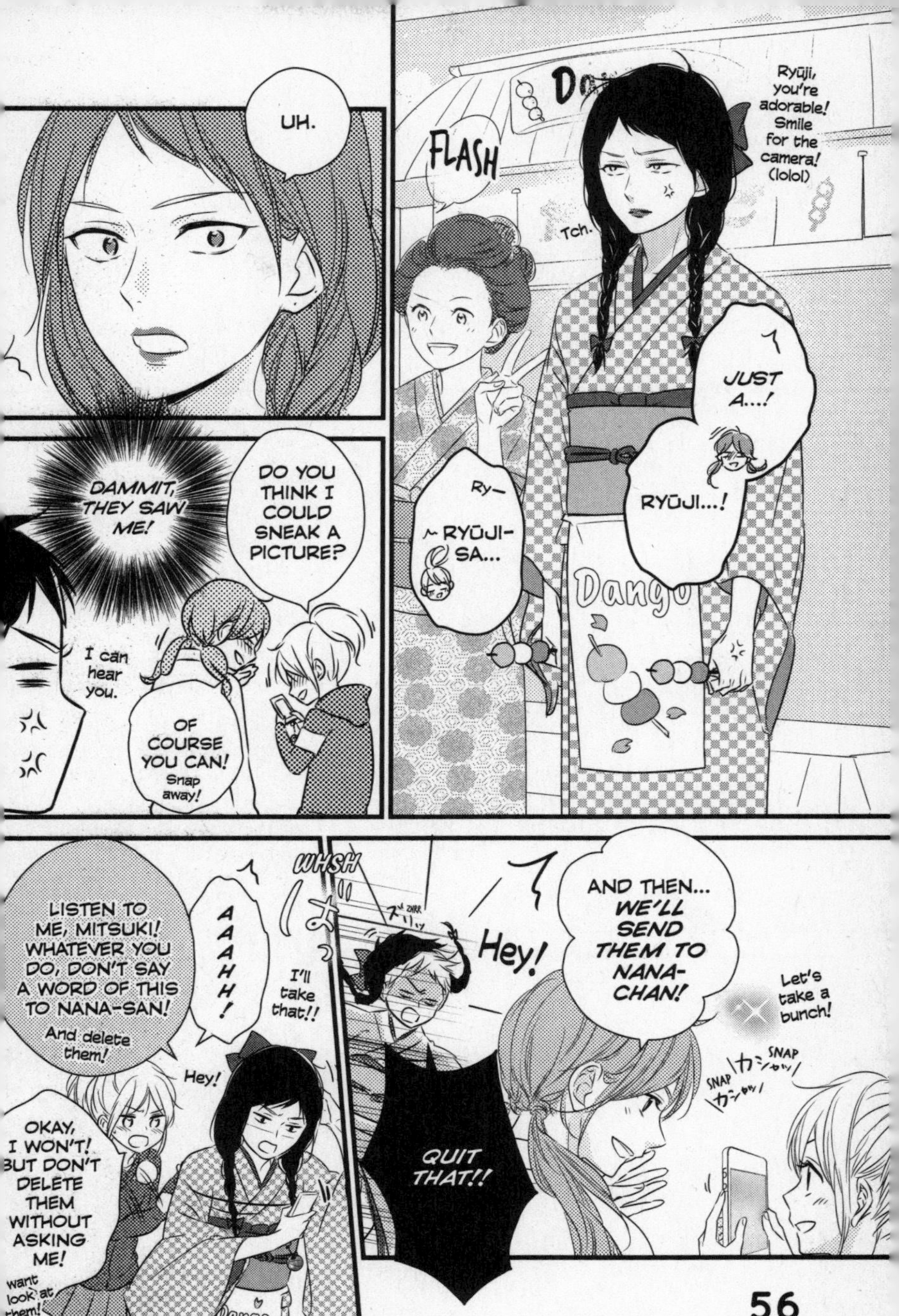

Ryūji, you're adorable! Smile for the camera! (lolol)
FLASH
Tch.
JUST A...!
RYŪJI...!
Ry— RYŪJI-SA...
Dango
UH.
DO YOU THINK I COULD SNEAK A PICTURE?
DAMMIT, THEY SAW ME!
OF COURSE YOU CAN! Snap away!
I can hear you.
AND THEN... WE'LL SEND THEM TO NANA-CHAN!
Let's take a bunch!
SNAP
SNAP
Hey!
WHSH
ZHRR
QUIT THAT!!
AAAAHH!
I'll take that!!
LISTEN TO ME, MITSUKI! WHATEVER YOU DO, DON'T SAY A WORD OF THIS TO NANA-SAN!
And delete them!
Hey!
OKAY, I WON'T! BUT DON'T DELETE THEM WITHOUT ASKING ME!
want look at them!
Dango

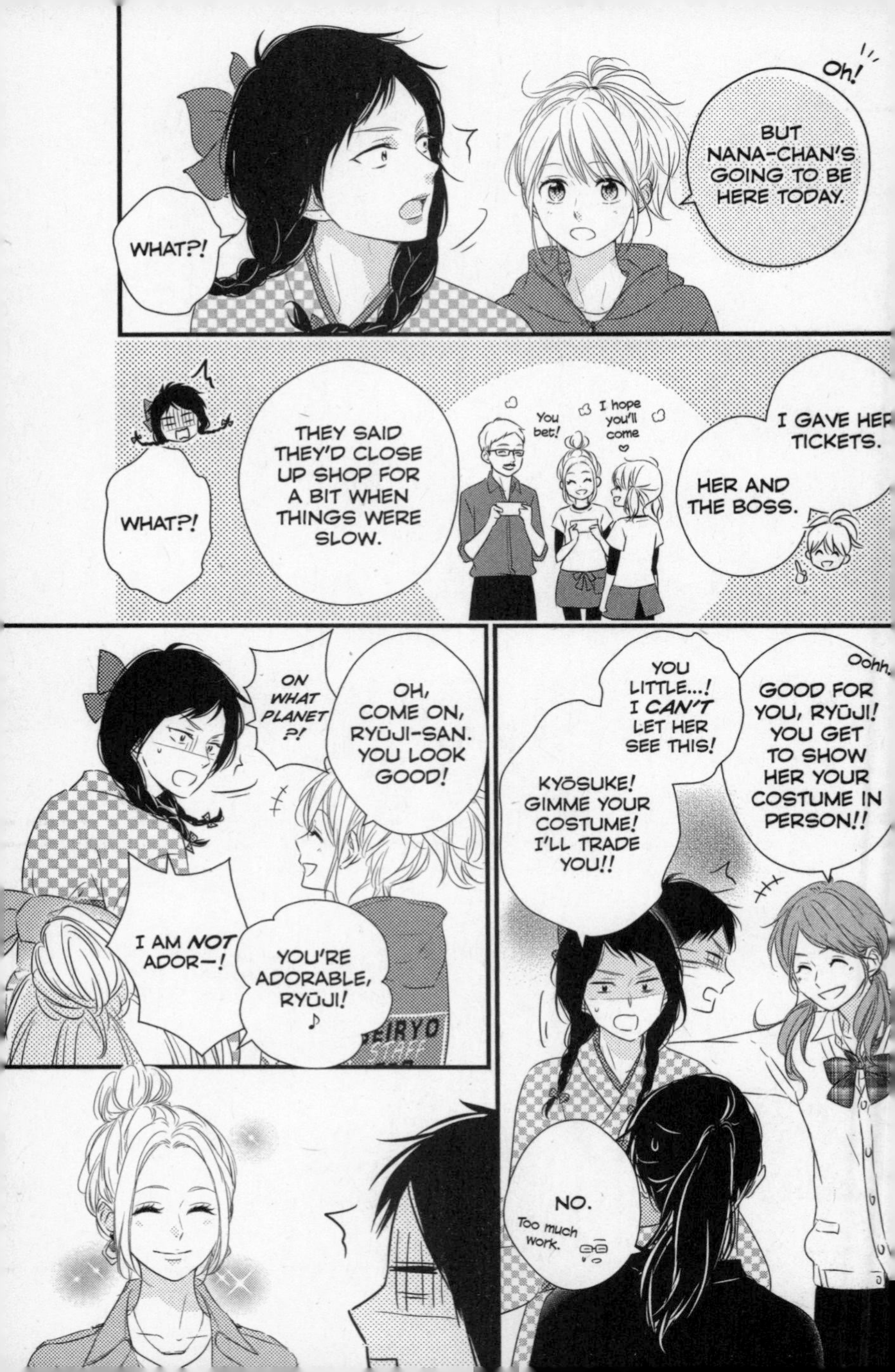

Oh!
BUT NANA-CHAN'S GOING TO BE HERE TODAY.
WHAT?!
I GAVE HER TICKETS.
HER AND THE BOSS.
I hope you'll come
You bet!
THEY SAID THEY'D CLOSE UP SHOP FOR A BIT WHEN THINGS WERE SLOW.
WHAT?!
Oohh.
GOOD FOR YOU, RYŪJI! YOU GET TO SHOW HER YOUR COSTUME IN PERSON!!
YOU LITTLE...! I CAN'T LET HER SEE THIS!
KYŌSUKE! GIMME YOUR COSTUME! I'LL TRADE YOU!!
NO.
Too much work.
OH, COME ON, RYŪJI-SAN. YOU LOOK GOOD!
ON WHAT PLANET?!
YOU'RE ADORABLE, RYŪJI! ♪
I AM NOT ADOR—!

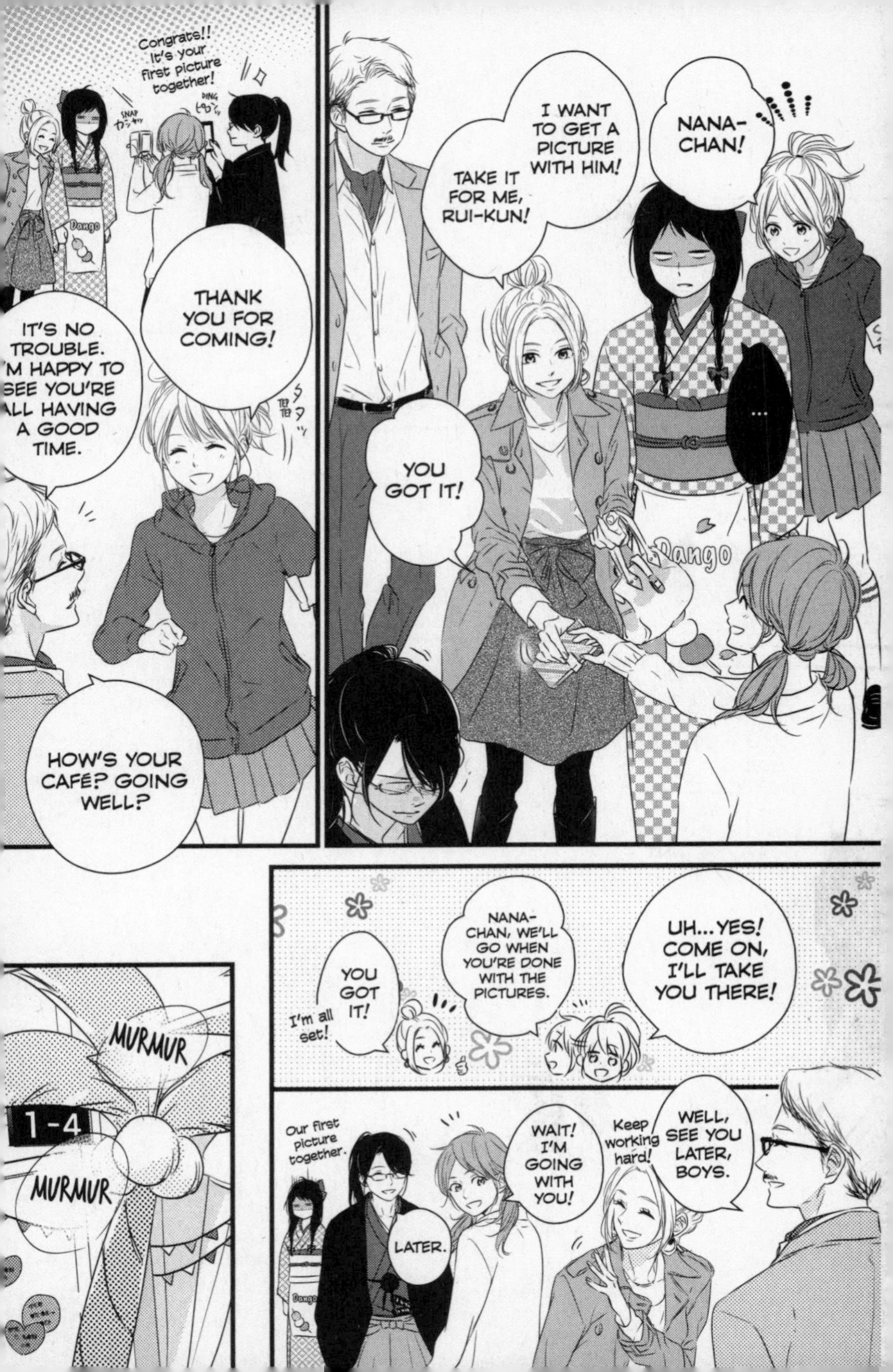
NANA-CHAN!
I WANT TO GET A PICTURE WITH HIM!
TAKE IT FOR ME, RUI-KUN!
...
YOU GOT IT!
Congrats!! It's your first picture together!
DING
SNAP
THANK YOU FOR COMING!
TEP TEP
IT'S NO TROUBLE. 'M HAPPY TO SEE YOU'RE LL HAVING A GOOD TIME.
HOW'S YOUR CAFÉ? GOING WELL?
UH...YES! COME ON, I'LL TAKE YOU THERE!
NANA-CHAN, WE'LL GO WHEN YOU'RE DONE WITH THE PICTURES.
YOU GOT IT!
I'm all set!
WELL, SEE YOU LATER, BOYS.
Keep working hard!
WAIT! I'M GOING WITH YOU!
Our first picture together.
LATER.
MURMUR
1-4
MURMUR

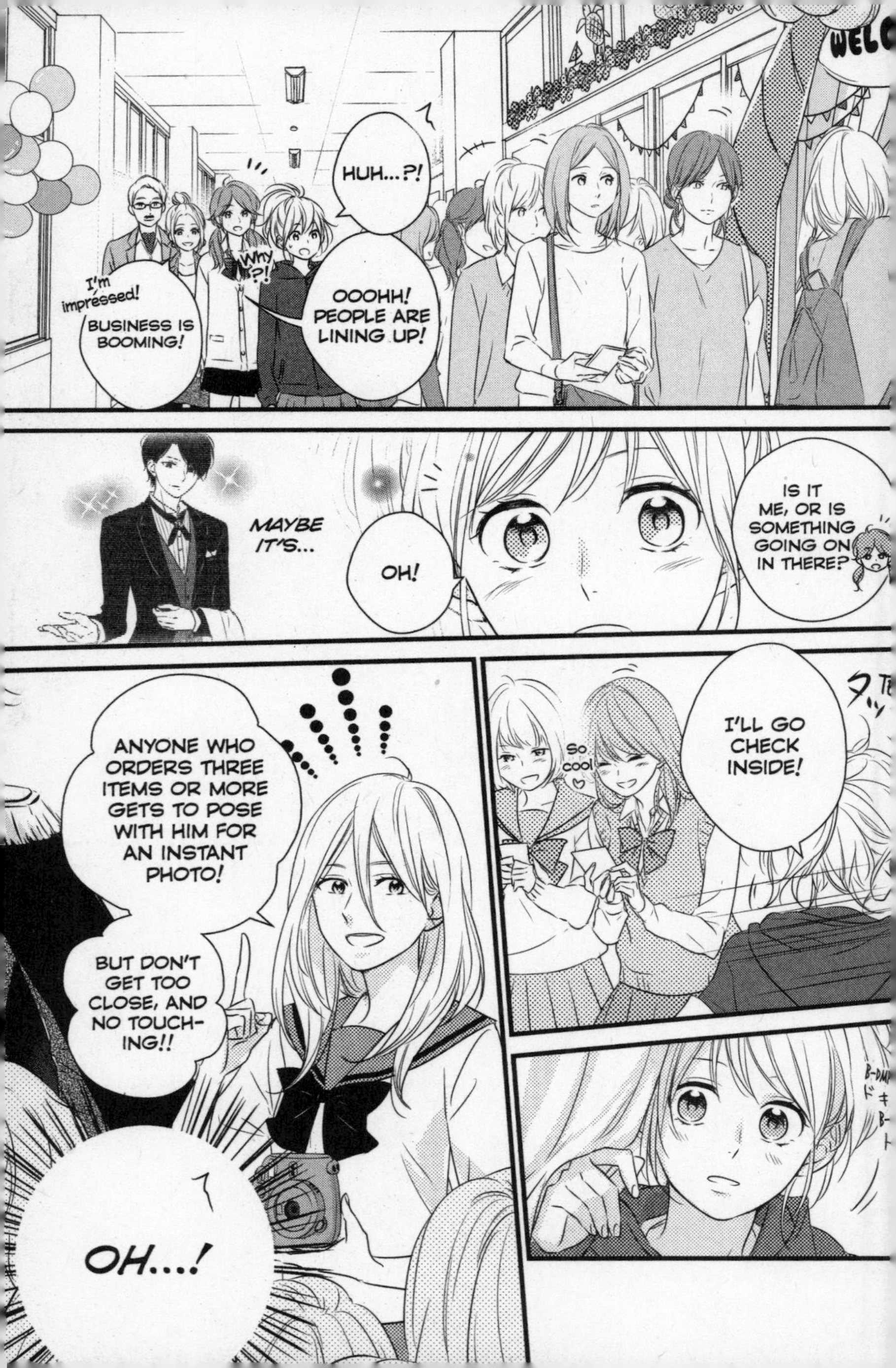
WELC
HUH...?!
OOOHH! PEOPLE ARE LINING UP!
Why?!
I'm impressed!
BUSINESS IS BOOMING!
IS IT ME, OR IS SOMETHING GOING ON IN THERE?
OH!
MAYBE IT'S...
I'LL GO CHECK INSIDE!
So cool
ANYONE WHO ORDERS THREE ITEMS OR MORE GETS TO POSE WITH HIM FOR AN INSTANT PHOTO!
BUT DON'T GET TOO CLOSE, AND NO TOUCHING!!
OH...!

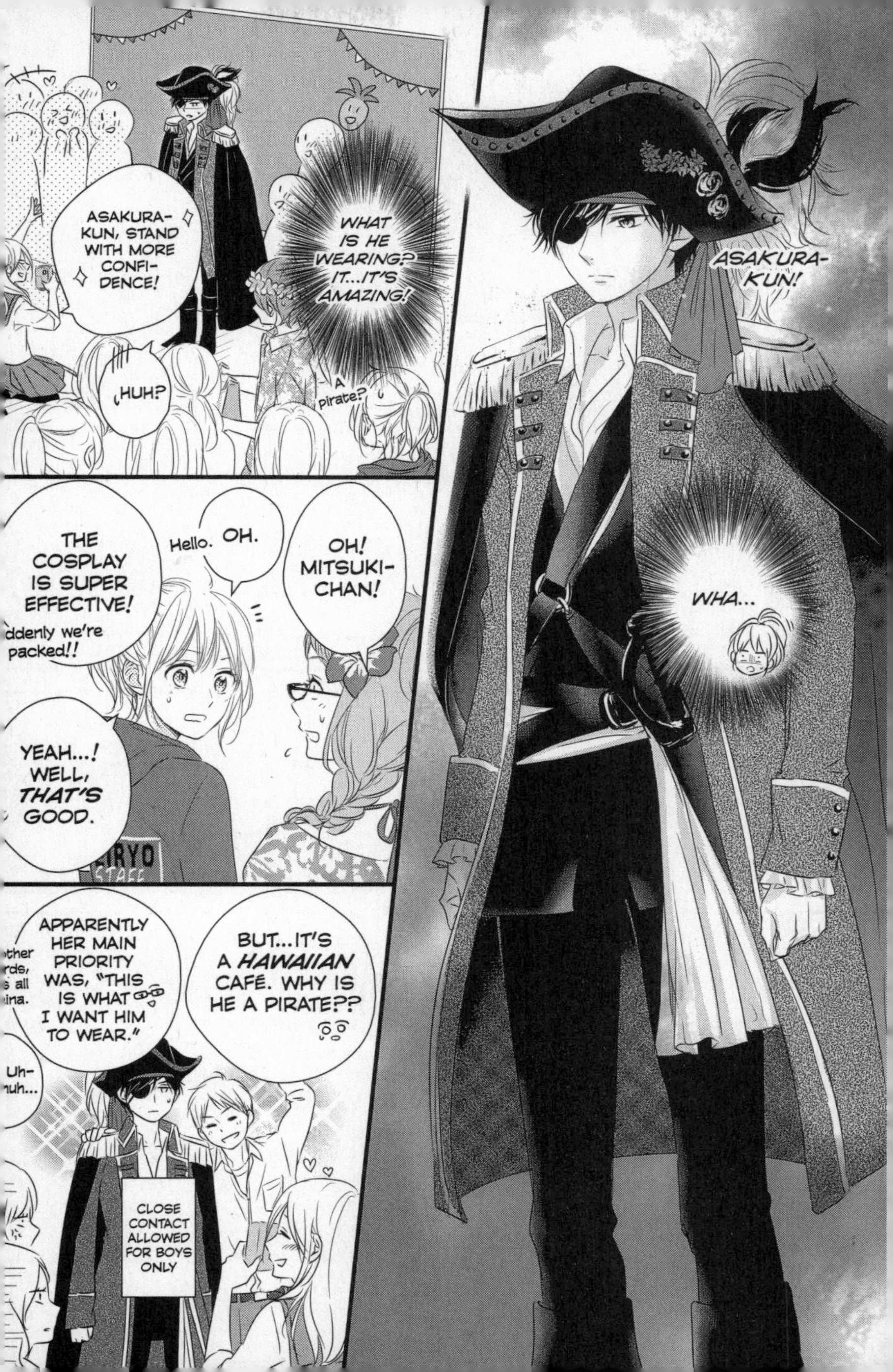
ASAKURA-KUN!
WHA...
WHAT IS HE WEARING? IT...IT'S AMAZING!
ASAKURA-KUN, STAND WITH MORE CONFIDENCE!
A pirate?
HUH?
OH! MITSUKI-CHAN!
Hello. OH.
THE COSPLAY IS SUPER EFFECTIVE!
ddenly we're packed!!
YEAH...! WELL, *THAT'S* GOOD.
BUT...IT'S A *HAWAIIAN* CAFÉ. WHY IS HE A PIRATE??
APPARENTLY HER MAIN PRIORITY WAS, "THIS IS WHAT I WANT HIM TO WEAR."
CLOSE CONTACT ALLOWED FOR BOYS ONLY

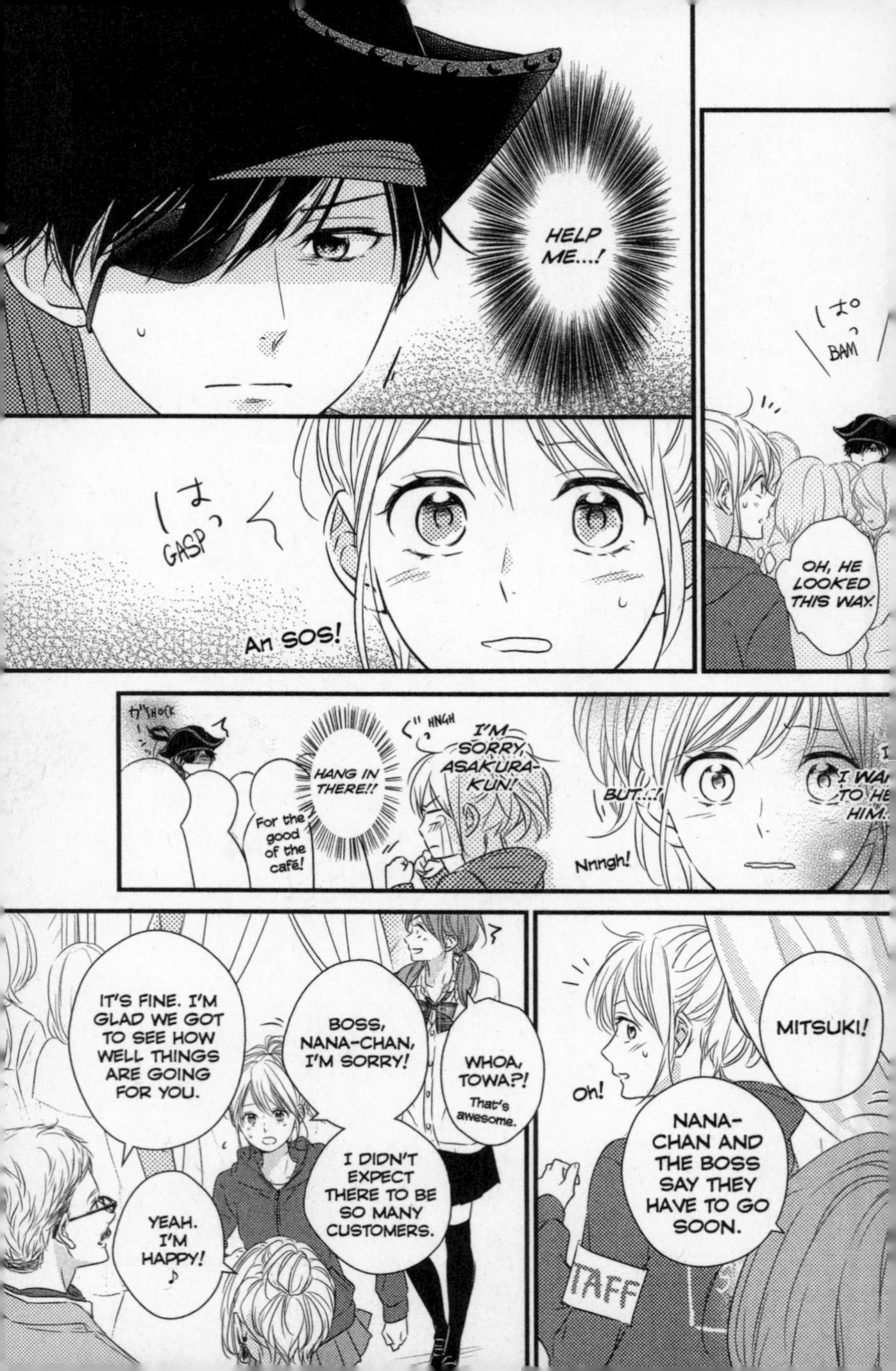

ぱっ
BAM
OH, HE LOOKED THIS WAY.
HELP ME...!
はっ
GASP
An SOS!
BUT...!
Nnngh!
I'M SORRY, ASAKURA-KUN!
HNGH
HANG IN THERE!!
For the good of the café!
SHOCK
MITSUKI!
Oh!
NANA-CHAN AND THE BOSS SAY THEY HAVE TO GO SOON.
TAFF
WHOA, TOWA?!
That's awesome.
BOSS, NANA-CHAN, I'M SORRY!
I DIDN'T EXPECT THERE TO BE SO MANY CUSTOMERS.
IT'S FINE. I'M GLAD WE GOT TO SEE HOW WELL THINGS ARE GOING FOR YOU.
YEAH. I'M HAPPY! ♪

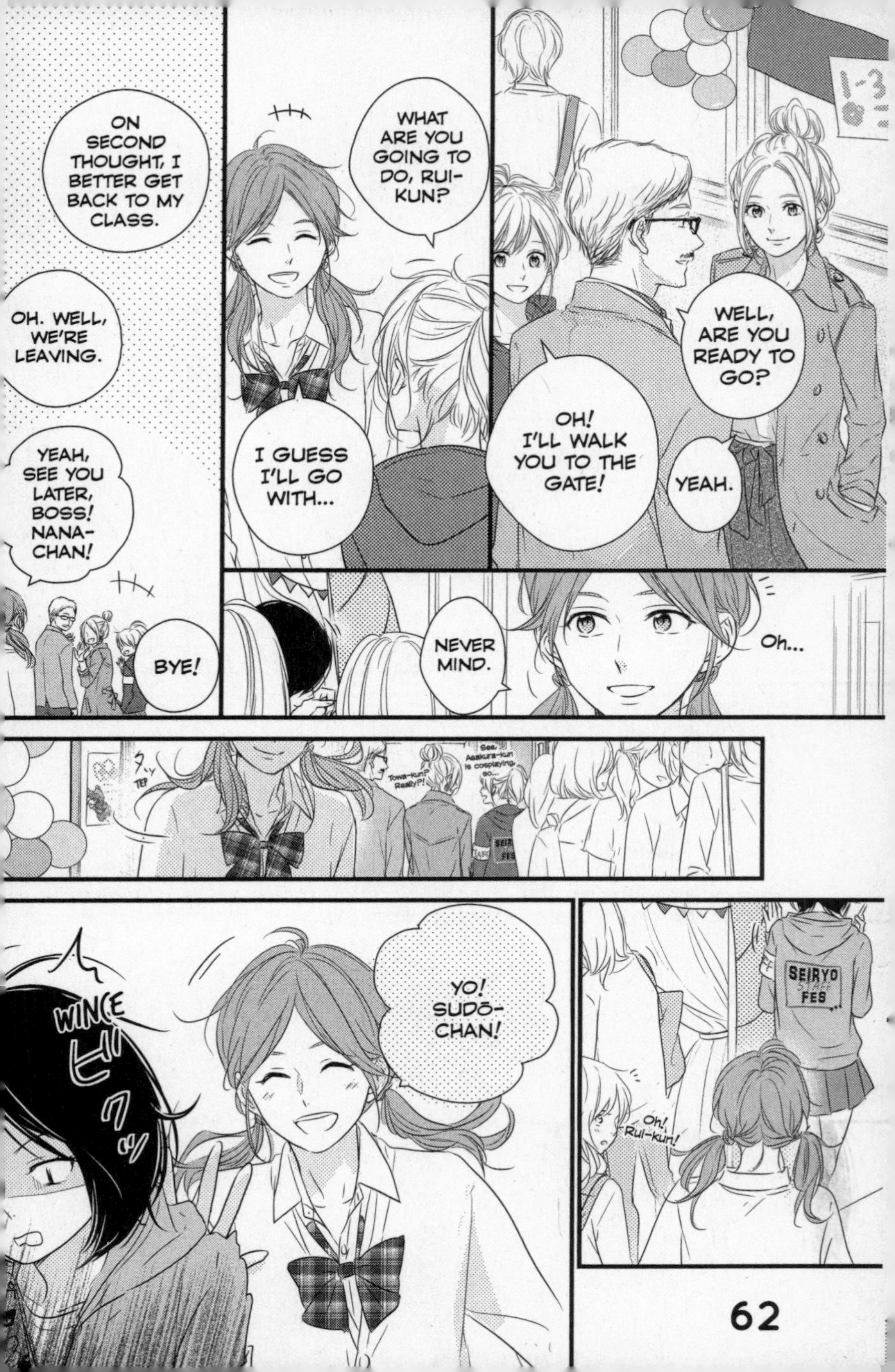
WELL, ARE YOU READY TO GO?
YEAH.
OH! I'LL WALK YOU TO THE GATE!
WHAT ARE YOU GOING TO DO, RUI-KUN?
I GUESS I'LL GO WITH...
Oh...
NEVER MIND.
ON SECOND THOUGHT, I BETTER GET BACK TO MY CLASS.
OH. WELL, WE'RE LEAVING.
YEAH, SEE YOU LATER, BOSS! NANA-CHAN!
BYE!
See, Asakura-kun is cosplaying, so...
Towa-kun? Really?!
TEP
SEIRYO FES
Oh! Rui-kun!
SEIRYO STAFF FES
YO! SUDŌ-CHAN!
WINCE

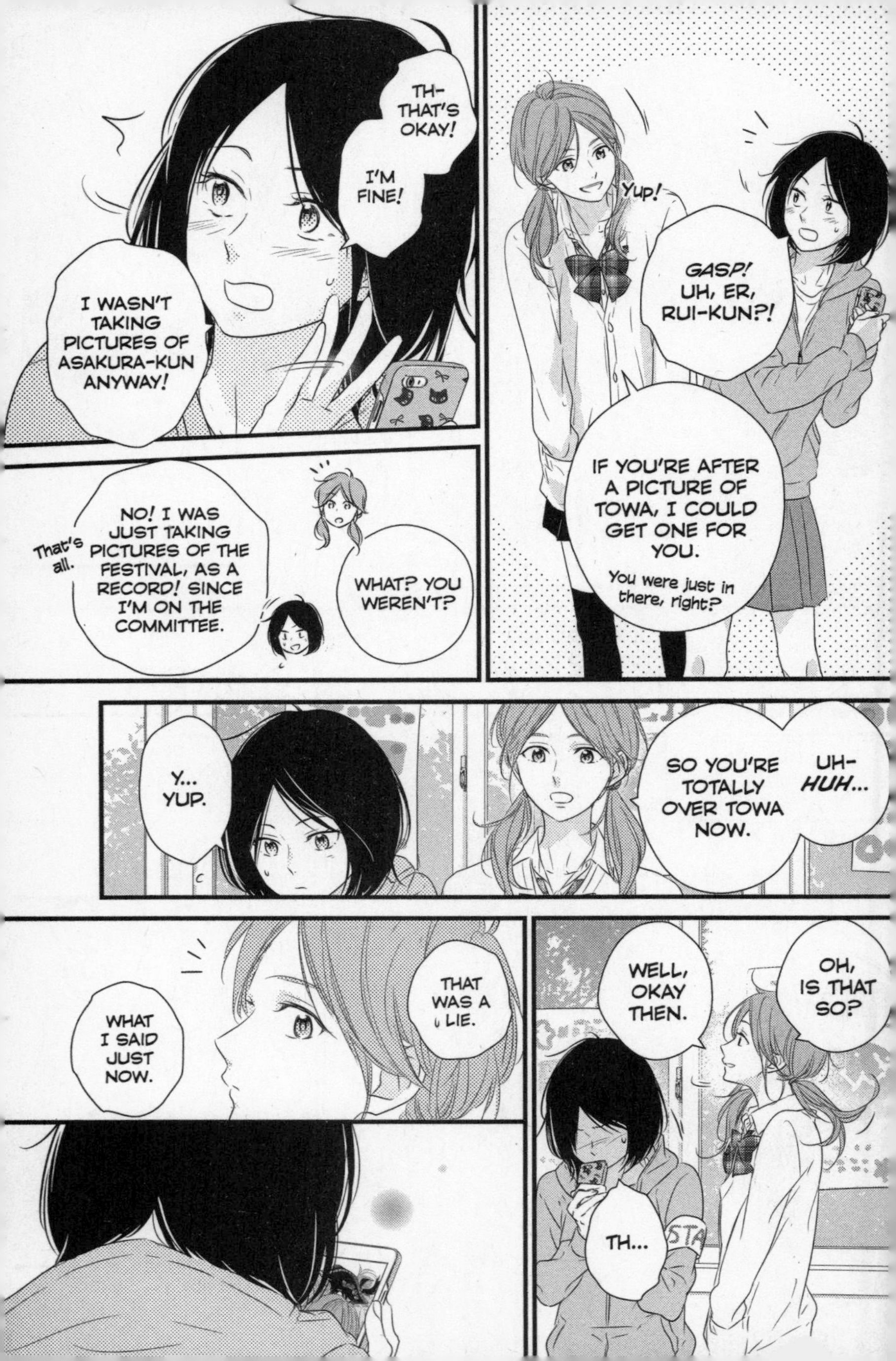
GASP! UH, ER, RUI-KUN?!
Yup!
IF YOU'RE AFTER A PICTURE OF TOWA, I COULD GET ONE FOR YOU.
You were just in there, right?
TH- THAT'S OKAY!
I'M FINE!
I WASN'T TAKING PICTURES OF ASAKURA-KUN ANYWAY!
WHAT? YOU WEREN'T?
NO! I WAS JUST TAKING PICTURES OF THE FESTIVAL, AS A RECORD! SINCE I'M ON THE COMMITTEE.
That's all.
UH-HUH...
SO YOU'RE TOTALLY OVER TOWA NOW.
Y... YUP.
OH, IS THAT SO?
WELL, OKAY THEN.
TH...
THAT WAS A LIE.
WHAT I SAID JUST NOW.

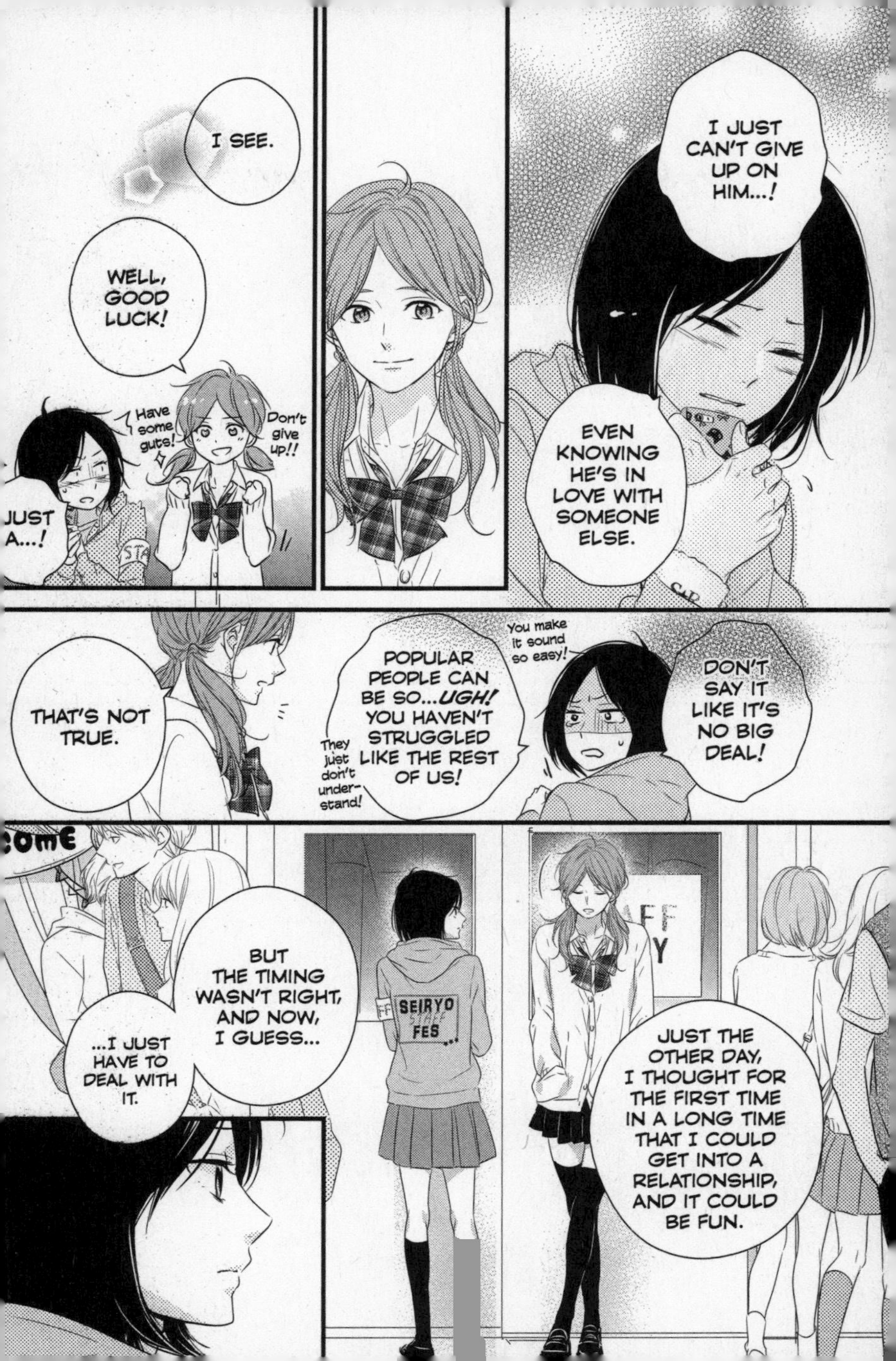
I JUST CAN'T GIVE UP ON HIM...!
EVEN KNOWING HE'S IN LOVE WITH SOMEONE ELSE.
I SEE.
WELL, GOOD LUCK!
Don't give up!!
Have some guts!
JUST A...!
DON'T SAY IT LIKE IT'S NO BIG DEAL!
You make it sound so easy!
POPULAR PEOPLE CAN BE SO...*UGH!* YOU HAVEN'T STRUGGLED LIKE THE REST OF US!
They just don't under-stand!
THAT'S NOT TRUE.
JUST THE OTHER DAY, I THOUGHT FOR THE FIRST TIME IN A LONG TIME THAT I COULD GET INTO A RELATIONSHIP, AND IT COULD BE FUN.
SEIRYO FES
BUT THE TIMING WASN'T RIGHT, AND NOW, I GUESS...
...I JUST HAVE TO DEAL WITH IT.

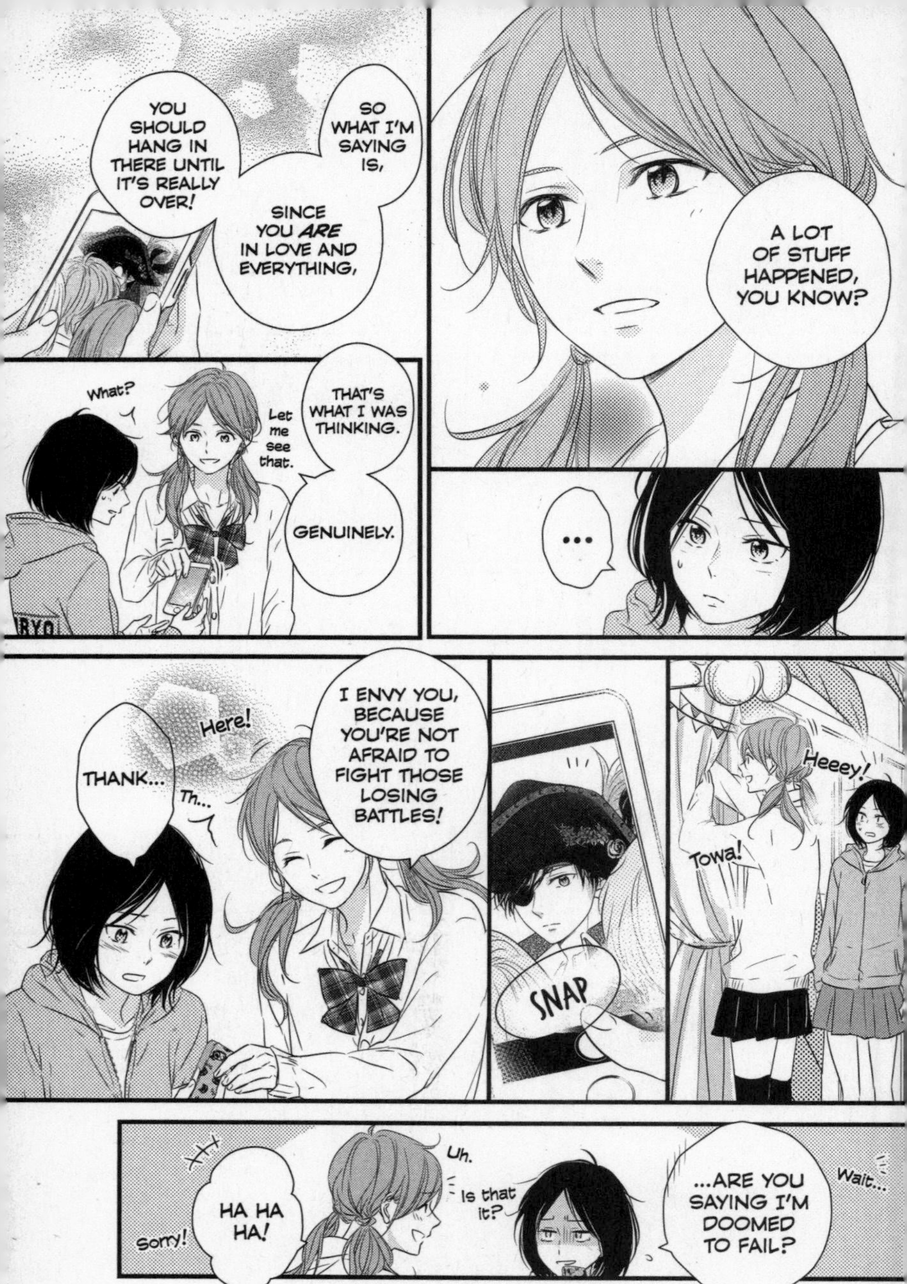
A LOT OF STUFF HAPPENED, YOU KNOW?
SO WHAT I'M SAYING IS,
SINCE YOU *ARE* IN LOVE AND EVERYTHING,
YOU SHOULD HANG IN THERE UNTIL IT'S REALLY OVER!
...
THAT'S WHAT I WAS THINKING.
GENUINELY.
Let me see that.
What?
Heeey!
Towa!
SNAP
I ENVY YOU, BECAUSE YOU'RE NOT AFRAID TO FIGHT THOSE LOSING BATTLES!
Here!
Th...
THANK...
Wait...
...ARE YOU SAYING I'M DOOMED TO FAIL?
Uh.
Is that it?
HA HA HA!
Sorry!

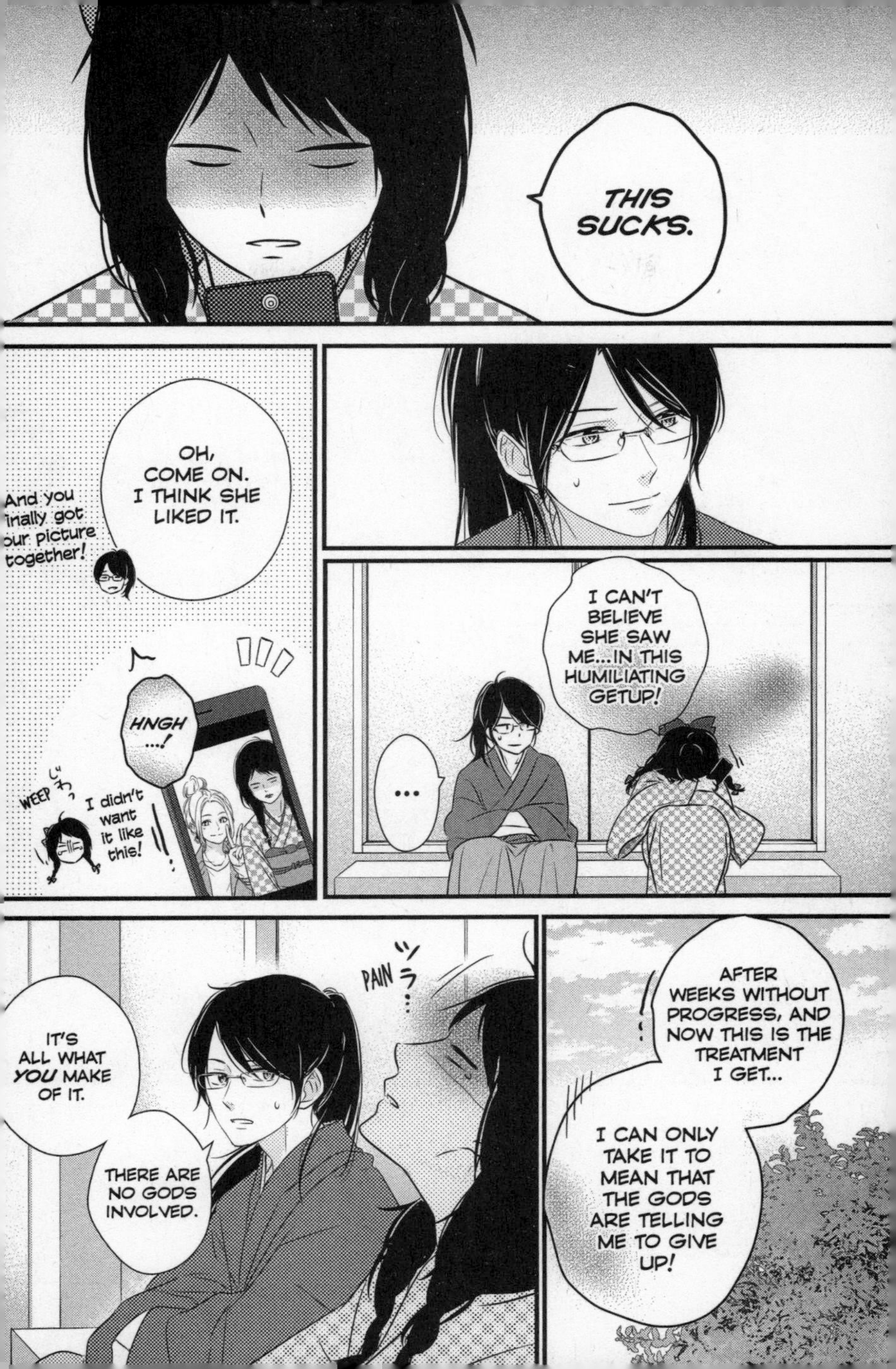
THIS SUCKS.
I CAN'T BELIEVE SHE SAW ME...IN THIS HUMILIATING GETUP!
...
OH, COME ON. I THINK SHE LIKED IT.
And you inally got our picture together!
HNGH ...!
WEEP
I didn't want it like this!
AFTER WEEKS WITHOUT PROGRESS, AND NOW THIS IS THE TREATMENT I GET...
I CAN ONLY TAKE IT TO MEAN THAT THE GODS ARE TELLING ME TO GIVE UP!
PAIN
IT'S ALL WHAT YOU MAKE OF IT.
THERE ARE NO GODS INVOLVED.

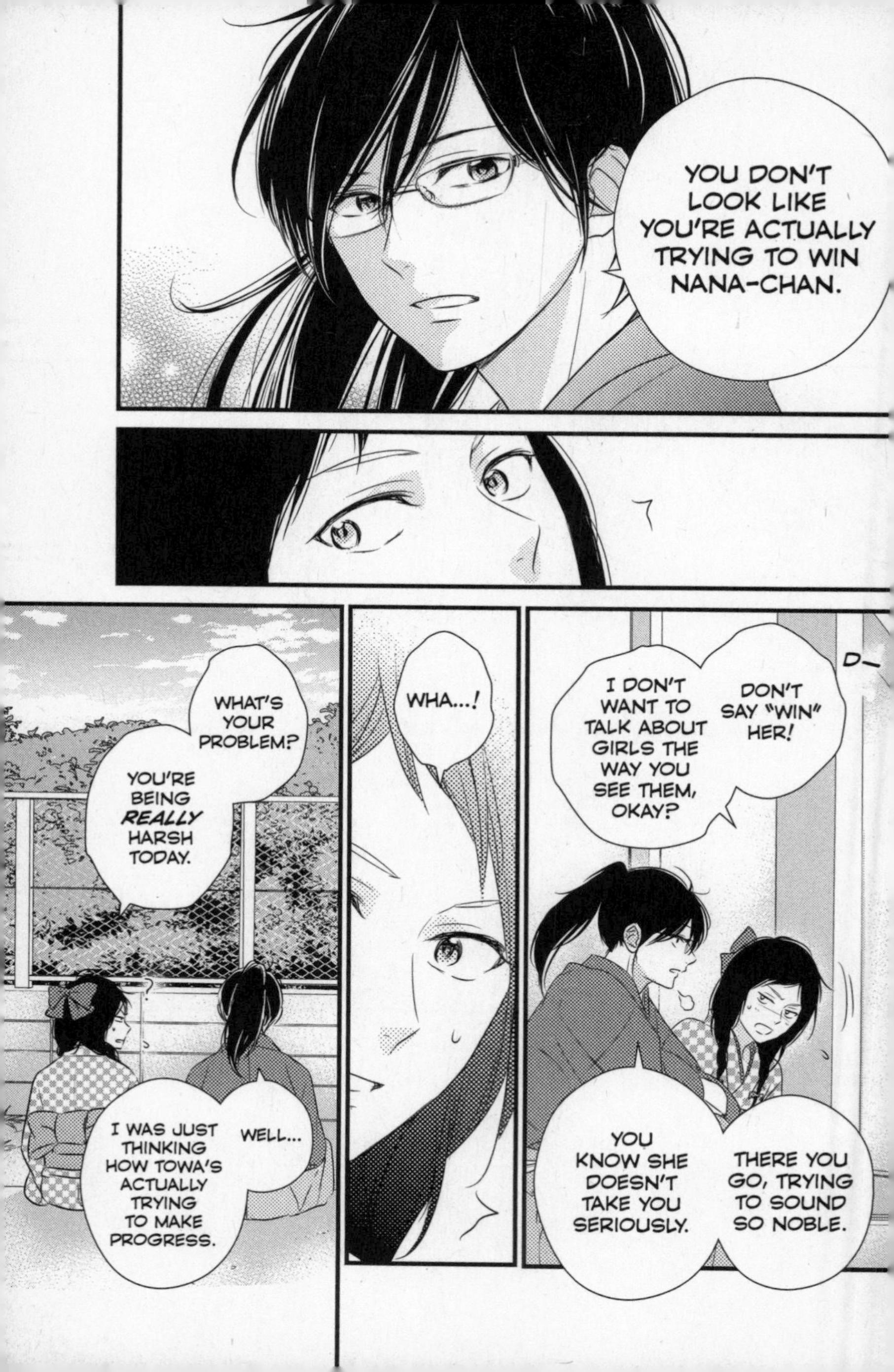
YOU DON'T LOOK LIKE YOU'RE ACTUALLY TRYING TO WIN NANA-CHAN.
D—
DON'T SAY "WIN" HER!
I DON'T WANT TO TALK ABOUT GIRLS THE WAY YOU SEE THEM, OKAY?
THERE YOU GO, TRYING TO SOUND SO NOBLE.
YOU KNOW SHE DOESN'T TAKE YOU SERIOUSLY.
WHA...!
WHAT'S YOUR PROBLEM?
YOU'RE BEING *REALLY* HARSH TODAY.
WELL...
I WAS JUST THINKING HOW TOWA'S ACTUALLY TRYING TO MAKE PROGRESS.

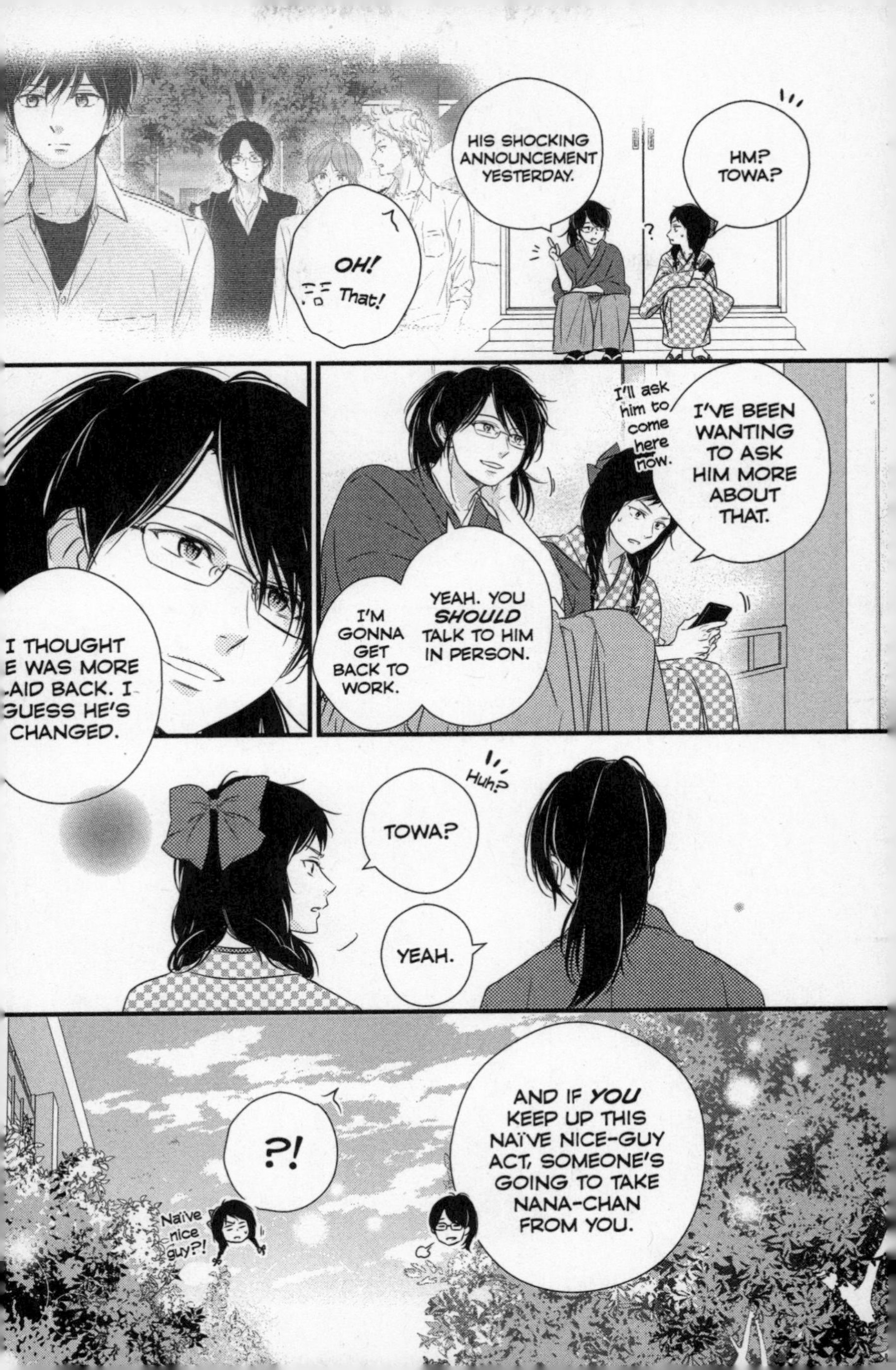
HM? TOWA?
HIS SHOCKING ANNOUNCEMENT YESTERDAY.
OH! That!
I'VE BEEN WANTING TO ASK HIM MORE ABOUT THAT.
I'll ask him to come here now.
YEAH. YOU SHOULD TALK TO HIM IN PERSON.
I'M GONNA GET BACK TO WORK.
I THOUGHT E WAS MORE AID BACK. I GUESS HE'S CHANGED.
Huh?
TOWA?
YEAH.
AND IF YOU KEEP UP THIS NAÏVE NICE-GUY ACT, SOMEONE'S GOING TO TAKE NANA-CHAN FROM YOU.
?!
Naïve nice guy?!

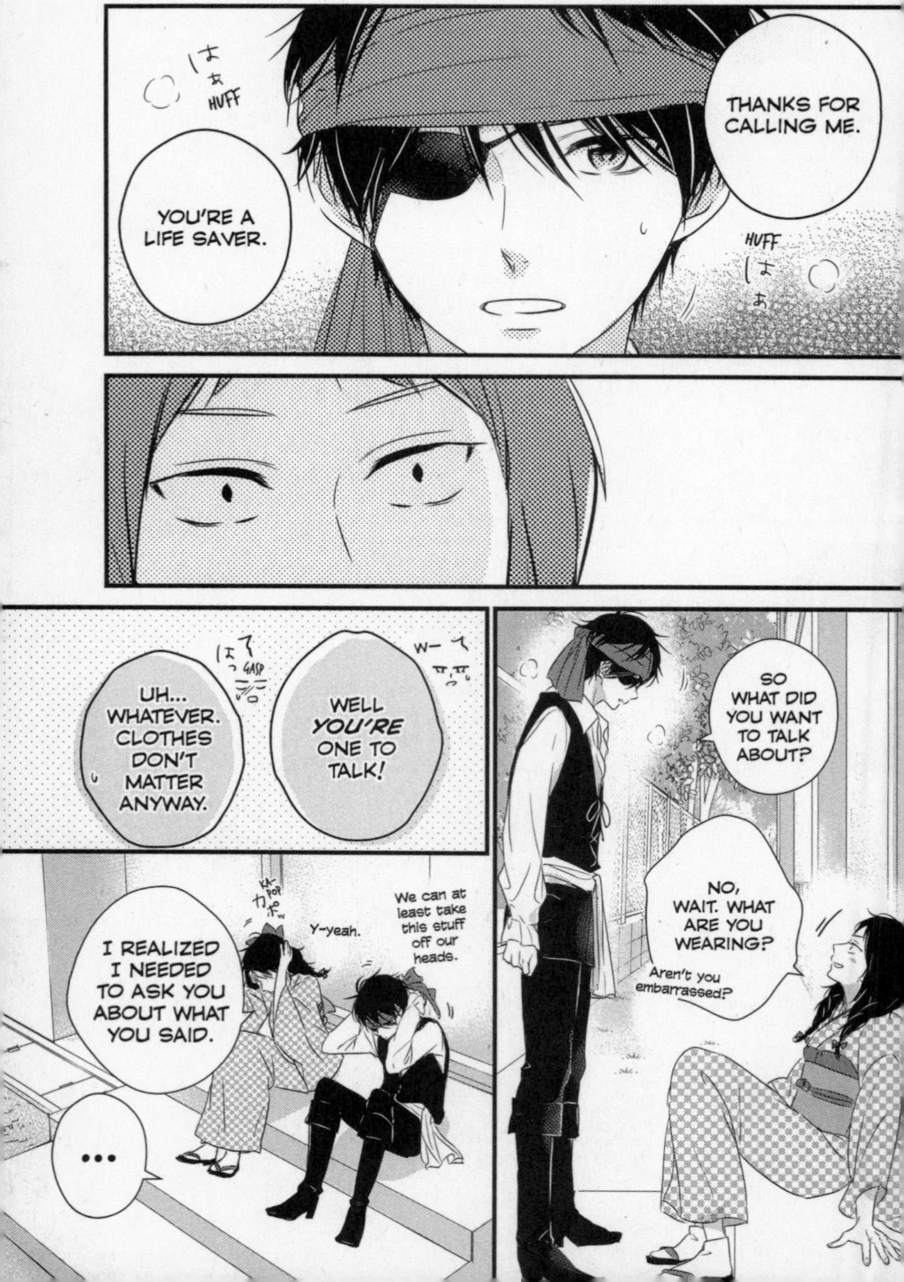
THANKS FOR CALLING ME.
HUFF
はぁ
HUFF
はぁ
YOU'RE A LIFE SAVER.
SO WHAT DID YOU WANT TO TALK ABOUT?
NO, WAIT. WHAT ARE YOU WEARING?
Aren't you embarrassed?
WELL *YOU'RE* ONE TO TALK!
UH... WHATEVER. CLOTHES DON'T MATTER ANYWAY.
GASP
We can at least take this stuff off our heads.
Y-yeah.
KA-POP
カポッ
I REALIZED I NEEDED TO ASK YOU ABOUT WHAT YOU SAID.
...

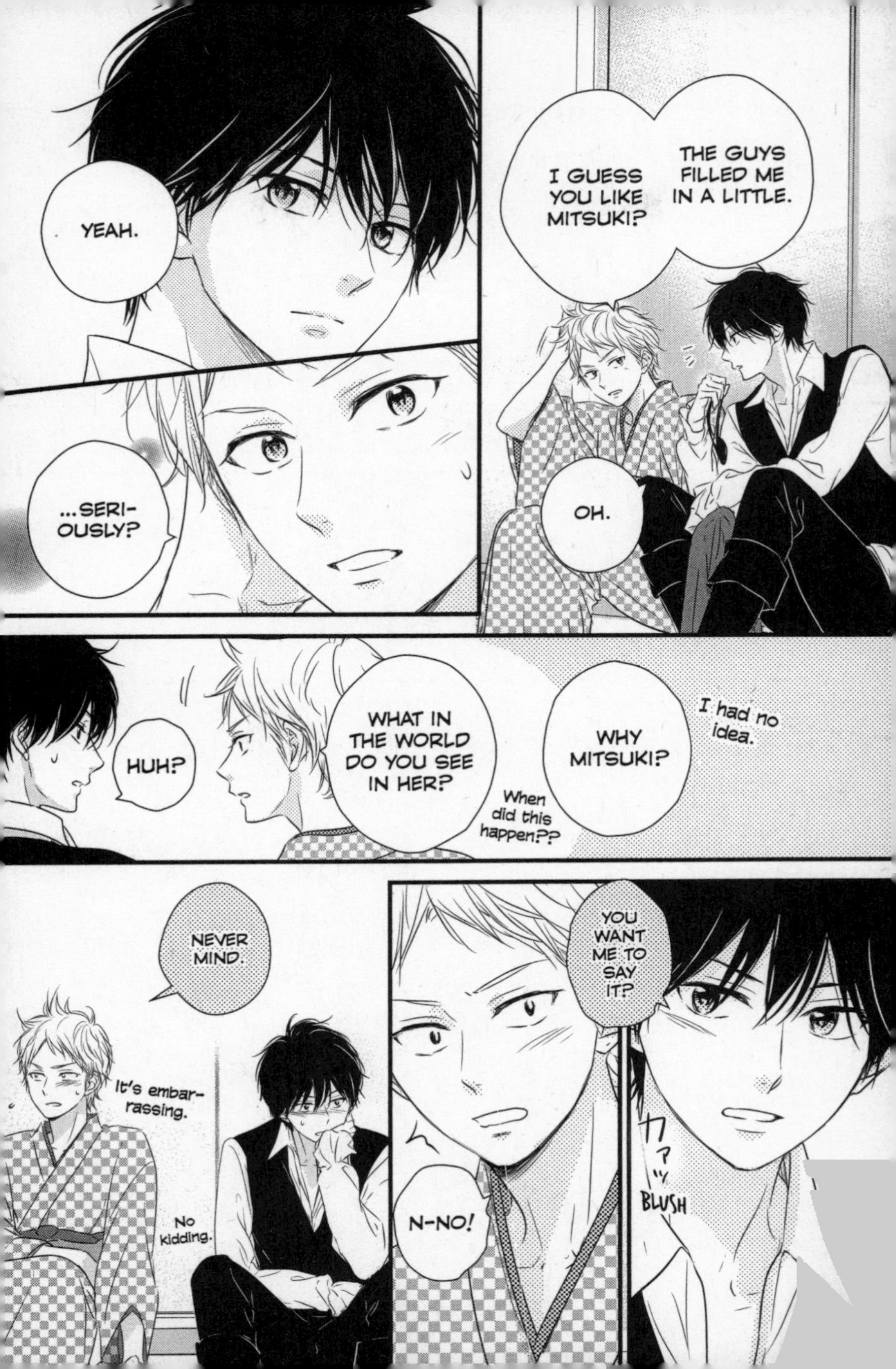
THE GUYS FILLED ME IN A LITTLE.
I GUESS YOU LIKE MITSUKI?
OH.
YEAH.
...SERI-OUSLY?
I had no idea.
WHY MITSUKI?
When did this happen??
WHAT IN THE WORLD DO YOU SEE IN HER?
HUH?
YOU WANT ME TO SAY IT?
BLUSH
N-NO!
NEVER MIND.
It's embar-rassing.
No kidding.

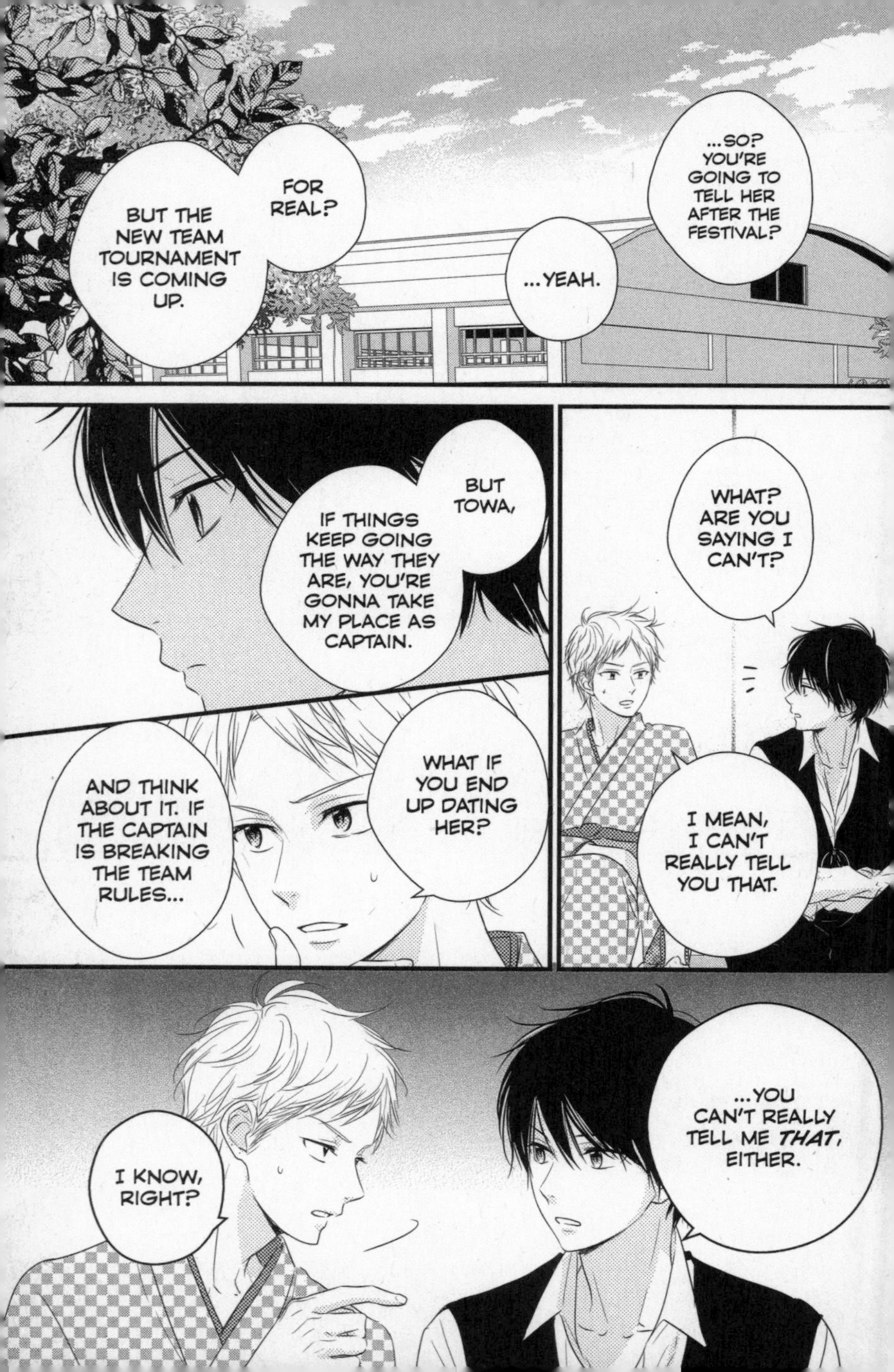
...SO? YOU'RE GOING TO TELL HER AFTER THE FESTIVAL?
...YEAH.
FOR REAL?
BUT THE NEW TEAM TOURNAMENT IS COMING UP.
BUT TOWA,
IF THINGS KEEP GOING THE WAY THEY ARE, YOU'RE GONNA TAKE MY PLACE AS CAPTAIN.
WHAT IF YOU END UP DATING HER?
AND THINK ABOUT IT. IF THE CAPTAIN IS BREAKING THE TEAM RULES...
WHAT? ARE YOU SAYING I CAN'T?
I MEAN, I CAN'T REALLY TELL YOU THAT.
...YOU CAN'T REALLY TELL ME *THAT*, EITHER.
I KNOW, RIGHT?

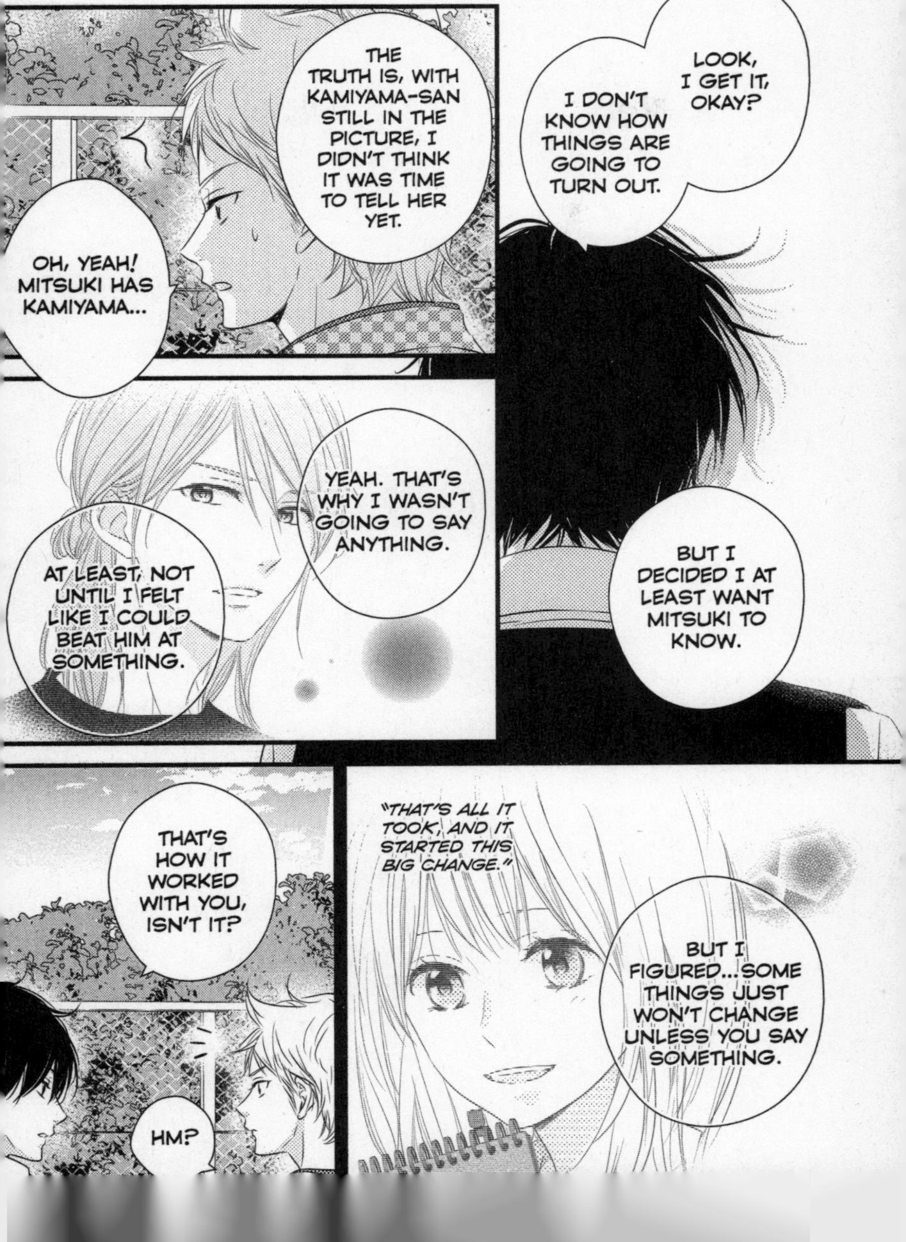
LOOK, I GET IT, OKAY?
I DON'T KNOW HOW THINGS ARE GOING TO TURN OUT.
BUT I DECIDED I AT LEAST WANT MITSUKI TO KNOW.
THE TRUTH IS, WITH KAMIYAMA-SAN STILL IN THE PICTURE, I DIDN'T THINK IT WAS TIME TO TELL HER YET.
OH, YEAH! MITSUKI HAS KAMIYAMA...
YEAH. THAT'S WHY I WASN'T GOING TO SAY ANYTHING.
AT LEAST, NOT UNTIL I FELT LIKE I COULD BEAT HIM AT SOMETHING.
"THAT'S ALL IT TOOK, AND IT STARTED THIS BIG CHANGE."
BUT I FIGURED... SOME THINGS JUST WON'T CHANGE UNLESS YOU SAY SOMETHING.
THAT'S HOW IT WORKED WITH YOU, ISN'T IT?
HM?

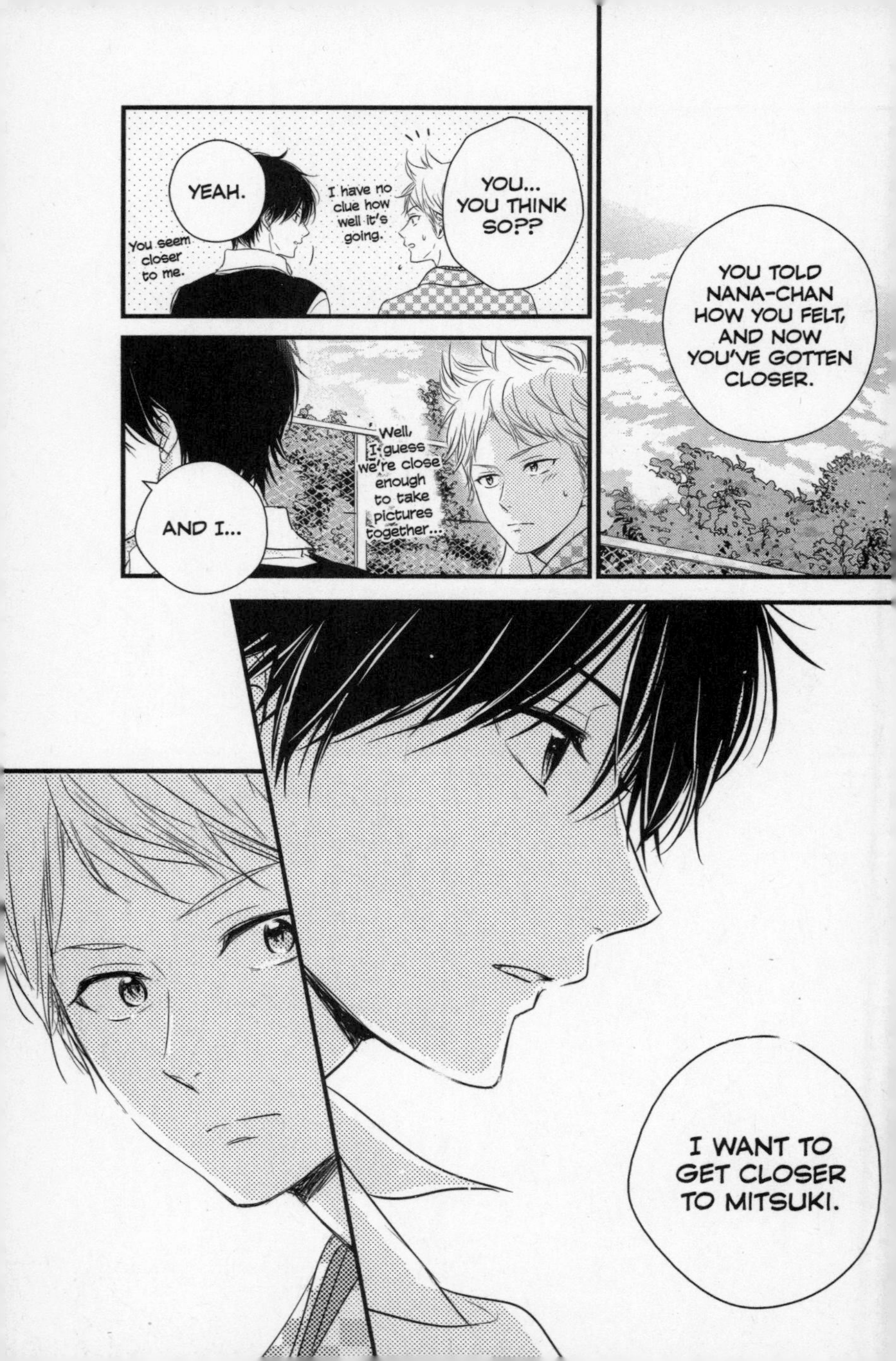
YOU TOLD NANA-CHAN HOW YOU FELT, AND NOW YOU'VE GOTTEN CLOSER.
YOU... YOU THINK SO??
I have no clue how well it's going.
YEAH.
You seem closer to me.
Well, I guess we're close enough to take pictures together...
AND I...
I WANT TO GET CLOSER TO MITSUKI.

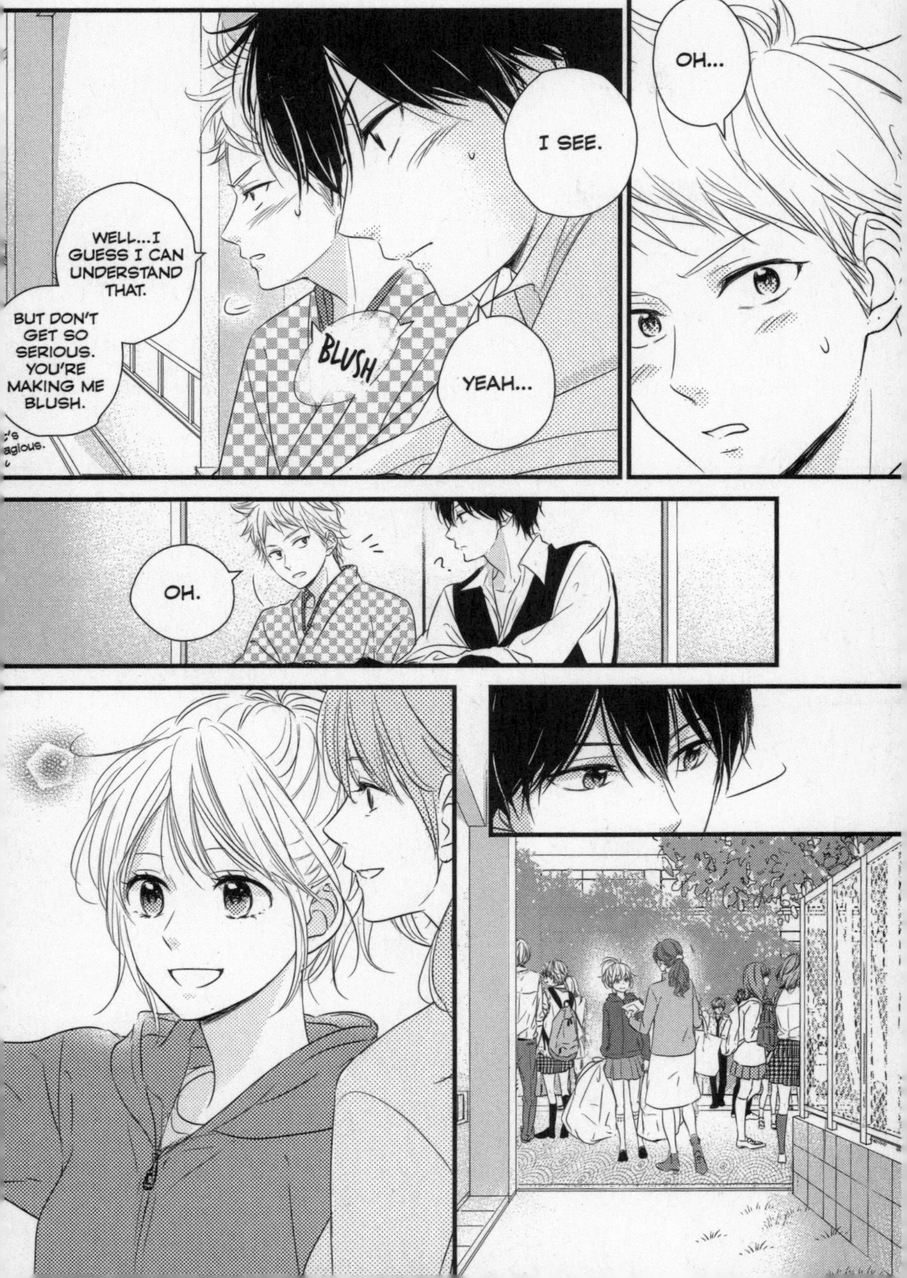
OH...
I SEE.
YEAH...
BLUSH
WELL...I GUESS I CAN UNDERSTAND THAT.
BUT DON'T GET SO SERIOUS. YOU'RE MAKING ME BLUSH.
OH.

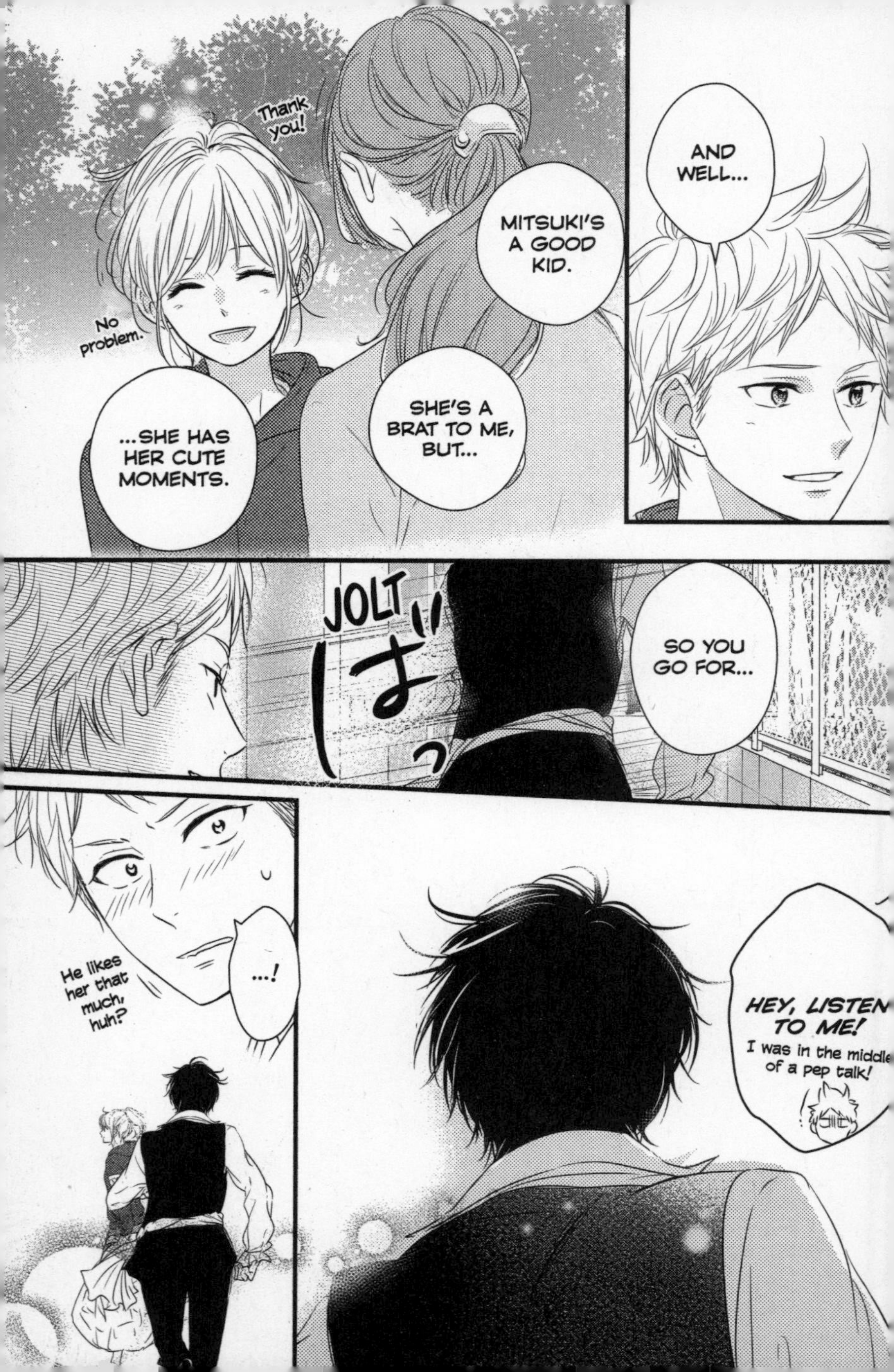
AND WELL...
MITSUKI'S A GOOD KID.
Thank you!
SHE'S A BRAT TO ME, BUT...
No problem.
...SHE HAS HER CUTE MOMENTS.
SO YOU GO FOR...
JOLT
HEY, LISTEN TO ME!
I was in the middle of a pep talk!
...!
He likes her that much, huh?

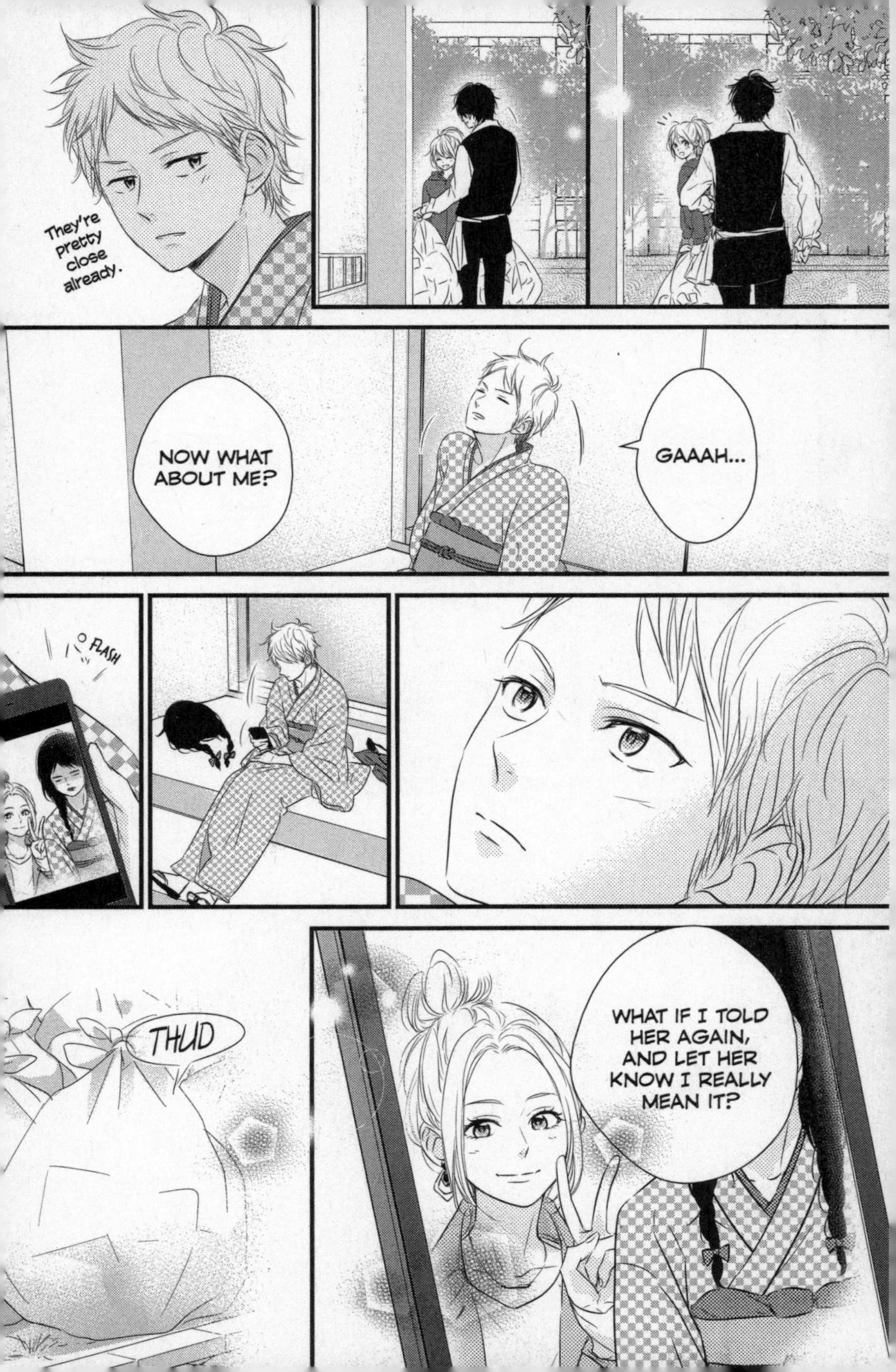
They're pretty close already.
GAAAH...
NOW WHAT ABOUT ME?
FLASH
WHAT IF I TOLD HER AGAIN, AND LET HER KNOW I REALLY MEAN IT?
THUD

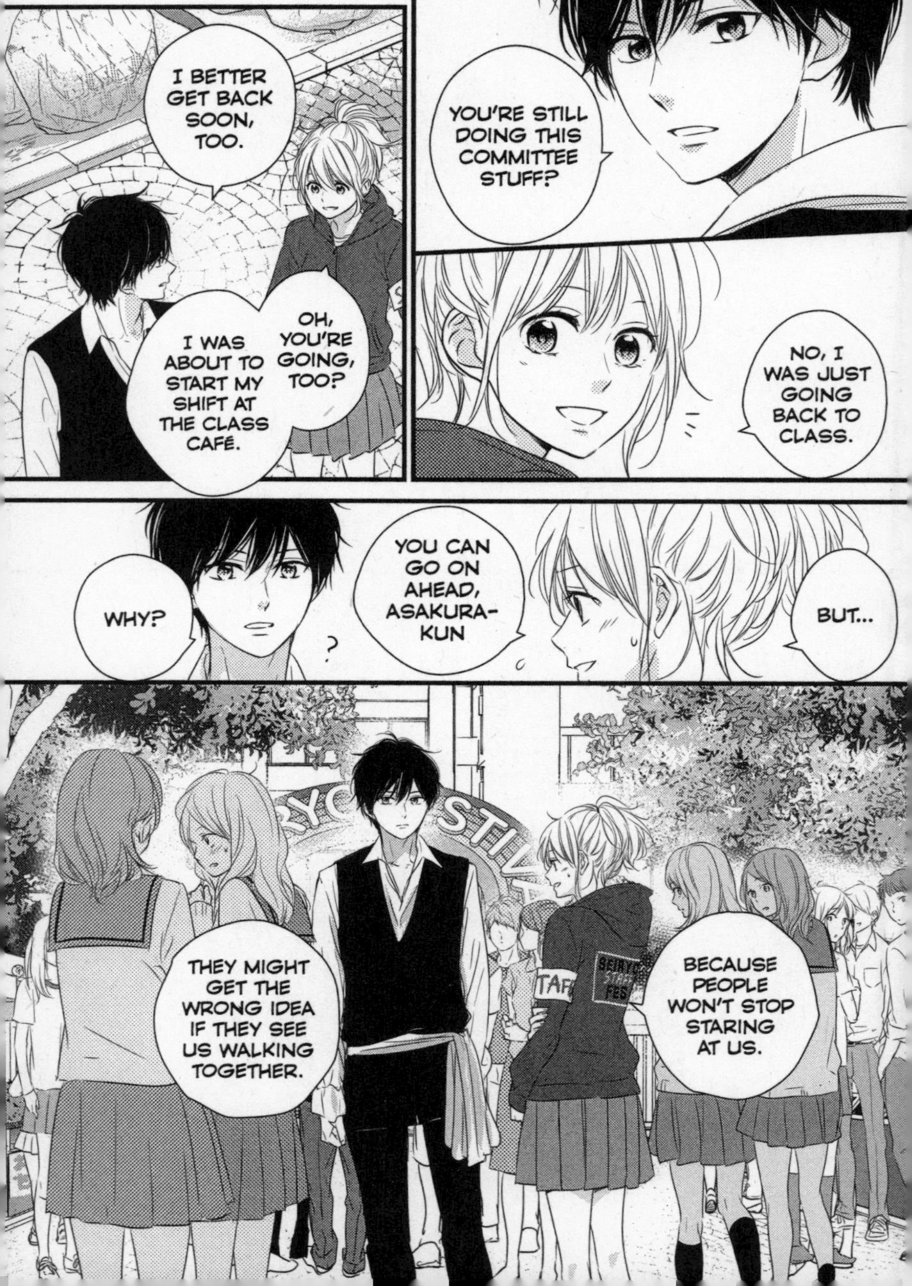
YOU'RE STILL DOING THIS COMMITTEE STUFF?
NO, I WAS JUST GOING BACK TO CLASS.
I BETTER GET BACK SOON, TOO.
OH, YOU'RE GOING, TOO? I WAS ABOUT TO START MY SHIFT AT THE CLASS CAFÉ.
BUT...
YOU CAN GO ON AHEAD, ASAKURA-KUN
WHY?
BECAUSE PEOPLE WON'T STOP STARING AT US.
THEY MIGHT GET THE WRONG IDEA IF THEY SEE US WALKING TOGETHER.

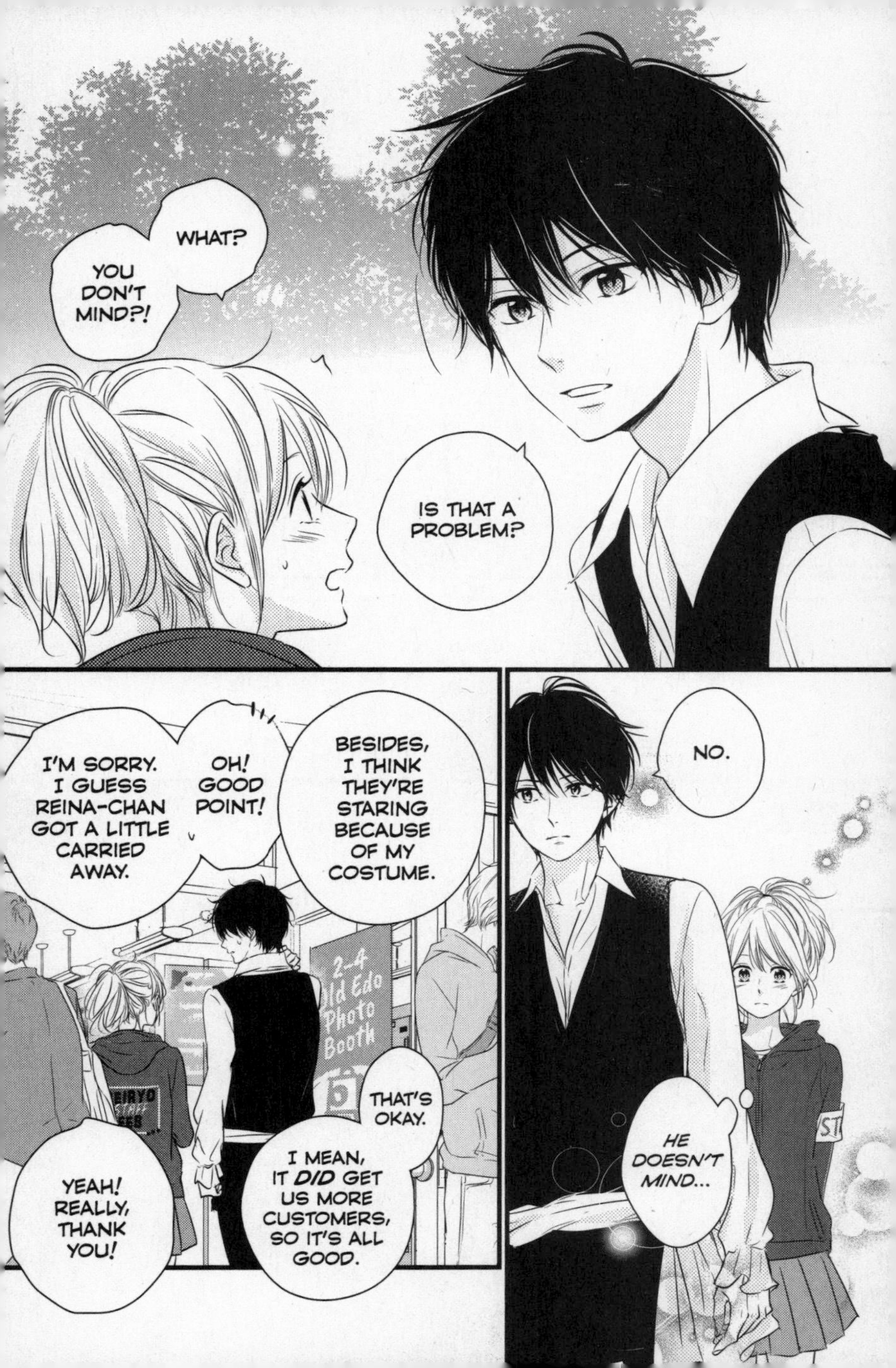
WHAT? YOU DON'T MIND?!
IS THAT A PROBLEM?
NO.
HE DOESN'T MIND...
BESIDES, I THINK THEY'RE STARING BECAUSE OF MY COSTUME.
OH! GOOD POINT!
I'M SORRY. I GUESS REINA-CHAN GOT A LITTLE CARRIED AWAY.
2-4 Old Edo Photo Booth
THAT'S OKAY.
I MEAN, IT *DID* GET US MORE CUSTOMERS, SO IT'S ALL GOOD.
YEAH! REALLY, THANK YOU!

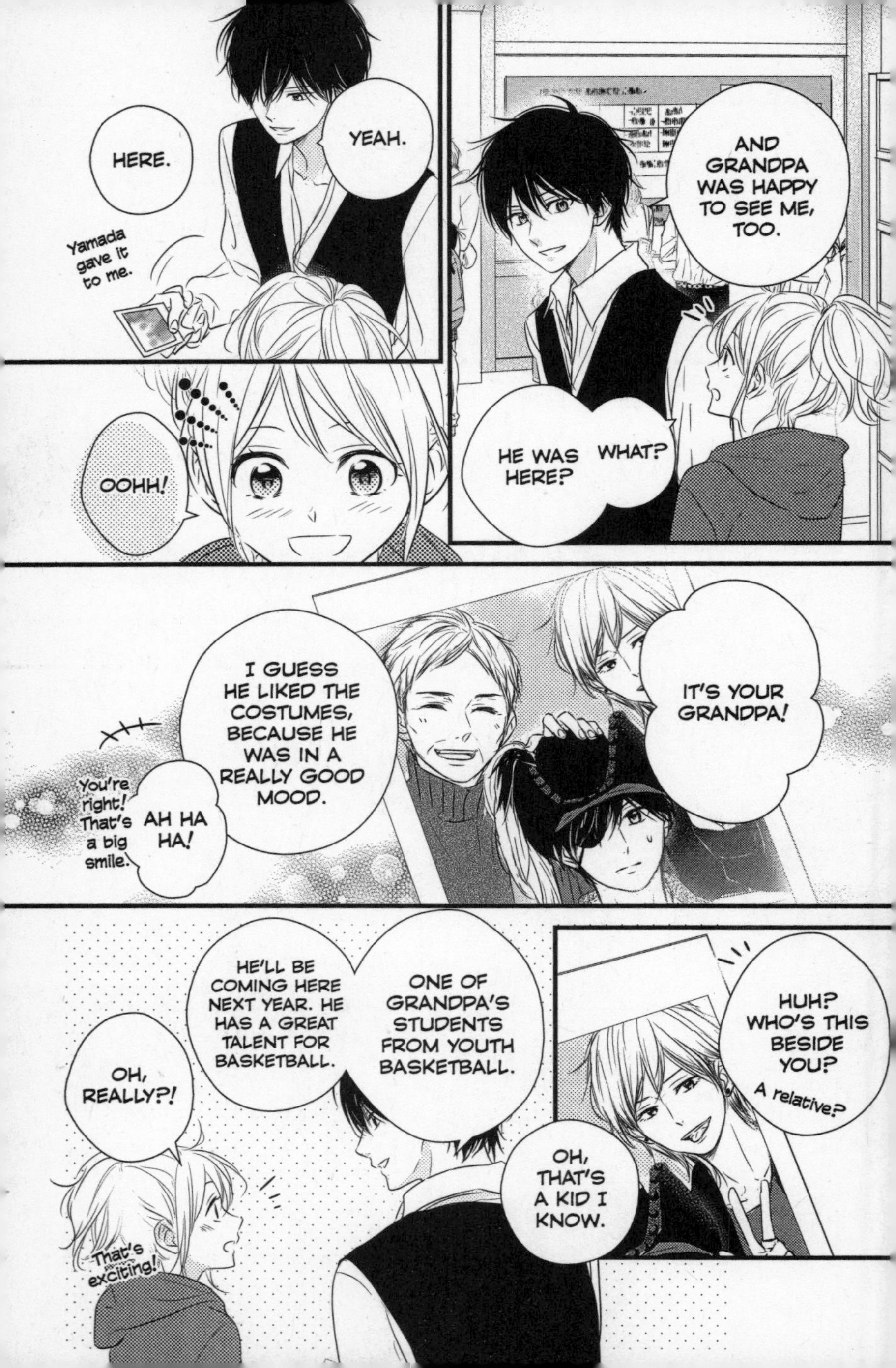
AND GRANDPA WAS HAPPY TO SEE ME, TOO.
WHAT?
HE WAS HERE?
YEAH.
HERE.
Yamada gave it to me.
OOHH!
IT'S YOUR GRANDPA!
I GUESS HE LIKED THE COSTUMES, BECAUSE HE WAS IN A REALLY GOOD MOOD.
AH HA HA!
You're right! That's a big smile.
HUH? WHO'S THIS BESIDE YOU?
A relative?
OH, THAT'S A KID I KNOW.
ONE OF GRANDPA'S STUDENTS FROM YOUTH BASKETBALL.
HE'LL BE COMING HERE NEXT YEAR. HE HAS A GREAT TALENT FOR BASKETBALL.
OH, REALLY?!
That's exciting!

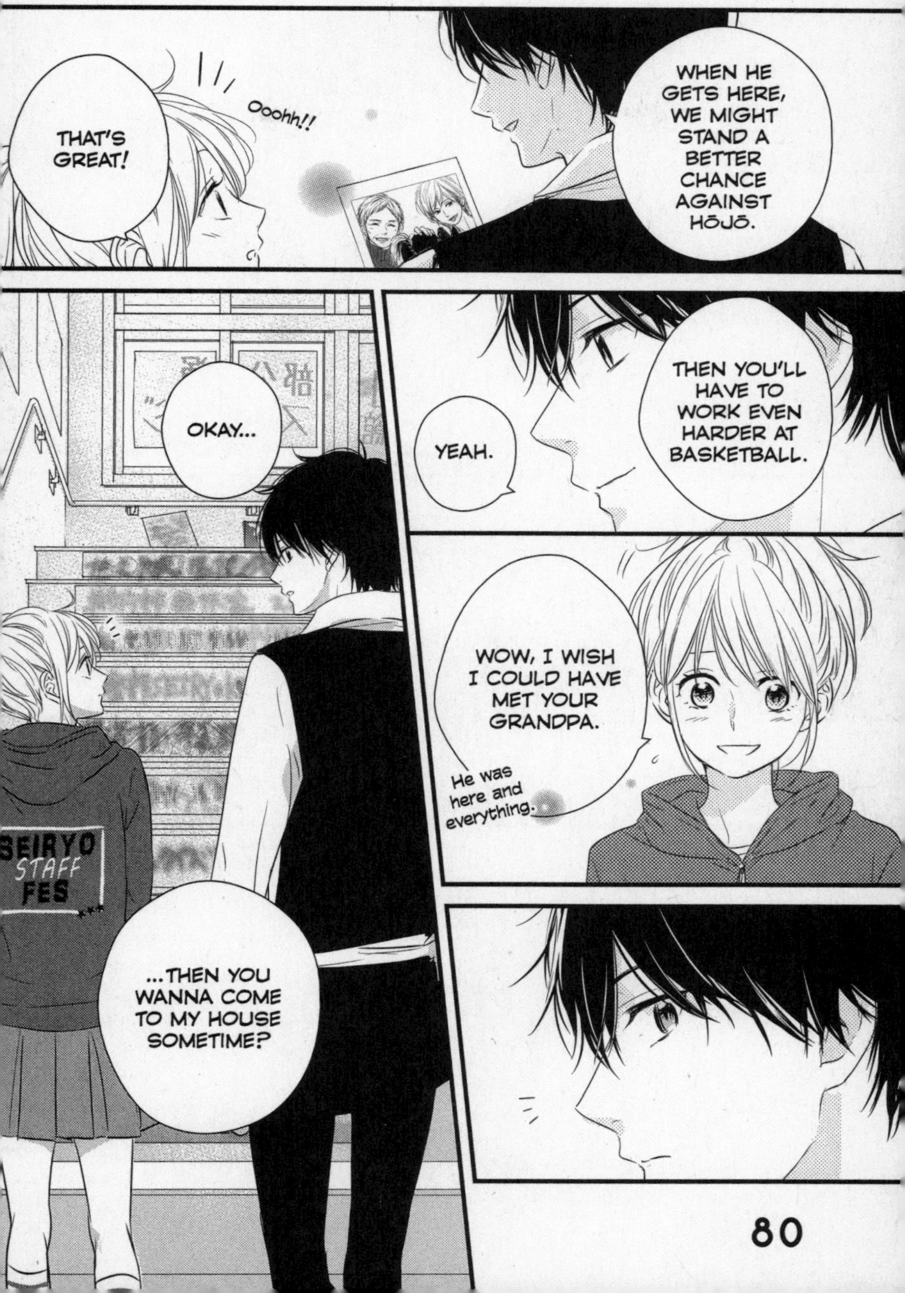
WHEN HE GETS HERE, WE MIGHT STAND A BETTER CHANCE AGAINST HŌJŌ.
Ooohh!!
THAT'S GREAT!
THEN YOU'LL HAVE TO WORK EVEN HARDER AT BASKETBALL.
YEAH.
WOW, I WISH I COULD HAVE MET YOUR GRANDPA.
He was here and everything.
OKAY...
SEIRYO STAFF FES
...THEN YOU WANNA COME TO MY HOUSE SOMETIME?

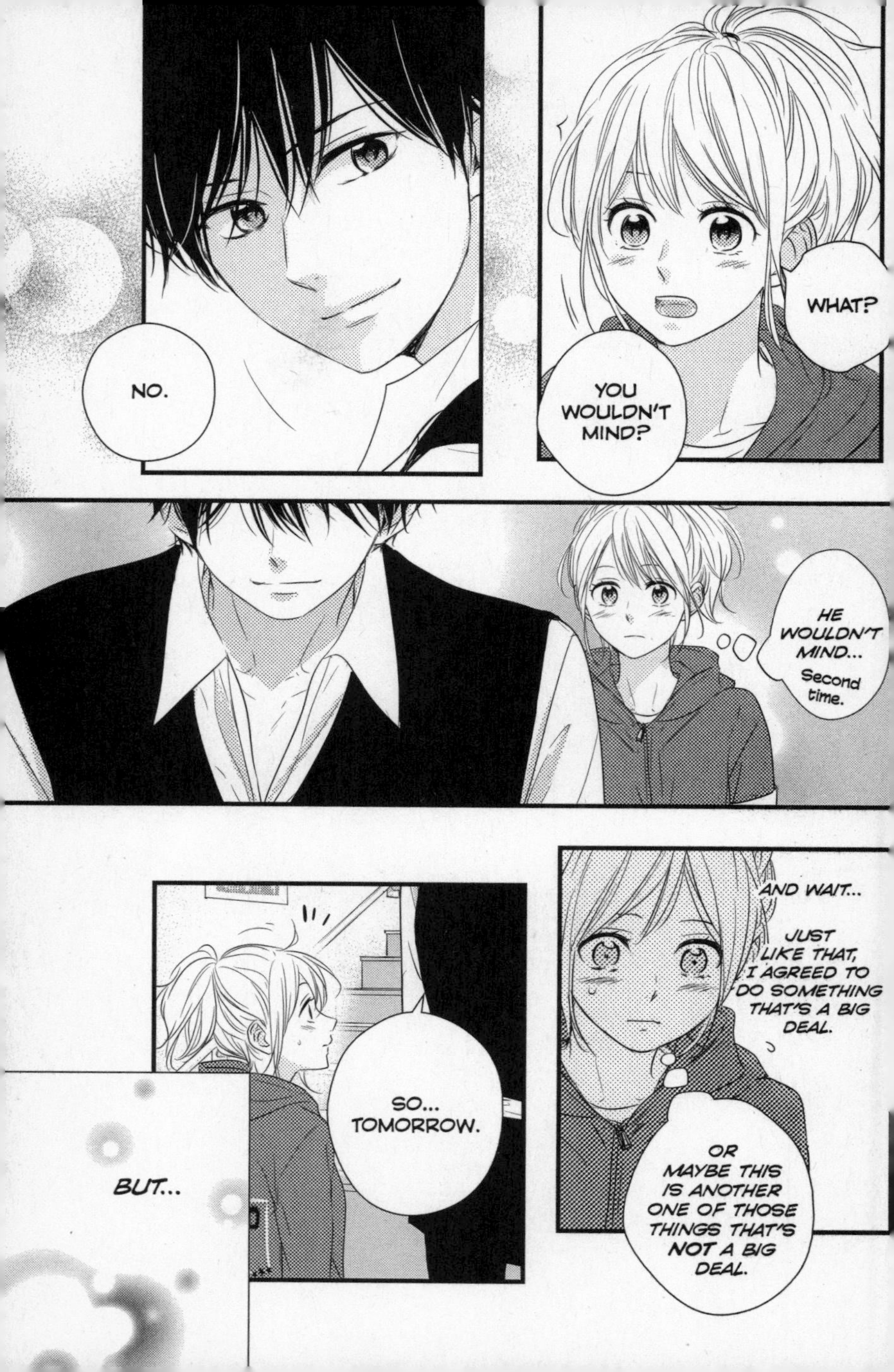
WHAT?
YOU WOULDN'T MIND?
NO.
HE WOULDN'T MIND... Second time.
AND WAIT...
JUST LIKE THAT, I AGREED TO DO SOMETHING THAT'S A BIG DEAL.
OR MAYBE THIS IS ANOTHER ONE OF THOSE THINGS THAT'S NOT A BIG DEAL.
SO... TOMORROW.
BUT...

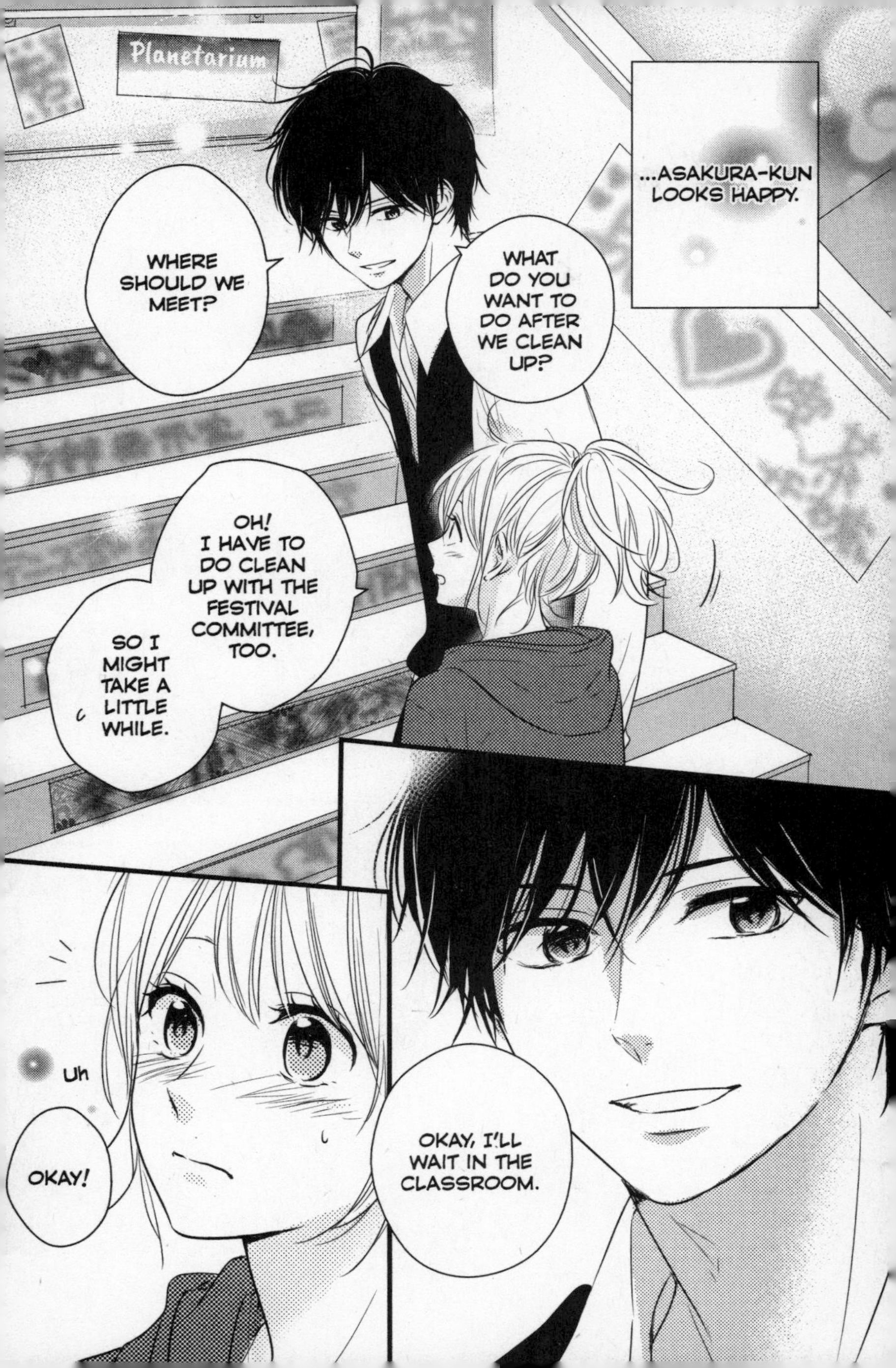
...ASAKURA-KUN LOOKS HAPPY.
WHAT DO YOU WANT TO DO AFTER WE CLEAN UP?
Planetarium
WHERE SHOULD WE MEET?
OH! I HAVE TO DO CLEAN UP WITH THE FESTIVAL COMMITTEE, TOO.
SO I MIGHT TAKE A LITTLE WHILE.
OKAY, I'LL WAIT IN THE CLASSROOM.
Uh
OKAY!

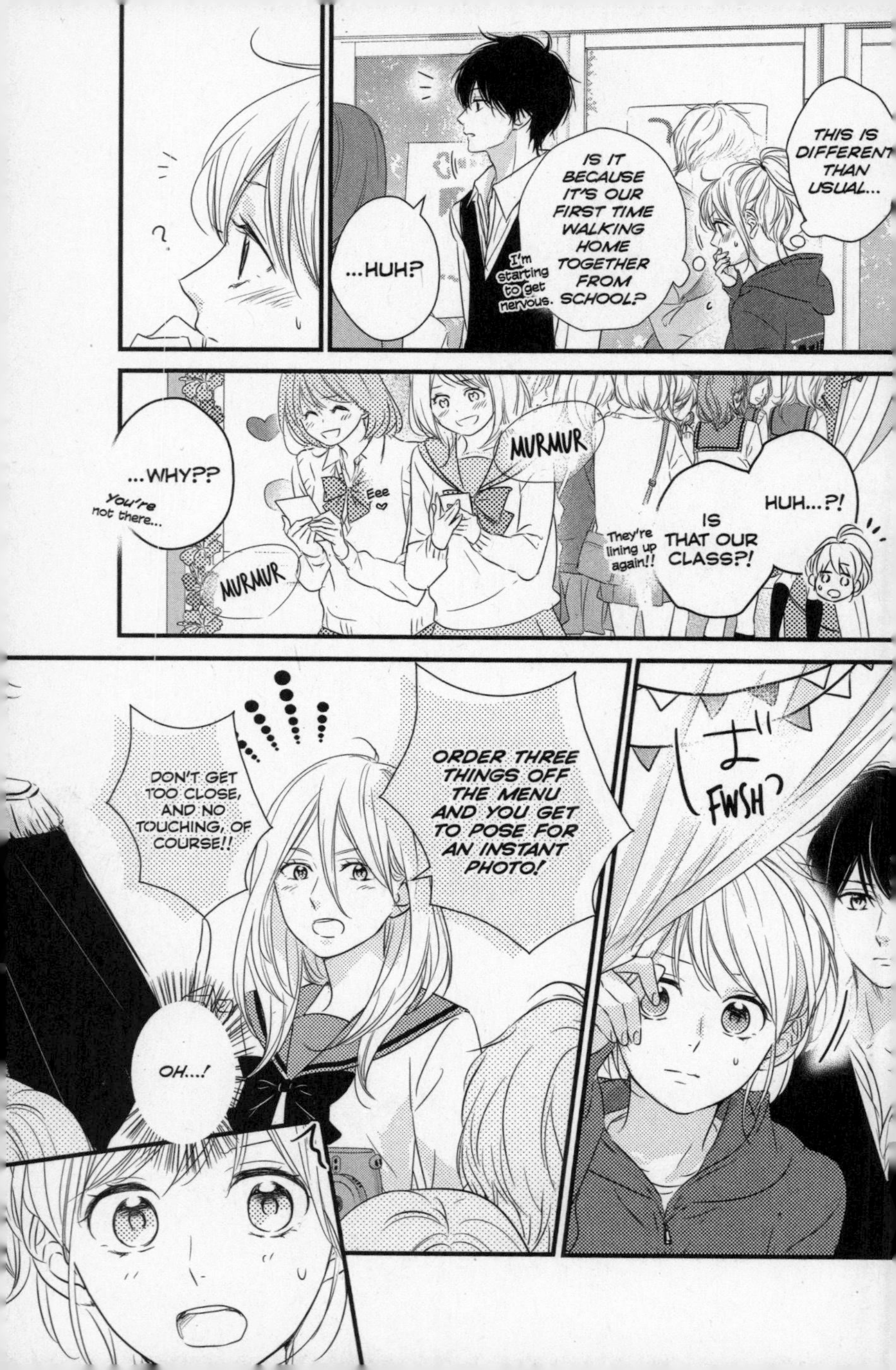
THIS IS DIFFERENT THAN USUAL...
IS IT BECAUSE IT'S OUR FIRST TIME WALKING HOME TOGETHER FROM SCHOOL?
I'm starting to get nervous.
...HUH?
HUH...?!
IS THAT OUR CLASS?!
They're lining up again!!
MURMUR
Eee
MURMUR
...WHY??
You're not there...
FWSH
ORDER THREE THINGS OFF THE MENU AND YOU GET TO POSE FOR AN INSTANT PHOTO!
DON'T GET TOO CLOSE, AND NO TOUCHING, OF COURSE!!
OH...!

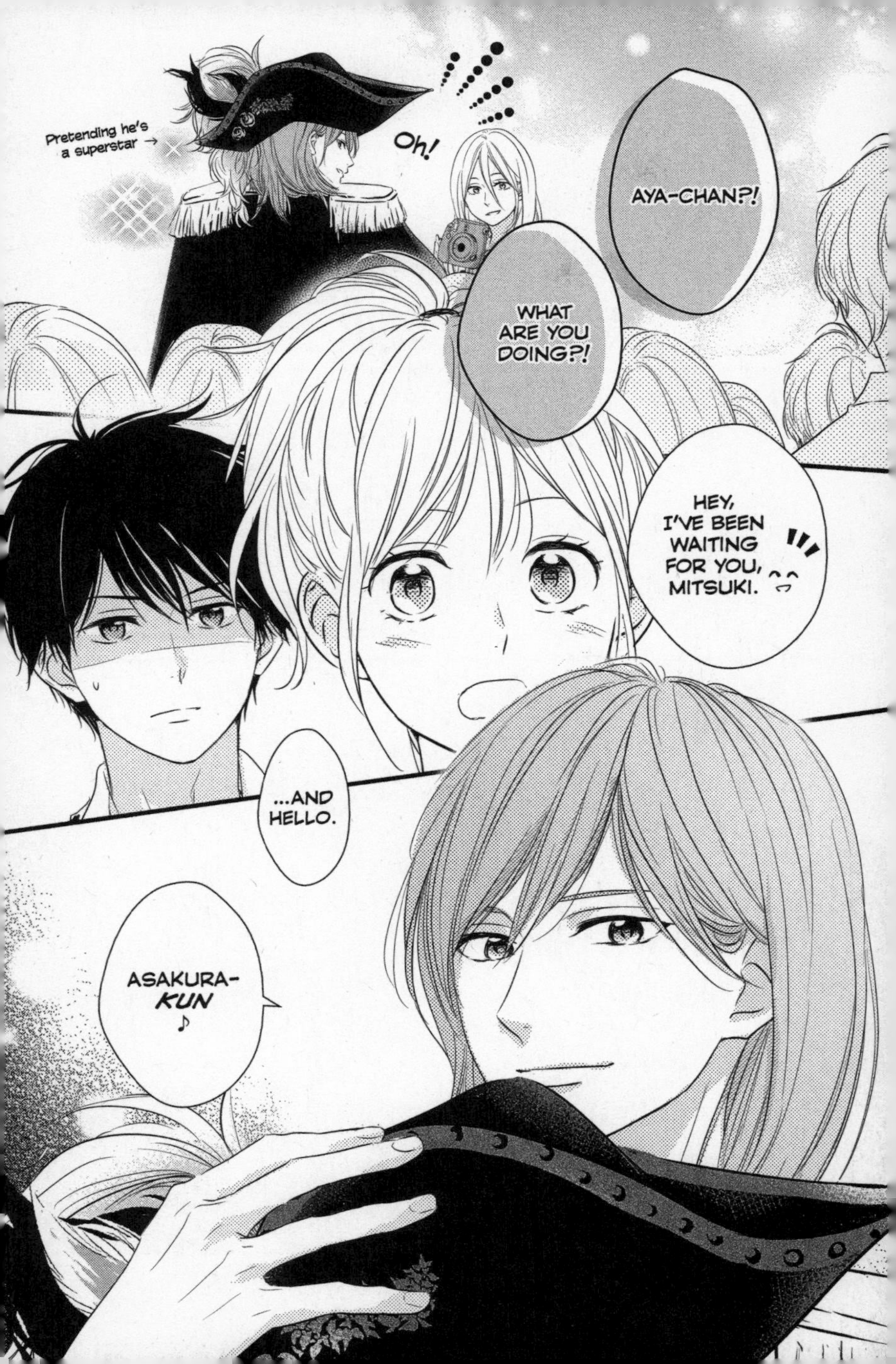
AYA-CHAN?!
WHAT ARE YOU DOING?!
Oh!
Pretending he's a superstar →
HEY, I'VE BEEN WAITING FOR YOU, MITSUKI.
...AND HELLO.
ASAKURA-KUN ♪

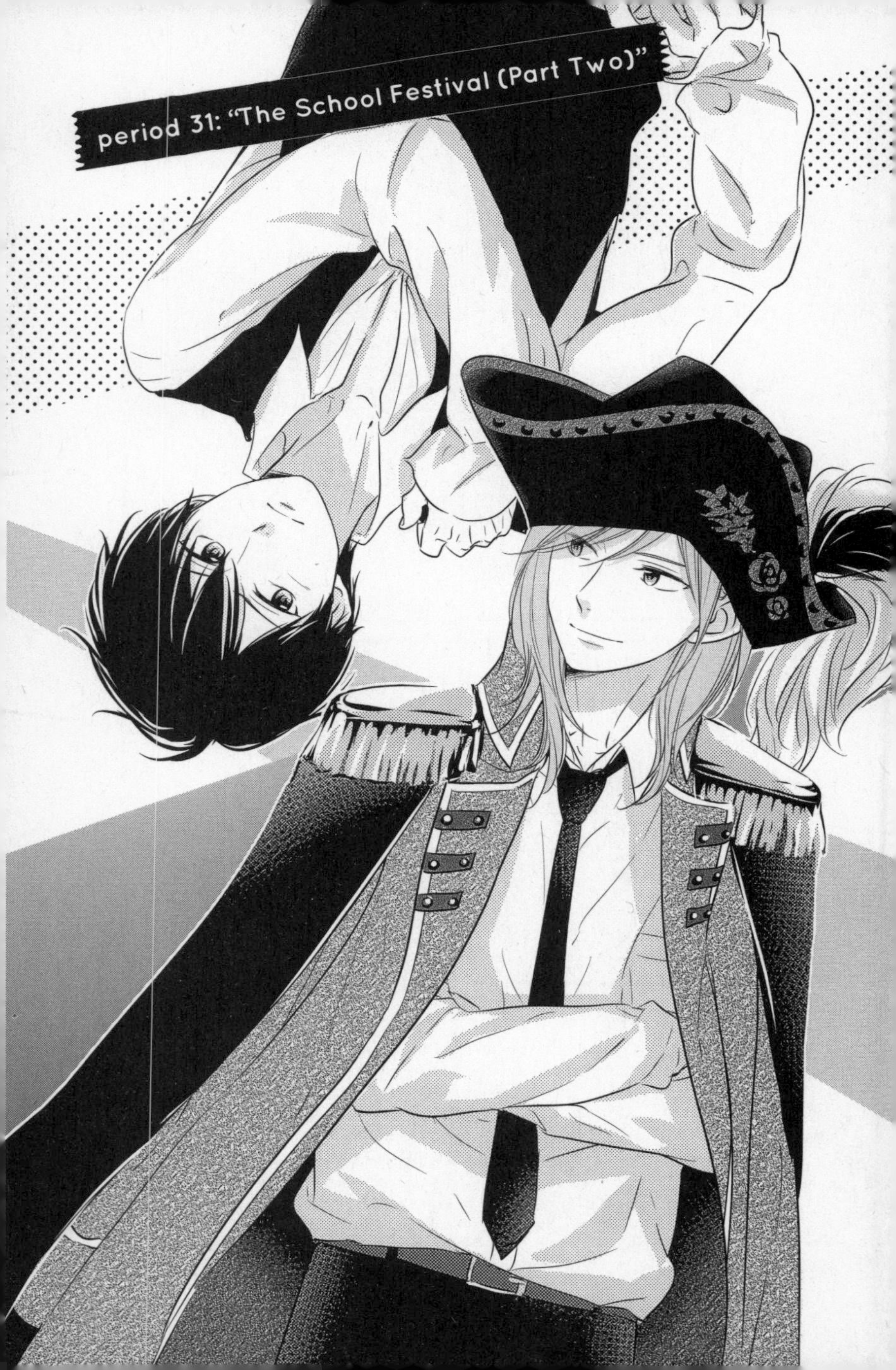
period 31: "The School Festival (Part Two)"

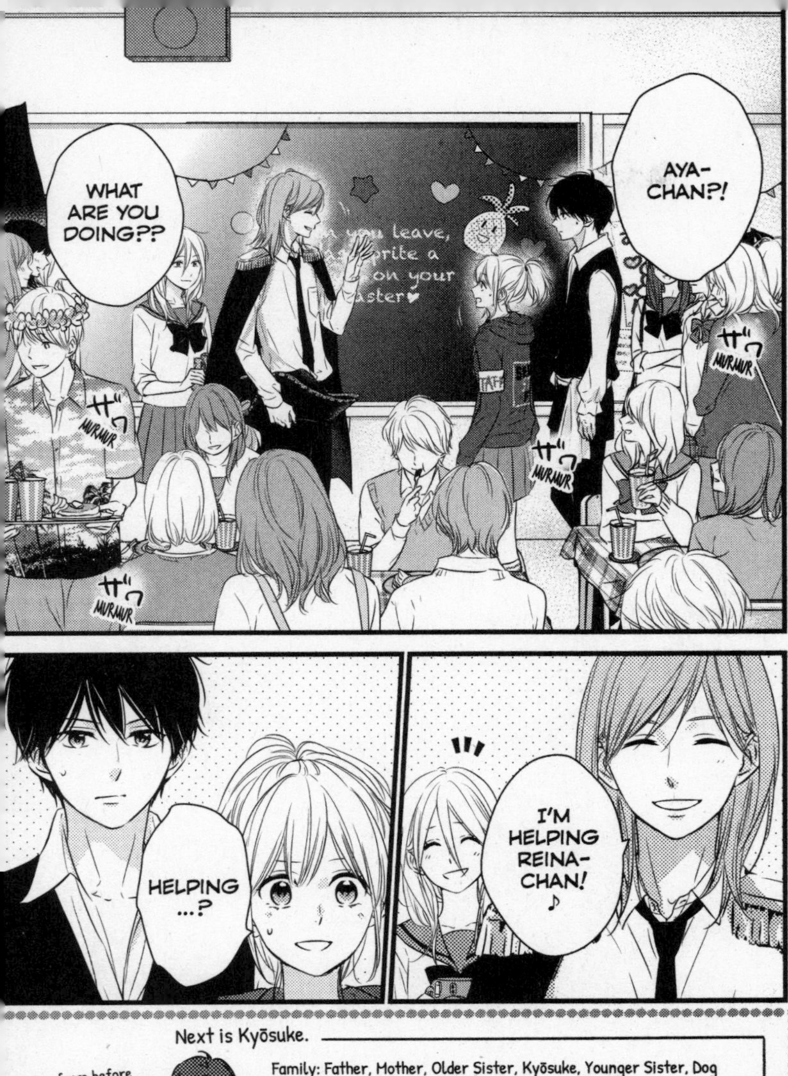
AYA-CHAN?!
ザワ MURMUR
ザワ MURMUR
WHAT ARE YOU DOING??
ザワ MURMUR
ザワ MURMUR
I'M HELPING REINA-CHAN! ♪
HELPING ...?

Next is Kyōsuke.

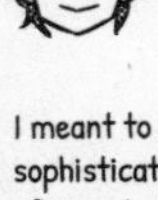

Family: Father, Mother, Older Sister, Kyōsuke, Younger Sister, Dog
Apparently his older sister (in college) and younger sister (in middle school) are gorgeous (according to Rui).

Design from before the series started

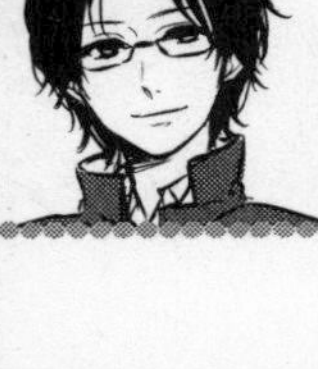

I meant to draw a caring, older-brother type, but at some point he morphed into a sexy, sophisticated guy. Maybe it's because in his early character notes, I wrote, "his knowledge of risqué stuff is on a different level" (ha ha). Dealing with his stubborn sisters has taught him how to be good with women. Apparently I originally called him Sōsuke. His character design isn't that different.

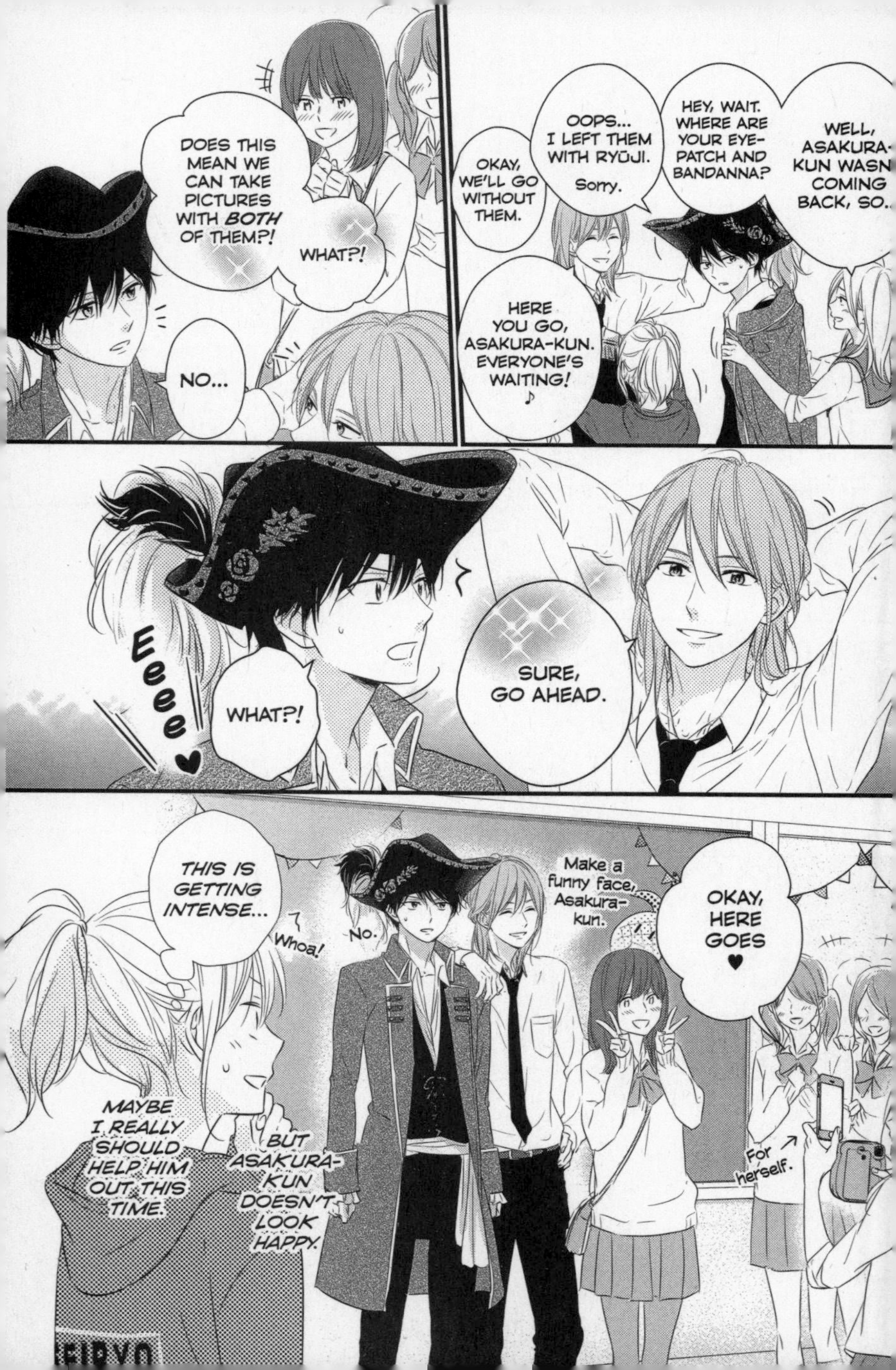
WELL, ASAKURA-KUN WASN COMING BACK, SO...
HEY, WAIT. WHERE ARE YOUR EYE-PATCH AND BANDANNA?
OOPS... I LEFT THEM WITH RYŪJI.
Sorry.
OKAY, WE'LL GO WITHOUT THEM.
HERE YOU GO, ASAKURA-KUN. EVERYONE'S WAITING! ♪
DOES THIS MEAN WE CAN TAKE PICTURES WITH *BOTH* OF THEM?!
WHAT?!
NO...
SURE, GO AHEAD.
WHAT?!
Eeee♥
OKAY, HERE GOES ♥
For herself.
Make a funny face, Asakura-kun.
No.
Whoa!
THIS IS GETTING INTENSE...
BUT ASAKURA-KUN DOESN'T LOOK HAPPY.
MAYBE I REALLY SHOULD HELP HIM OUT THIS TIME.

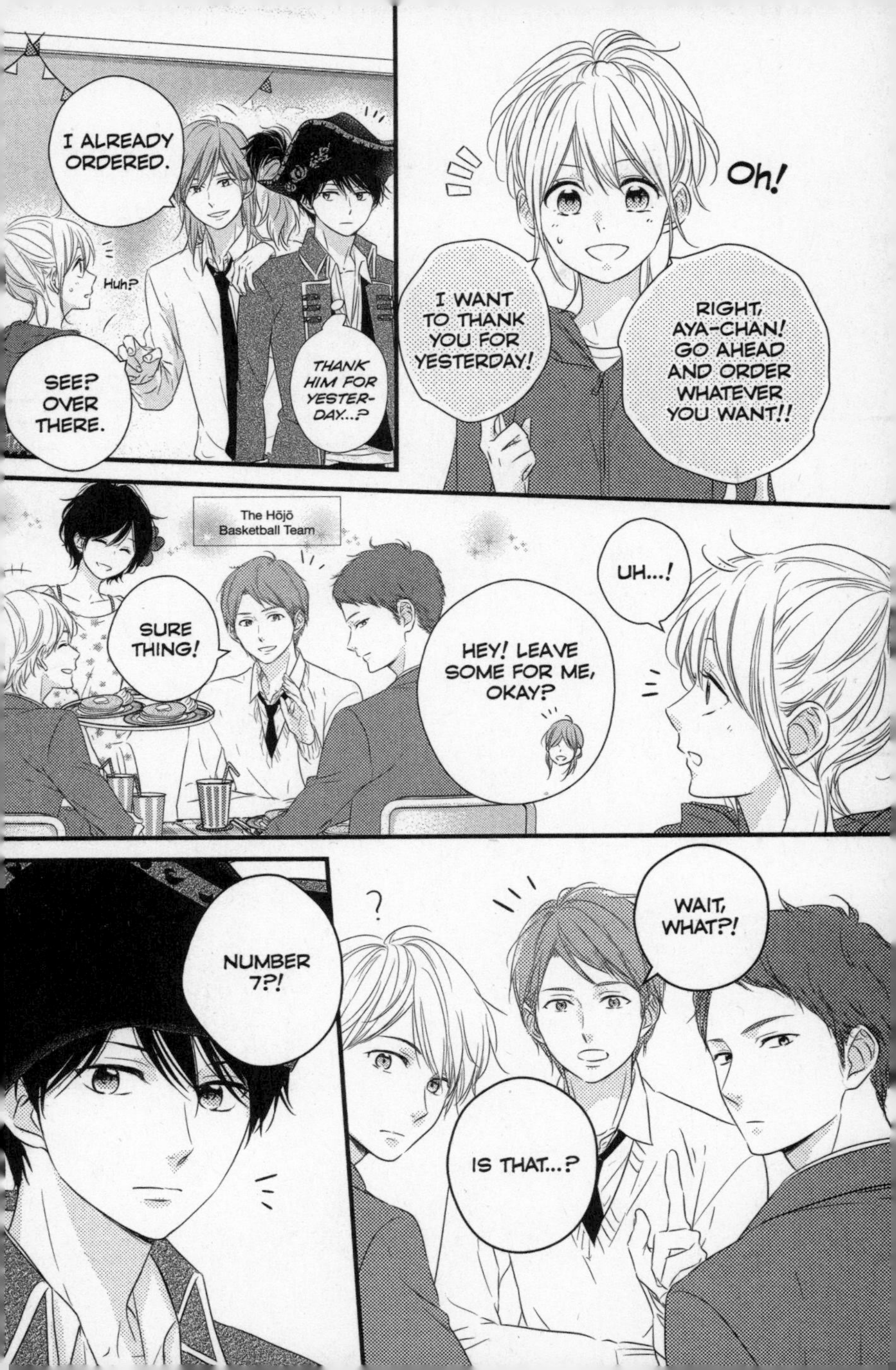
Oh!
RIGHT, AYA-CHAN! GO AHEAD AND ORDER WHATEVER YOU WANT!!
I WANT TO THANK YOU FOR YESTERDAY!
I ALREADY ORDERED.
Huh?
THANK HIM FOR YESTER-DAY...?
SEE? OVER THERE.
UH...!
HEY! LEAVE SOME FOR ME, OKAY?
SURE THING!
The Hōjō Basketball Team
WAIT, WHAT?!
IS THAT...?
NUMBER 7?!

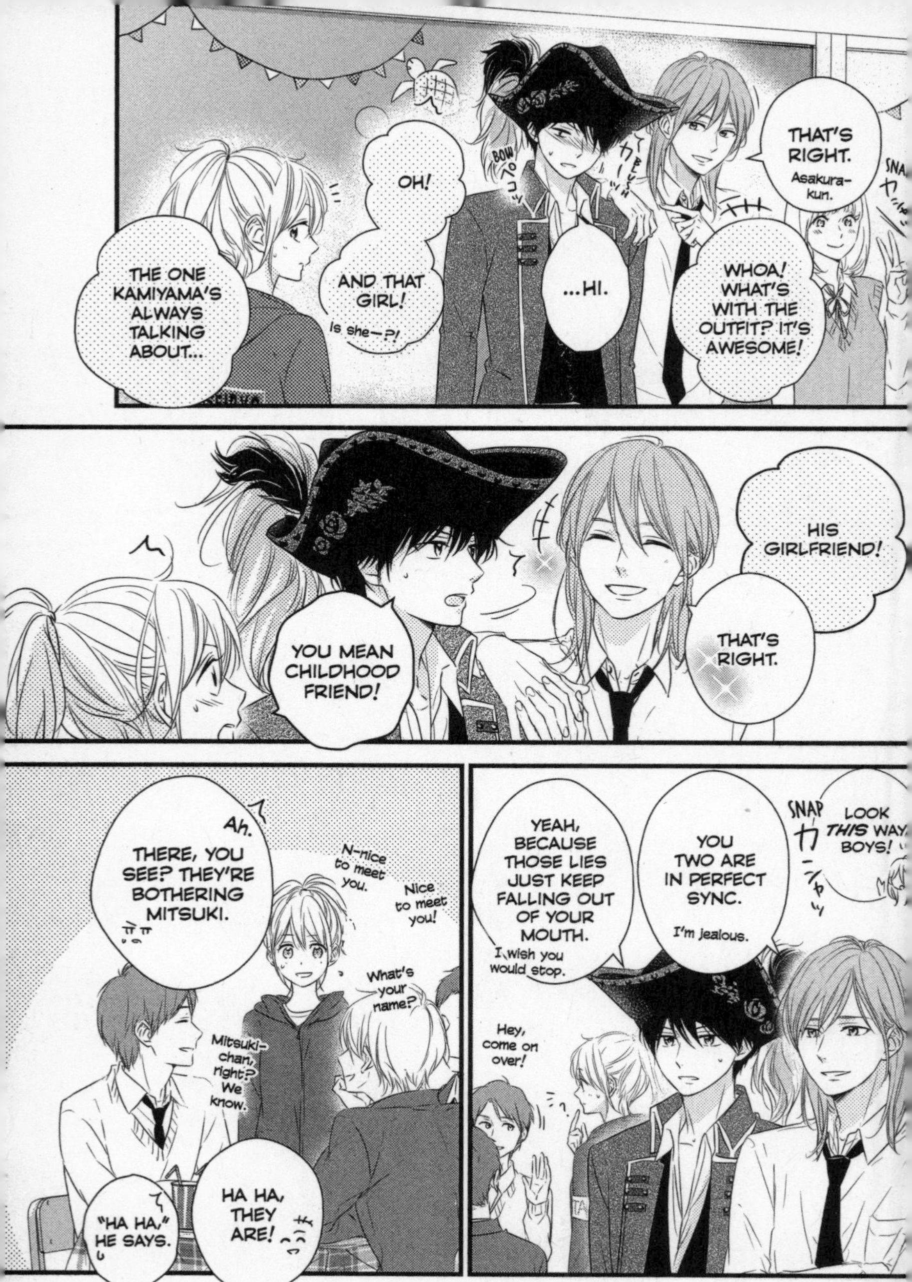
THAT'S RIGHT.
Asakura-kun.
WHOA! WHAT'S WITH THE OUTFIT? IT'S AWESOME!
BLUSH
...HI.
BOW
OH!
AND THAT GIRL!
is she—?!
THE ONE KAMIYAMA'S ALWAYS TALKING ABOUT...
HIS GIRLFRIEND!
THAT'S RIGHT.
YOU MEAN CHILDHOOD FRIEND!
SNAP
LOOK THIS WAY, BOYS!
YOU TWO ARE IN PERFECT SYNC.
I'm jealous.
YEAH, BECAUSE THOSE LIES JUST KEEP FALLING OUT OF YOUR MOUTH.
I wish you would stop.
Hey, come on over!
Nice to meet you!
N-nice to meet you.
Ah.
THERE, YOU SEE? THEY'RE BOTHERING MITSUKI.
What's your name?
Mitsuki-chan, right? We know.
HA HA, THEY ARE!
"HA HA," HE SAYS.

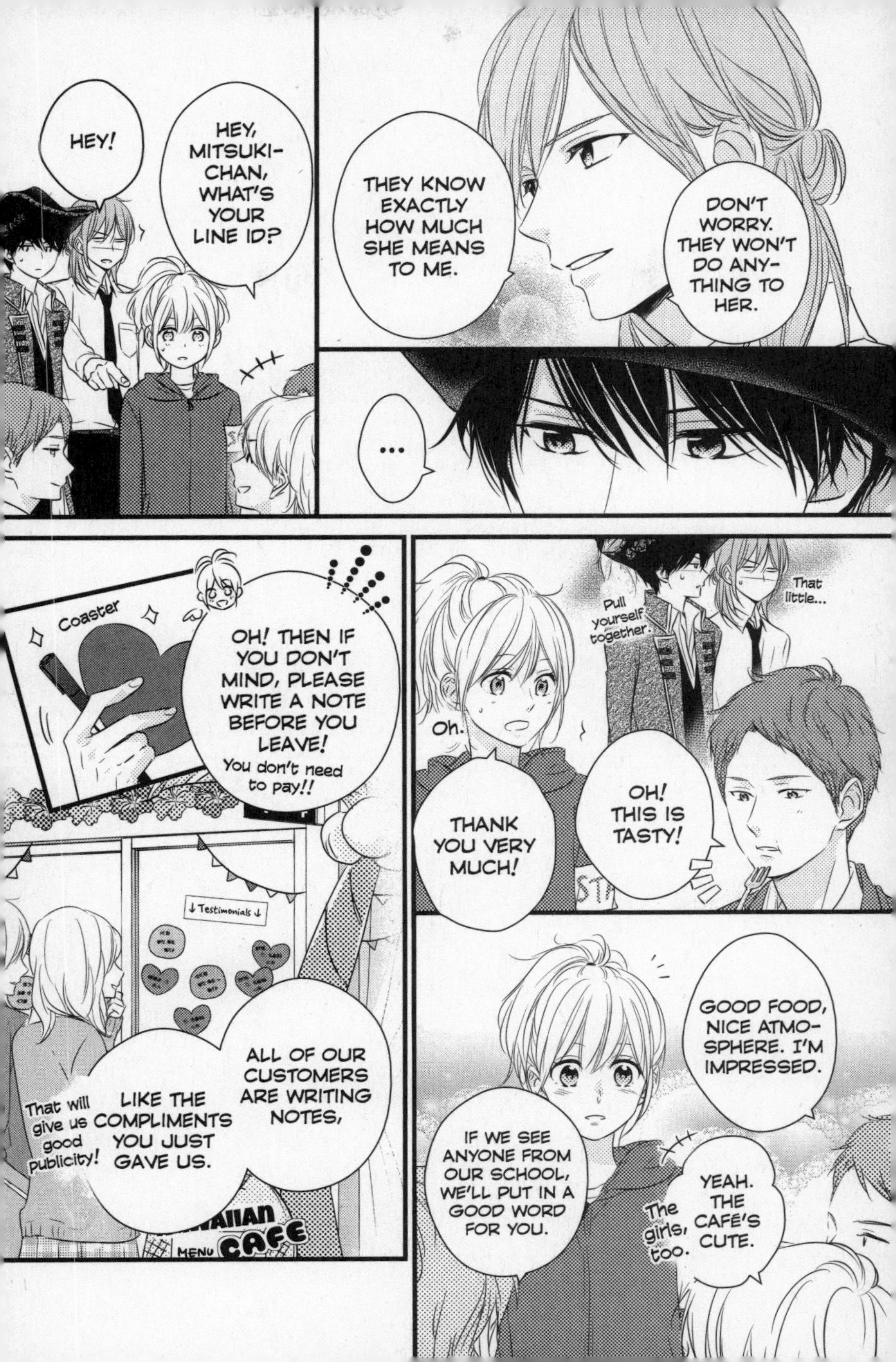
DON'T WORRY. THEY WON'T DO ANYTHING TO HER.
THEY KNOW EXACTLY HOW MUCH SHE MEANS TO ME.
...
HEY, MITSUKI-CHAN, WHAT'S YOUR LINE ID?
HEY!
That little...
Pull yourself together.
OH! THIS IS TASTY!
Oh.
THANK YOU VERY MUCH!
GOOD FOOD, NICE ATMOSPHERE. I'M IMPRESSED.
YEAH. THE CAFÉ'S CUTE.
The girls, too.
IF WE SEE ANYONE FROM OUR SCHOOL, WE'LL PUT IN A GOOD WORD FOR YOU.
OH! THEN IF YOU DON'T MIND, PLEASE WRITE A NOTE BEFORE YOU LEAVE!
You don't need to pay!!
Coaster
↓ Testimonials ↓
ALL OF OUR CUSTOMERS ARE WRITING NOTES,
LIKE THE COMPLIMENTS YOU JUST GAVE US.
That will give us good publicity!
MENU
CAFE

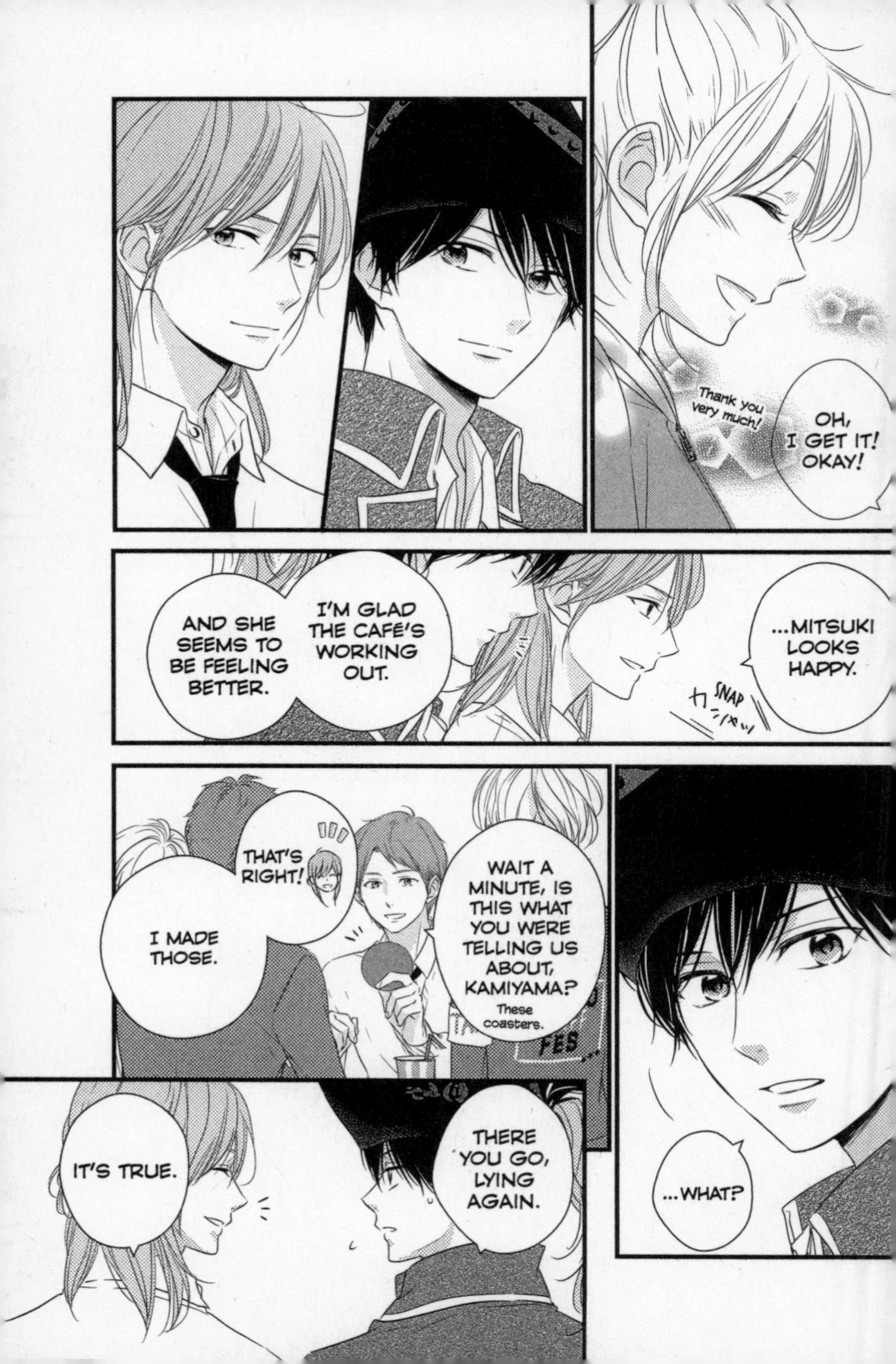
OH, I GET IT! OKAY!
Thank you very much!
...MITSUKI LOOKS HAPPY.
SNAP
I'M GLAD THE CAFÉ'S WORKING OUT.
AND SHE SEEMS TO BE FEELING BETTER.
...WHAT?
WAIT A MINUTE, IS THIS WHAT YOU WERE TELLING US ABOUT, KAMIYAMA?
These coasters.
THAT'S RIGHT!
I MADE THOSE.
FES
THERE YOU GO, LYING AGAIN.
IT'S TRUE.

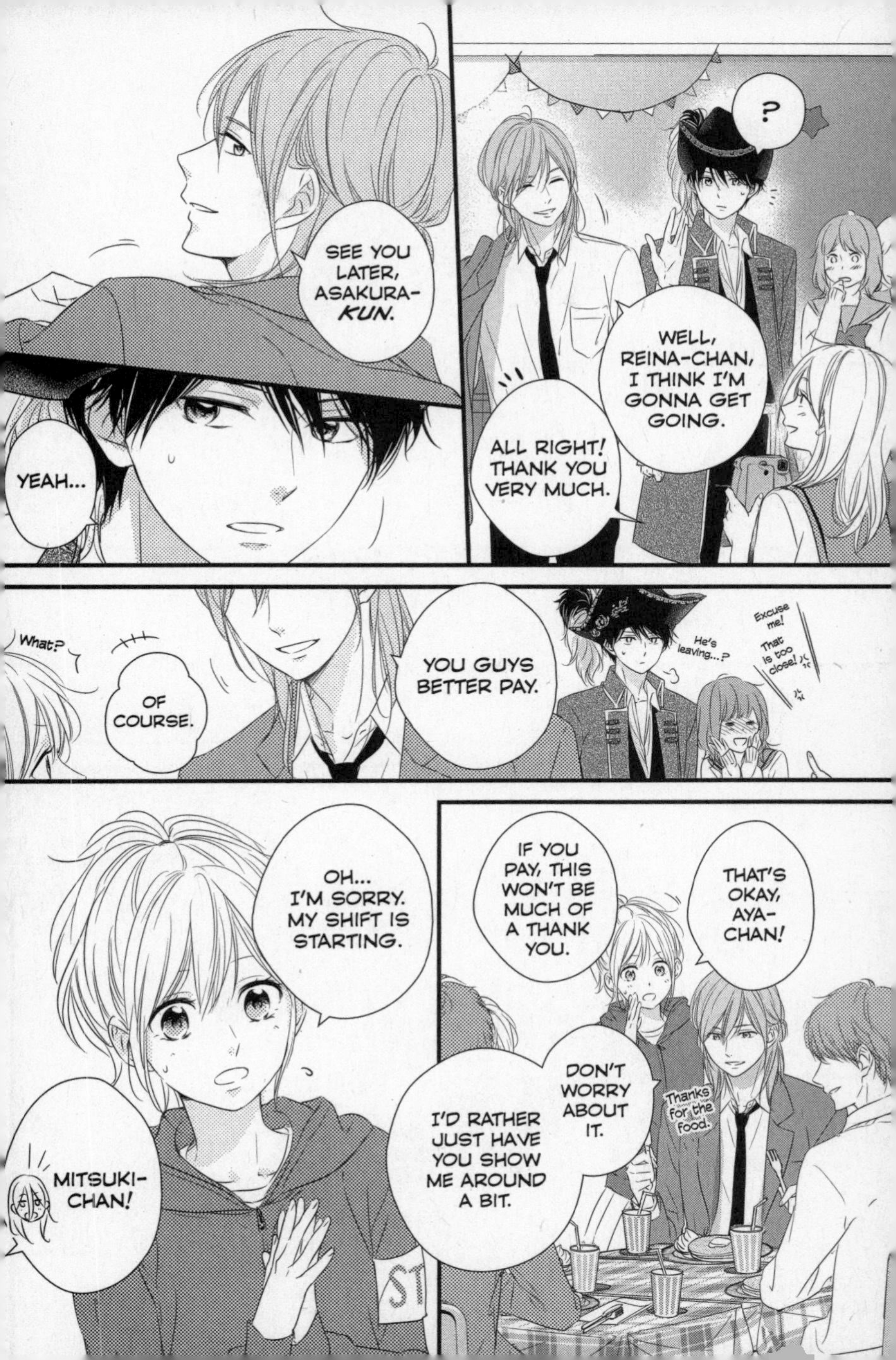
?
WELL, REINA-CHAN, I THINK I'M GONNA GET GOING.
ALL RIGHT! THANK YOU VERY MUCH.
SEE YOU LATER, ASAKURA-*KUN*.
YEAH...
Excuse me! That is too close!
He's leaving...?
YOU GUYS BETTER PAY.
OF COURSE.
What?
THAT'S OKAY, AYA-CHAN!
IF YOU PAY, THIS WON'T BE MUCH OF A THANK YOU.
DON'T WORRY ABOUT IT.
Thanks for the food.
I'D RATHER JUST HAVE YOU SHOW ME AROUND A BIT.
OH... I'M SORRY. MY SHIFT IS STARTING.
MITSUKI-CHAN!

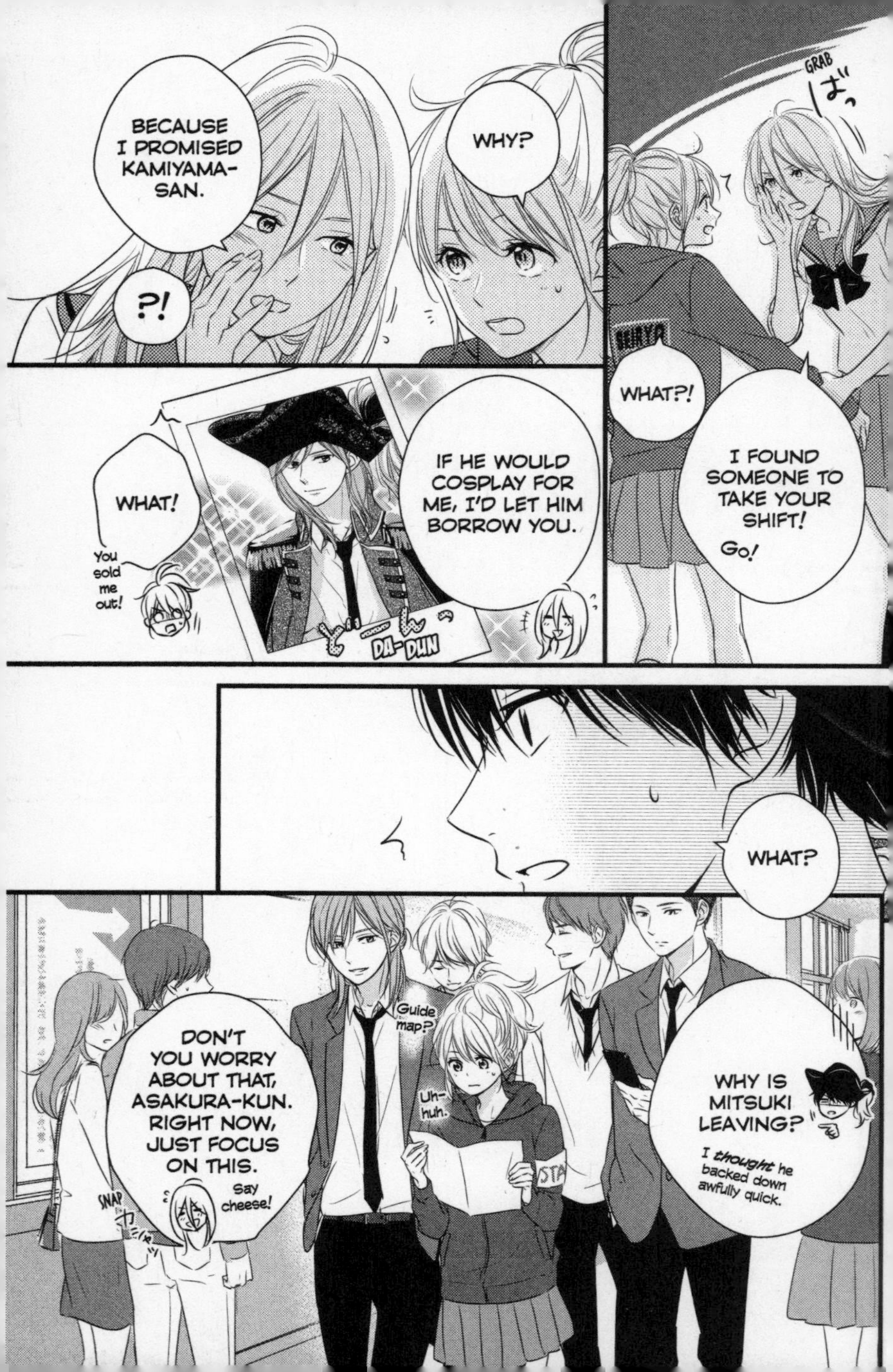
GRAB
WHAT?!
I FOUND SOMEONE TO TAKE YOUR SHIFT!
Go!
WHY?
BECAUSE I PROMISED KAMIYAMA-SAN.
?!
IF HE WOULD COSPLAY FOR ME, I'D LET HIM BORROW YOU.
DA-DUN
WHAT!
You sold me out!
WHAT?
WHY IS MITSUKI LEAVING?
I *thought* he backed down awfully quick.
Guide map?
Uh-huh.
DON'T YOU WORRY ABOUT THAT, ASAKURA-KUN. RIGHT NOW, JUST FOCUS ON THIS.
Say cheese!
SNAP

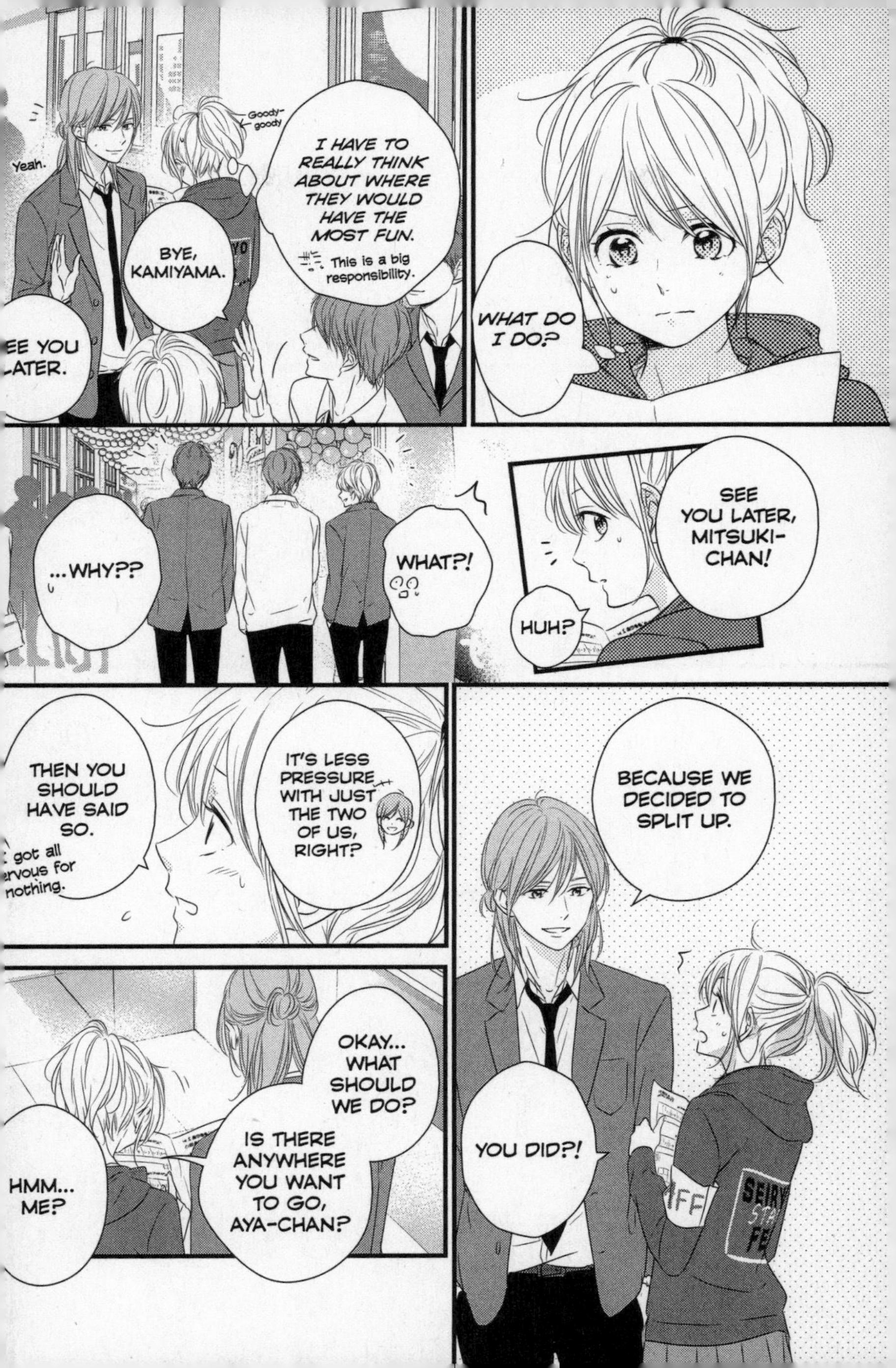

WHAT DO I DO?
I HAVE TO REALLY THINK ABOUT WHERE THEY WOULD HAVE THE MOST FUN.
This is a big responsibility.
Goody-goody
BYE, KAMIYAMA.
Yeah.
EE YOU ATER.
SEE YOU LATER, MITSUKI-CHAN!
HUH?
WHAT?!
...WHY??
BECAUSE WE DECIDED TO SPLIT UP.
YOU DID?!
IT'S LESS PRESSURE WITH JUST THE TWO OF US, RIGHT?
THEN YOU SHOULD HAVE SAID SO.
got all ervous for nothing.
OKAY... WHAT SHOULD WE DO?
IS THERE ANYWHERE YOU WANT TO GO, AYA-CHAN?
HMM... ME?

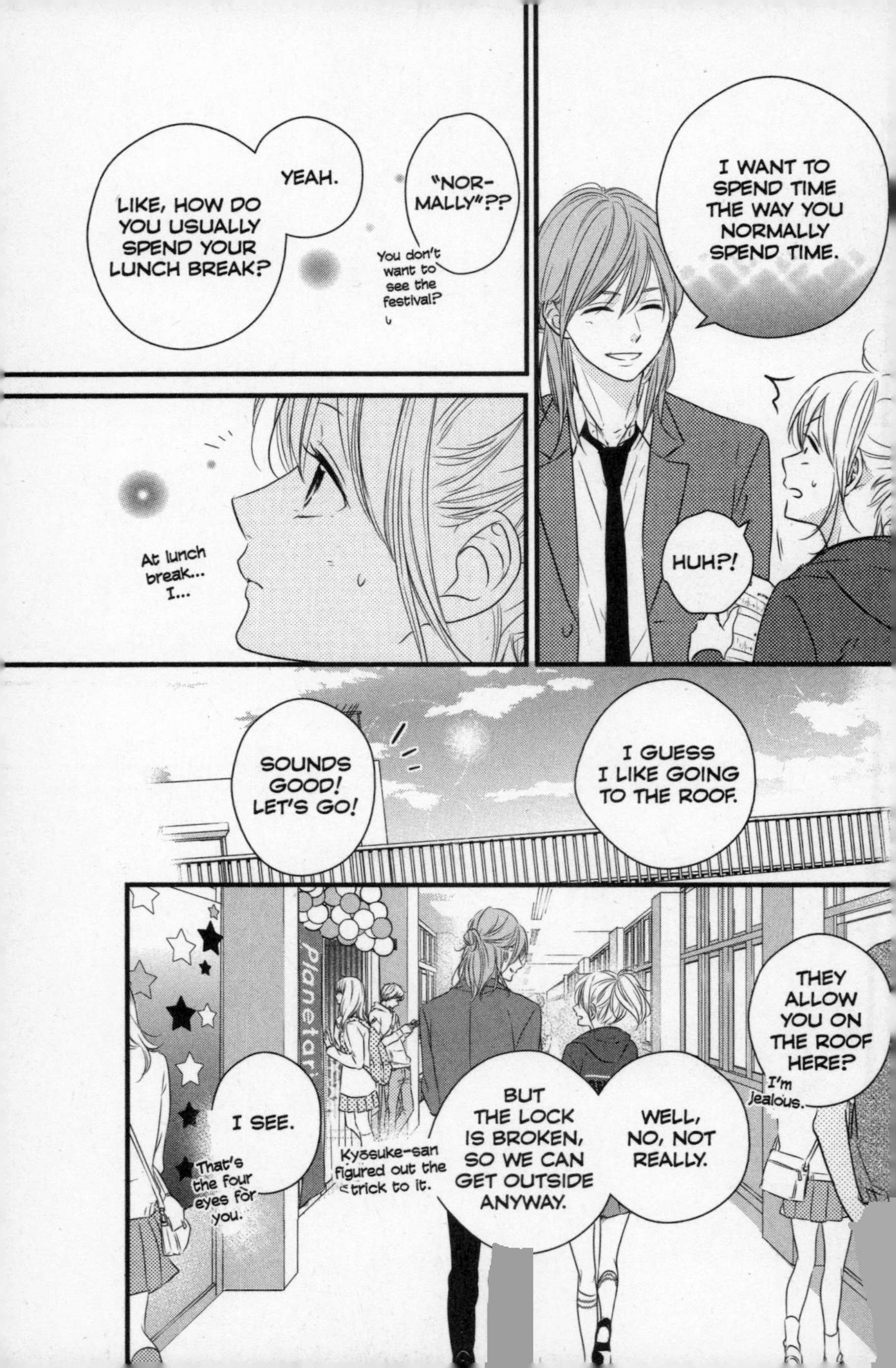
I WANT TO SPEND TIME THE WAY YOU NORMALLY SPEND TIME.
HUH?!
"NOR-MALLY"??
You don't want to see the festival?
YEAH.
LIKE, HOW DO YOU USUALLY SPEND YOUR LUNCH BREAK?
At lunch break... I...
I GUESS I LIKE GOING TO THE ROOF.
SOUNDS GOOD! LET'S GO!
THEY ALLOW YOU ON THE ROOF HERE?
I'm jealous.
WELL, NO, NOT REALLY.
BUT THE LOCK IS BROKEN, SO WE CAN GET OUTSIDE ANYWAY.
Kyosuke-san figured out the trick to it.
I SEE.
That's the four eyes for you.

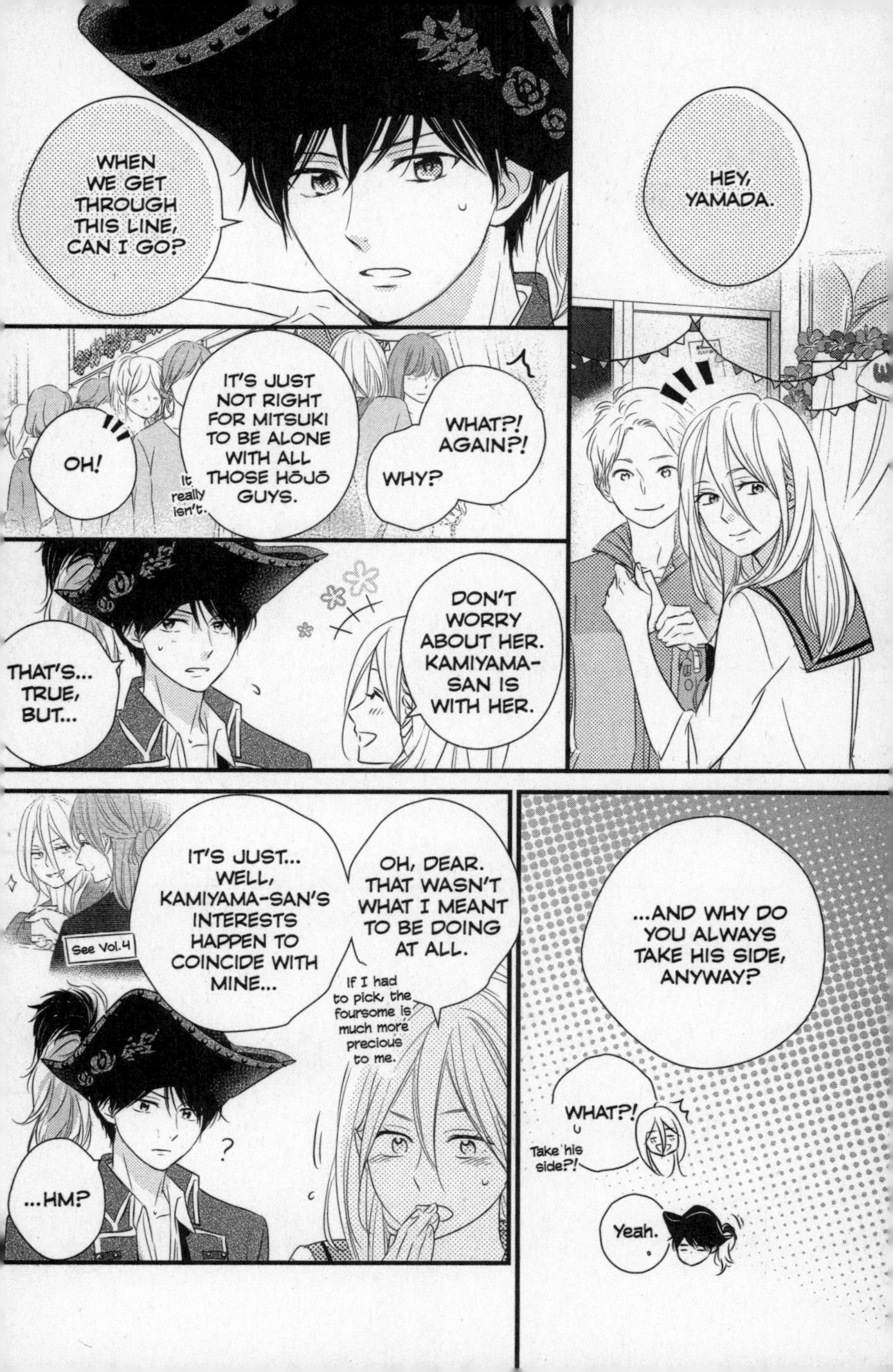
HEY, YAMADA.
WHEN WE GET THROUGH THIS LINE, CAN I GO?
WHAT?! AGAIN?!
WHY?
IT'S JUST NOT RIGHT FOR MITSUKI TO BE ALONE WITH ALL THOSE HŌJŌ GUYS.
It really isn't.
OH!
DON'T WORRY ABOUT HER. KAMIYAMA-SAN IS WITH HER.
THAT'S... TRUE, BUT...
...AND WHY DO YOU ALWAYS TAKE HIS SIDE, ANYWAY?
WHAT?!
Take his side?!
Yeah.
OH, DEAR. THAT WASN'T WHAT I MEANT TO BE DOING AT ALL.
IT'S JUST... WELL, KAMIYAMA-SAN'S INTERESTS HAPPEN TO COINCIDE WITH MINE...
If I had to pick, the foursome is much more precious to me.
See Vol.4
...HM?

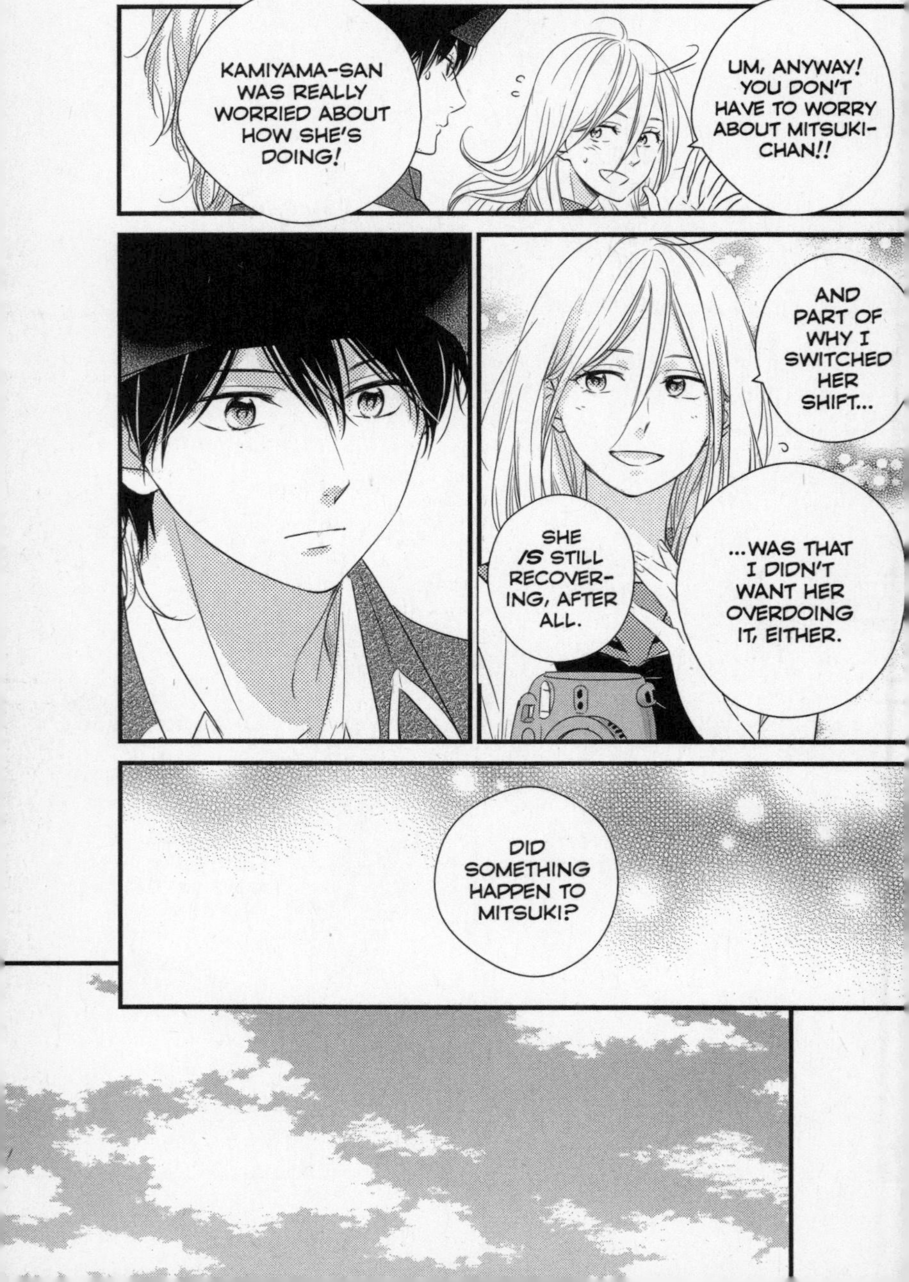
UM, ANYWAY! YOU DON'T HAVE TO WORRY ABOUT MITSUKI-CHAN!!
KAMIYAMA-SAN WAS REALLY WORRIED ABOUT HOW SHE'S DOING!
AND PART OF WHY I SWITCHED HER SHIFT...
...WAS THAT I DIDN'T WANT HER OVERDOING IT, EITHER.
SHE IS STILL RECOVERING, AFTER ALL.
DID SOMETHING HAPPEN TO MITSUKI?

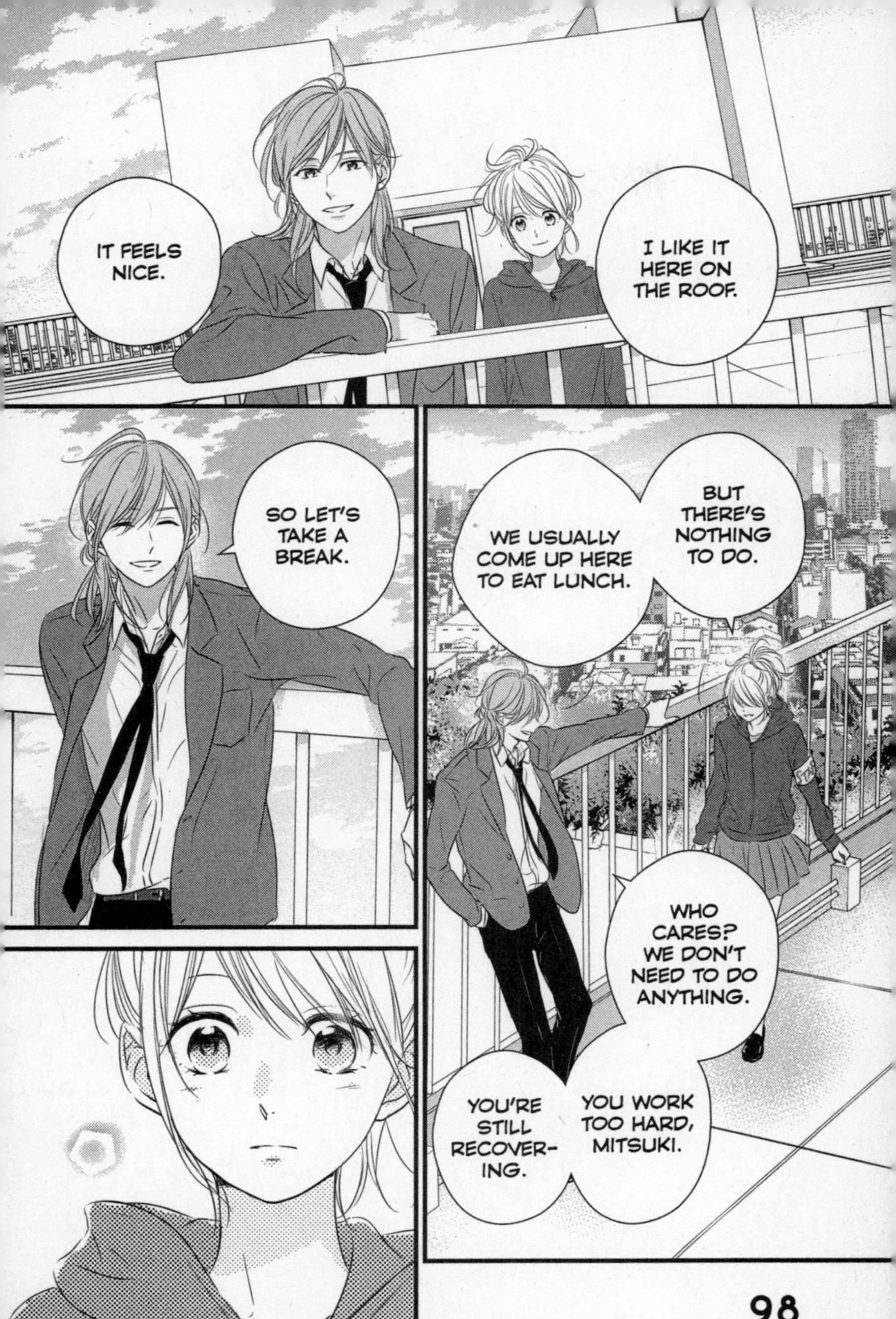
I LIKE IT HERE ON THE ROOF.
IT FEELS NICE.
BUT THERE'S NOTHING TO DO.
WE USUALLY COME UP HERE TO EAT LUNCH.
WHO CARES? WE DON'T NEED TO DO ANYTHING.
YOU WORK TOO HARD, MITSUKI.
YOU'RE STILL RECOVER-ING.
SO LET'S TAKE A BREAK.

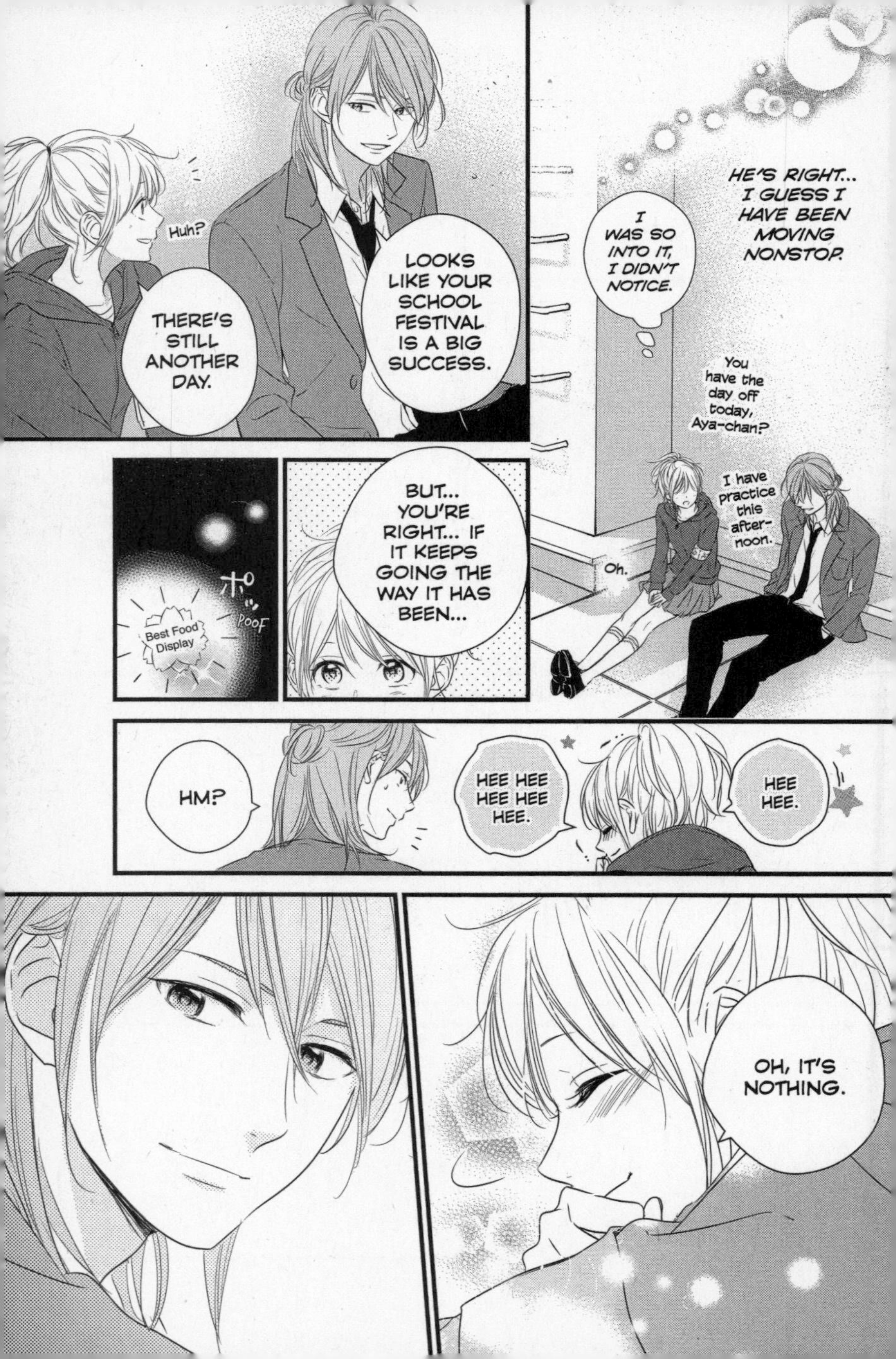
HE'S RIGHT... I GUESS I HAVE BEEN MOVING NONSTOP.
I WAS SO INTO IT, I DIDN'T NOTICE.
You have the day off today, Aya-chan?
I have practice this afternoon.
Oh.
LOOKS LIKE YOUR SCHOOL FESTIVAL IS A BIG SUCCESS.
Huh?
THERE'S STILL ANOTHER DAY.
BUT... YOU'RE RIGHT... IF IT KEEPS GOING THE WAY IT HAS BEEN...
POOF
Best Food Display
HEE HEE.
HEE HEE HEE HEE HEE.
HM?
OH, IT'S NOTHING.

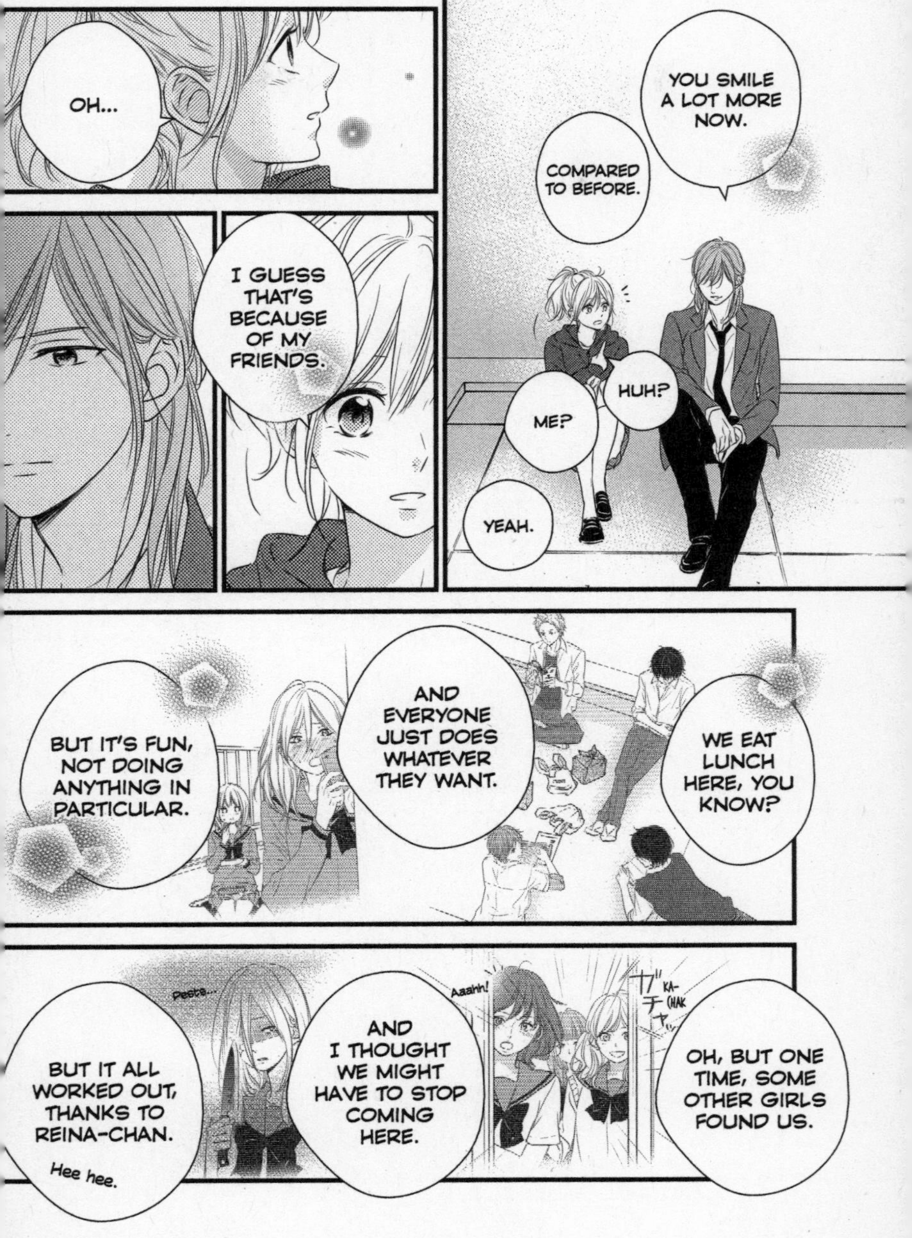
YOU SMILE A LOT MORE NOW.
COMPARED TO BEFORE.
HUH?
ME?
YEAH.
OH...
I GUESS THAT'S BECAUSE OF MY FRIENDS.
WE EAT LUNCH HERE, YOU KNOW?
AND EVERYONE JUST DOES WHATEVER THEY WANT.
BUT IT'S FUN, NOT DOING ANYTHING IN PARTICULAR.
KA-CHAK
OH, BUT ONE TIME, SOME OTHER GIRLS FOUND US.
Aaahh!
AND I THOUGHT WE MIGHT HAVE TO STOP COMING HERE.
Pesta...
BUT IT ALL WORKED OUT, THANKS TO REINA-CHAN.
Hee hee.

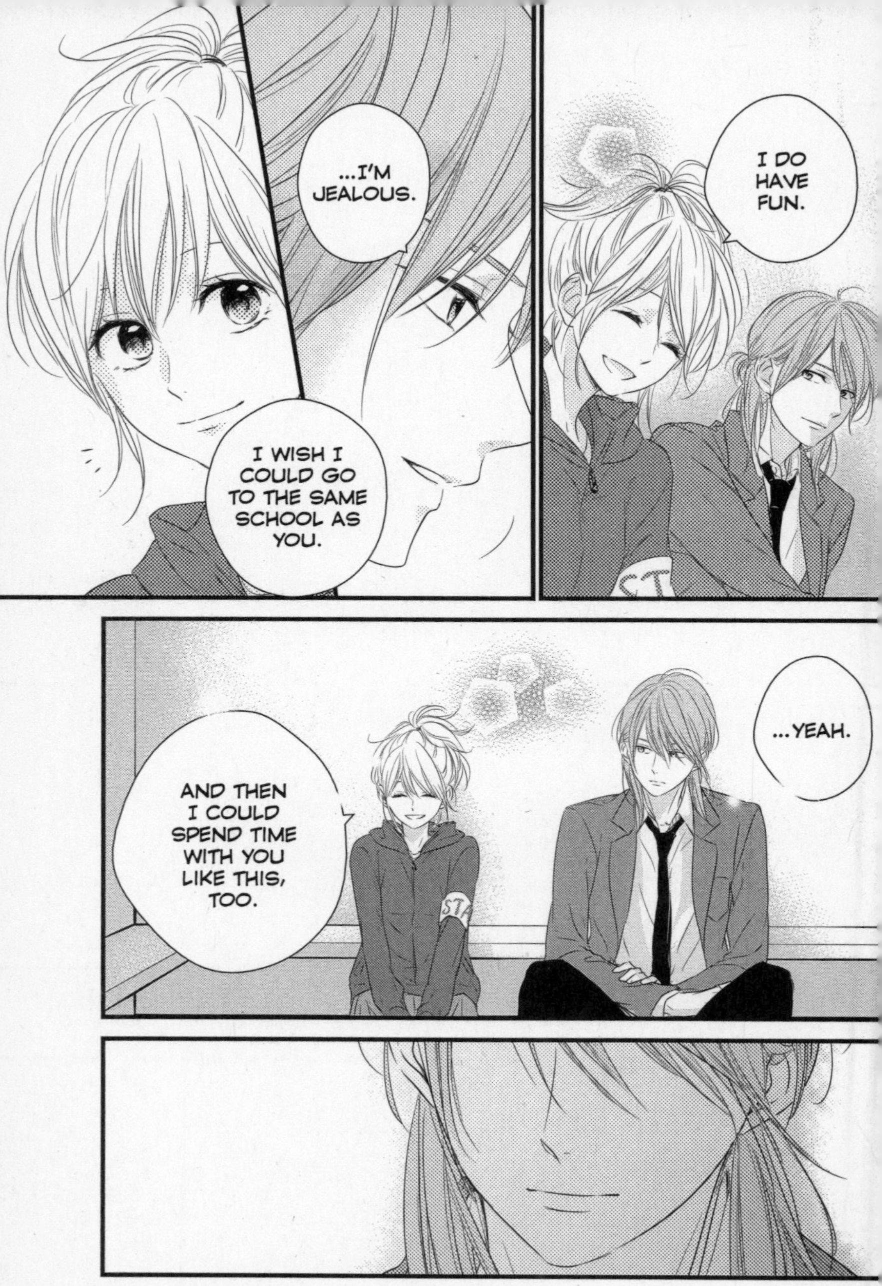
I DO HAVE FUN.
...I'M JEALOUS.
I WISH I COULD GO TO THE SAME SCHOOL AS YOU.
...YEAH.
AND THEN I COULD SPEND TIME WITH YOU LIKE THIS, TOO.

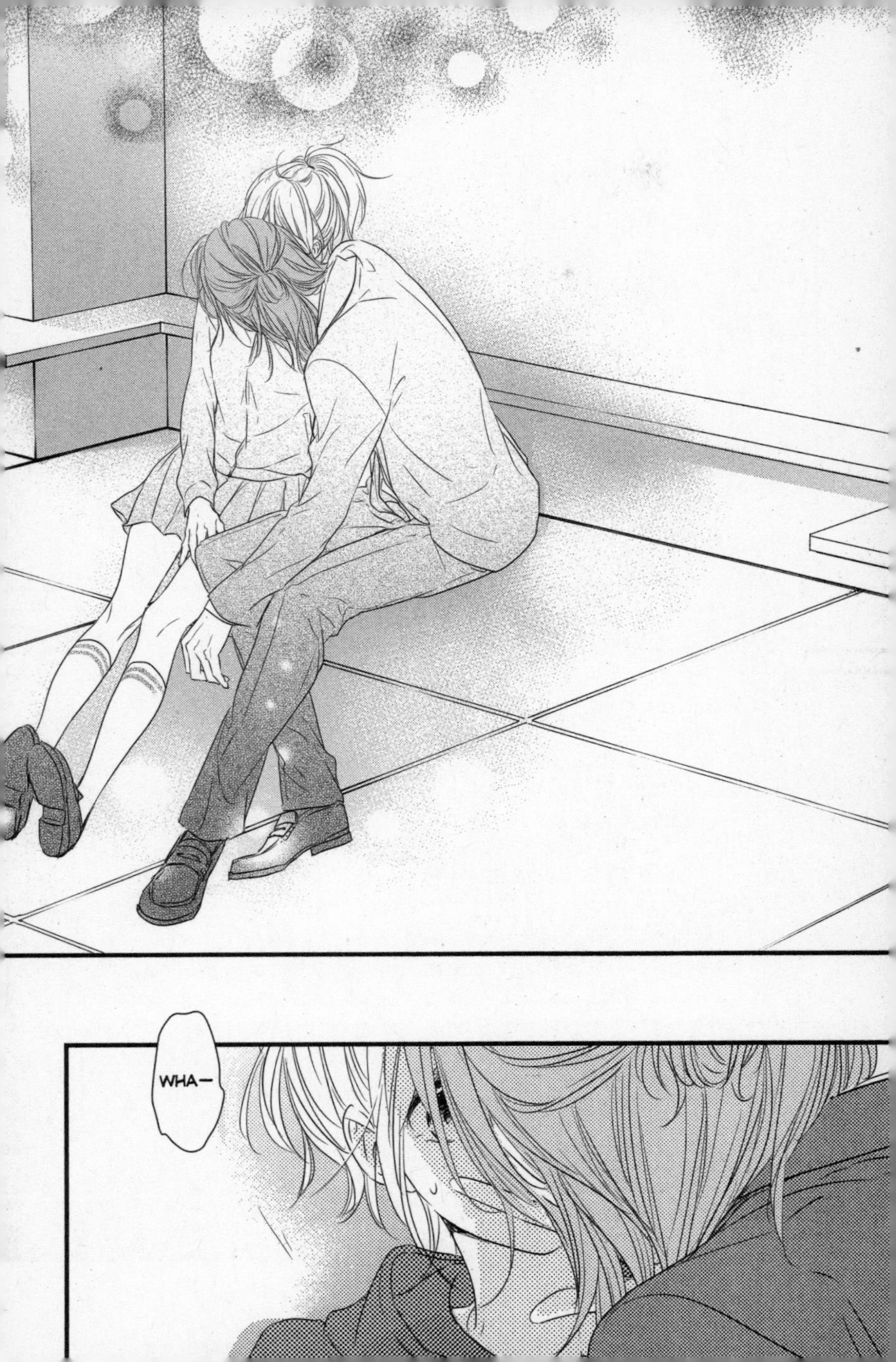
WHA—

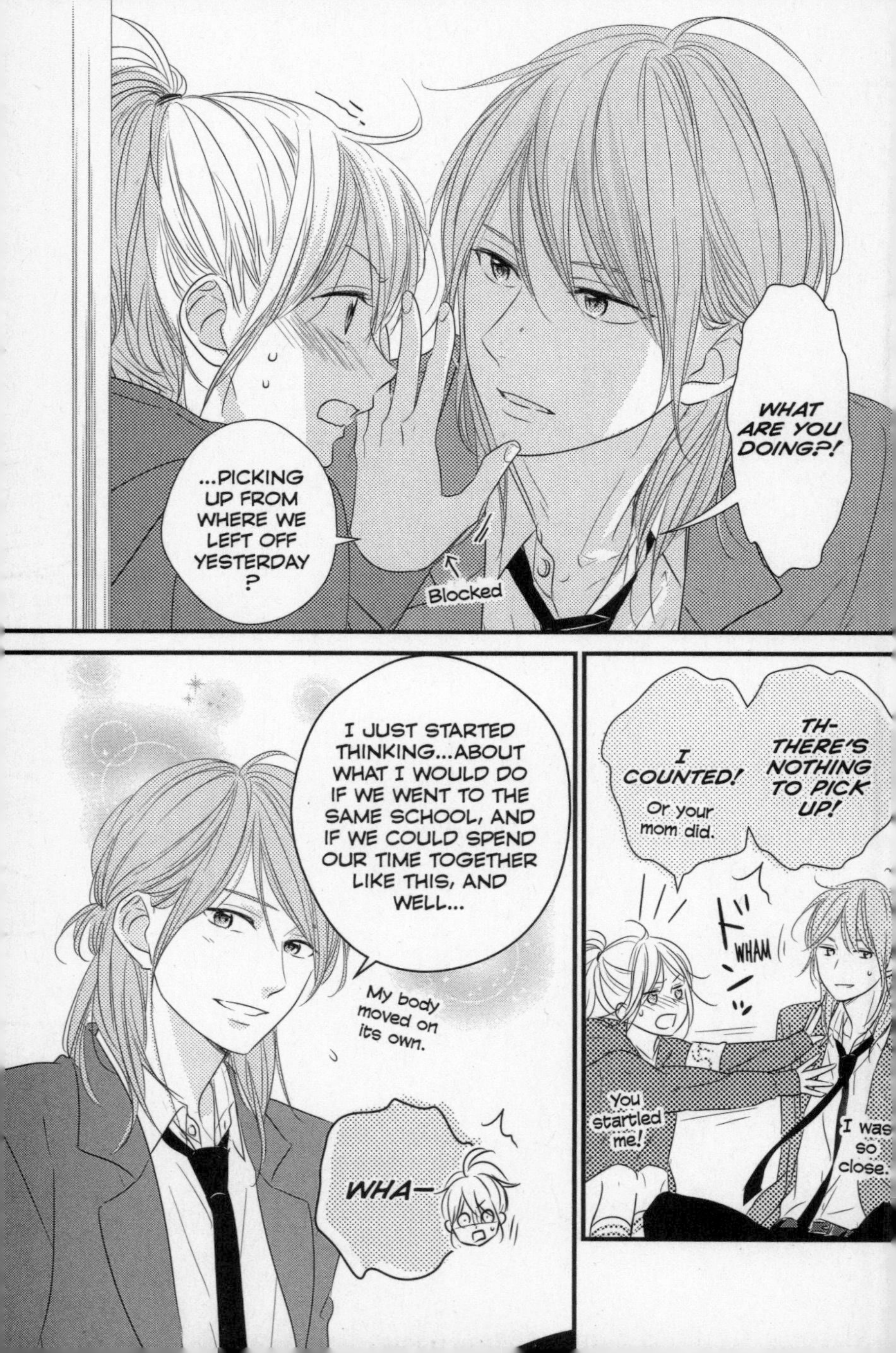
WHAT ARE YOU DOING?!
...PICKING UP FROM WHERE WE LEFT OFF YESTERDAY?
Blocked
TH-THERE'S NOTHING TO PICK UP!
I COUNTED!
Or your mom did.
WHAM
You startled me!
I was so close.
I JUST STARTED THINKING...ABOUT WHAT I WOULD DO IF WE WENT TO THE SAME SCHOOL, AND IF WE COULD SPEND OUR TIME TOGETHER LIKE THIS, AND WELL...
My body moved on its own.
WHA—

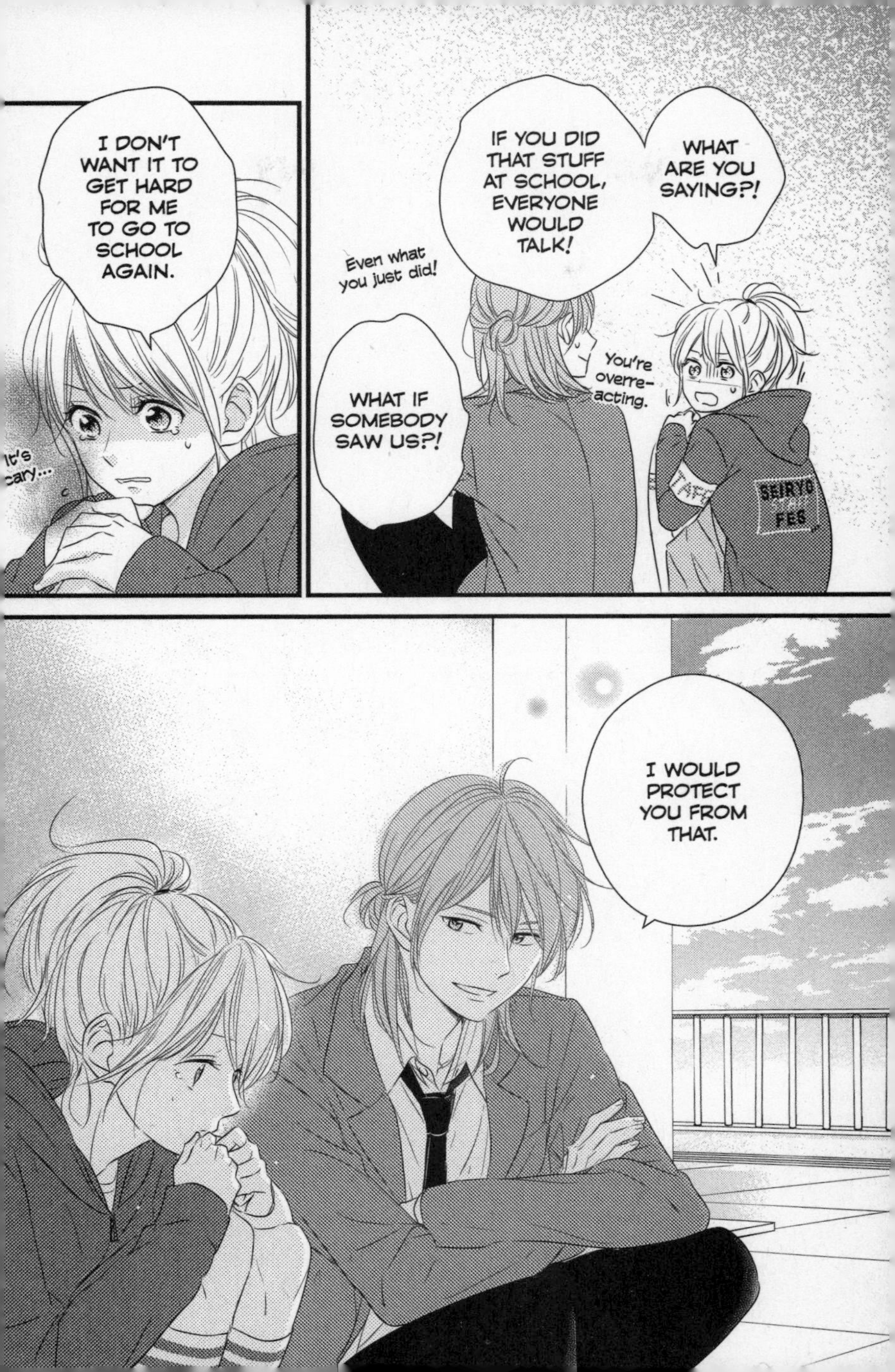
WHAT ARE YOU SAYING?!
IF YOU DID THAT STUFF AT SCHOOL, EVERYONE WOULD TALK!
Even what you just did!
You're overre-acting.
SEIRYO FES
WHAT IF SOMEBODY SAW US?!
I DON'T WANT IT TO GET HARD FOR ME TO GO TO SCHOOL AGAIN.
It's cary...
I WOULD PROTECT YOU FROM THAT.

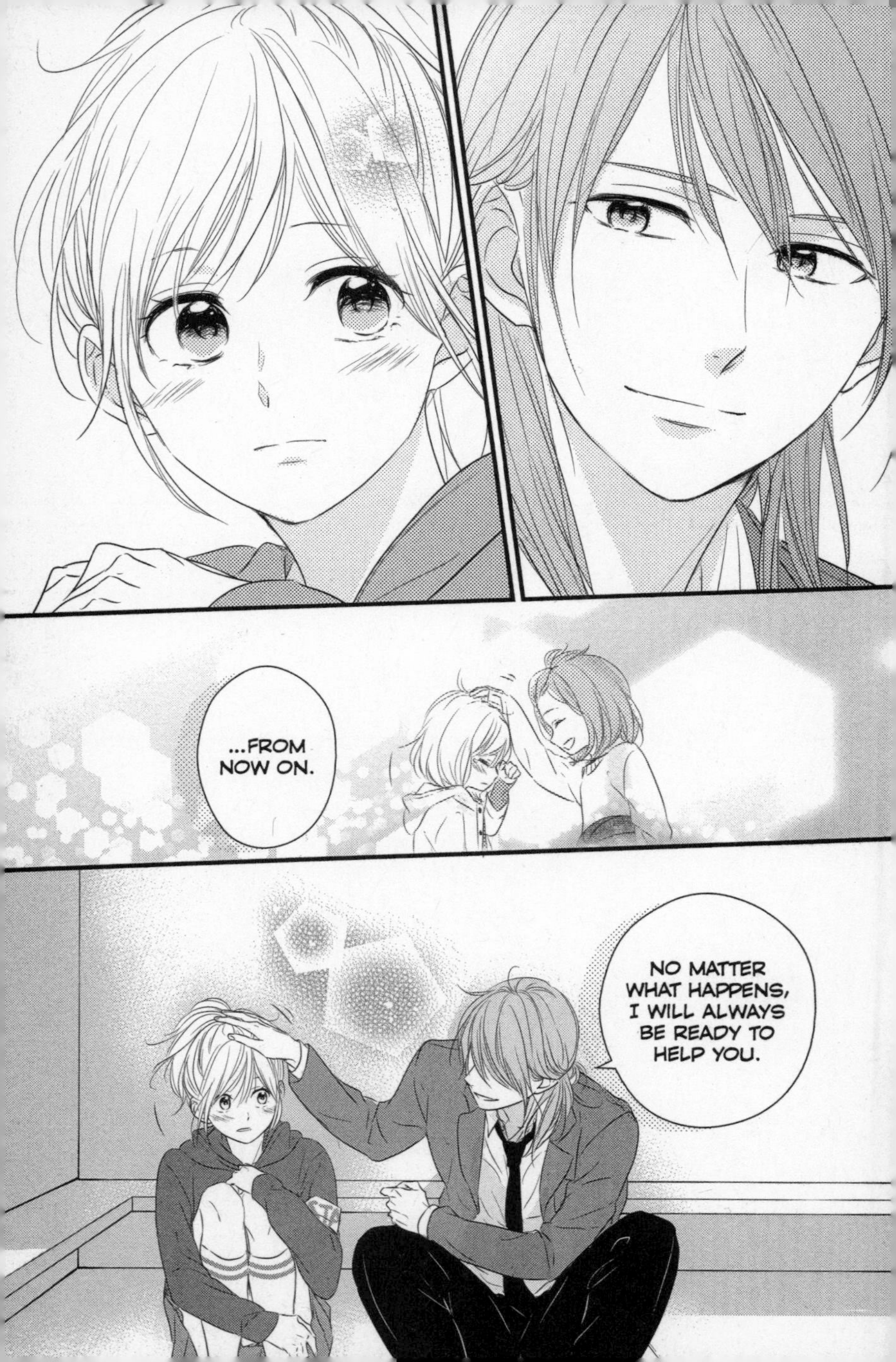
...FROM NOW ON.
NO MATTER WHAT HAPPENS, I WILL ALWAYS BE READY TO HELP YOU.

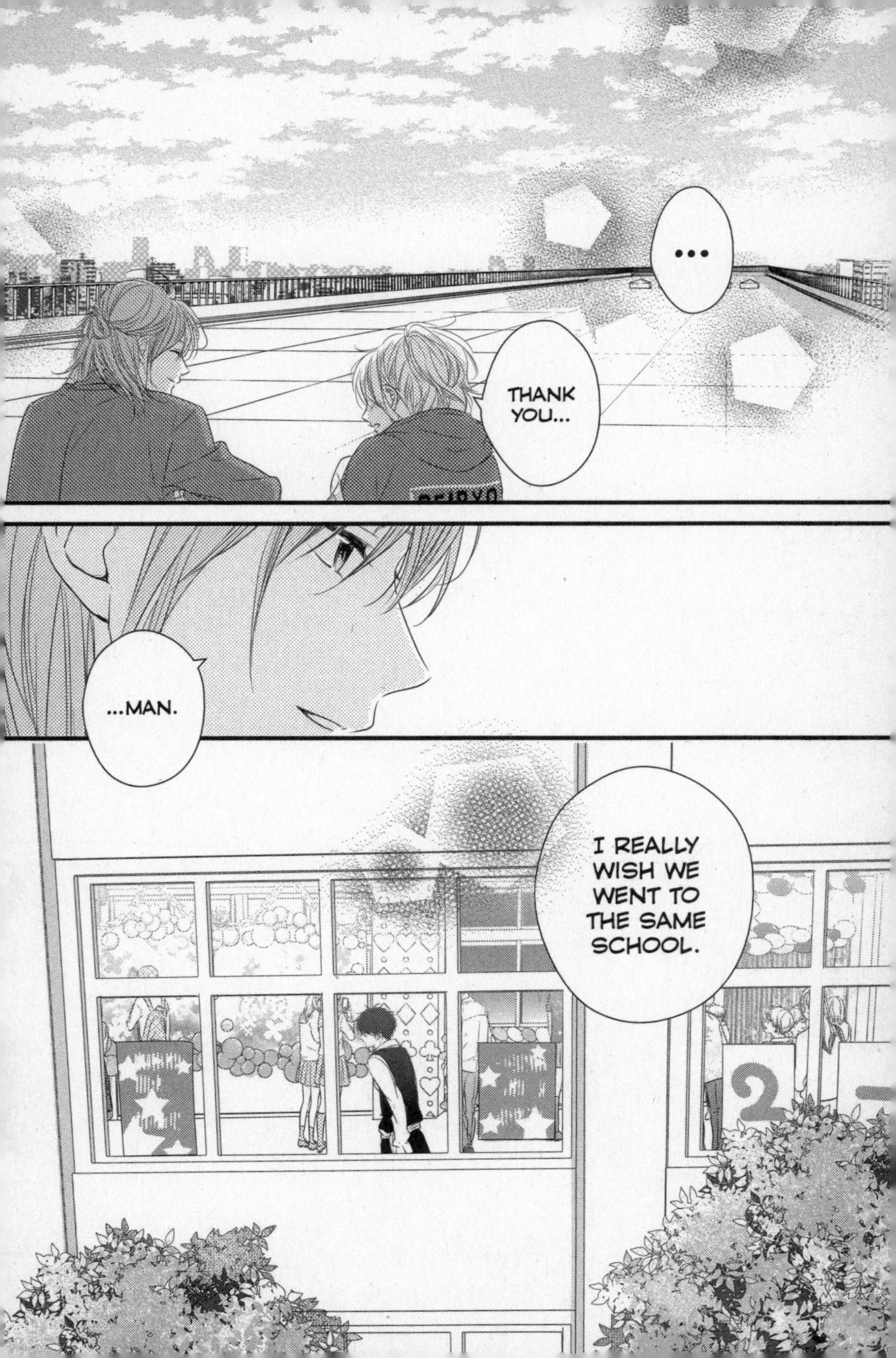
...
THANK YOU...
...MAN.
I REALLY WISH WE WENT TO THE SAME SCHOOL.

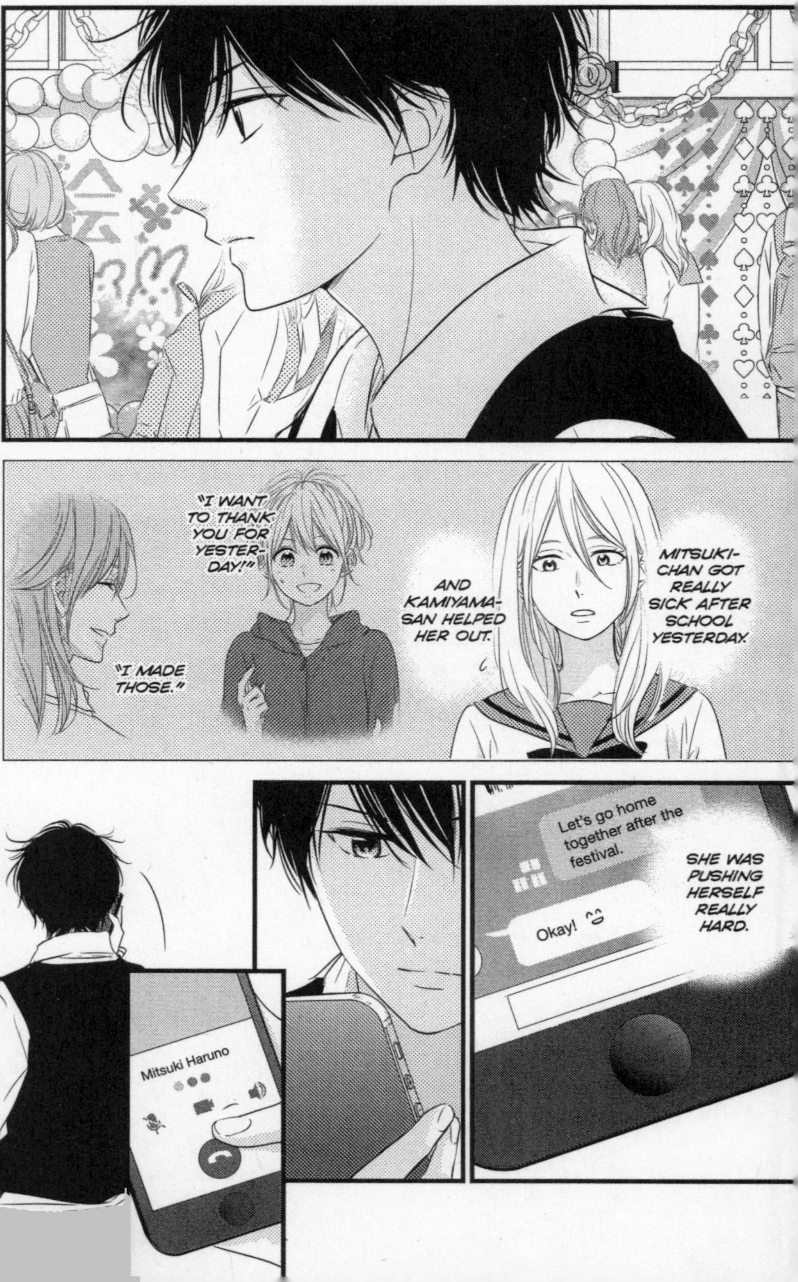
MITSUKI-CHAN GOT REALLY SICK AFTER SCHOOL YESTERDAY.
AND KAMIYAMA-SAN HELPED HER OUT.
"I WANT TO THANK YOU FOR YESTER-DAY!"
"I MADE THOSE."
Let's go home together after the festival.
Okay!
SHE WAS PUSHING HERSELF REALLY HARD.
Mitsuki Haruno

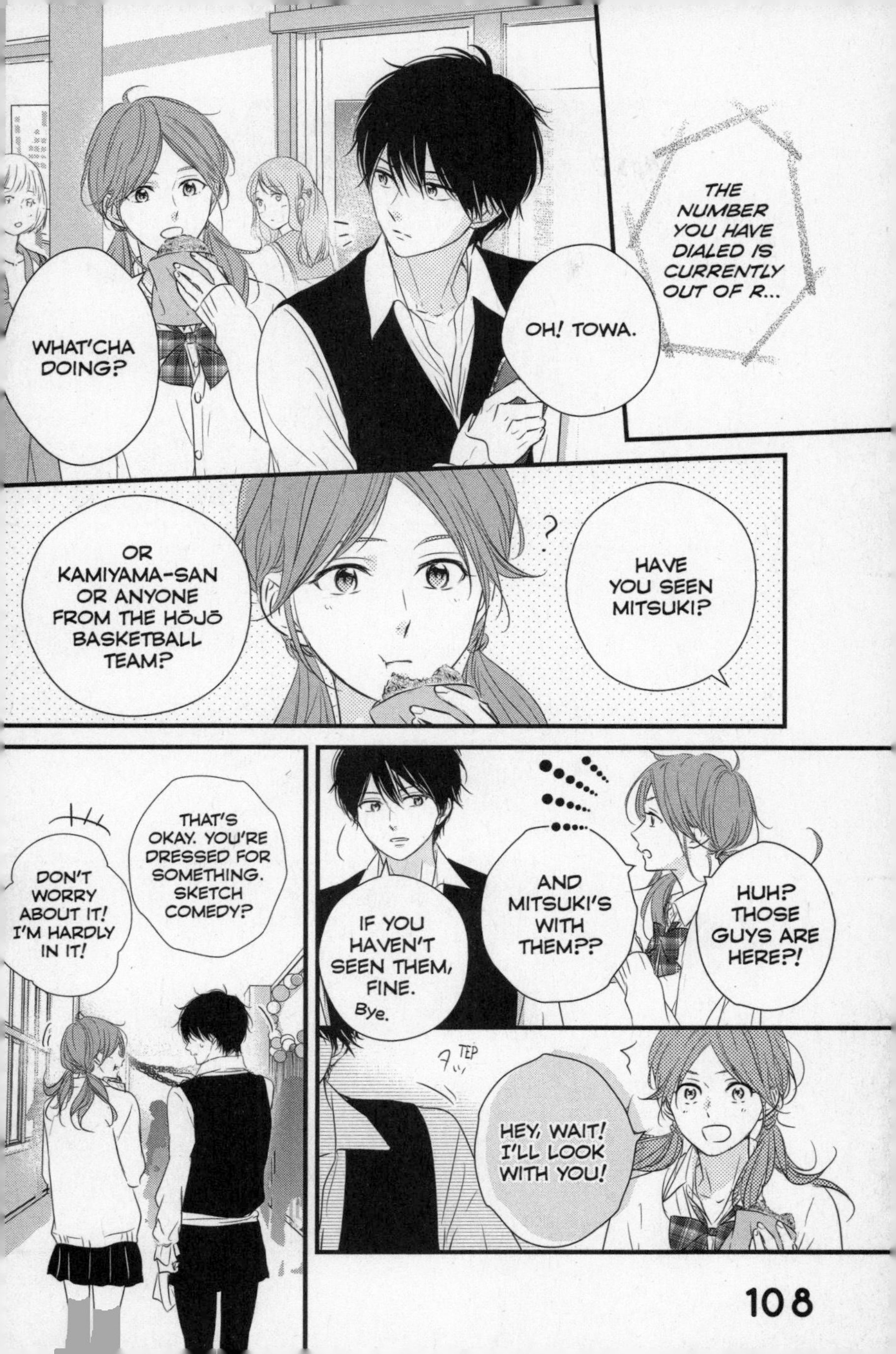
THE NUMBER YOU HAVE DIALED IS CURRENTLY OUT OF R...
OH! TOWA.
WHAT'CHA DOING?
HAVE YOU SEEN MITSUKI?
OR KAMIYAMA-SAN OR ANYONE FROM THE HŌJŌ BASKETBALL TEAM?
HUH? THOSE GUYS ARE HERE?!
AND MITSUKI'S WITH THEM??
IF YOU HAVEN'T SEEN THEM, FINE.
Bye.
TEP
HEY, WAIT! I'LL LOOK WITH YOU!
THAT'S OKAY. YOU'RE DRESSED FOR SOMETHING. SKETCH COMEDY?
DON'T WORRY ABOUT IT! I'M HARDLY IN IT!

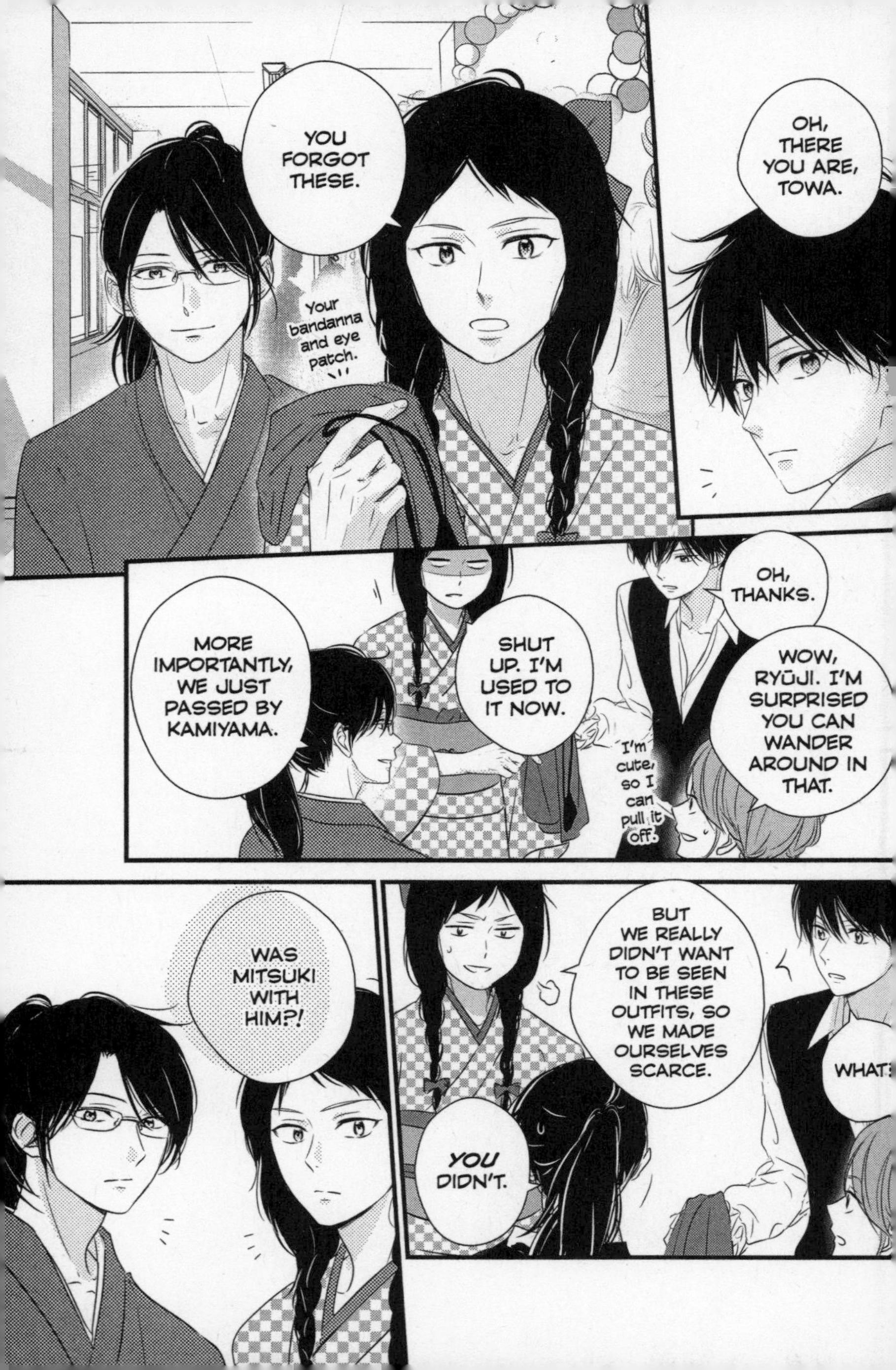

OH, THERE YOU ARE, TOWA.
YOU FORGOT THESE.
Your bandanna and eye patch.
OH, THANKS.
WOW, RYŪJI. I'M SURPRISED YOU CAN WANDER AROUND IN THAT.
I'm cute, so I can pull it off.
SHUT UP. I'M USED TO IT NOW.
MORE IMPORTANTLY, WE JUST PASSED BY KAMIYAMA.
WHAT
BUT WE REALLY DIDN'T WANT TO BE SEEN IN THESE OUTFITS, SO WE MADE OURSELVES SCARCE.
YOU DIDN'T.
WAS MITSUKI WITH HIM?!

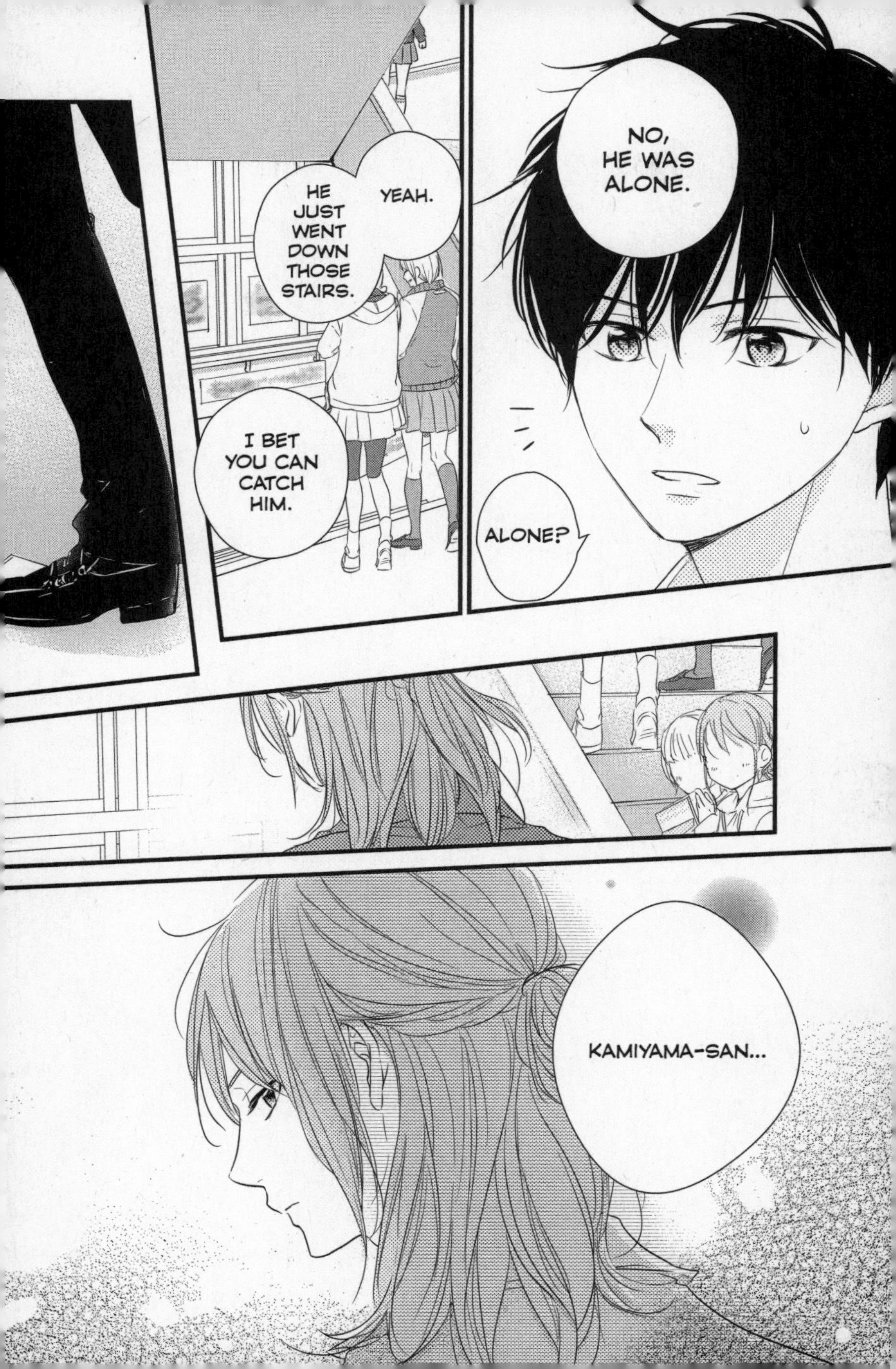

NO, HE WAS ALONE.
ALONE?
YEAH.
HE JUST WENT DOWN THOSE STAIRS.
I BET YOU CAN CATCH HIM.
KAMIYAMA-SAN...

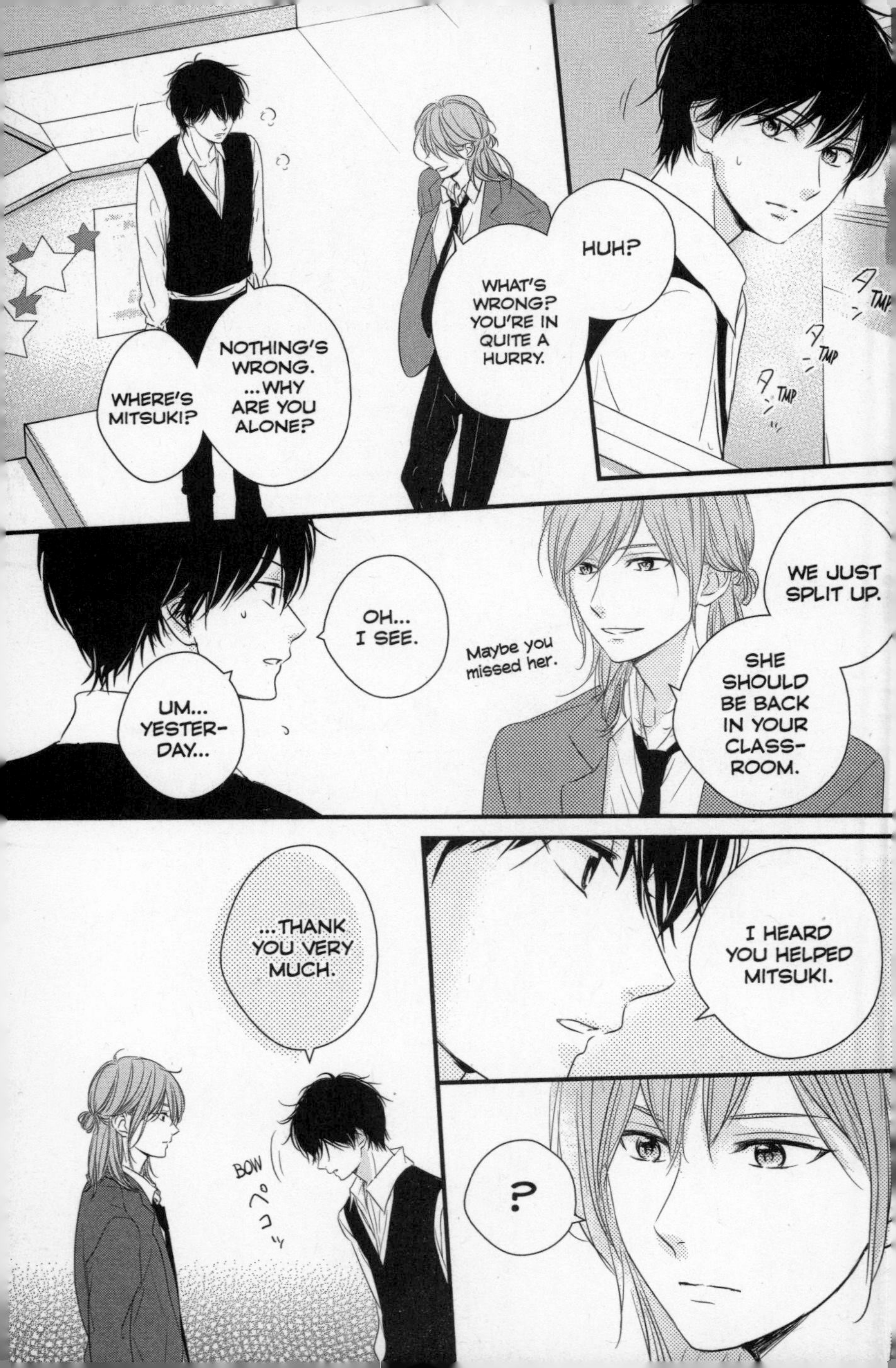
TMP
TMP
TMP
HUH?
WHAT'S WRONG? YOU'RE IN QUITE A HURRY.
NOTHING'S WRONG. ...WHY ARE YOU ALONE?
WHERE'S MITSUKI?
WE JUST SPLIT UP.
SHE SHOULD BE BACK IN YOUR CLASSROOM.
Maybe you missed her.
OH... I SEE.
UM... YESTERDAY...
I HEARD YOU HELPED MITSUKI.
?
...THANK YOU VERY MUCH.
BOW
ペコッ

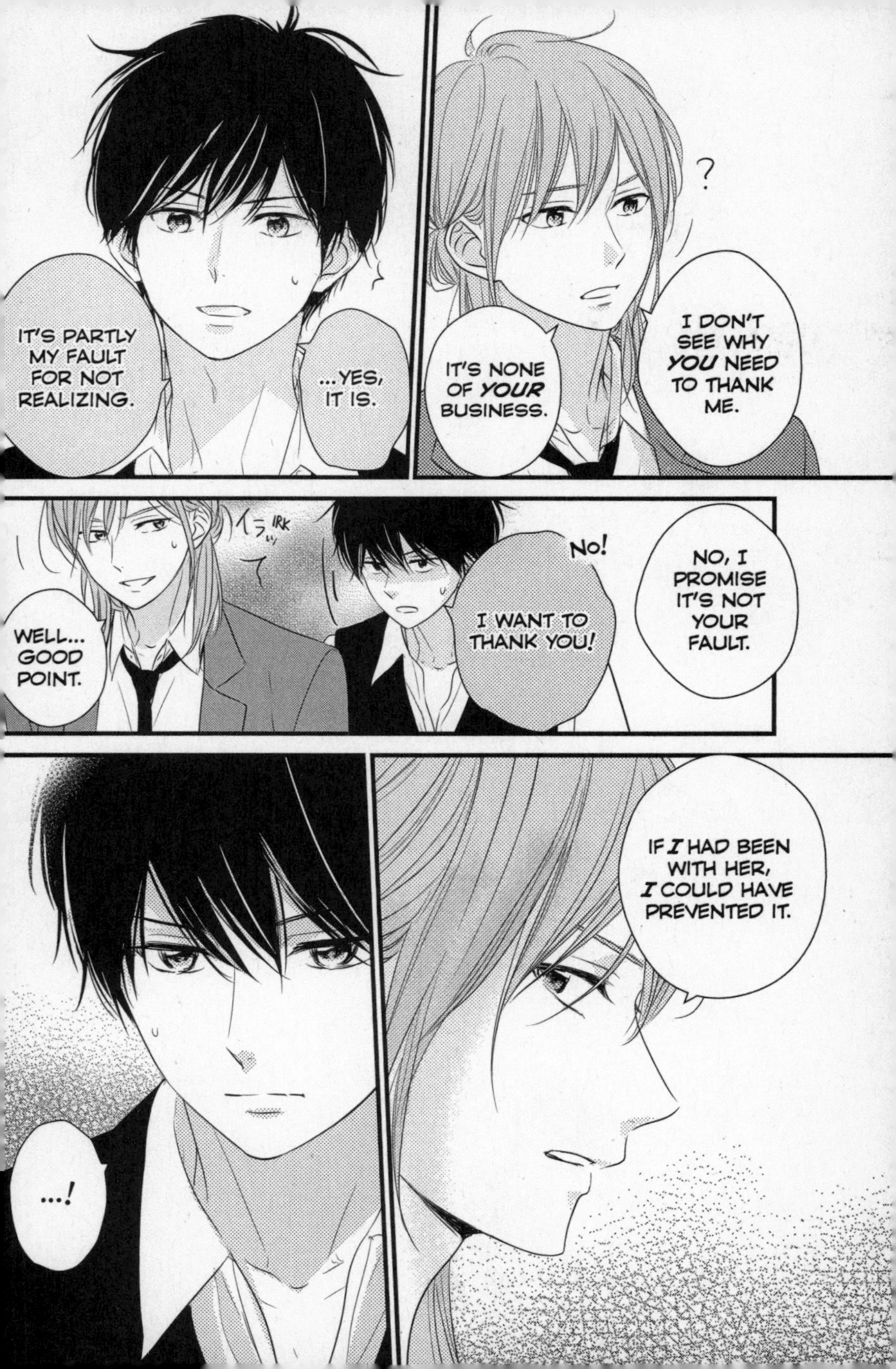
?
I DON'T SEE WHY *YOU* NEED TO THANK ME.
IT'S NONE OF *YOUR* BUSINESS.
IT'S PARTLY MY FAULT FOR NOT REALIZING.
...YES, IT IS.
NO, I PROMISE IT'S NOT YOUR FAULT.
No!
I WANT TO THANK YOU!
IRK
WELL... GOOD POINT.
IF *I* HAD BEEN WITH HER, *I* COULD HAVE PREVENTED IT.
...!

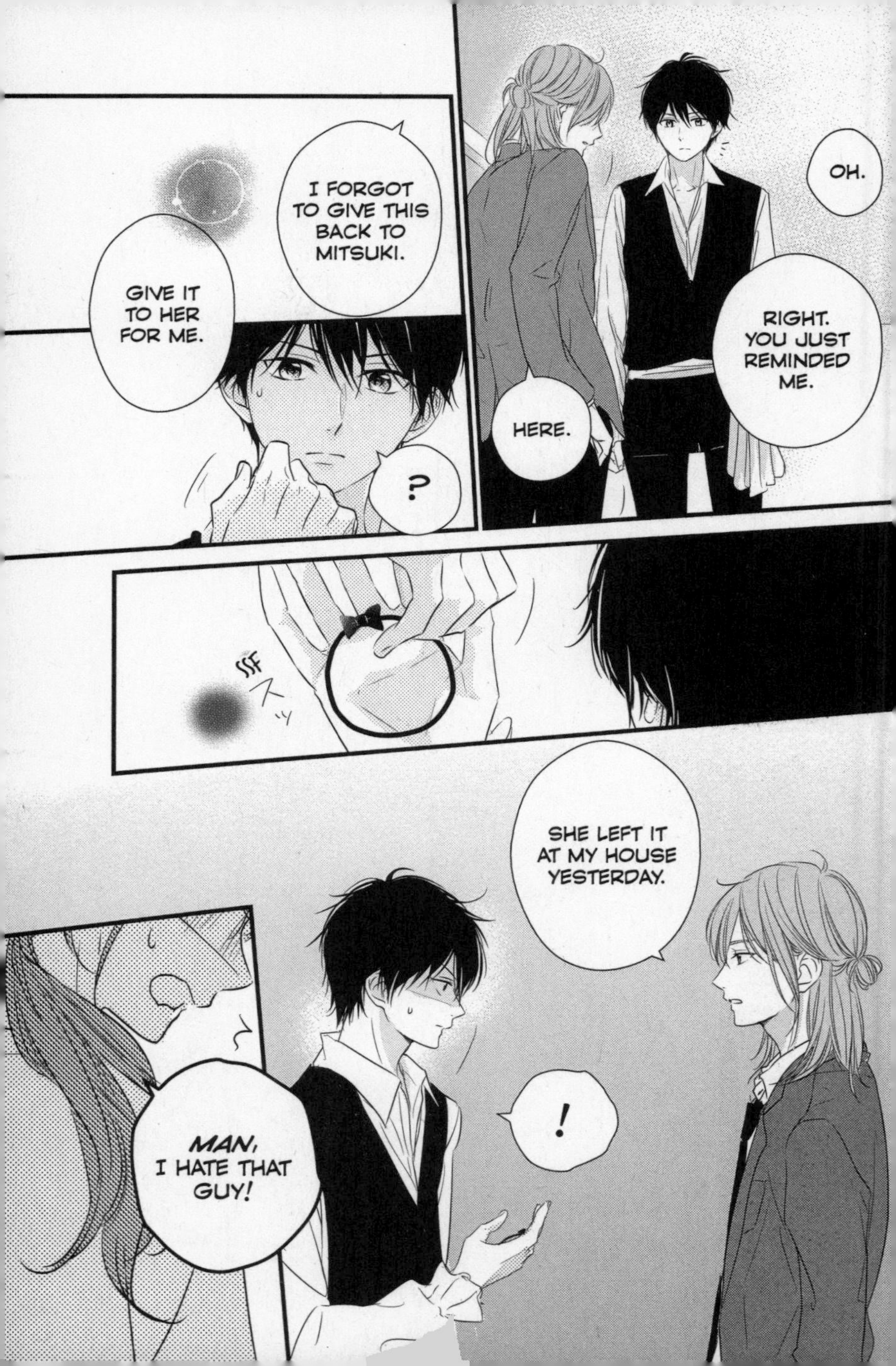
OH.
RIGHT. YOU JUST REMINDED ME.
HERE.
I FORGOT TO GIVE THIS BACK TO MITSUKI.
GIVE IT TO HER FOR ME.
?
SSF
スッ
SHE LEFT IT AT MY HOUSE YESTERDAY.
!
MAN, I HATE THAT GUY!

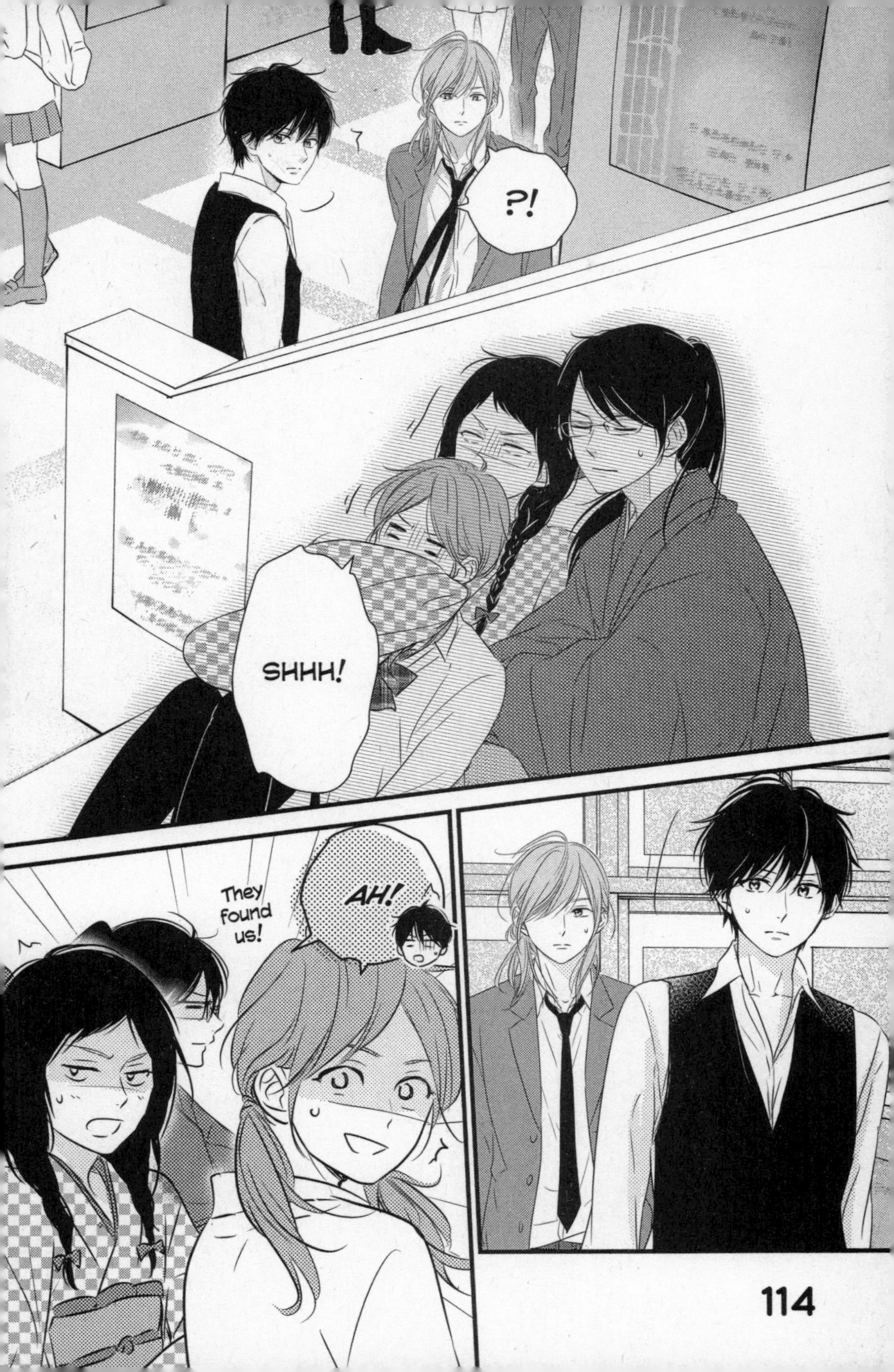
?!
SHHH!
AH!
They found us!

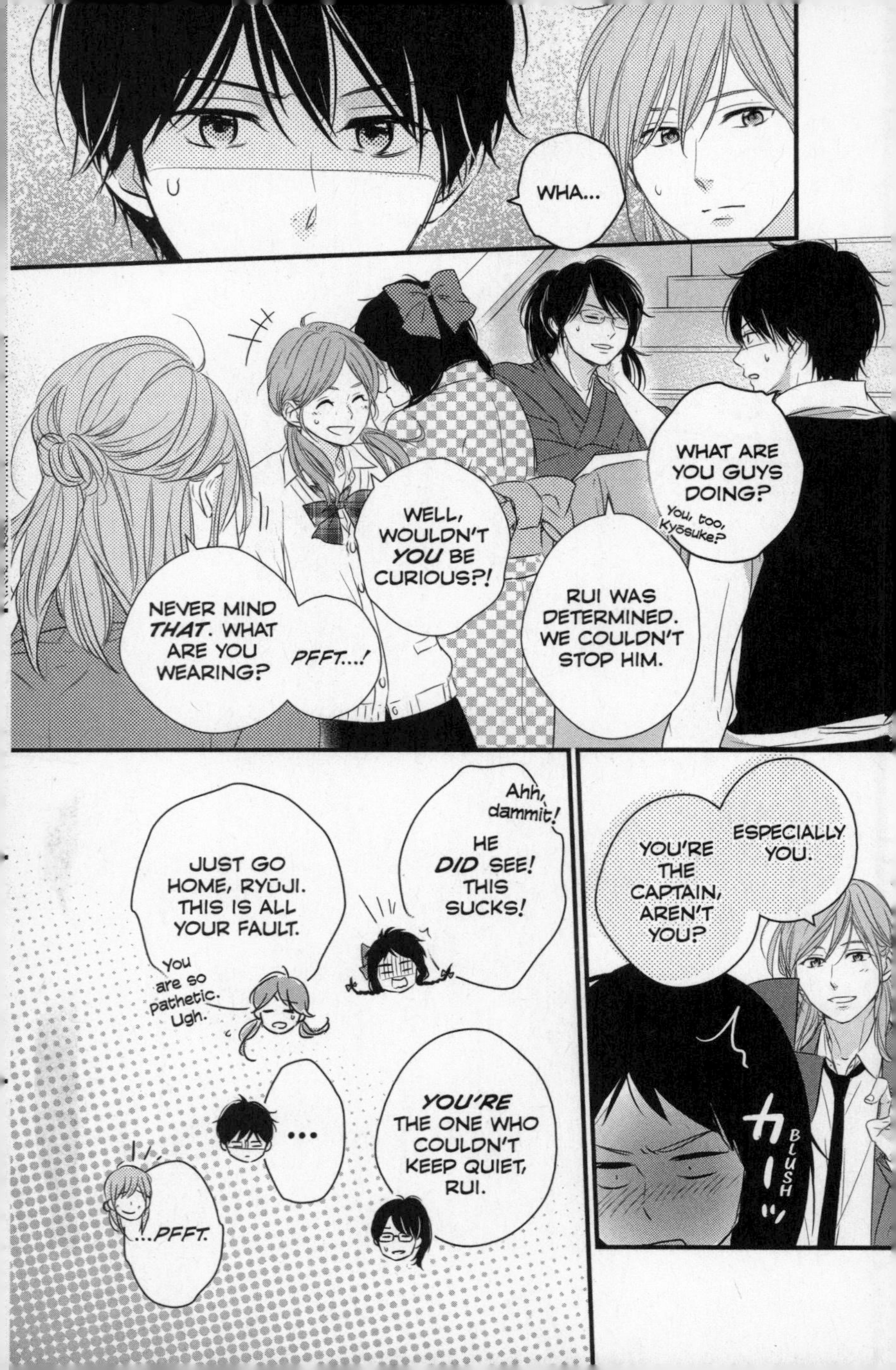
WHA...
WHAT ARE YOU GUYS DOING?
You, too, Kyōsuke?
RUI WAS DETERMINED. WE COULDN'T STOP HIM.
WELL, WOULDN'T YOU BE CURIOUS?!
NEVER MIND THAT. WHAT ARE YOU WEARING?
PFFT...!
ESPECIALLY YOU.
YOU'RE THE CAPTAIN, AREN'T YOU?
BLUSH
Ahh, dammit!
HE DID SEE! THIS SUCKS!
JUST GO HOME, RYŪJI. THIS IS ALL YOUR FAULT.
You are so pathetic. Ugh.
YOU'RE THE ONE WHO COULDN'T KEEP QUIET, RUI.
...
...PFFT.

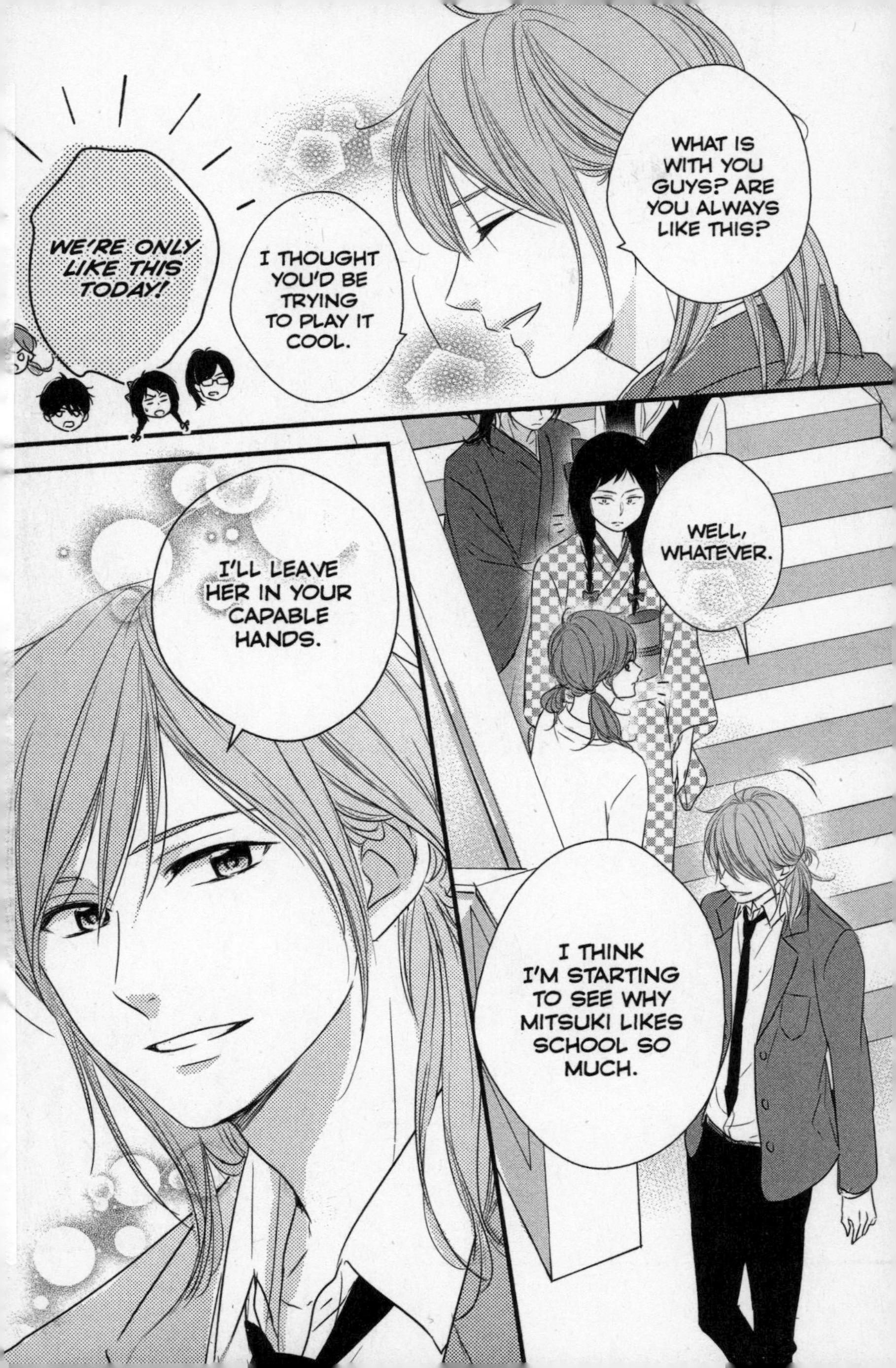
WHAT IS WITH YOU GUYS? ARE YOU ALWAYS LIKE THIS?
I THOUGHT YOU'D BE TRYING TO PLAY IT COOL.
WE'RE ONLY LIKE THIS TODAY!
WELL, WHATEVER.
I THINK I'M STARTING TO SEE WHY MITSUKI LIKES SCHOOL SO MUCH.
I'LL LEAVE HER IN YOUR CAPABLE HANDS.

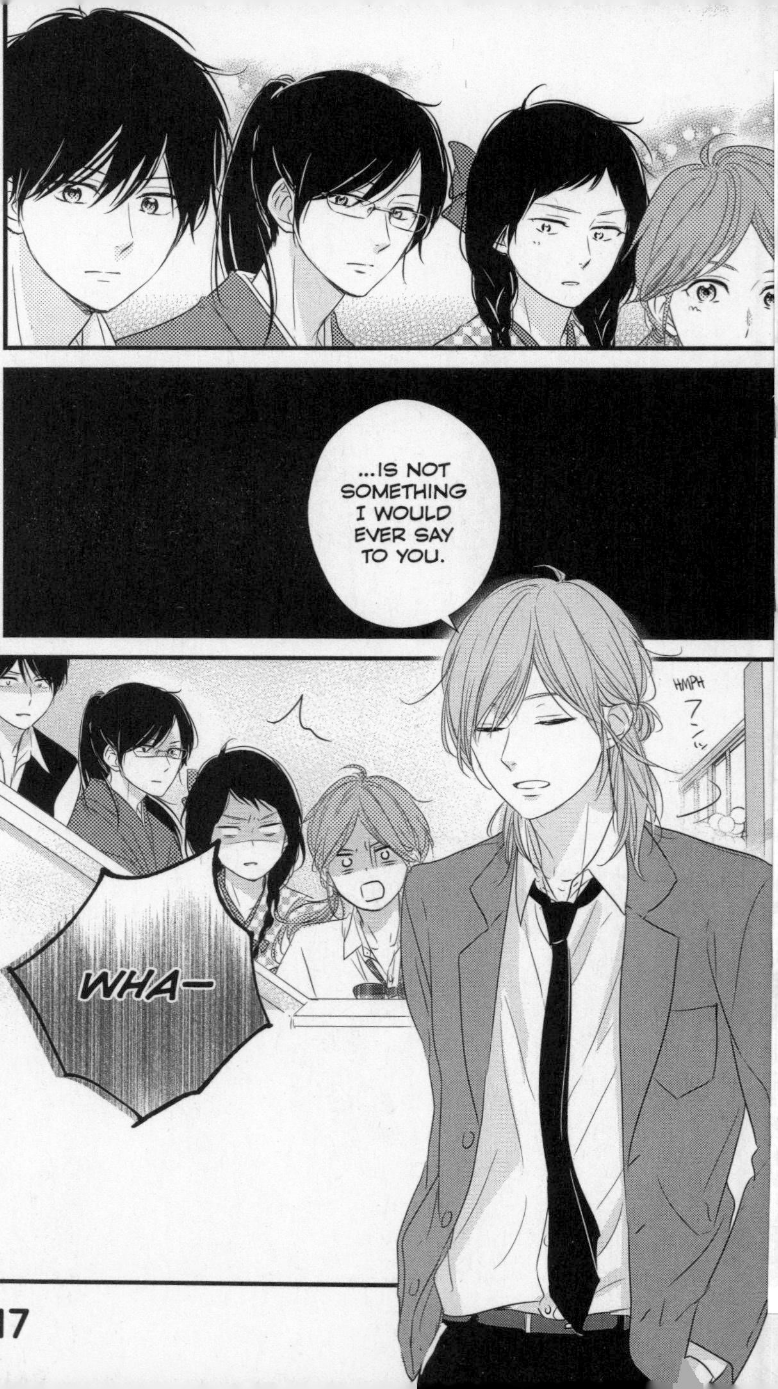
...IS NOT SOMETHING I WOULD EVER SAY TO YOU.
HMPH
WHA-

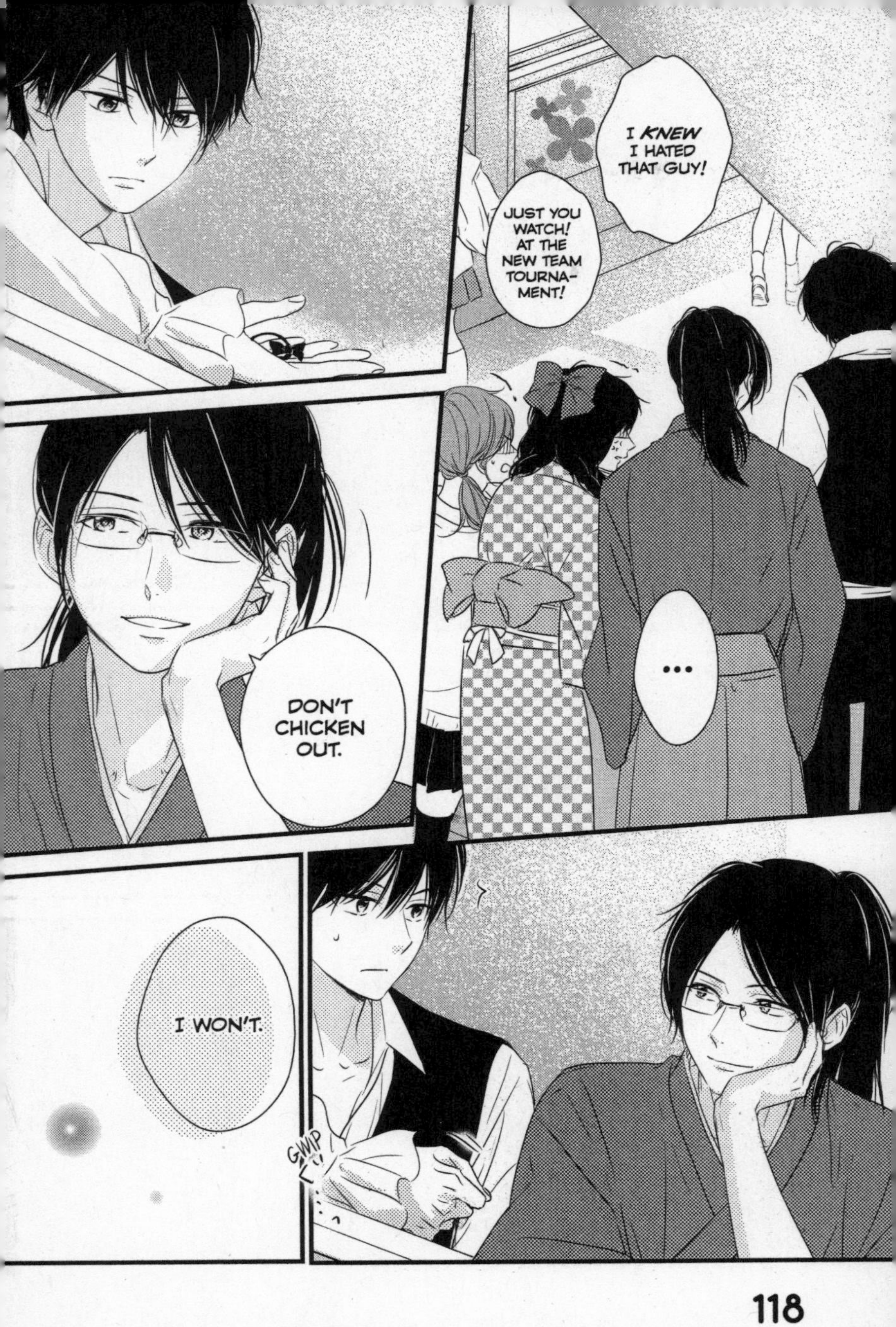
I KNEW I HATED THAT GUY!
JUST YOU WATCH! AT THE NEW TEAM TOURNAMENT!
...
DON'T CHICKEN OUT.
GWIP
I WON'T.

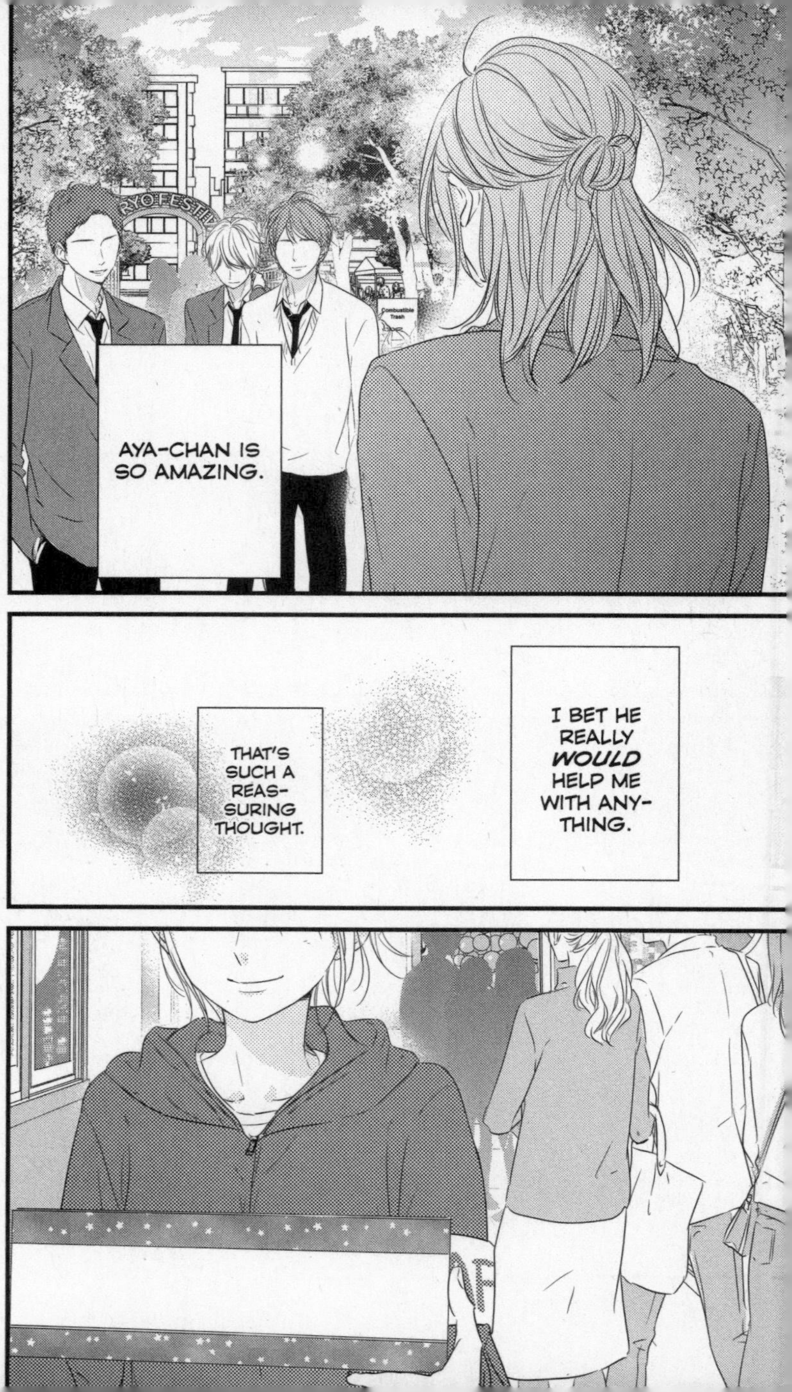
Combustible Trash
AYA-CHAN IS SO AMAZING.
I BET HE REALLY *WOULD* HELP ME WITH ANY-THING.
THAT'S SUCH A REAS-SURING THOUGHT.

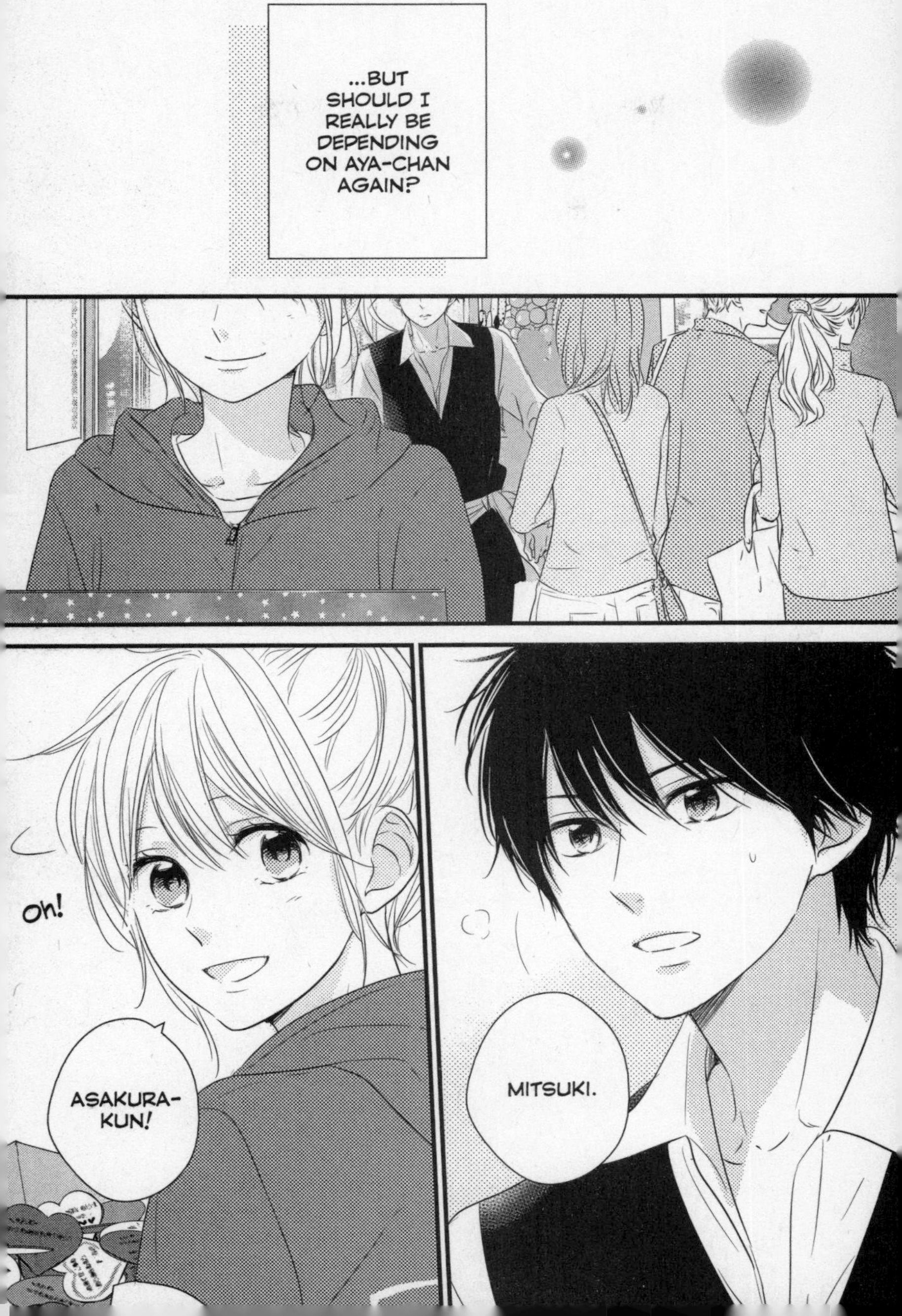
...BUT SHOULD I REALLY BE DEPENDING ON AYA-CHAN AGAIN?
MITSUKI.
Oh!
ASAKURA-KUN!

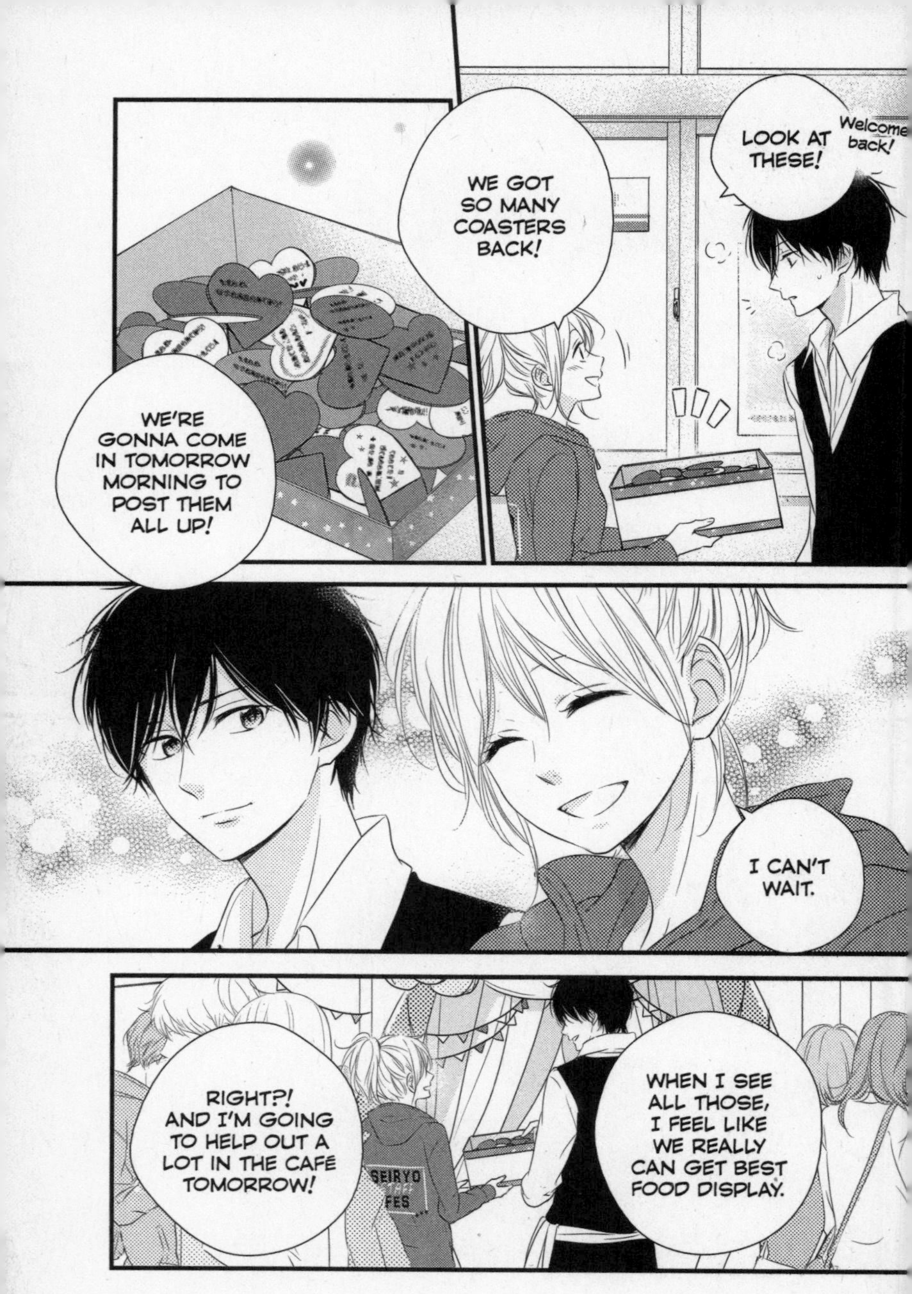
Welcome back!
LOOK AT THESE!
WE GOT SO MANY COASTERS BACK!
WE'RE GONNA COME IN TOMORROW MORNING TO POST THEM ALL UP!
I CAN'T WAIT.
WHEN I SEE ALL THOSE, I FEEL LIKE WE REALLY CAN GET BEST FOOD DISPLAY.
RIGHT?! AND I'M GOING TO HELP OUT A LOT IN THE CAFÉ TOMORROW!
SEIRYO FES

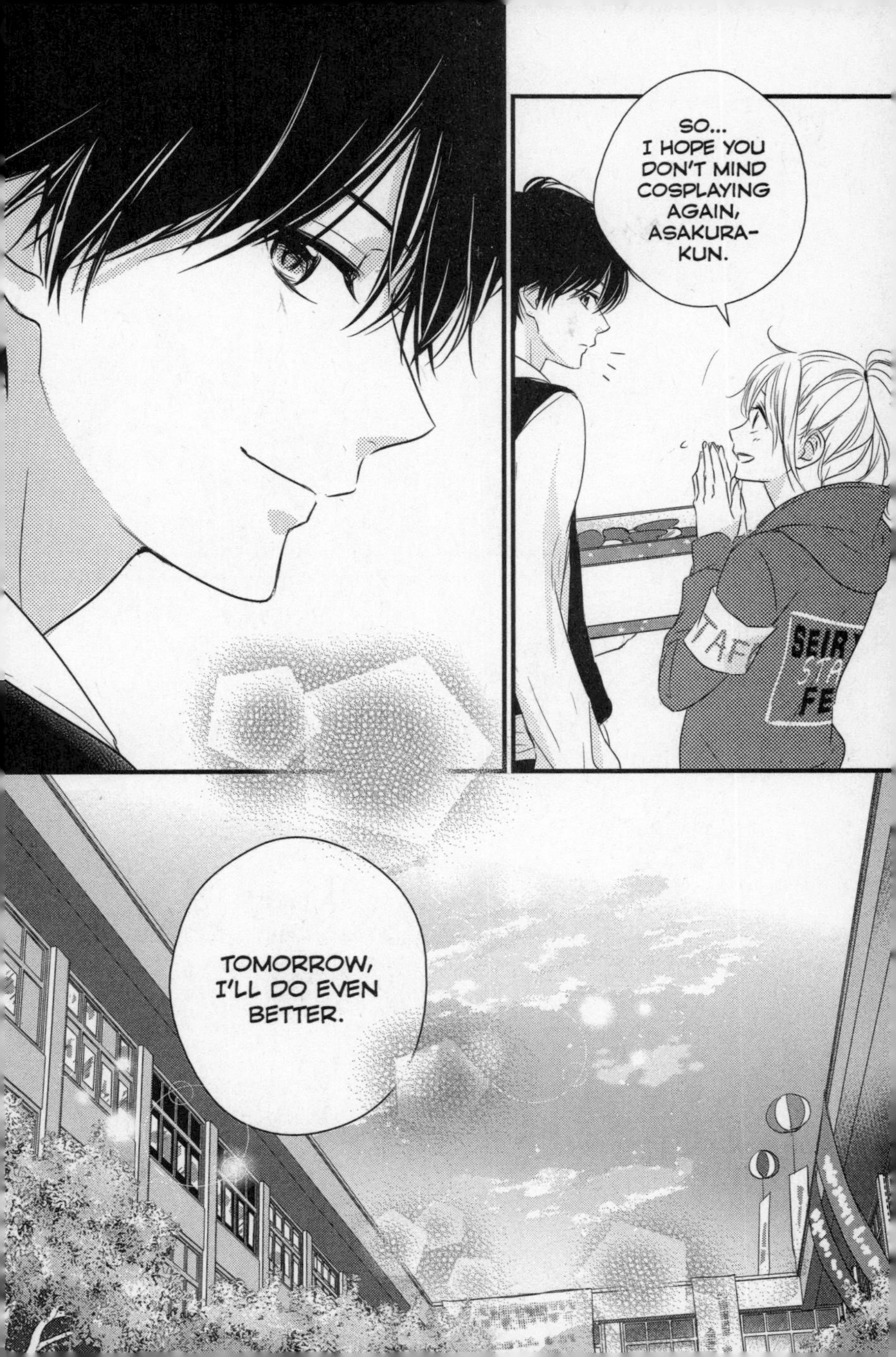
SO... I HOPE YOU DON'T MIND COSPLAYING AGAIN, ASAKURA-KUN.
TOMORROW, I'LL DO EVEN BETTER.

period 32: "The School Festival (Part Three)"

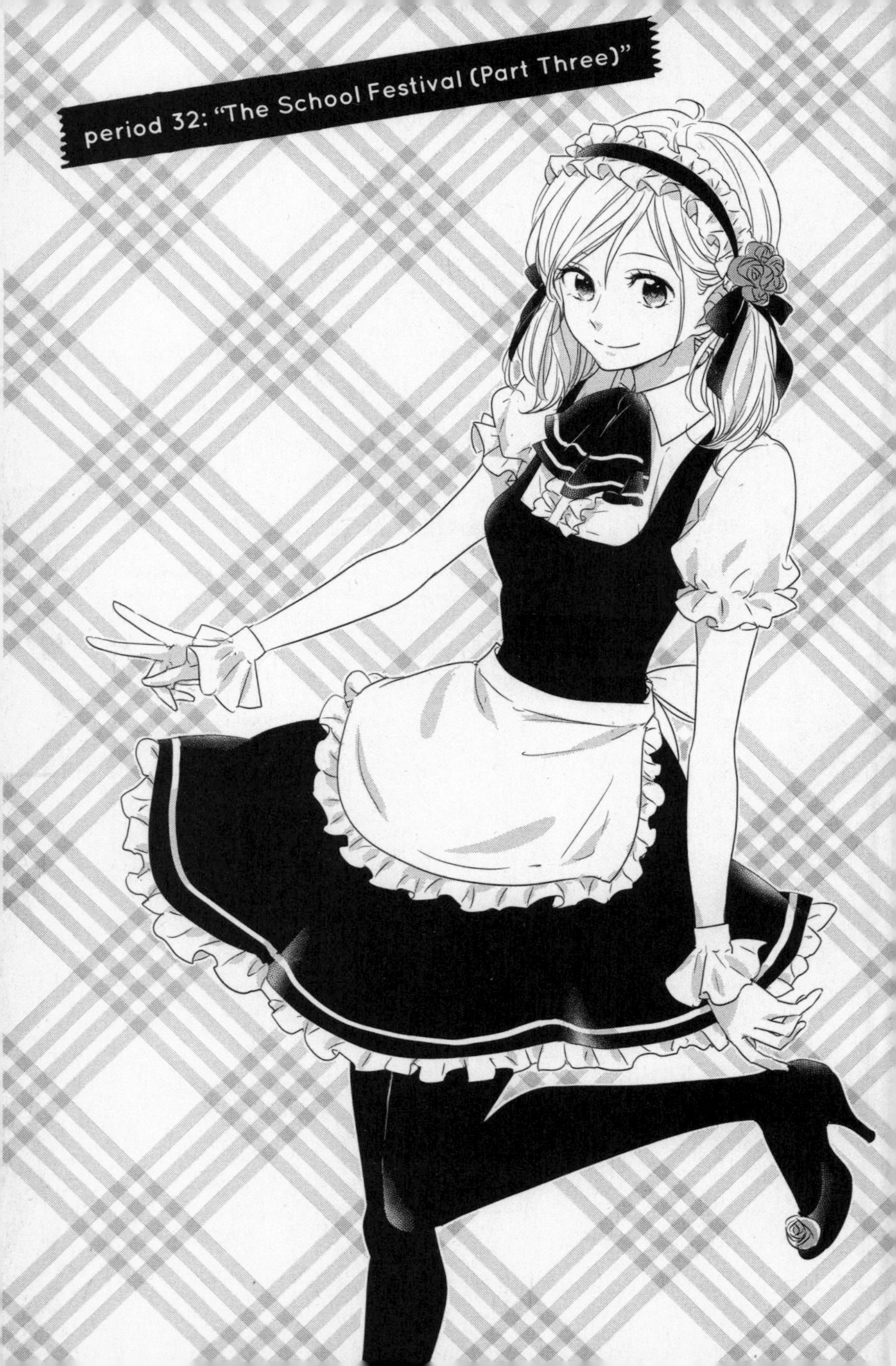

THE SECOND DAY OF THE FESTIVAL.
Good morning.
Good morning.
1-4
WELL, THAT'S ALL MY COASTERS.
ALL DONE OVER HERE, TOO!
So what are we gonna do about a wrap party?
WE GOT A LOT OF GOOD REVIEWS!
1-4 HAWAIIAN CAFE
MENU
OF COURSE, MOST OF THE COMMENTS WE GOT WERE, "ASAKURA-KUN IS SO HOT!"
Hang in there, Asakura-kun!
AH HA HA.
The pancakes are delicious
THAT MEANS THEY LIKED THE COSPLAY.
Woohoo! I got a picture with Towa-kun♥
OKAY, I'LL GO GET CHANGED.

Well, then! I'll work hard on Volume 8, too!! Let's meet again!

SPECIAL THANKS

To my editor; the Designer-sama; everyone on the Dessert editorial team; the photographer who took my research pictures Kin-sama; everyone who was involved in the creation of this work; Words Cafe-sama

My assistants Masuda-san, Aki-chan, my family,

And to all my readers. Thank you with all my heart.

Anashin
4/2017

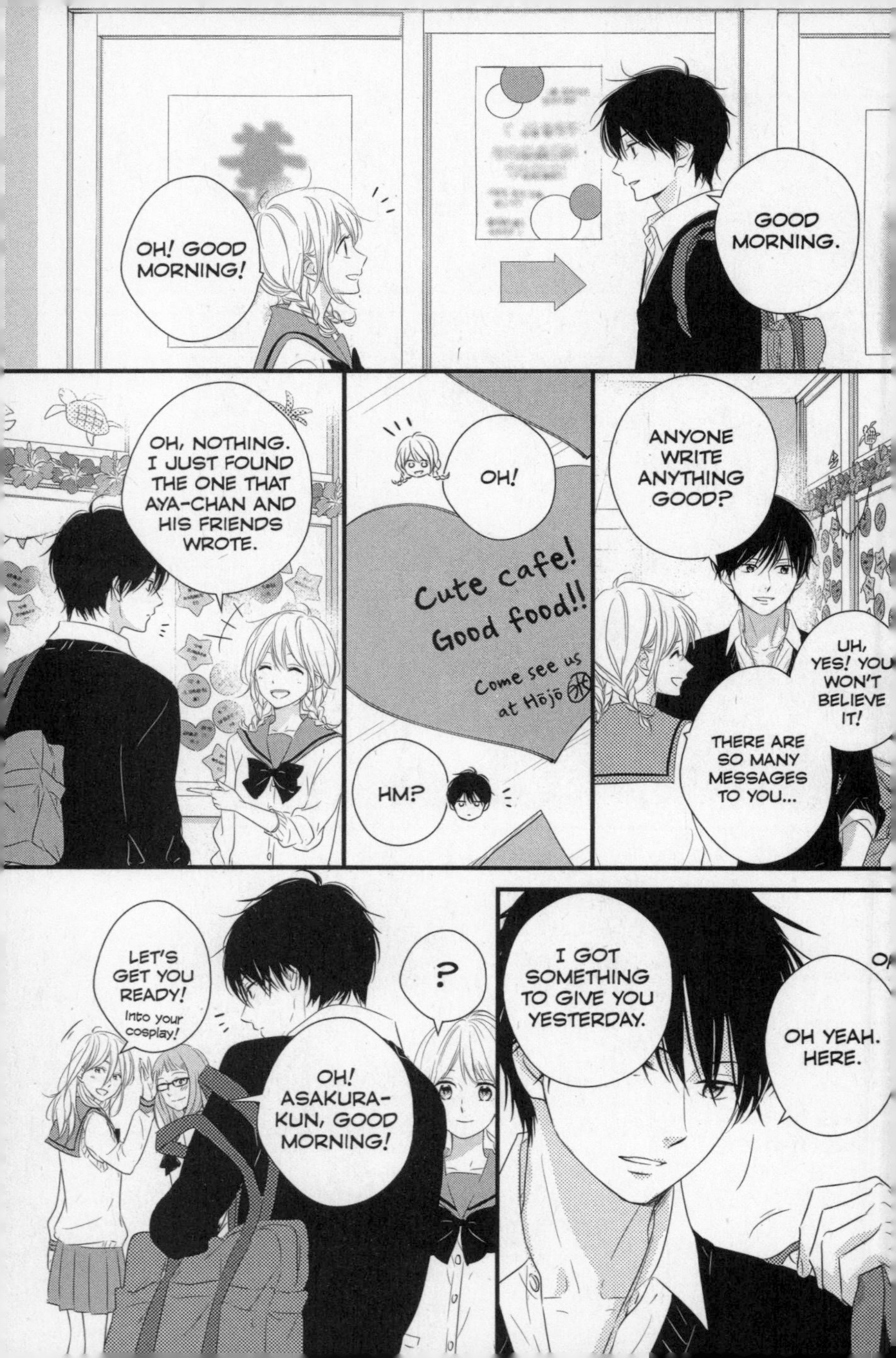
GOOD MORNING.
OH! GOOD MORNING!
ANYONE WRITE ANYTHING GOOD?
UH, YES! YOU WON'T BELIEVE IT!
THERE ARE SO MANY MESSAGES TO YOU...
OH!
Cute cafe! Good food!!
Come see us at Hōjō
HM?
OH, NOTHING. I JUST FOUND THE ONE THAT AYA-CHAN AND HIS FRIENDS WROTE.
OH YEAH. HERE.
I GOT SOMETHING TO GIVE YOU YESTERDAY.
?
LET'S GET YOU READY!
Into your cosplay!
OH! ASAKURA-KUN, GOOD MORNING!

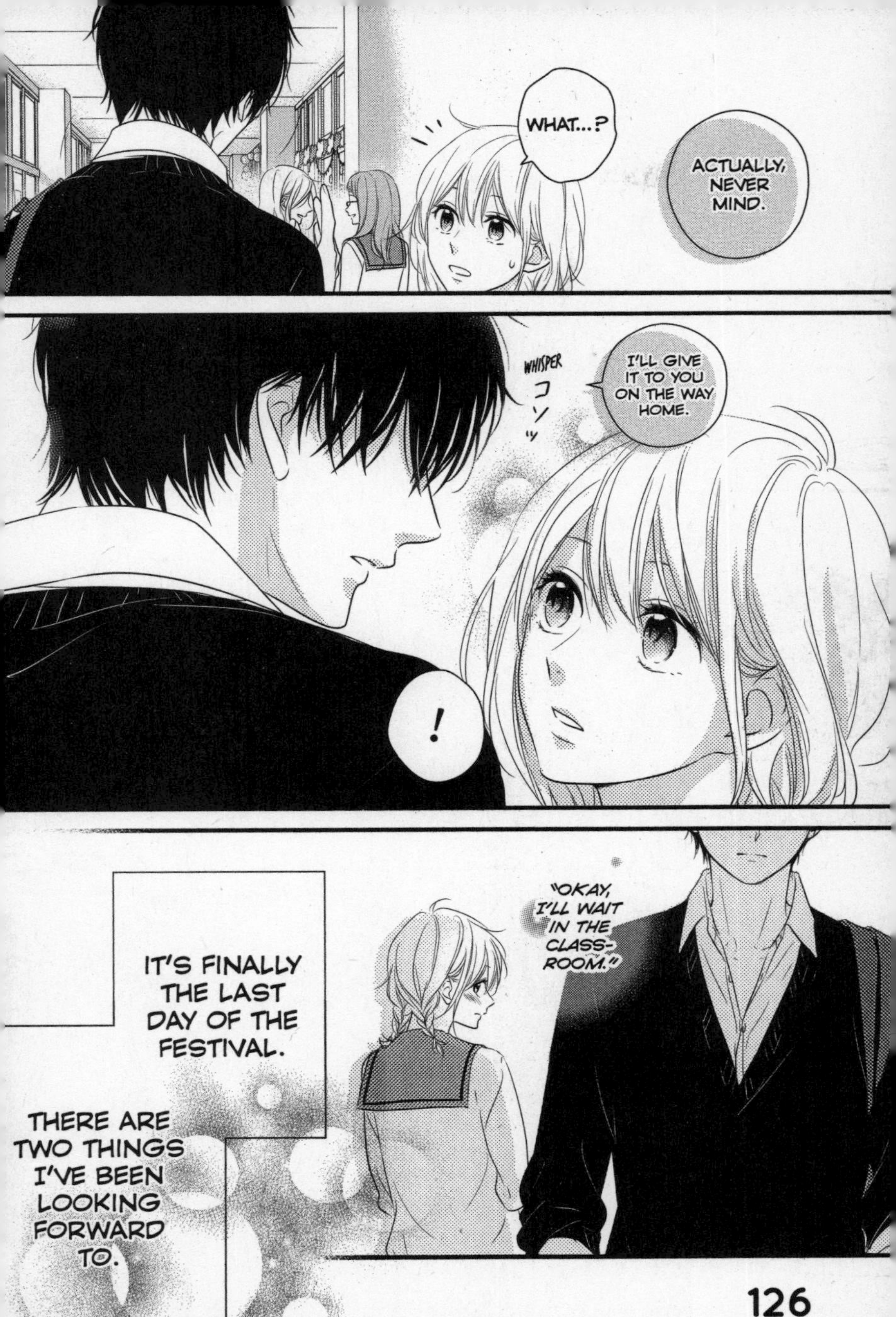
ACTUALLY, NEVER MIND.
WHAT...?
I'LL GIVE IT TO YOU ON THE WAY HOME.
WHISPER
コソッ
!
"OKAY, I'LL WAIT IN THE CLASS-ROOM."
IT'S FINALLY THE LAST DAY OF THE FESTIVAL.
THERE ARE TWO THINGS I'VE BEEN LOOKING FORWARD TO.

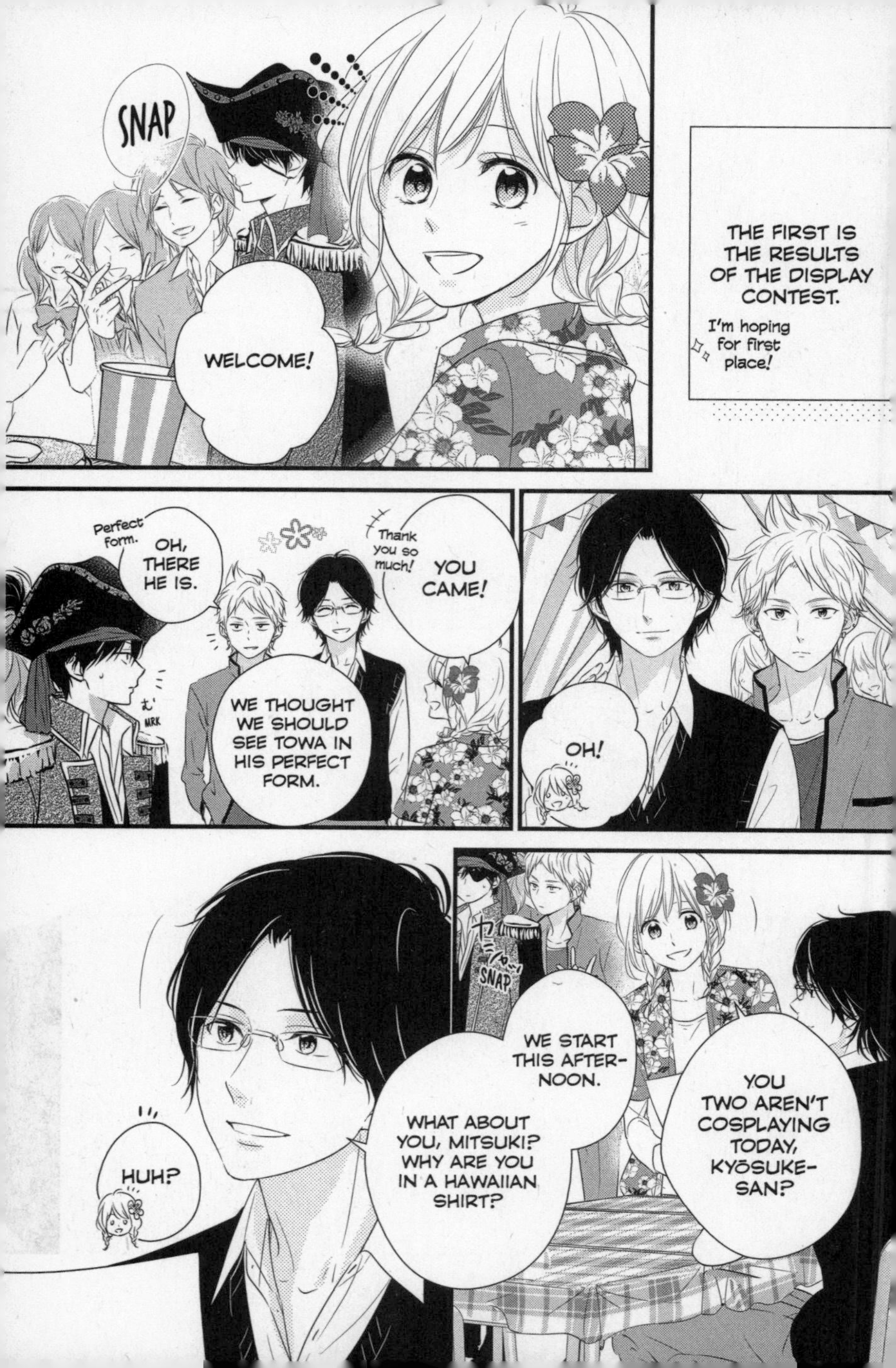
THE FIRST IS THE RESULTS OF THE DISPLAY CONTEST.
I'm hoping for first place!
SNAP
WELCOME!
OH!
YOU CAME!
Thank you so much!
WE THOUGHT WE SHOULD SEE TOWA IN HIS PERFECT FORM.
OH, THERE HE IS.
Perfect form.
MRK
YOU TWO AREN'T COSPLAYING TODAY, KYŌSUKE-SAN?
SNAP
WE START THIS AFTER-NOON.
WHAT ABOUT YOU, MITSUKI? WHY ARE YOU IN A HAWAIIAN SHIRT?
HUH?

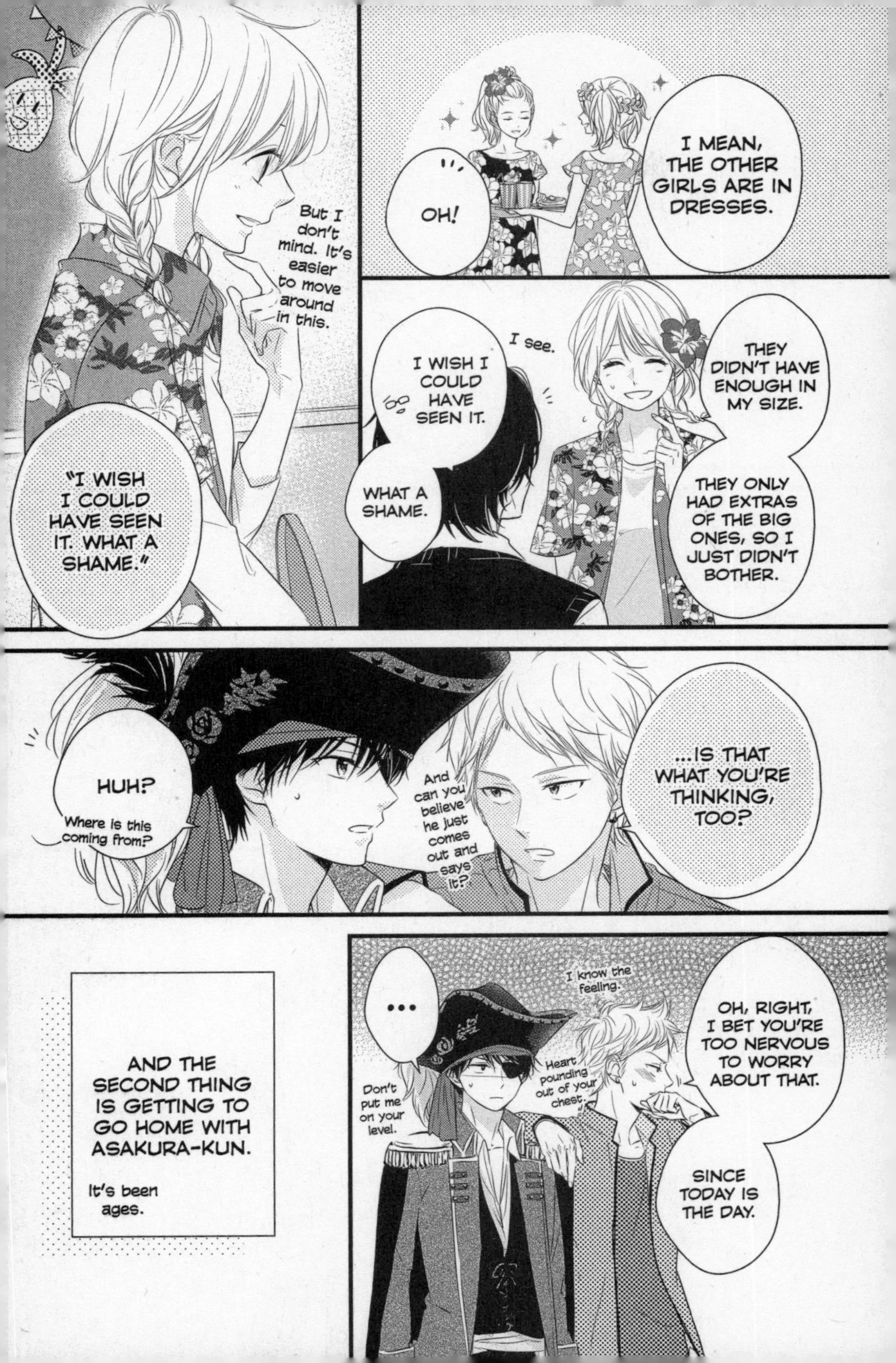
I MEAN, THE OTHER GIRLS ARE IN DRESSES.
OH!
THEY DIDN'T HAVE ENOUGH IN MY SIZE.
THEY ONLY HAD EXTRAS OF THE BIG ONES, SO I JUST DIDN'T BOTHER.
I see.
I WISH I COULD HAVE SEEN IT.
WHAT A SHAME.
But I don't mind. It's easier to move around in this.
"I WISH I COULD HAVE SEEN IT. WHAT A SHAME."
...IS THAT WHAT YOU'RE THINKING, TOO?
And can you believe he just comes out and says it?
HUH?
Where is this coming from?
OH, RIGHT, I BET YOU'RE TOO NERVOUS TO WORRY ABOUT THAT.
SINCE TODAY IS THE DAY.
I know the feeling.
Heart pounding out of your chest.
...
Don't put me on your level.
AND THE SECOND THING IS GETTING TO GO HOME WITH ASAKURA-KUN.
It's been ages.

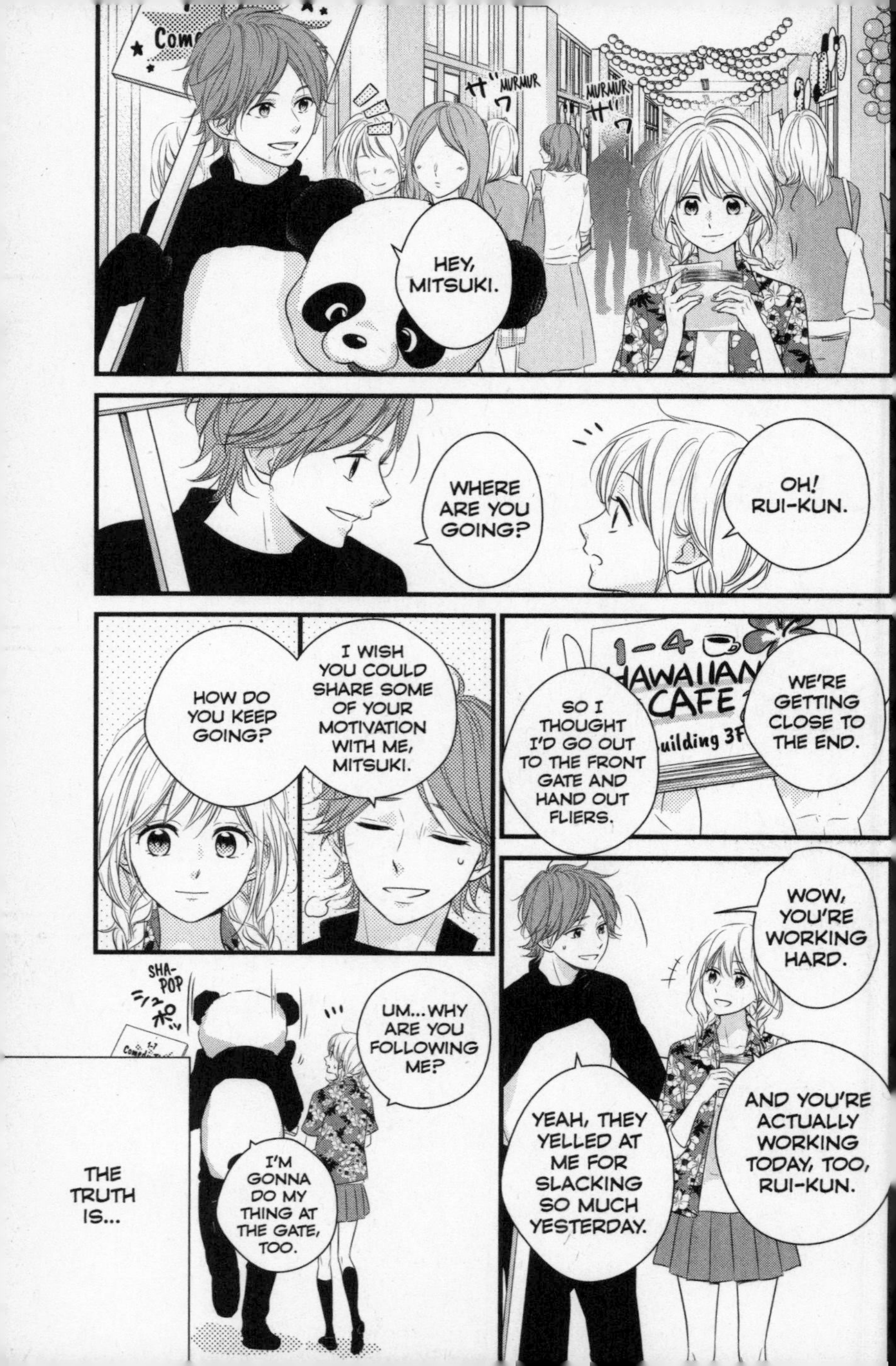
MURMUR
MURMUR
HEY, MITSUKI.
OH! RUI-KUN.
WHERE ARE YOU GOING?
WE'RE GETTING CLOSE TO THE END.
SO I THOUGHT I'D GO OUT TO THE FRONT GATE AND HAND OUT FLIERS.
I WISH YOU COULD SHARE SOME OF YOUR MOTIVATION WITH ME, MITSUKI.
HOW DO YOU KEEP GOING?
WOW, YOU'RE WORKING HARD.
AND YOU'RE ACTUALLY WORKING TODAY, TOO, RUI-KUN.
YEAH, THEY YELLED AT ME FOR SLACKING SO MUCH YESTERDAY.
UM...WHY ARE YOU FOLLOWING ME?
SHA-POP
I'M GONNA DO MY THING AT THE GATE, TOO.
THE TRUTH IS...

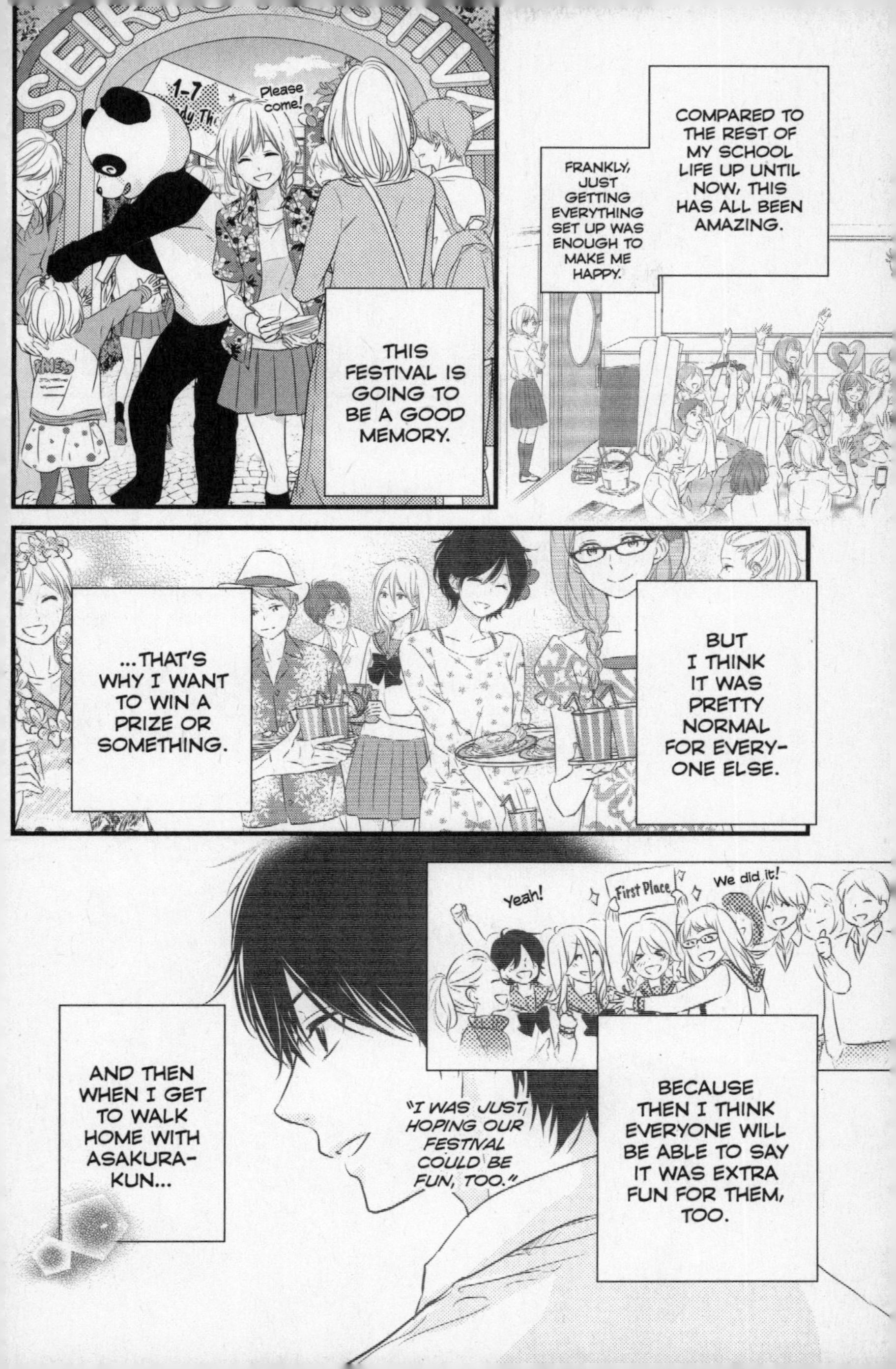
COMPARED TO THE REST OF MY SCHOOL LIFE UP UNTIL NOW, THIS HAS ALL BEEN AMAZING.
FRANKLY, JUST GETTING EVERYTHING SET UP WAS ENOUGH TO MAKE ME HAPPY.
Please come!
1-7
THIS FESTIVAL IS GOING TO BE A GOOD MEMORY.
BUT I THINK IT WAS PRETTY NORMAL FOR EVERY-ONE ELSE.
...THAT'S WHY I WANT TO WIN A PRIZE OR SOMETHING.
We did it!
First Place
Yeah!
BECAUSE THEN I THINK EVERYONE WILL BE ABLE TO SAY IT WAS EXTRA FUN FOR THEM, TOO.
"I WAS JUST HOPING OUR FESTIVAL COULD BE FUN, TOO."
AND THEN WHEN I GET TO WALK HOME WITH ASAKURA-KUN...

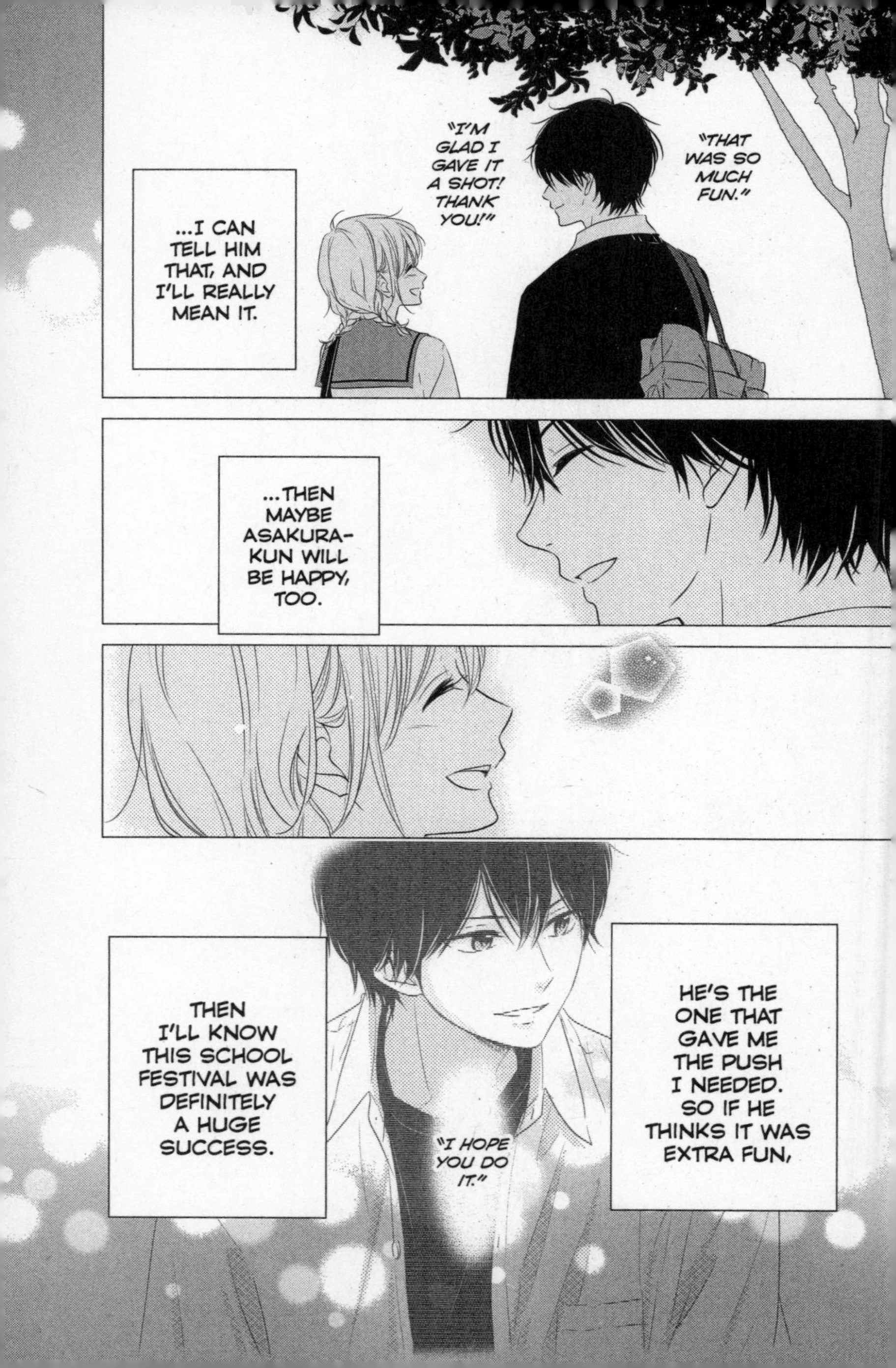
"THAT WAS SO MUCH FUN."
"I'M GLAD I GAVE IT A SHOT! THANK YOU!"
...I CAN TELL HIM THAT, AND I'LL REALLY MEAN IT.
...THEN MAYBE ASAKURA-KUN WILL BE HAPPY, TOO.
HE'S THE ONE THAT GAVE ME THE PUSH I NEEDED. SO IF HE THINKS IT WAS EXTRA FUN,
"I HOPE YOU DO IT."
THEN I'LL KNOW THIS SCHOOL FESTIVAL WAS DEFINITELY A HUGE SUCCESS.

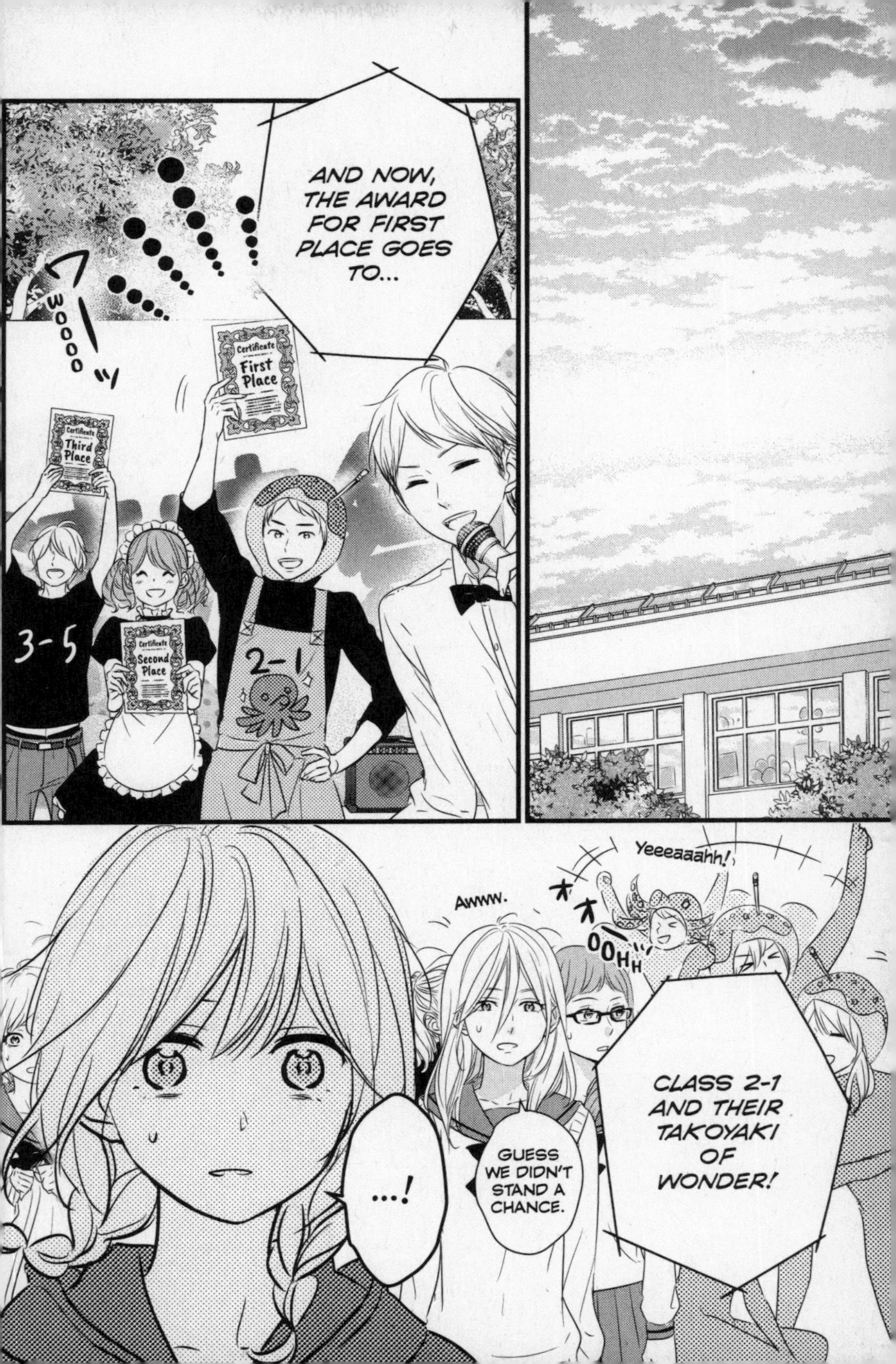
AND NOW, THE AWARD FOR FIRST PLACE GOES TO...
WOOOOO
Certificate First Place
Certificate Third Place
3-5
Certificate Second Place
2-1
CLASS 2-1 AND THEIR TAKOYAKI OF WONDER!
Yeeeaaaahh!
OOOHH
Awww.
GUESS WE DIDN'T STAND A CHANCE.
...!

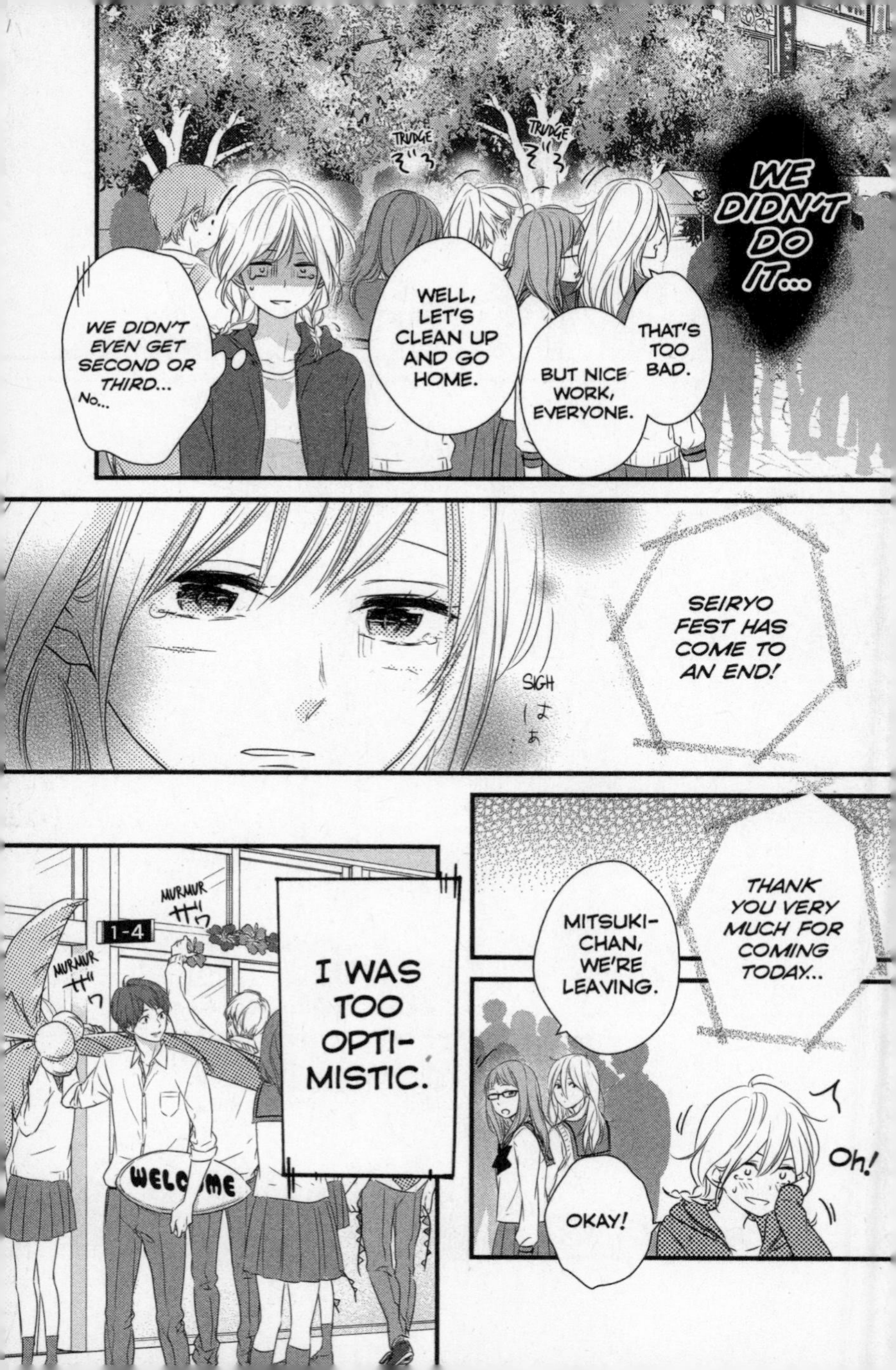
WE DIDN'T DO IT...
TRUDGE
TRUDGE
THAT'S TOO BAD.
BUT NICE WORK, EVERYONE.
WELL, LET'S CLEAN UP AND GO HOME.
WE DIDN'T EVEN GET SECOND OR THIRD... No...
SEIRYO FEST HAS COME TO AN END!
SIGH
THANK YOU VERY MUCH FOR COMING TODAY...
MITSUKI-CHAN, WE'RE LEAVING.
Oh!
OKAY!
I WAS TOO OPTI-MISTIC.
MURMUR
1-4
MURMUR
WELCOME

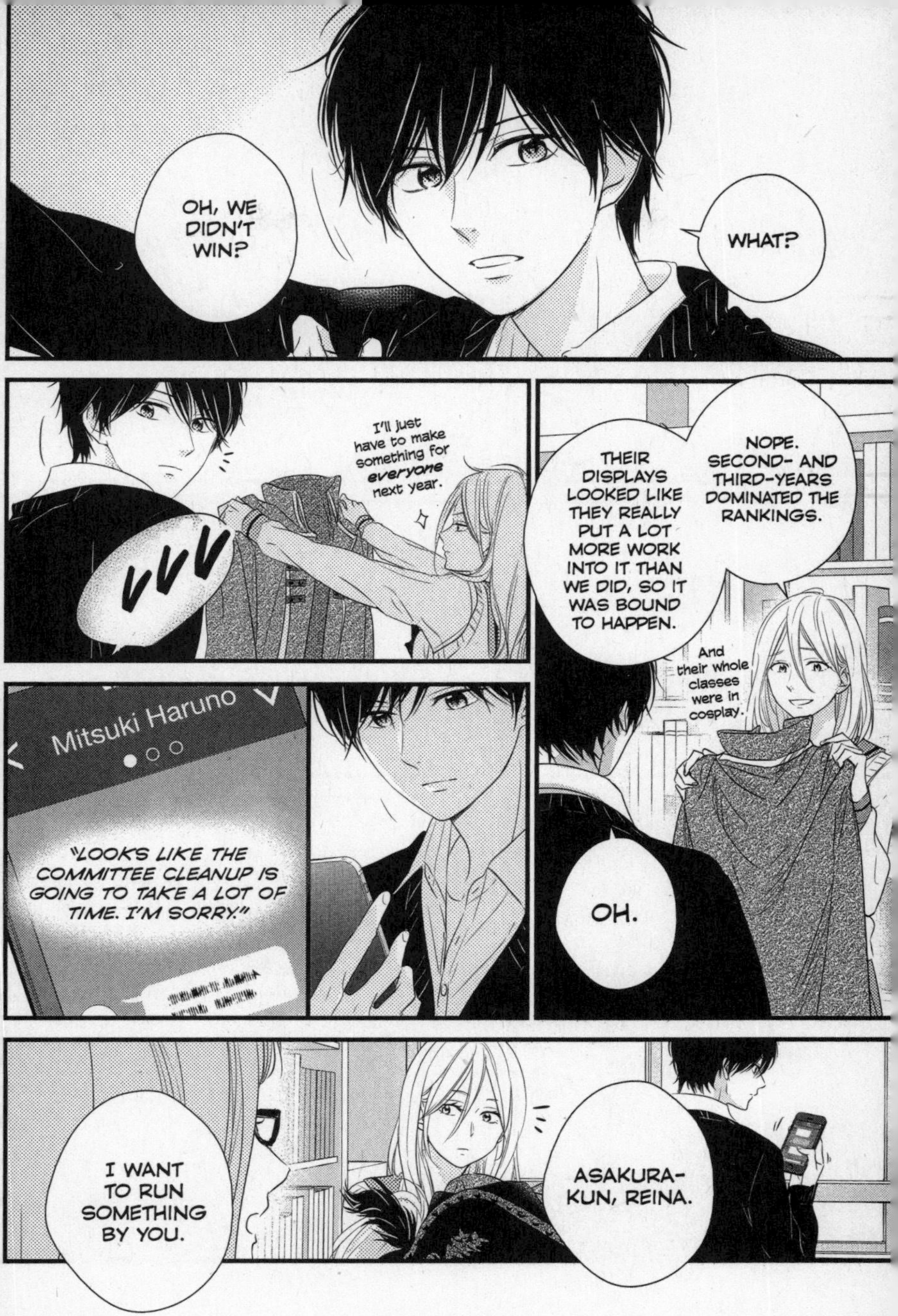
WHAT?
OH, WE DIDN'T WIN?
NOPE. SECOND- AND THIRD-YEARS DOMINATED THE RANKINGS.
THEIR DISPLAYS LOOKED LIKE THEY REALLY PUT A LOT MORE WORK INTO IT THAN WE DID, SO IT WAS BOUND TO HAPPEN.
And their whole classes were in cosplay.
OH.
I'll just have to make something for *everyone* next year.
VVV
Mitsuki Haruno
"LOOKS LIKE THE COMMITTEE CLEANUP IS GOING TO TAKE A LOT OF TIME. I'M SORRY."
ASAKURA-KUN, REINA.
I WANT TO RUN SOMETHING BY YOU.

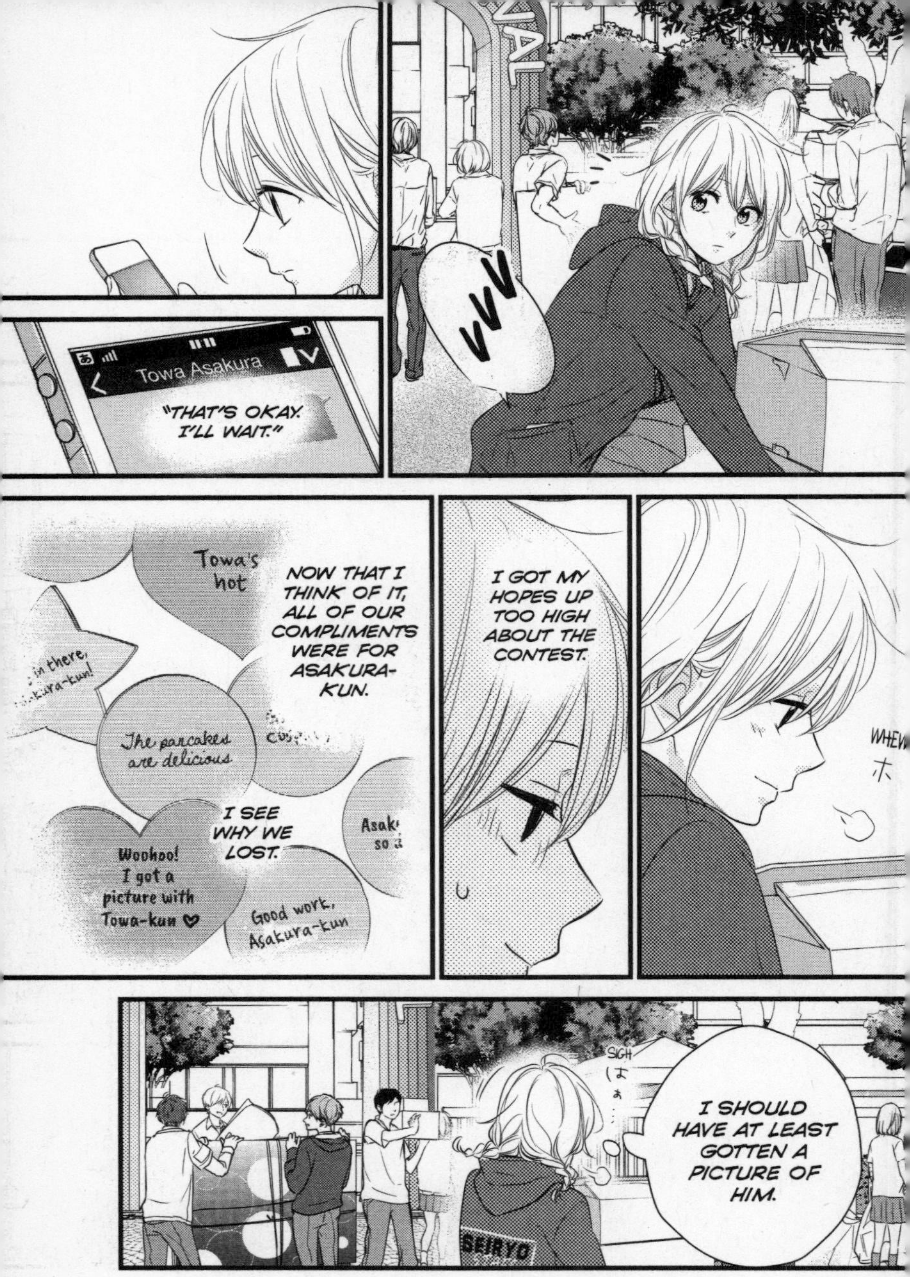

VVV
Towa Asakura
"THAT'S OKAY. I'LL WAIT."
WHEW
ホ
I GOT MY HOPES UP TOO HIGH ABOUT THE CONTEST.
NOW THAT I THINK OF IT, ALL OF OUR COMPLIMENTS WERE FOR ASAKURA-KUN.
Towa's hot
The pancakes are delicious
I SEE WHY WE LOST.
Woohoo! I got a picture with Towa-kun ♡
Good work, Asakura-kun
I SHOULD HAVE AT LEAST GOTTEN A PICTURE OF HIM.
SIGH
はぁ…
SEIRYO

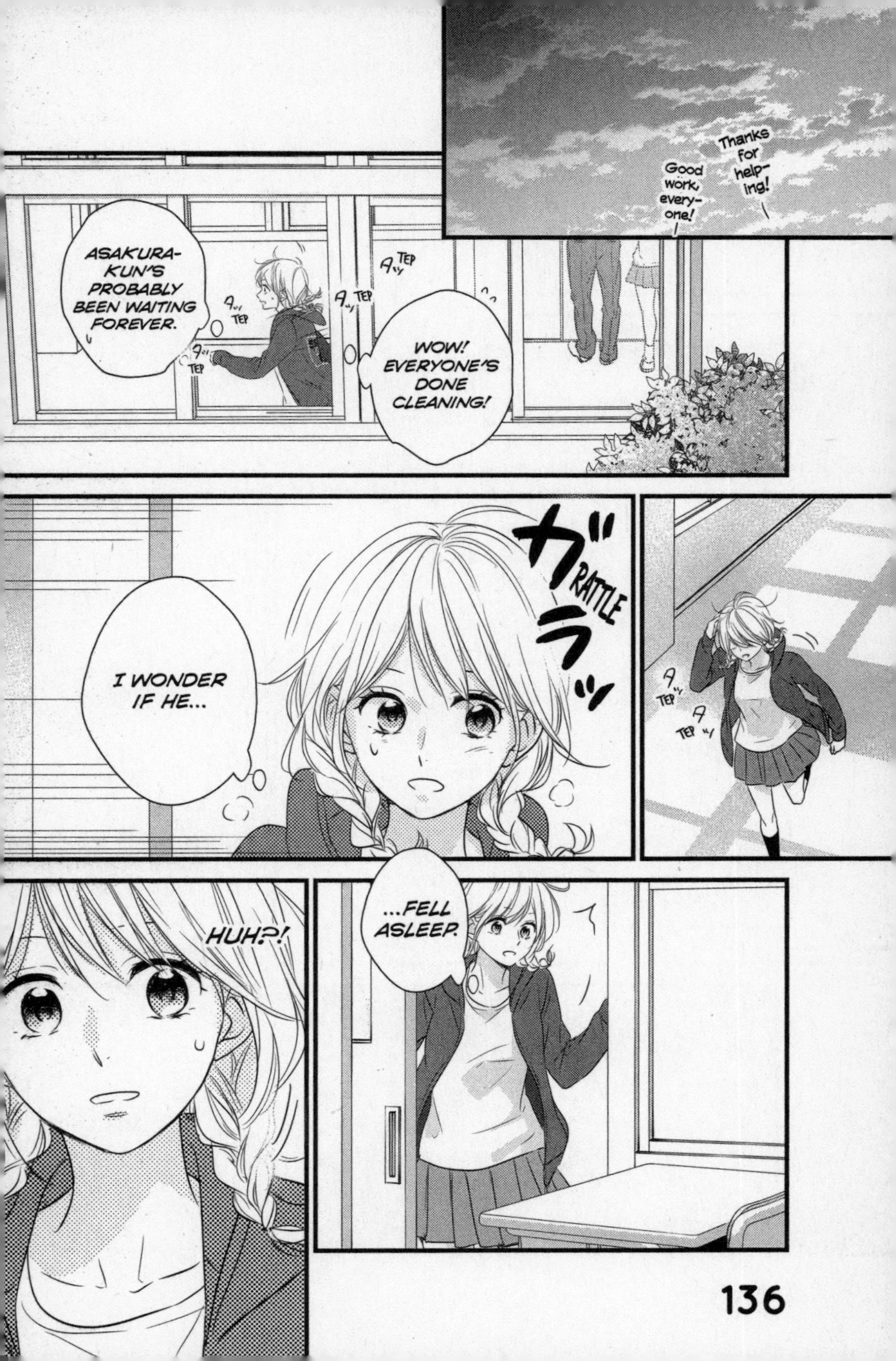
Thanks for helping!
Good work, everyone!
WOW! EVERYONE'S DONE CLEANING!
TEP
TEP
ASAKURA-KUN'S PROBABLY BEEN WAITING FOREVER.
TEP
TEP
TEP
TEP
RATTLE
I WONDER IF HE...
...FELL ASLEEP.
HUH?!

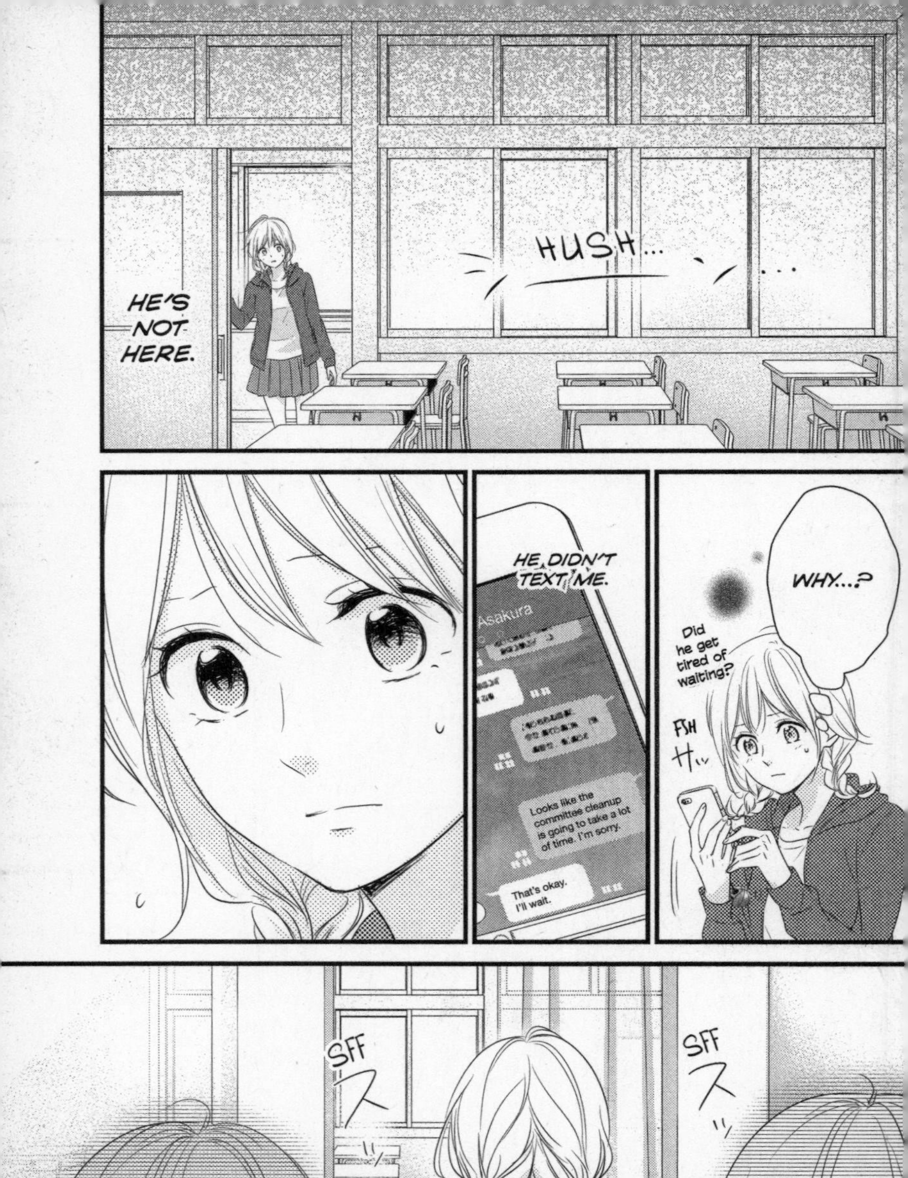
HUSH...
...
HE'S NOT HERE.
WHY...?
Did he get tired of waiting?
FSH
HE DIDN'T TEXT ME.
Asakura
Looks like the committee cleanup is going to take a lot of time. I'm sorry.
That's okay. I'll wait.
SFF
SFF

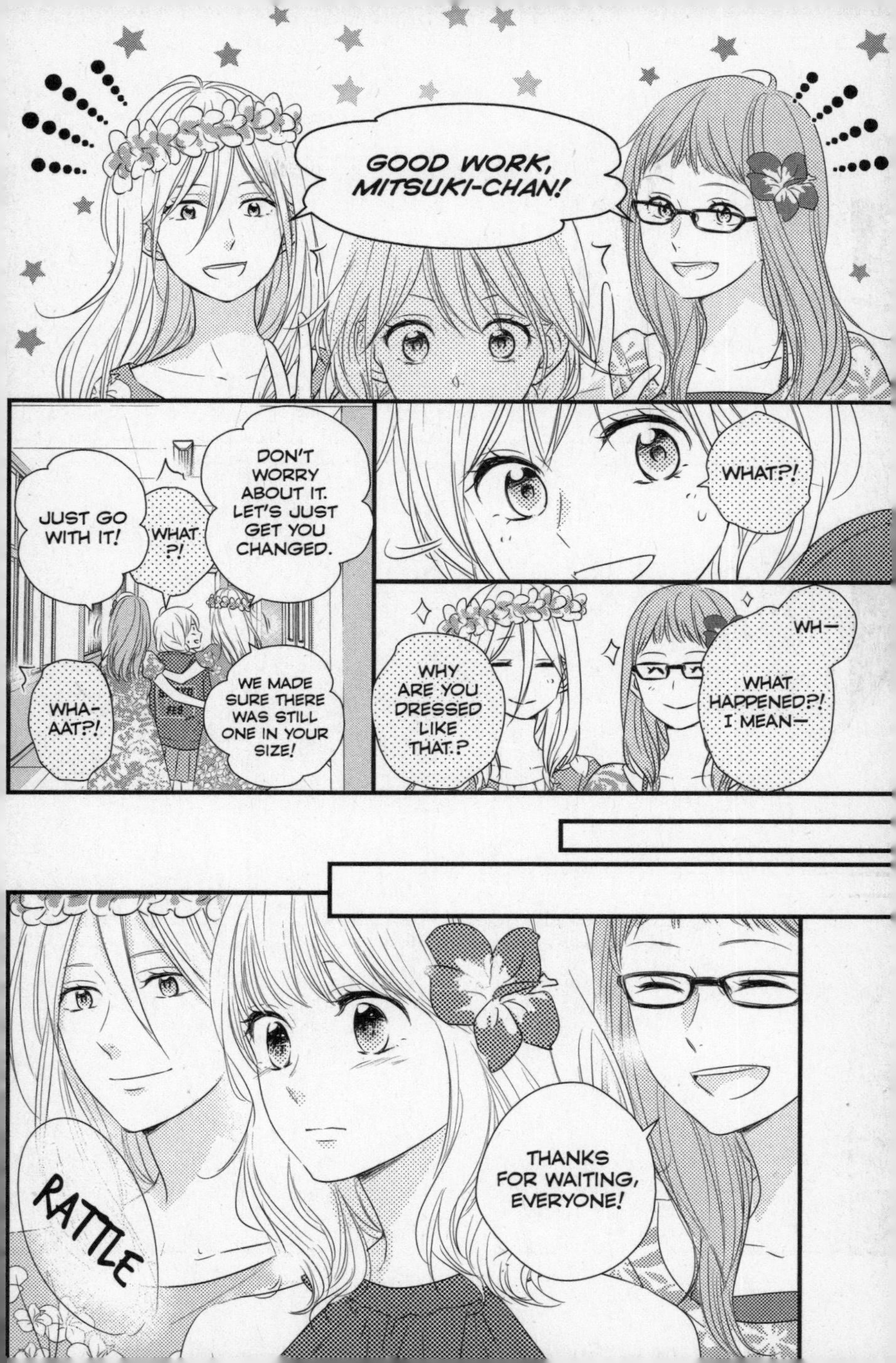
GOOD WORK, MITSUKI-CHAN!
WHAT?!
WH—
WHAT HAPPENED?! I MEAN—
WHY ARE YOU DRESSED LIKE THAT.?
DON'T WORRY ABOUT IT. LET'S JUST GET YOU CHANGED.
WHAT ?!
JUST GO WITH IT!
WE MADE SURE THERE WAS STILL ONE IN YOUR SIZE!
WHA-AAT?!
THANKS FOR WAITING, EVERYONE!
RATTLE

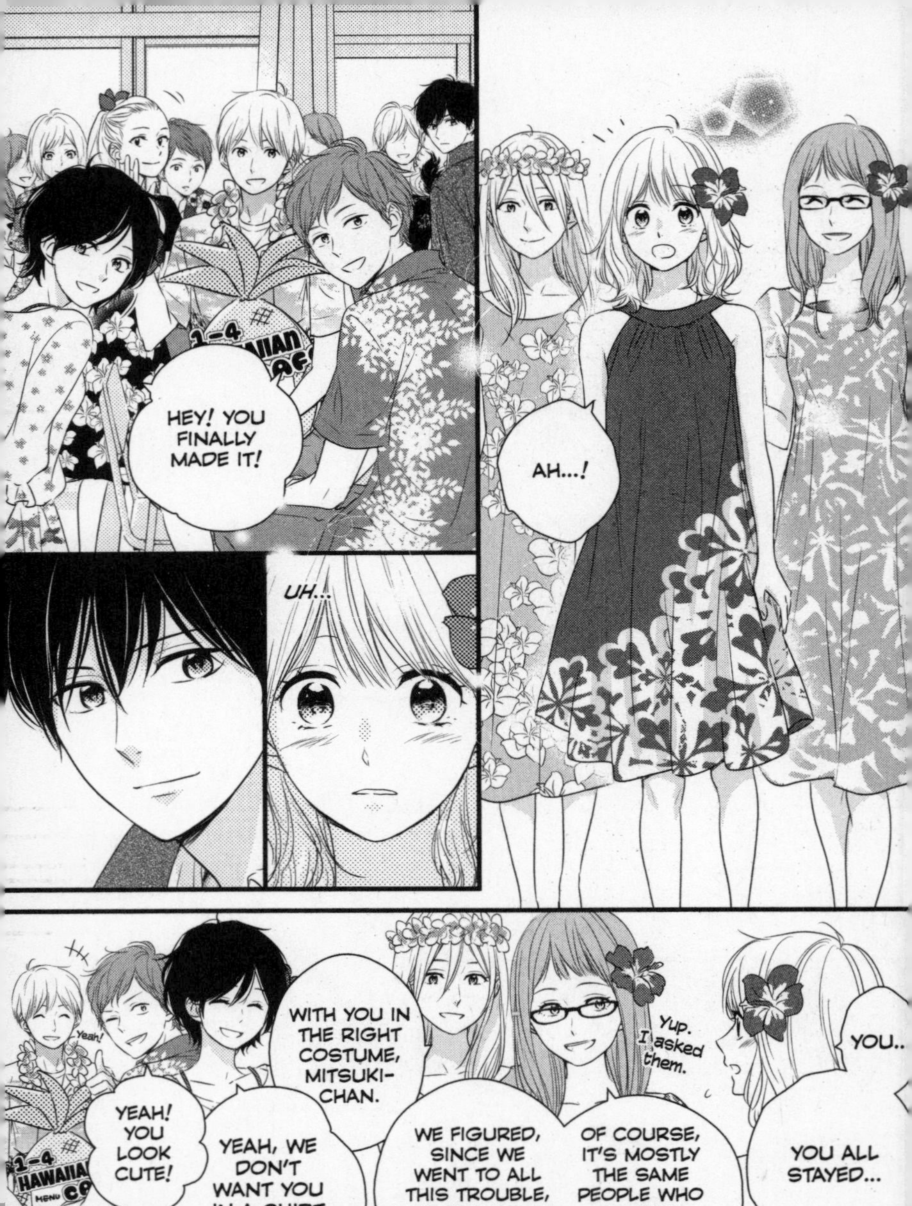
AH...!
HEY! YOU FINALLY MADE IT!
UH...
YOU...
YOU ALL STAYED...
Yup. I asked them.
OF COURSE, IT'S MOSTLY THE SAME PEOPLE WHO USUALLY STAYED TO HELP AFTER SCHOOL.
WE FIGURED, SINCE WE WENT TO ALL THIS TROUBLE, WE SHOULD AT LEAST TAKE A PICTURE.
WITH YOU IN THE RIGHT COSTUME, MITSUKI-CHAN.
YEAH, WE DON'T WANT YOU IN A SHIRT FOR THE PICTURE!
YEAH! YOU LOOK CUTE!
Yeah!

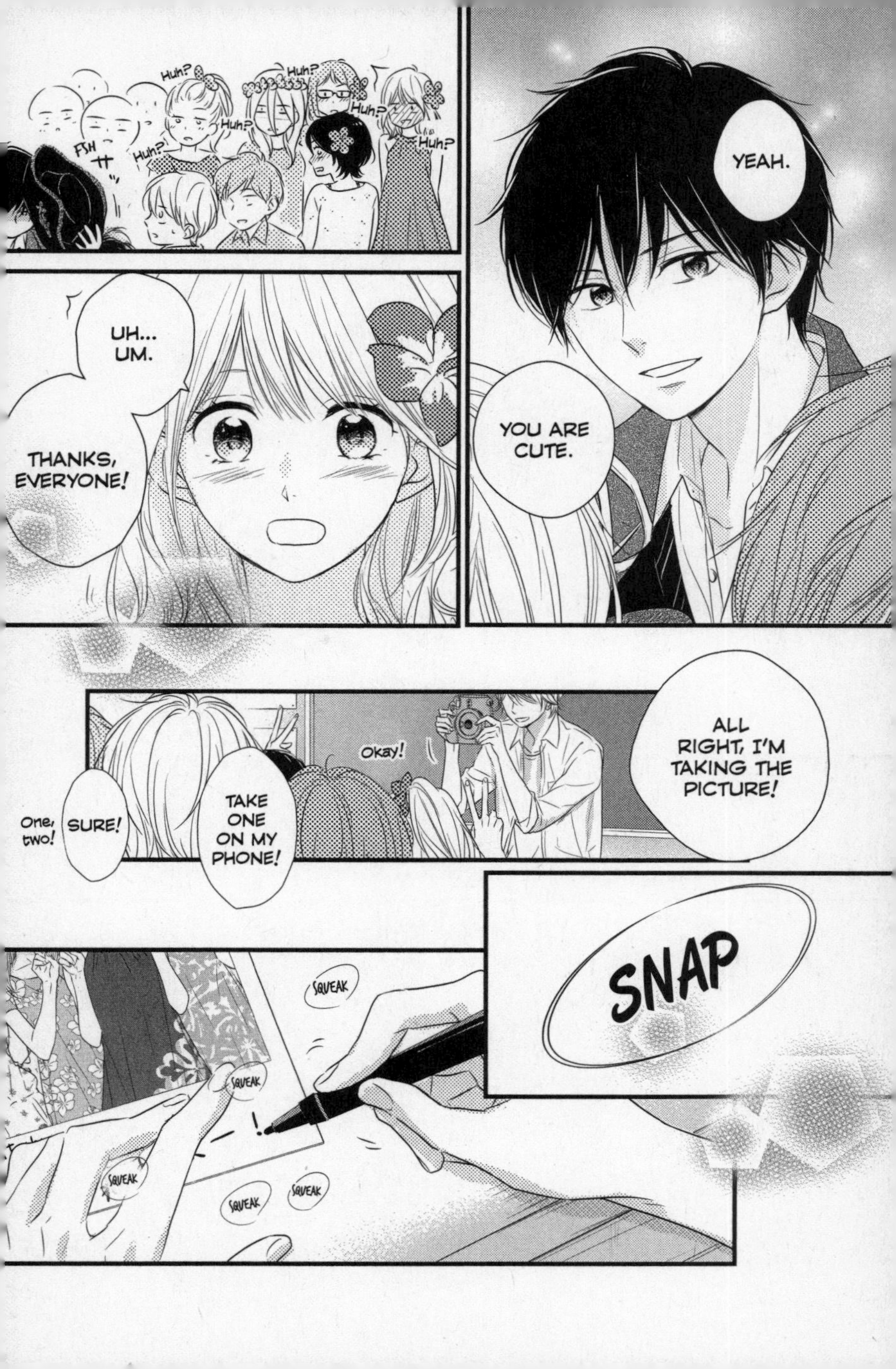

YEAH.
YOU ARE CUTE.
Huh?
Huh?
Huh?
Huh?
Huh?
Huh?
FSH
UH... UM.
THANKS, EVERYONE!
ALL RIGHT, I'M TAKING THE PICTURE!
Okay!
TAKE ONE ON MY PHONE!
SURE!
One, two!
SNAP
SQUEAK
SQUEAK
SQUEAK
SQUEAK
SQUEAK

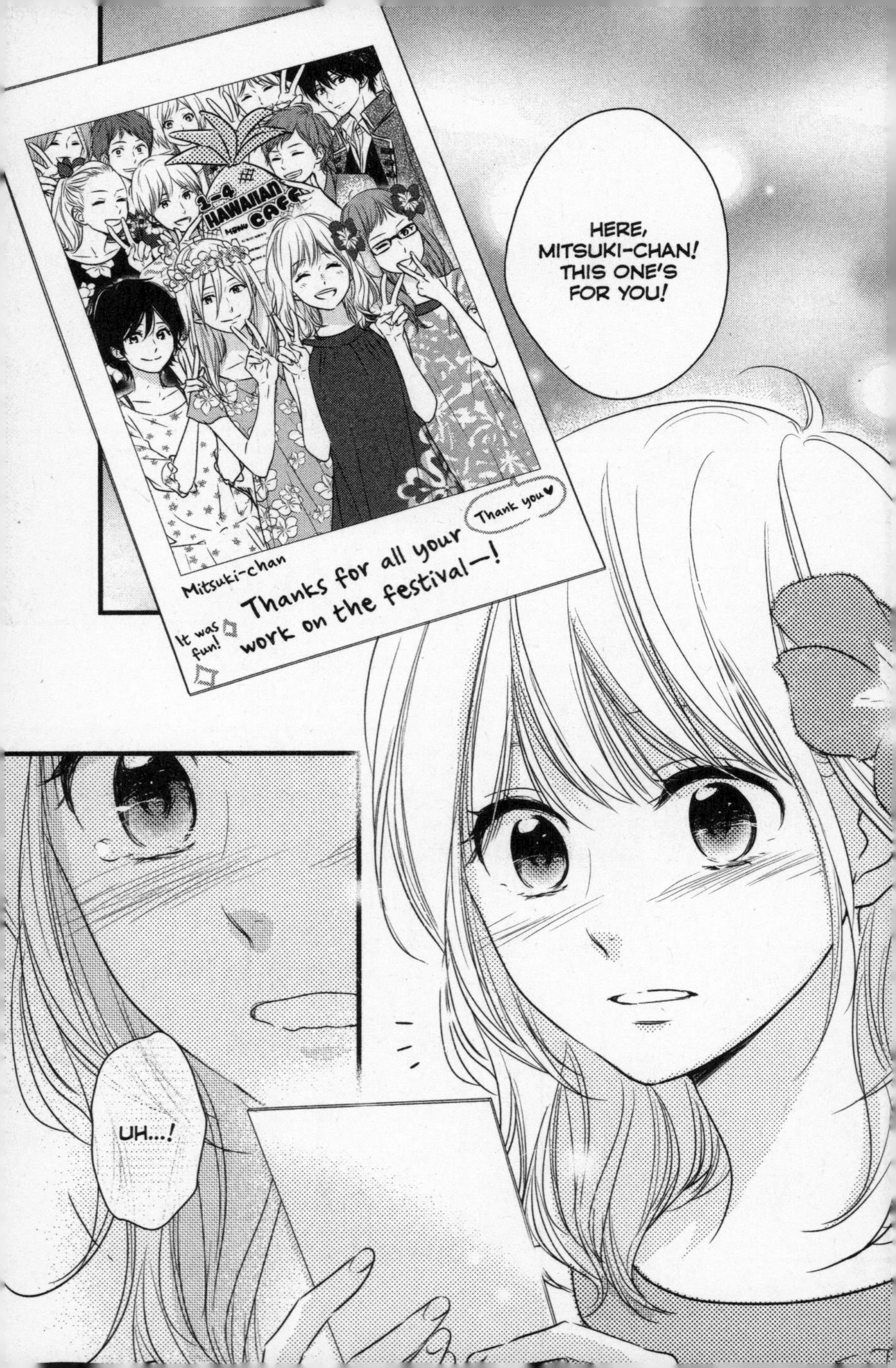
HERE, MITSUKI-CHAN! THIS ONE'S FOR YOU!
1-4 HAWAIIAN CAFE
Thank you♥
Mitsuki-chan
Thanks for all your work on the festival—!
It was fun!
UH...!

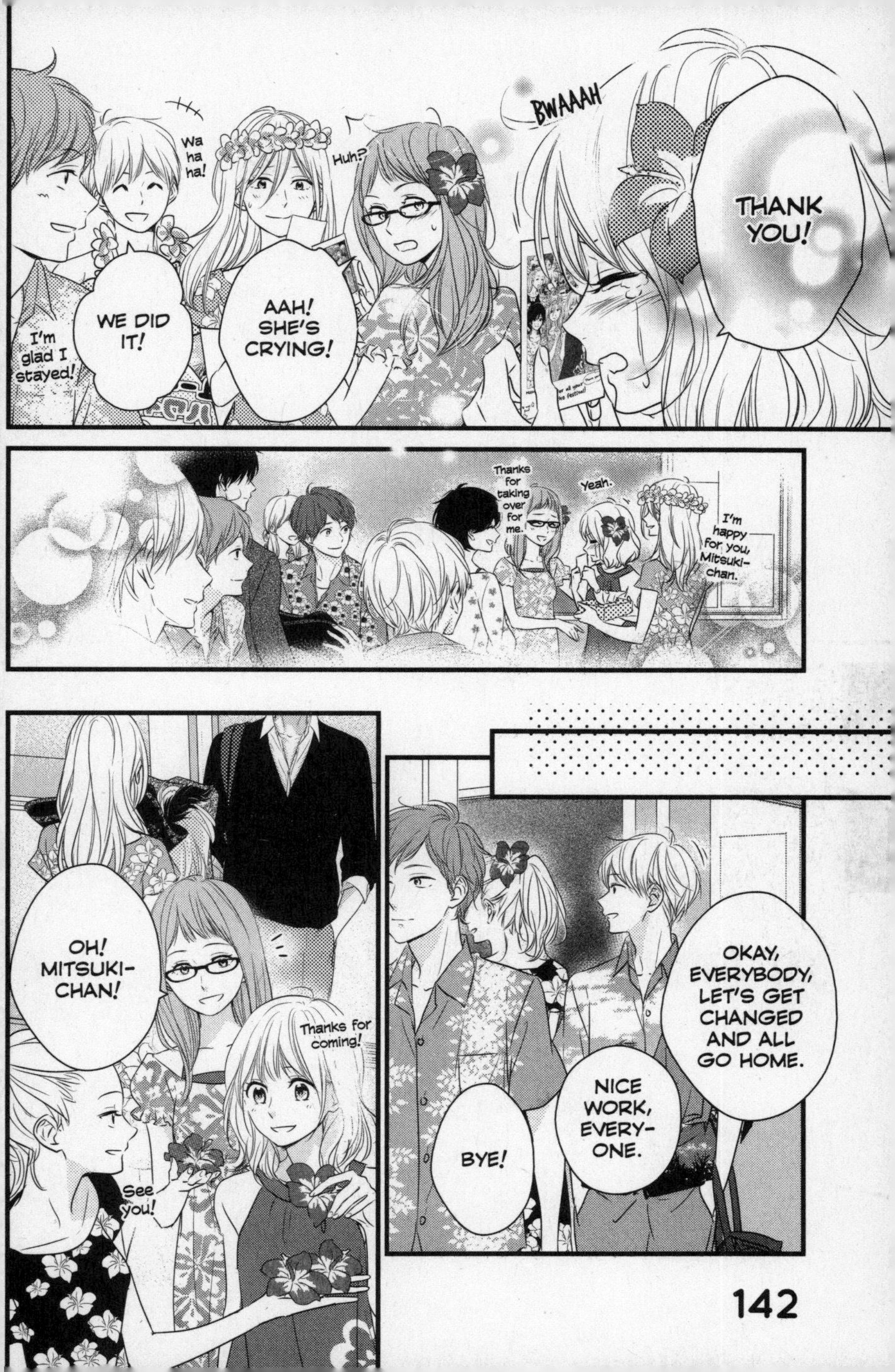
BWAAAH
THANK YOU!
Huh?
AAH! SHE'S CRYING!
Wa ha ha!
WE DID IT!
I'm glad I stayed!
I'm happy for you, Mitsuki-chan.
Yeah.
Thanks for taking over for me.
OKAY, EVERYBODY, LET'S GET CHANGED AND ALL GO HOME.
NICE WORK, EVERY-ONE.
BYE!
Thanks for coming!
OH! MITSUKI-CHAN!
See you!

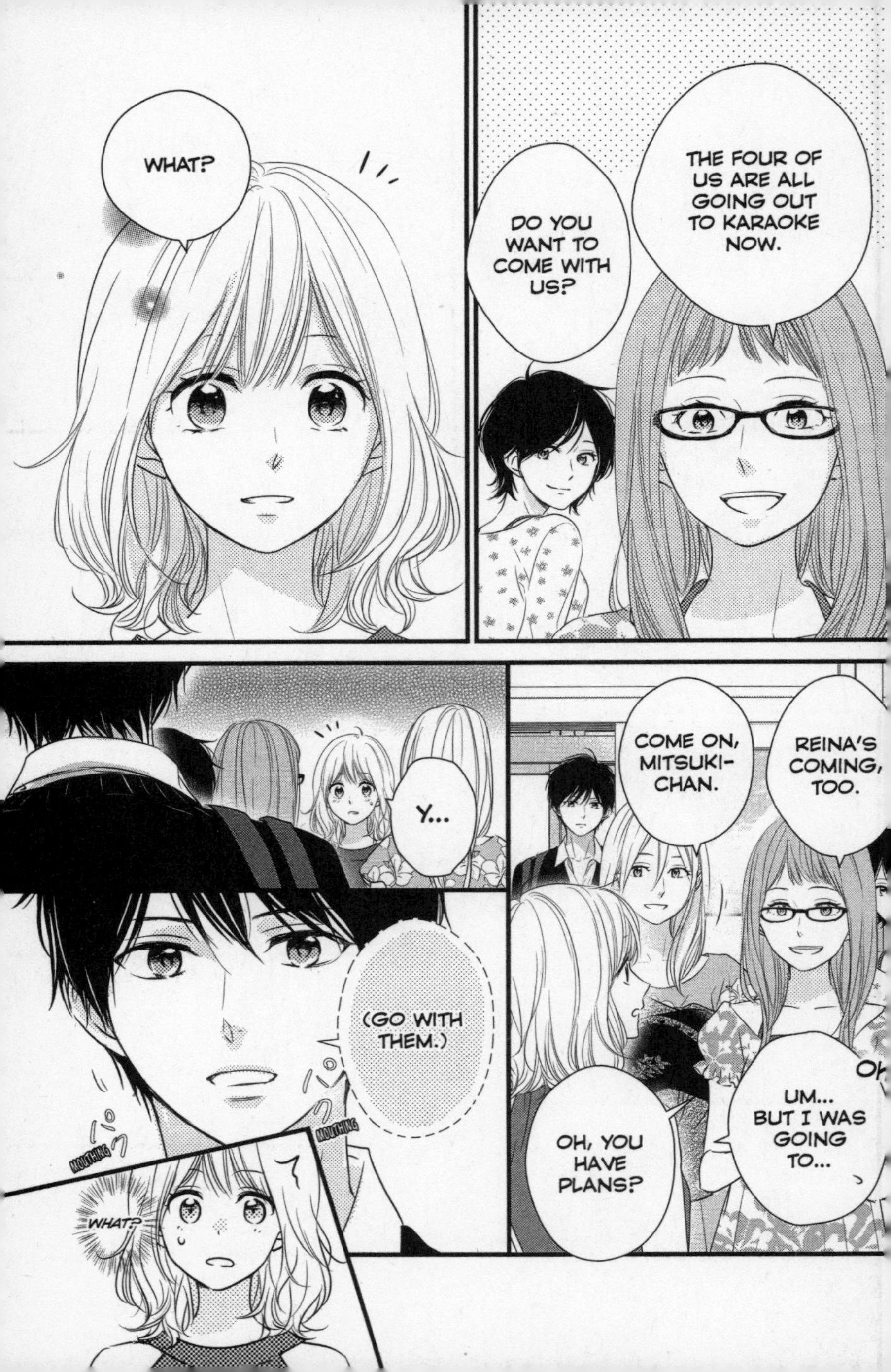
THE FOUR OF US ARE ALL GOING OUT TO KARAOKE NOW.
DO YOU WANT TO COME WITH US?
WHAT?
REINA'S COMING, TOO.
COME ON, MITSUKI-CHAN.
OH
UM... BUT I WAS GOING TO...
OH, YOU HAVE PLANS?
Y...
(GO WITH THEM.)
MOUTHING
MOUTHING
WHAT?

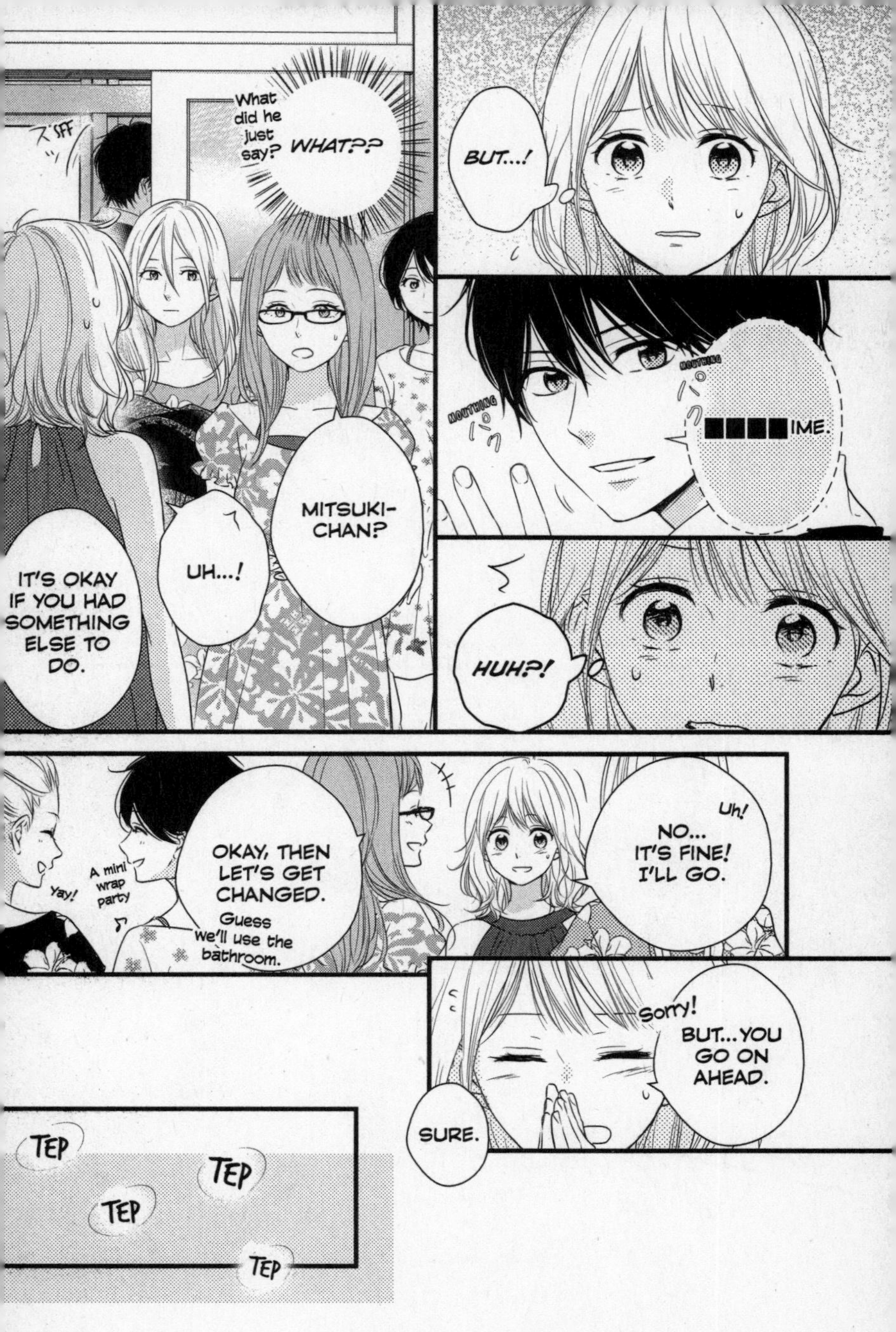
BUT...!
MOUTHING
MOUTHING
[redacted]IME.
HUH?!
What did he just say? WHAT??
SFF
MITSUKI-CHAN?
UH...!
IT'S OKAY IF YOU HAD SOMETHING ELSE TO DO.
Uh!
NO... IT'S FINE! I'LL GO.
OKAY, THEN LET'S GET CHANGED.
Guess we'll use the bathroom.
A mini wrap party
Yay!
Sorry!
BUT...YOU GO ON AHEAD.
SURE.
TEP
TEP
TEP
TEP

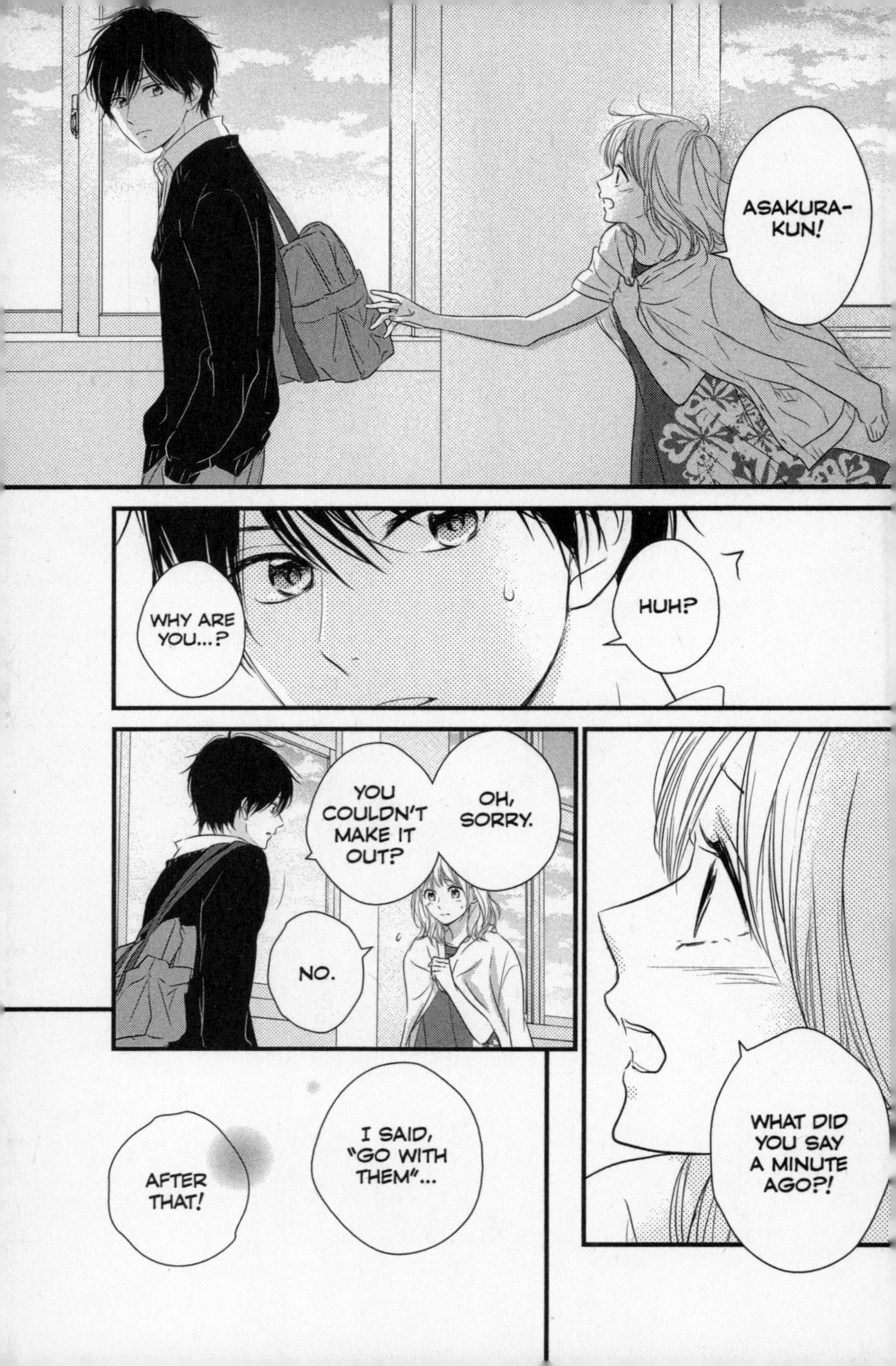

ASAKURA-KUN!
HUH?
WHY ARE YOU...?
OH, SORRY.
YOU COULDN'T MAKE IT OUT?
NO.
WHAT DID YOU SAY A MINUTE AGO?!
I SAID, "GO WITH THEM"...
AFTER THAT!

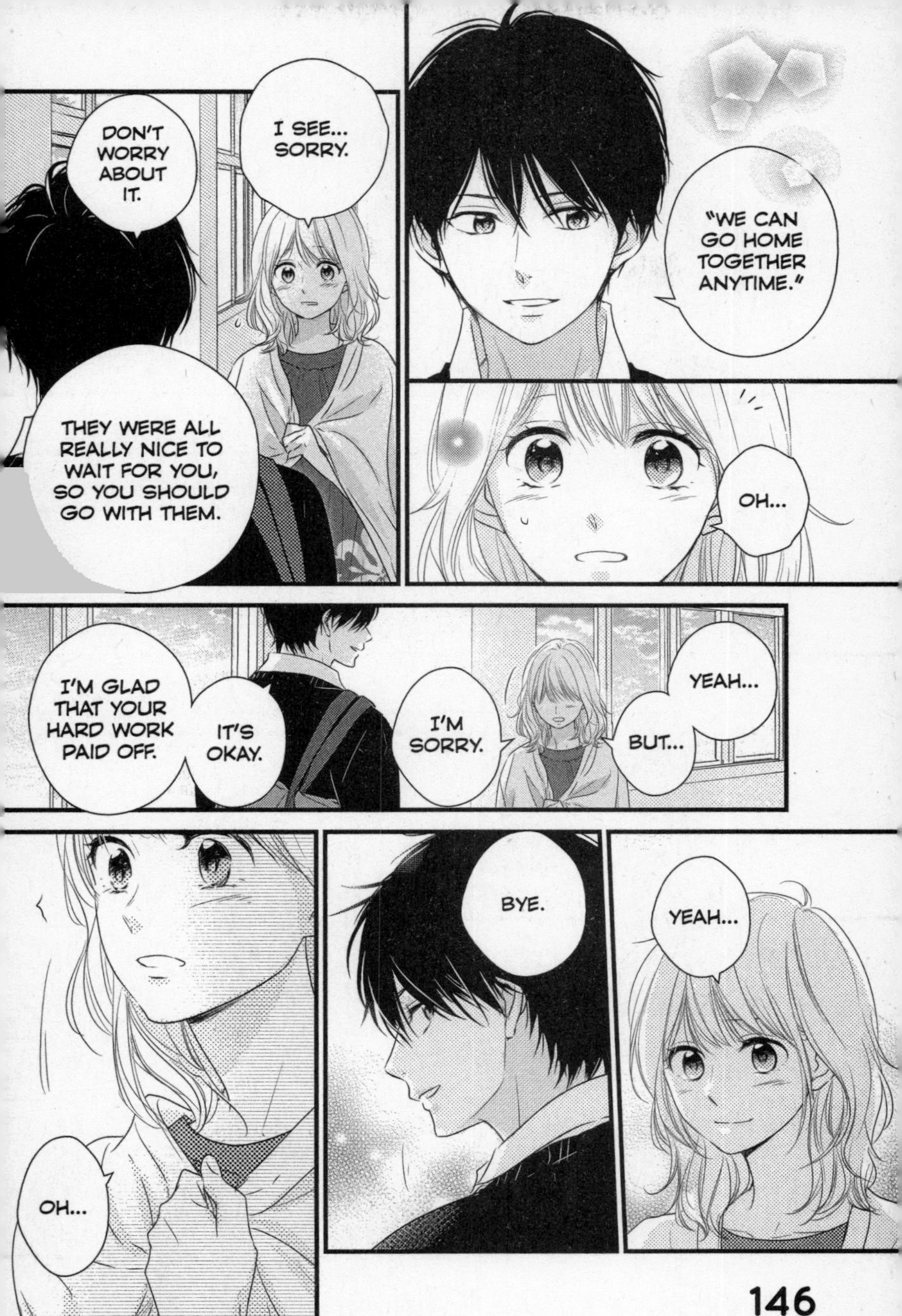
"WE CAN GO HOME TOGETHER ANYTIME."
OH...
I SEE... SORRY.
DON'T WORRY ABOUT IT.
THEY WERE ALL REALLY NICE TO WAIT FOR YOU, SO YOU SHOULD GO WITH THEM.
YEAH...
BUT...
I'M SORRY.
IT'S OKAY.
I'M GLAD THAT YOUR HARD WORK PAID OFF.
YEAH...
BYE.
OH...

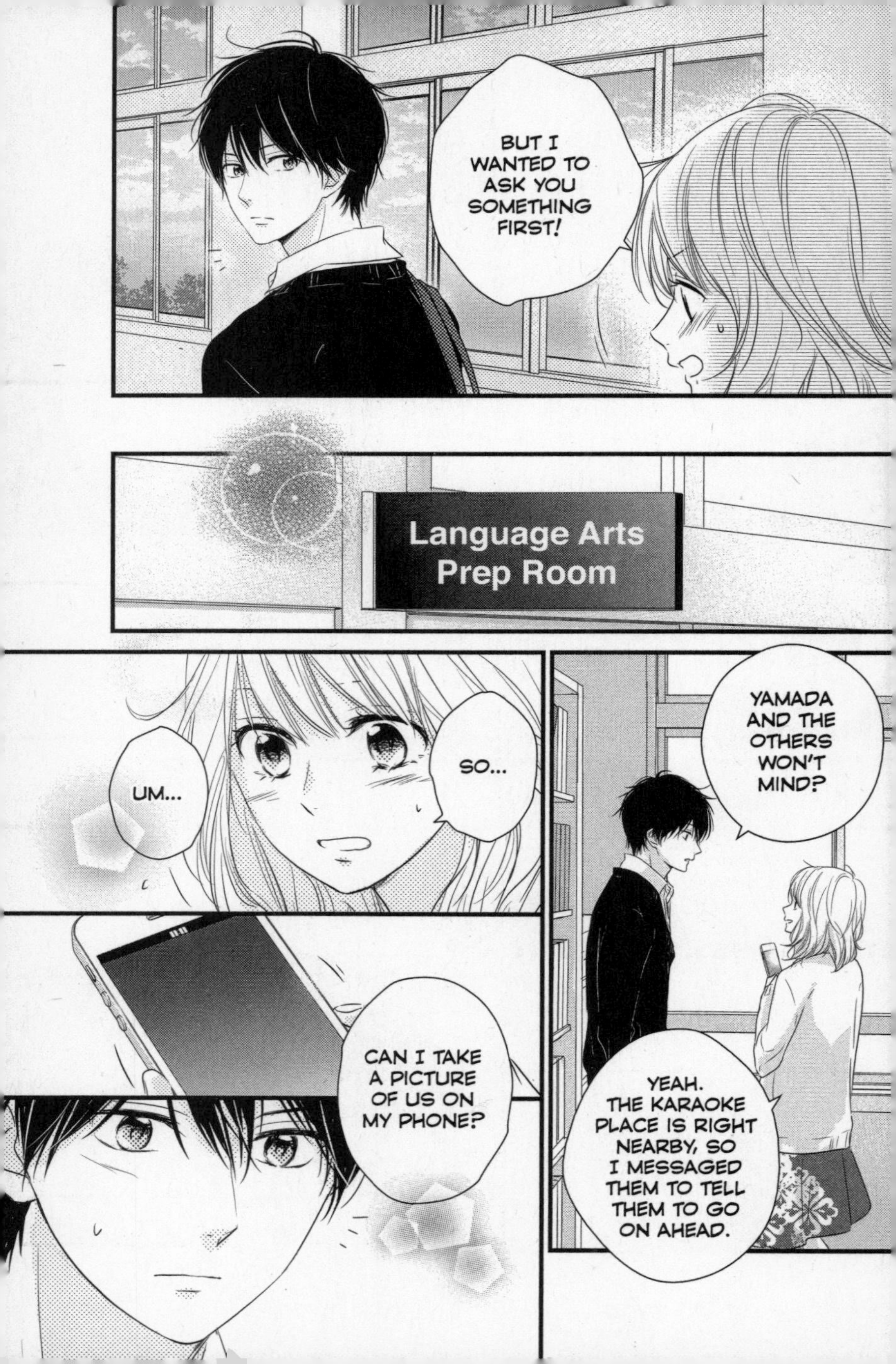

BUT I WANTED TO ASK YOU SOMETHING FIRST!
Language Arts Prep Room
YAMADA AND THE OTHERS WON'T MIND?
YEAH. THE KARAOKE PLACE IS RIGHT NEARBY, SO I MESSAGED THEM TO TELL THEM TO GO ON AHEAD.
SO...
UM...
CAN I TAKE A PICTURE OF US ON MY PHONE?

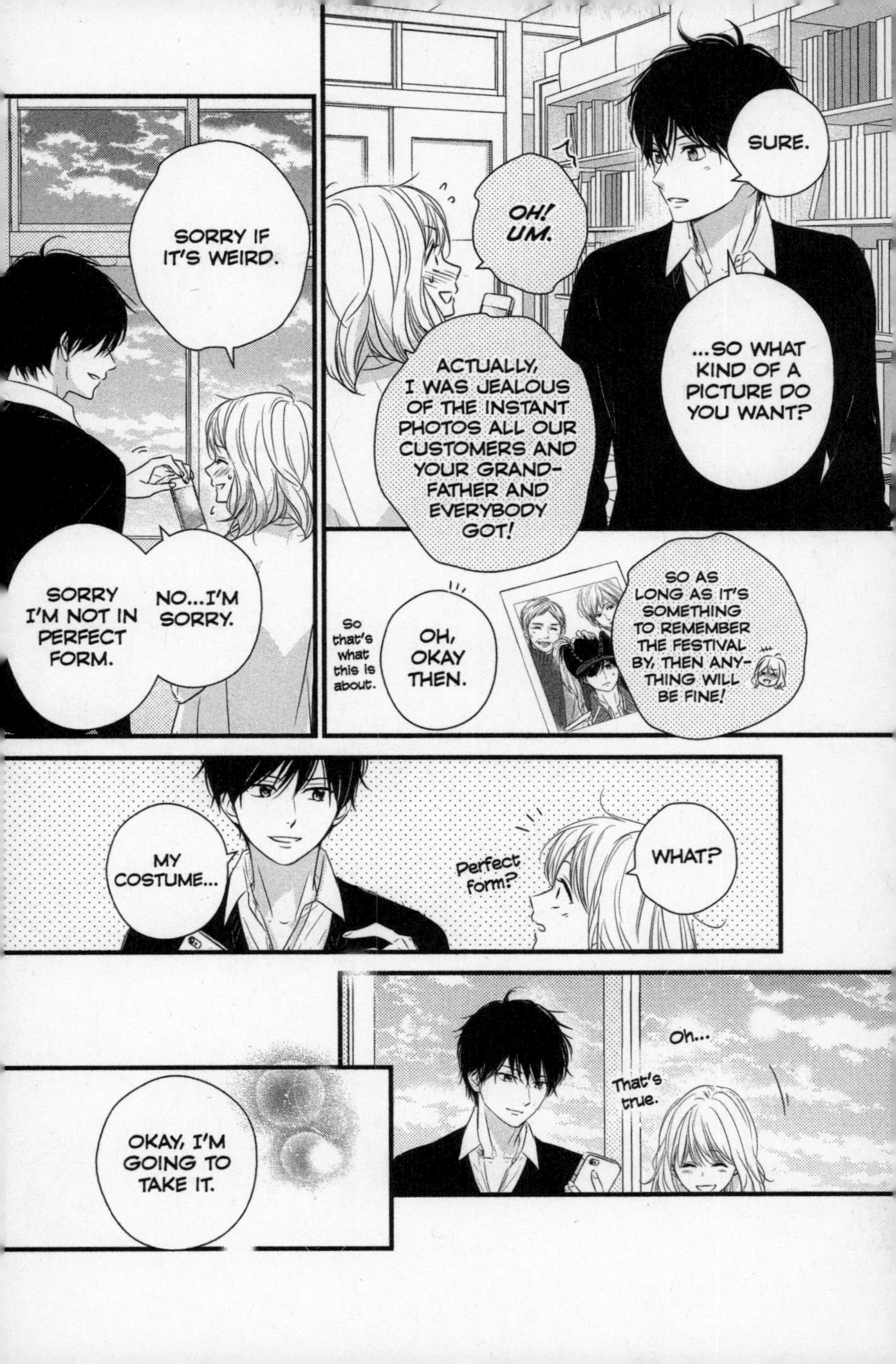
SURE.
OH! UM.
...SO WHAT KIND OF A PICTURE DO YOU WANT?
ACTUALLY, I WAS JEALOUS OF THE INSTANT PHOTOS ALL OUR CUSTOMERS AND YOUR GRAND-FATHER AND EVERYBODY GOT!
SO AS LONG AS IT'S SOMETHING TO REMEMBER THE FESTIVAL BY, THEN ANY-THING WILL BE FINE!
OH, OKAY THEN.
So that's what this is about.
SORRY IF IT'S WEIRD.
NO...I'M SORRY.
SORRY I'M NOT IN PERFECT FORM.
WHAT?
Perfect form?
MY COSTUME...
Oh...
That's true.
OKAY, I'M GOING TO TAKE IT.

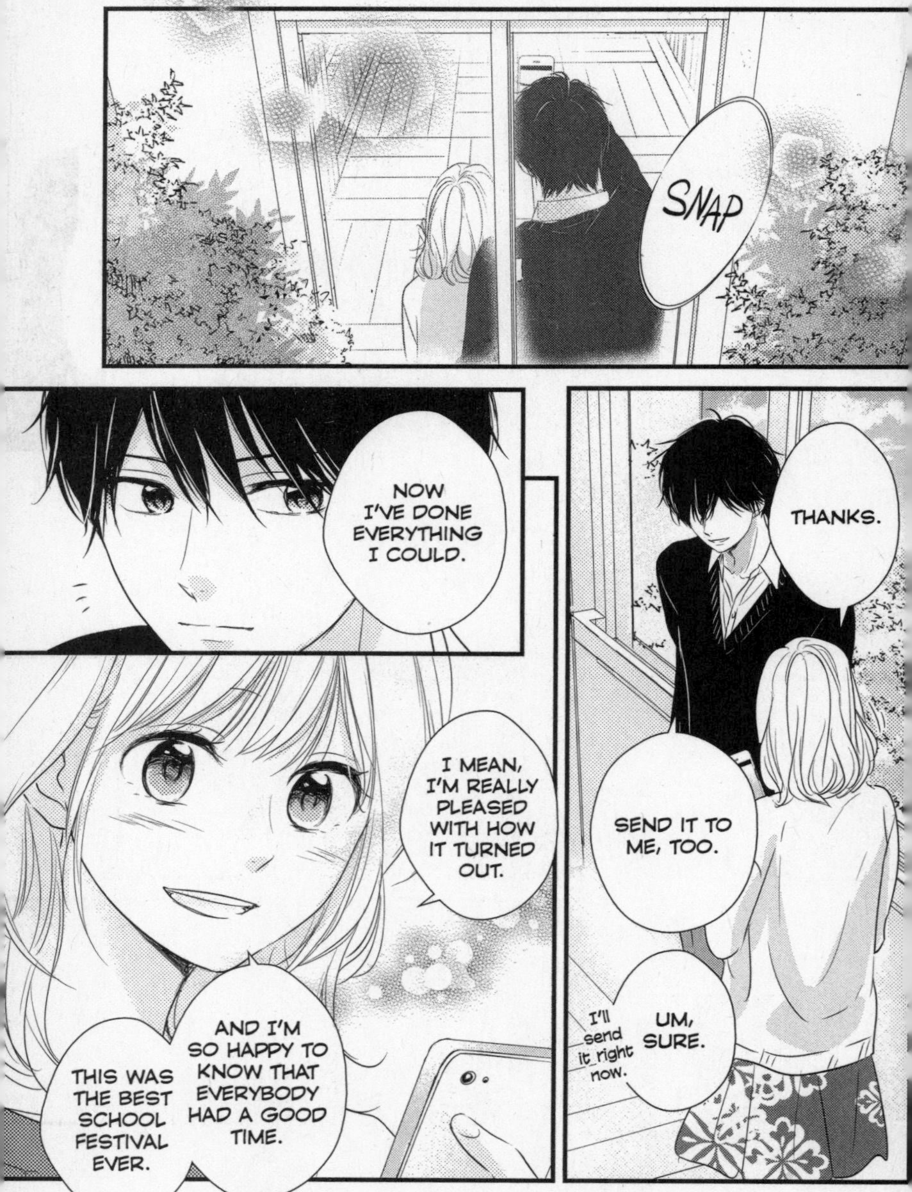
SNAP
THANKS.
SEND IT TO ME, TOO.
UM, SURE.
I'll send it right now.
NOW I'VE DONE EVERYTHING I COULD.
I MEAN, I'M REALLY PLEASED WITH HOW IT TURNED OUT.
AND I'M SO HAPPY TO KNOW THAT EVERYBODY HAD A GOOD TIME.
THIS WAS THE BEST SCHOOL FESTIVAL EVER.

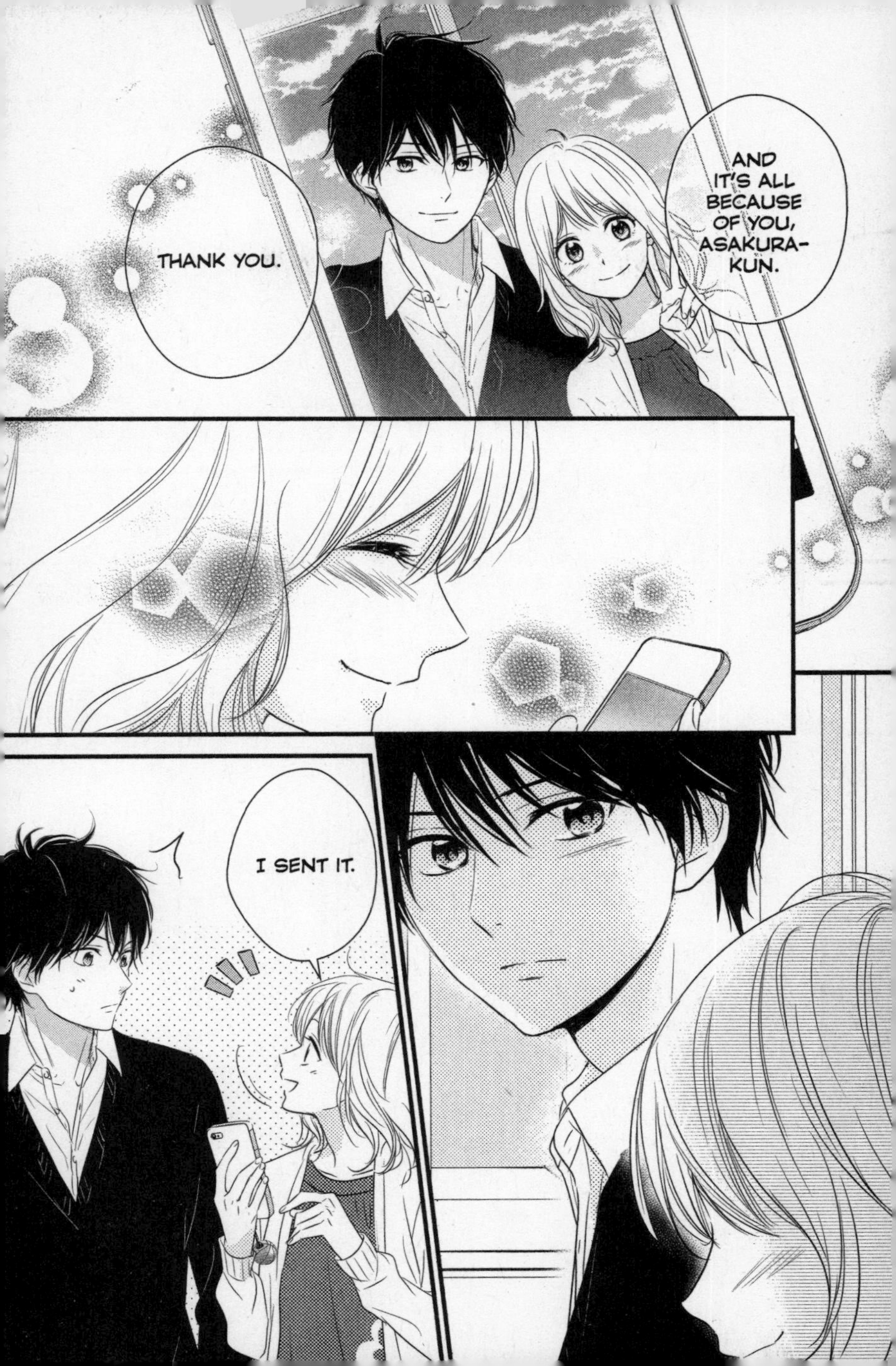
AND IT'S ALL BECAUSE OF YOU, ASAKURA-KUN.
THANK YOU.
I SENT IT.

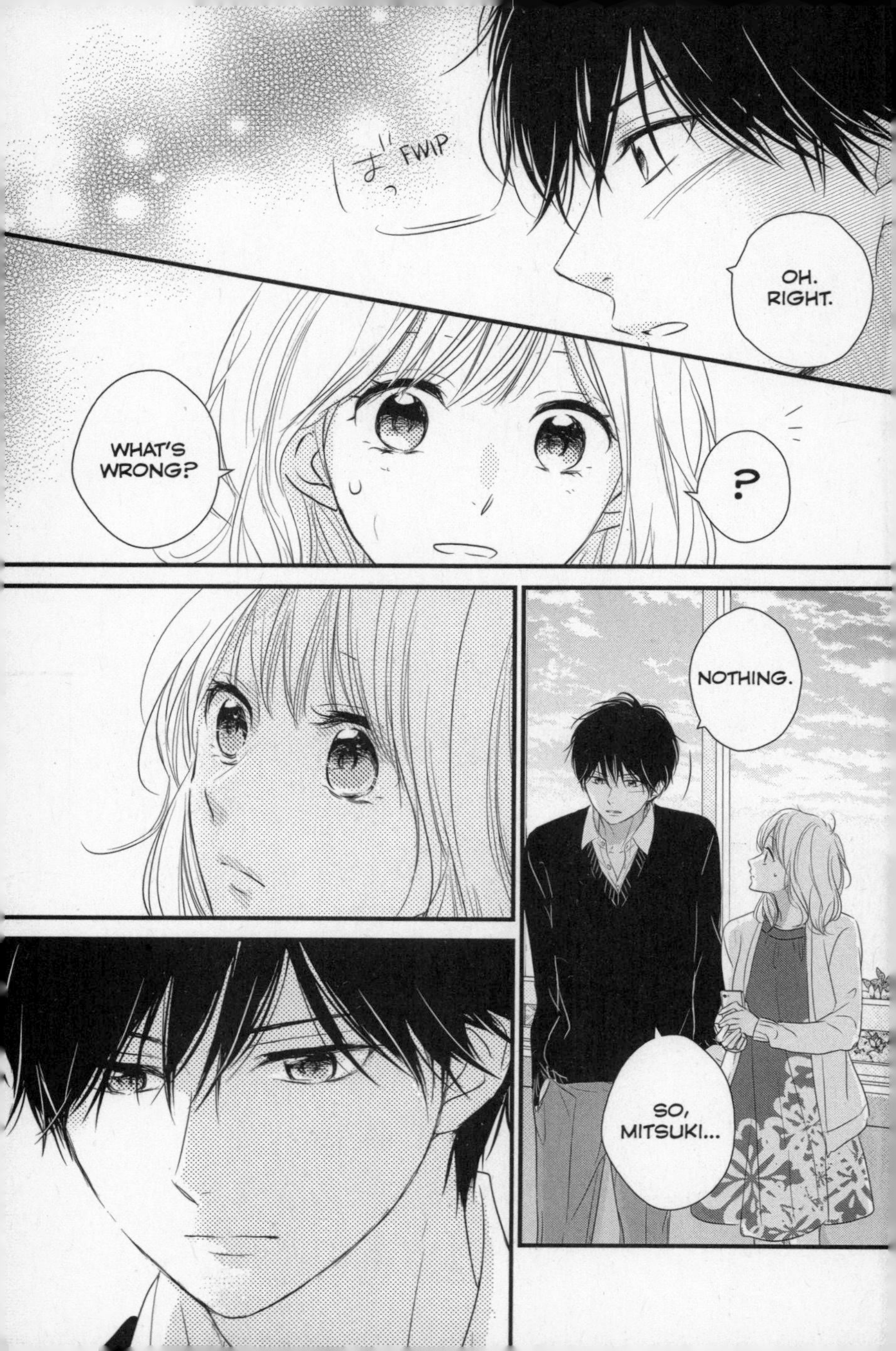
FWIP
OH. RIGHT.
?
WHAT'S WRONG?
NOTHING.
SO, MITSUKI...

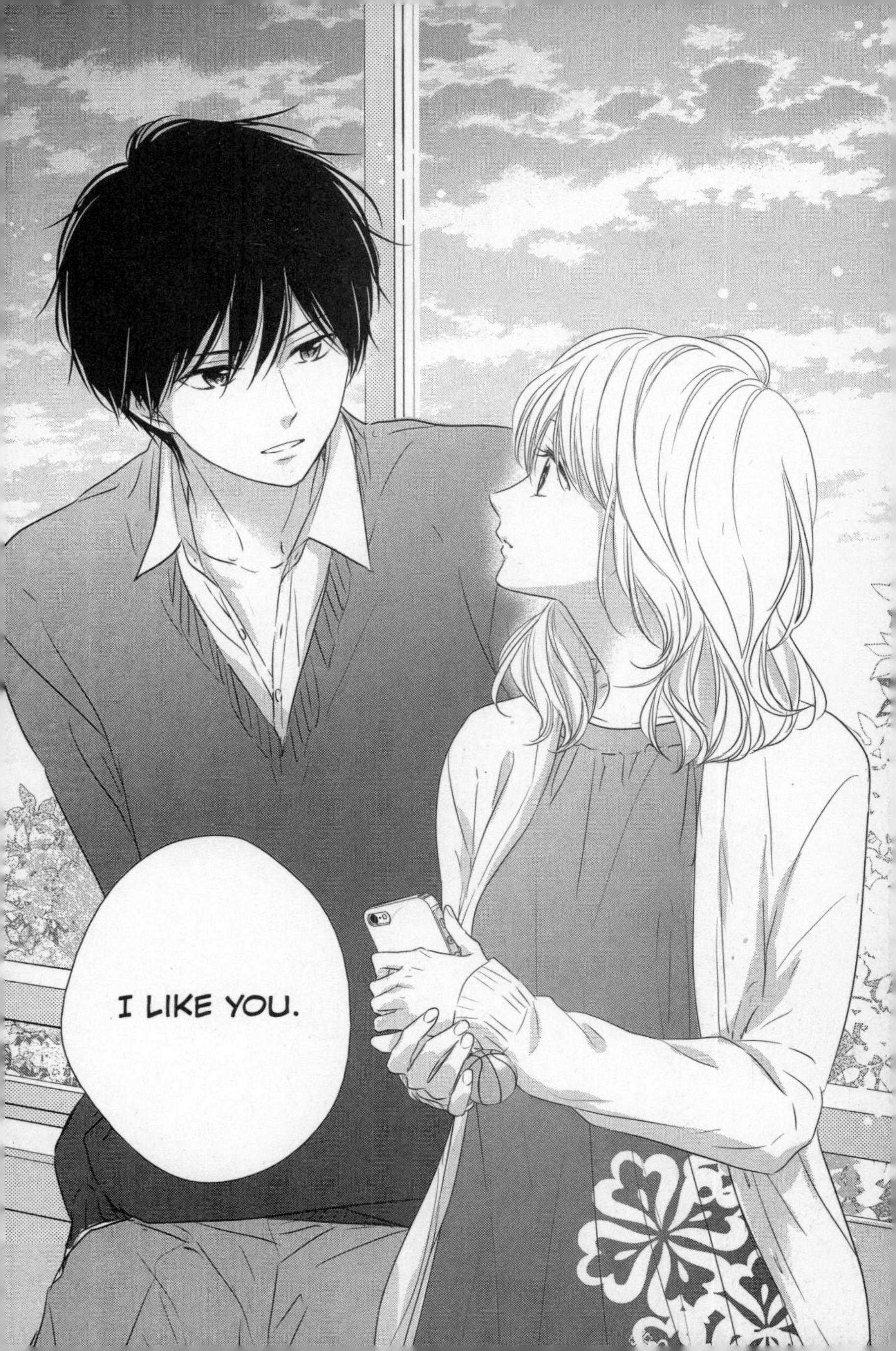
I LIKE YOU.

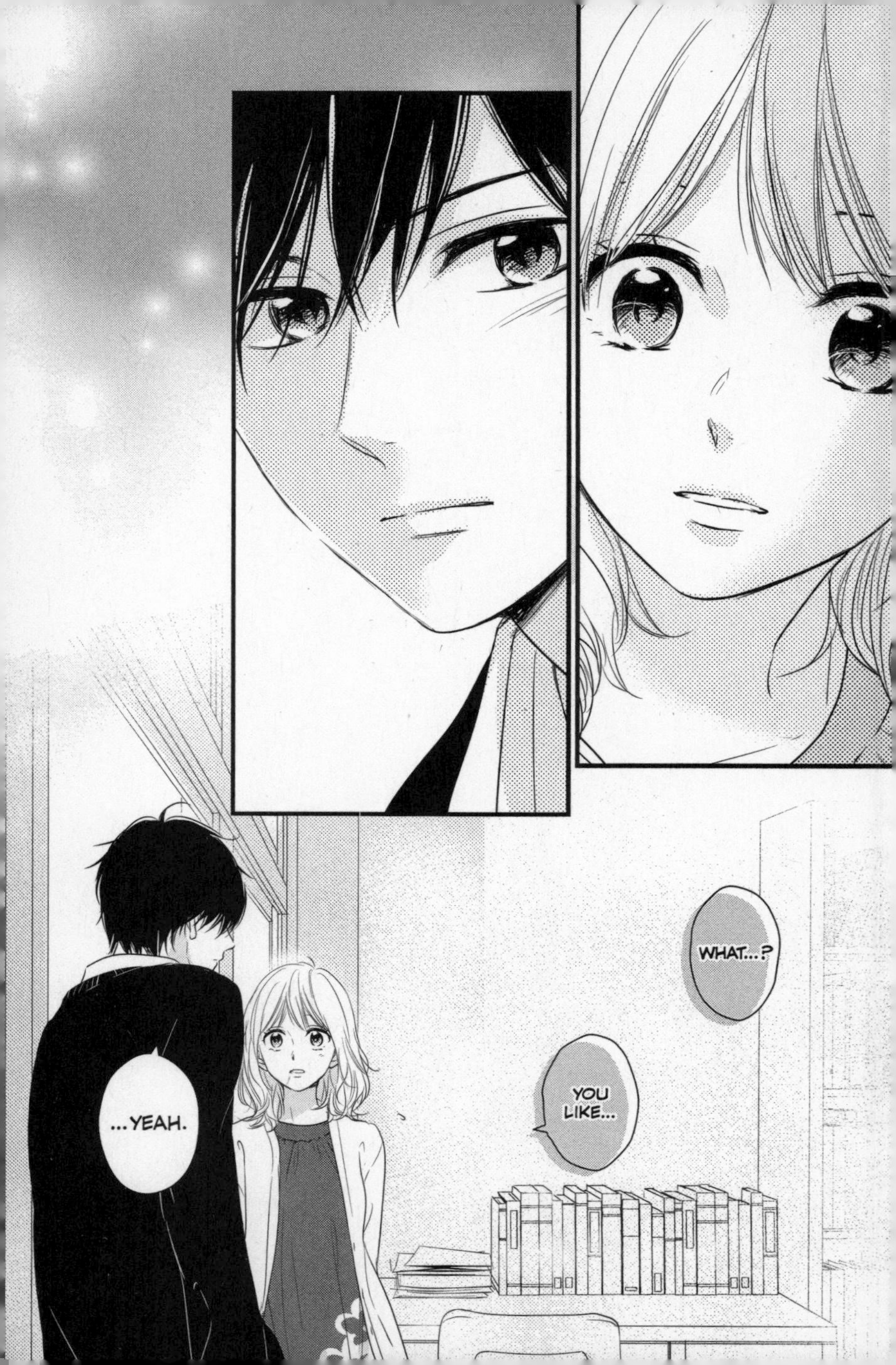
WHAT...?
YOU LIKE...
...YEAH.

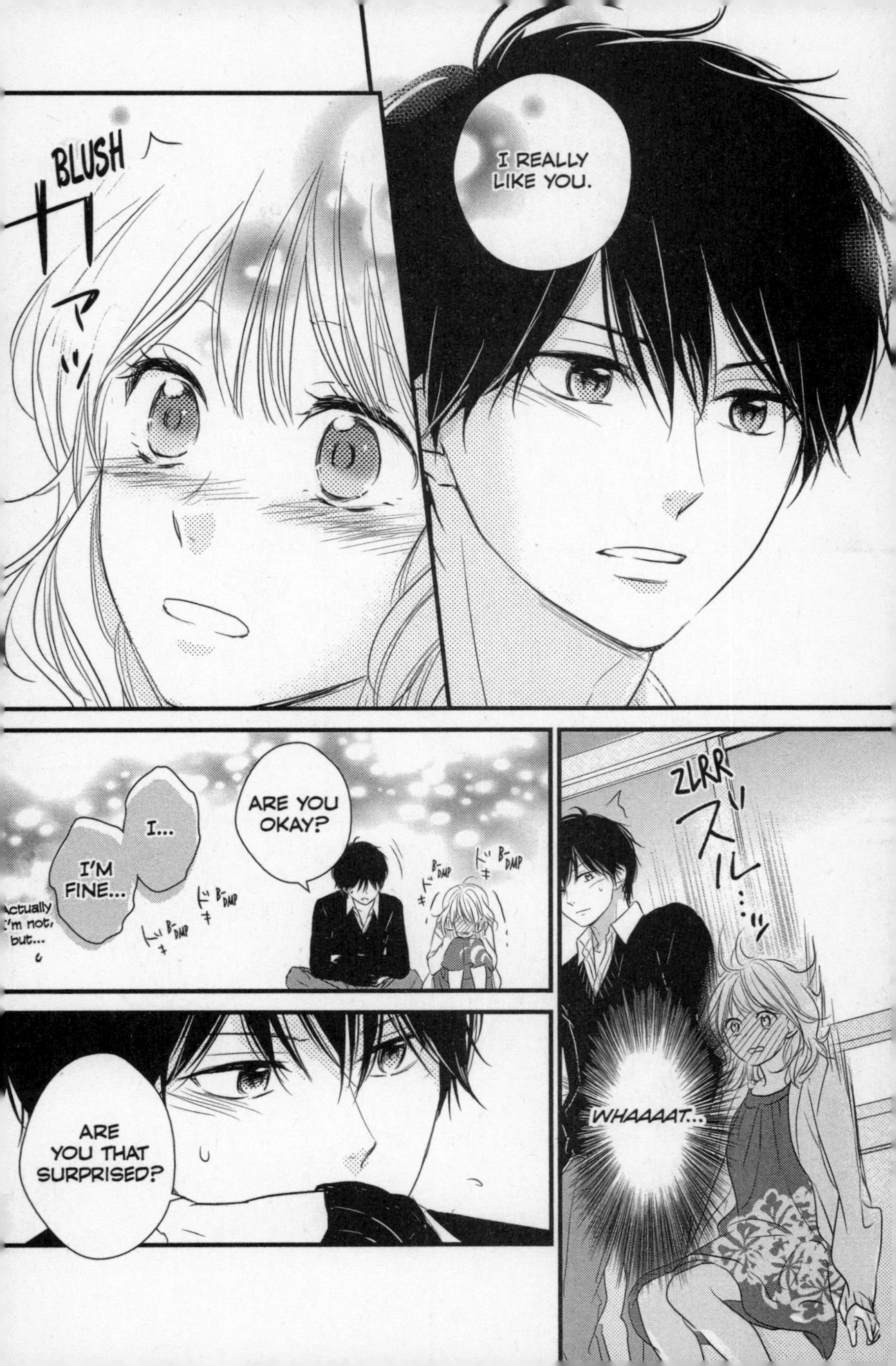
I REALLY LIKE YOU.
BLUSH
ZLRR
WHAAAAT...
ARE YOU OKAY?
I...
I'M FINE...
Actually I'm not, but...
B-DMP
B-DMP
B-DMP
B-DMP
ARE YOU THAT SURPRISED?

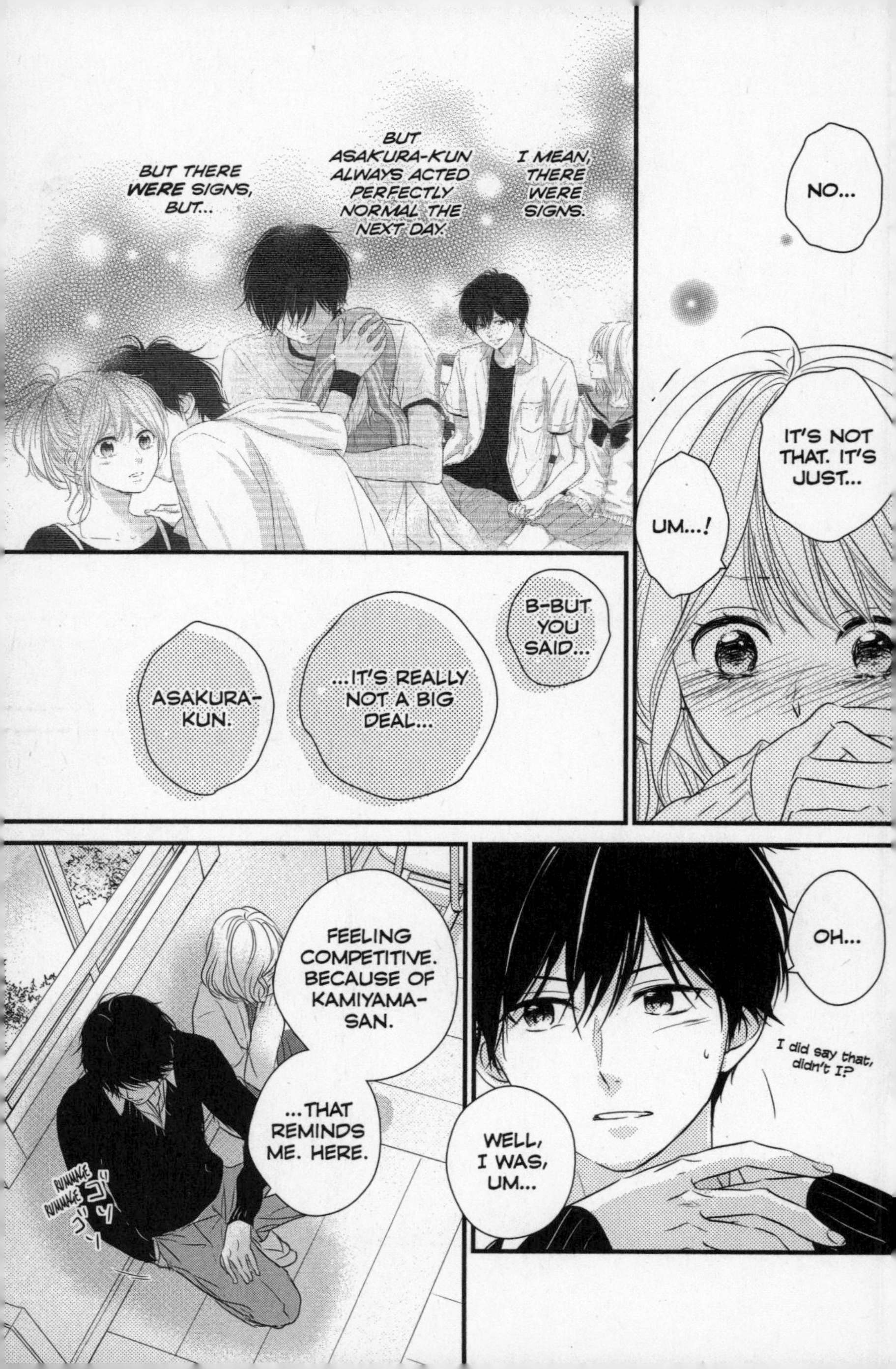
NO...
IT'S NOT THAT. IT'S JUST...
UM...!
I MEAN, THERE WERE SIGNS.
BUT ASAKURA-KUN ALWAYS ACTED PERFECTLY NORMAL THE NEXT DAY.
BUT THERE WERE SIGNS, BUT...
B-BUT YOU SAID...
...IT'S REALLY NOT A BIG DEAL...
ASAKURA-KUN.
OH...
I did say that, didn't I?
WELL, I WAS, UM...
FEELING COMPETITIVE. BECAUSE OF KAMIYAMA-SAN.
...THAT REMINDS ME. HERE.
RUMMAGE RUMMAGE

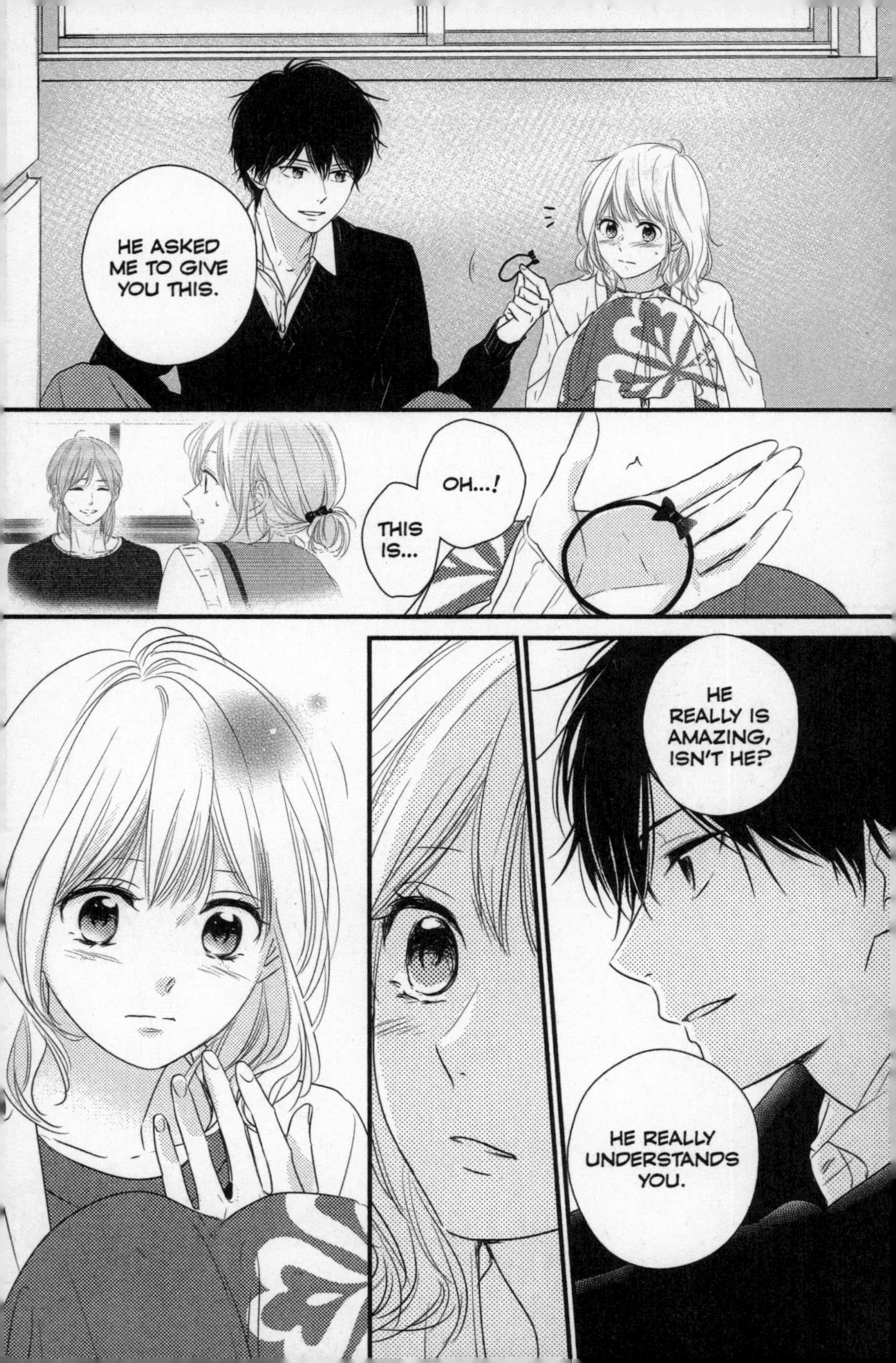
HE ASKED ME TO GIVE YOU THIS.
OH...!
THIS IS...
HE REALLY IS AMAZING, ISN'T HE?
HE REALLY UNDERSTANDS YOU.

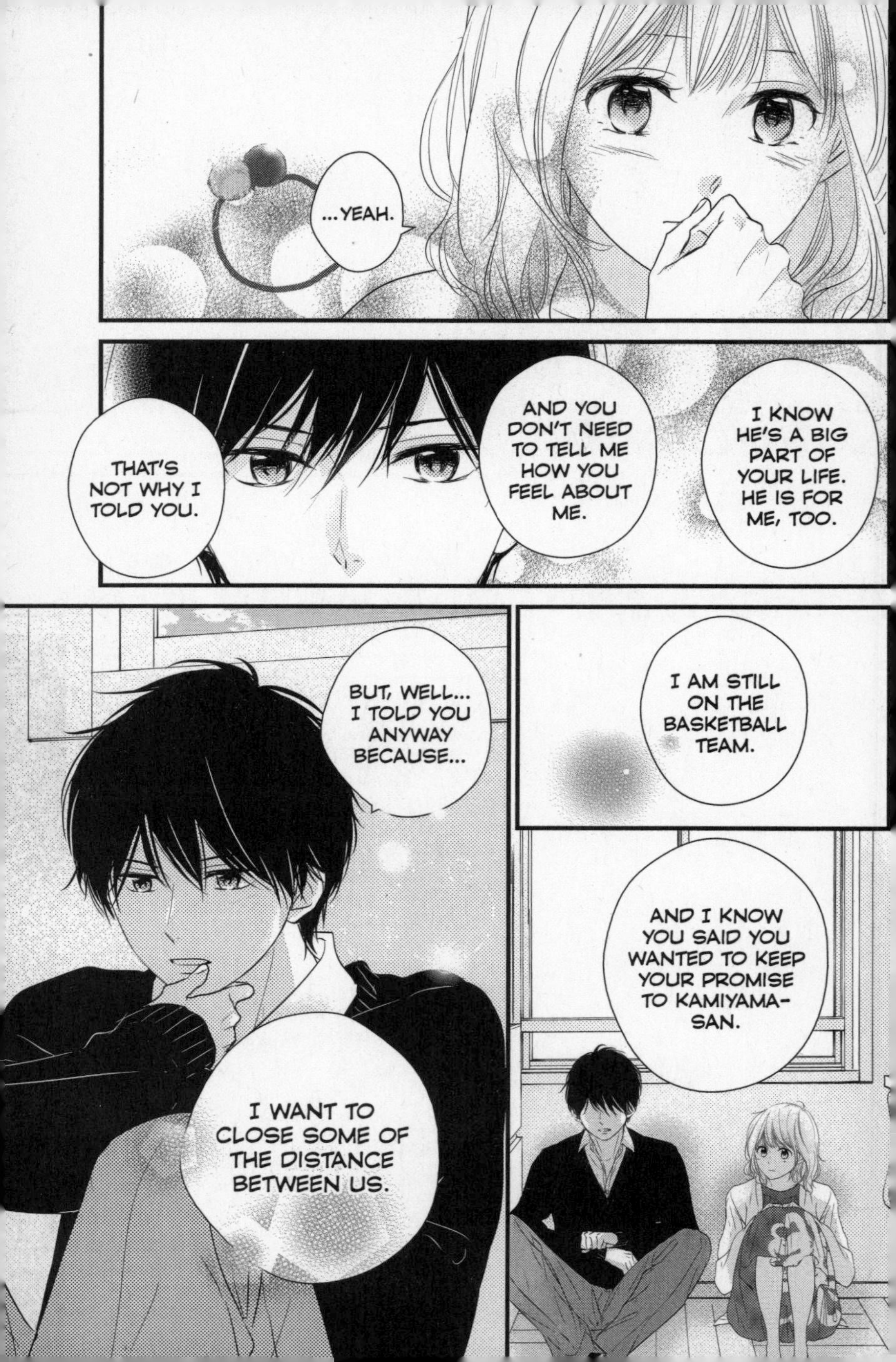

...YEAH.
I KNOW HE'S A BIG PART OF YOUR LIFE. HE IS FOR ME, TOO.
AND YOU DON'T NEED TO TELL ME HOW YOU FEEL ABOUT ME.
THAT'S NOT WHY I TOLD YOU.
I AM STILL ON THE BASKETBALL TEAM.
AND I KNOW YOU SAID YOU WANTED TO KEEP YOUR PROMISE TO KAMIYAMA-SAN.
BUT, WELL... I TOLD YOU ANYWAY BECAUSE...
I WANT TO CLOSE SOME OF THE DISTANCE BETWEEN US.

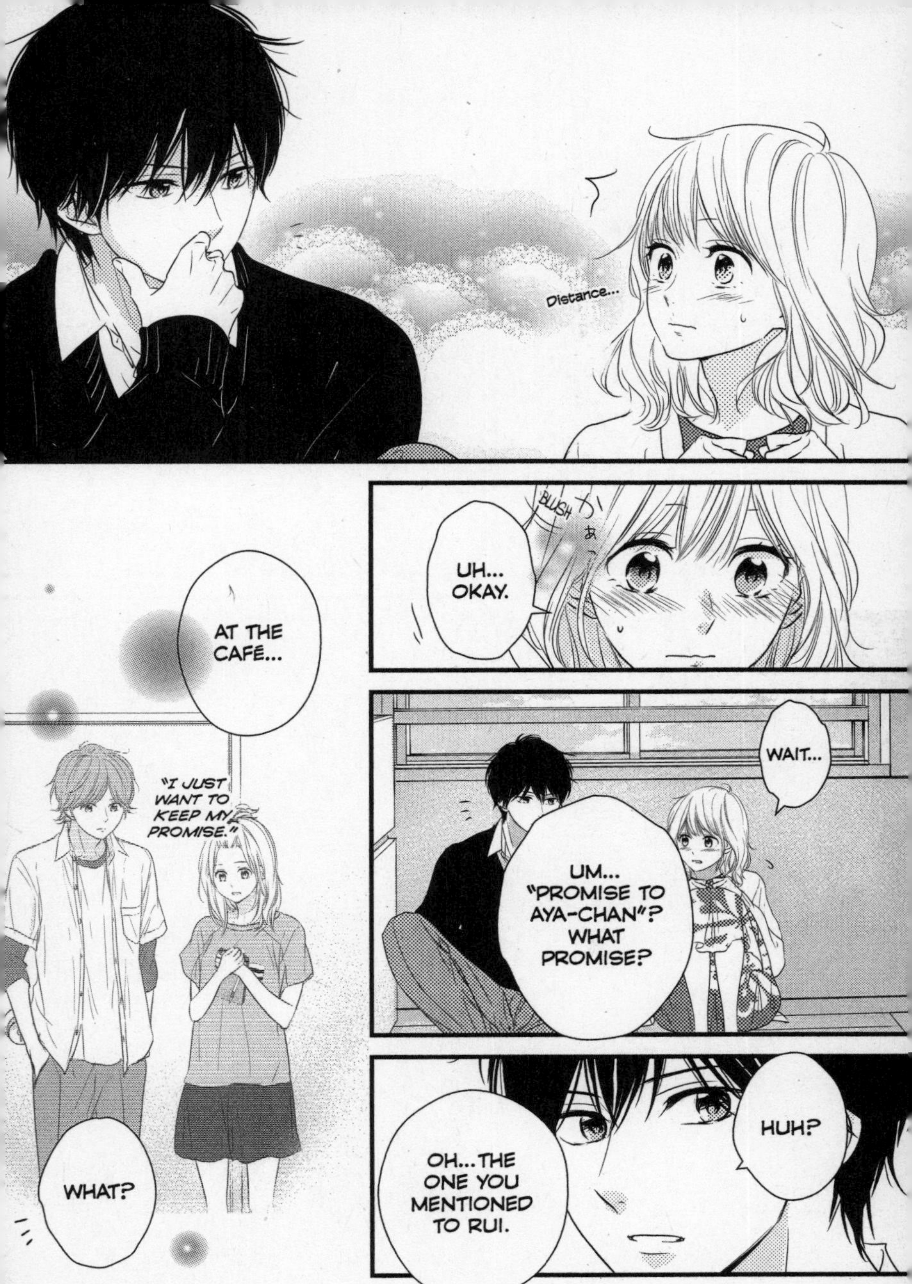
Distance...
BLUSH
UH... OKAY.
WAIT...
UM... "PROMISE TO AYA-CHAN"? WHAT PROMISE?
HUH?
OH...THE ONE YOU MENTIONED TO RUI.
AT THE CAFÉ...
"I JUST WANT TO KEEP MY PROMISE."
WHAT?

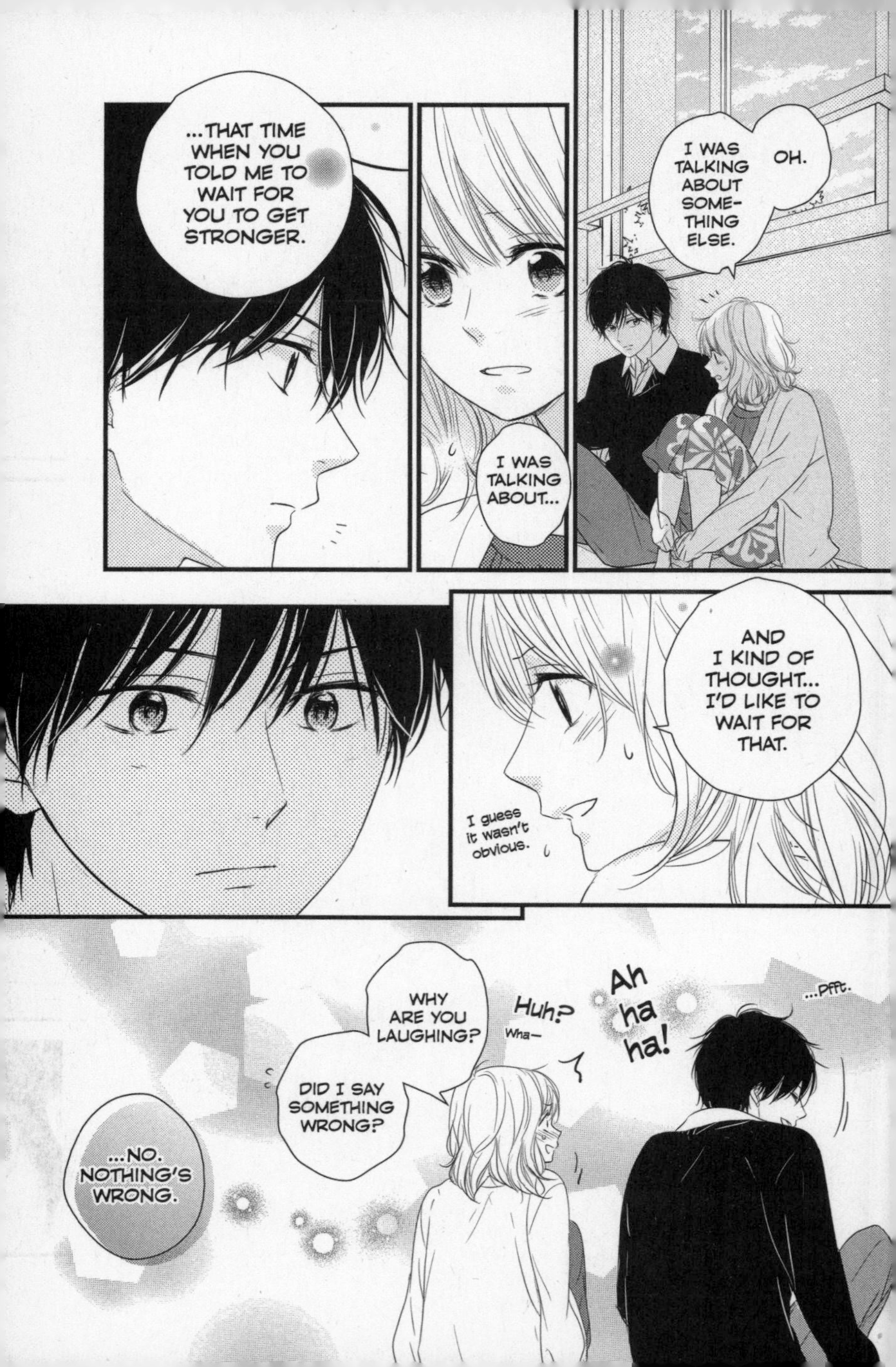
OH.
I WAS TALKING ABOUT SOMETHING ELSE.
I WAS TALKING ABOUT...
...THAT TIME WHEN YOU TOLD ME TO WAIT FOR YOU TO GET STRONGER.
AND I KIND OF THOUGHT... I'D LIKE TO WAIT FOR THAT.
I guess it wasn't obvious.
...Pfft.
Ah ha ha!
Huh?
Wha—
WHY ARE YOU LAUGHING?
DID I SAY SOMETHING WRONG?
...NO. NOTHING'S WRONG.

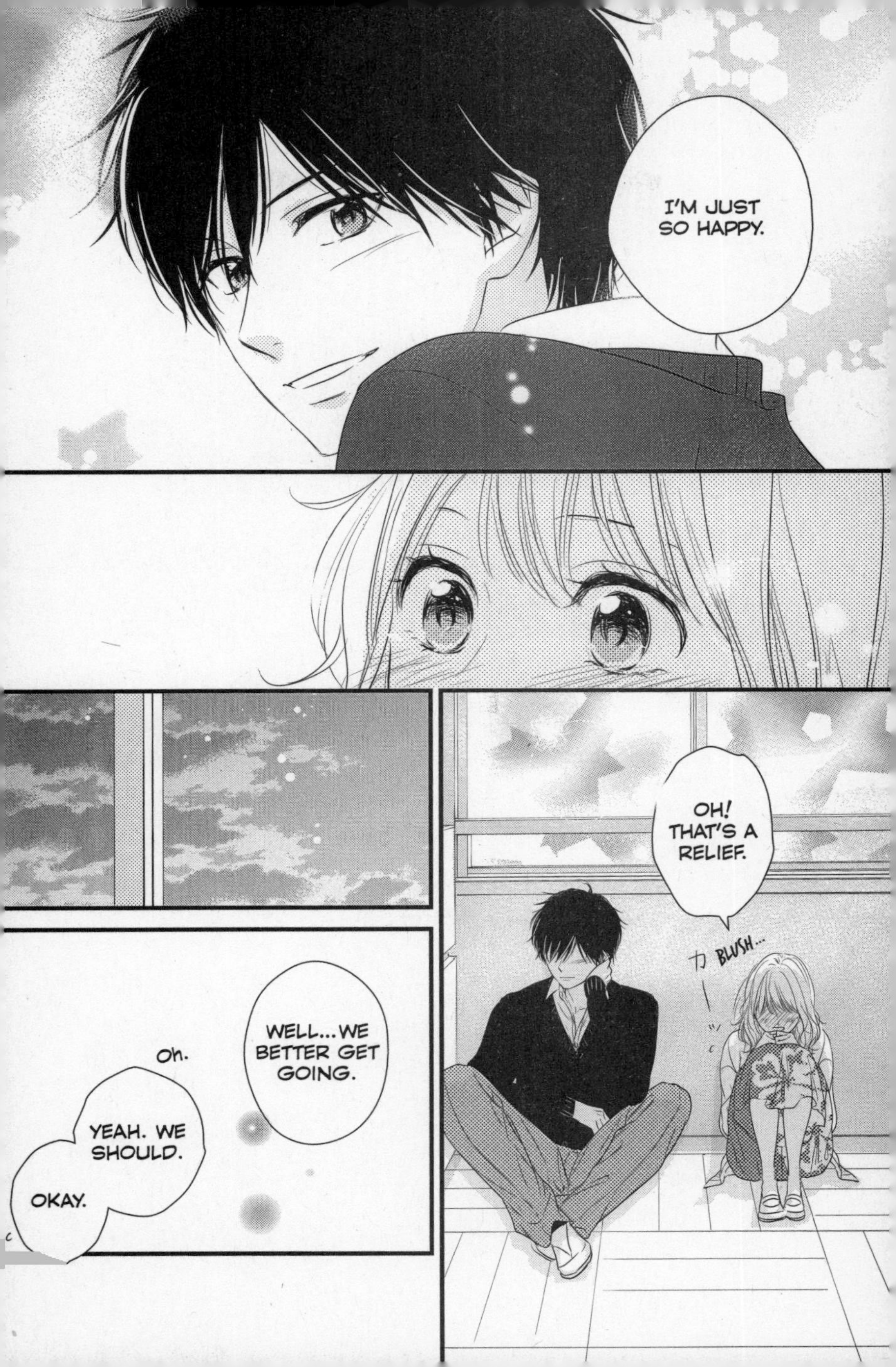
I'M JUST SO HAPPY.
OH! THAT'S A RELIEF.
BLUSH...
WELL...WE BETTER GET GOING.
Oh.
YEAH. WE SHOULD.
OKAY.

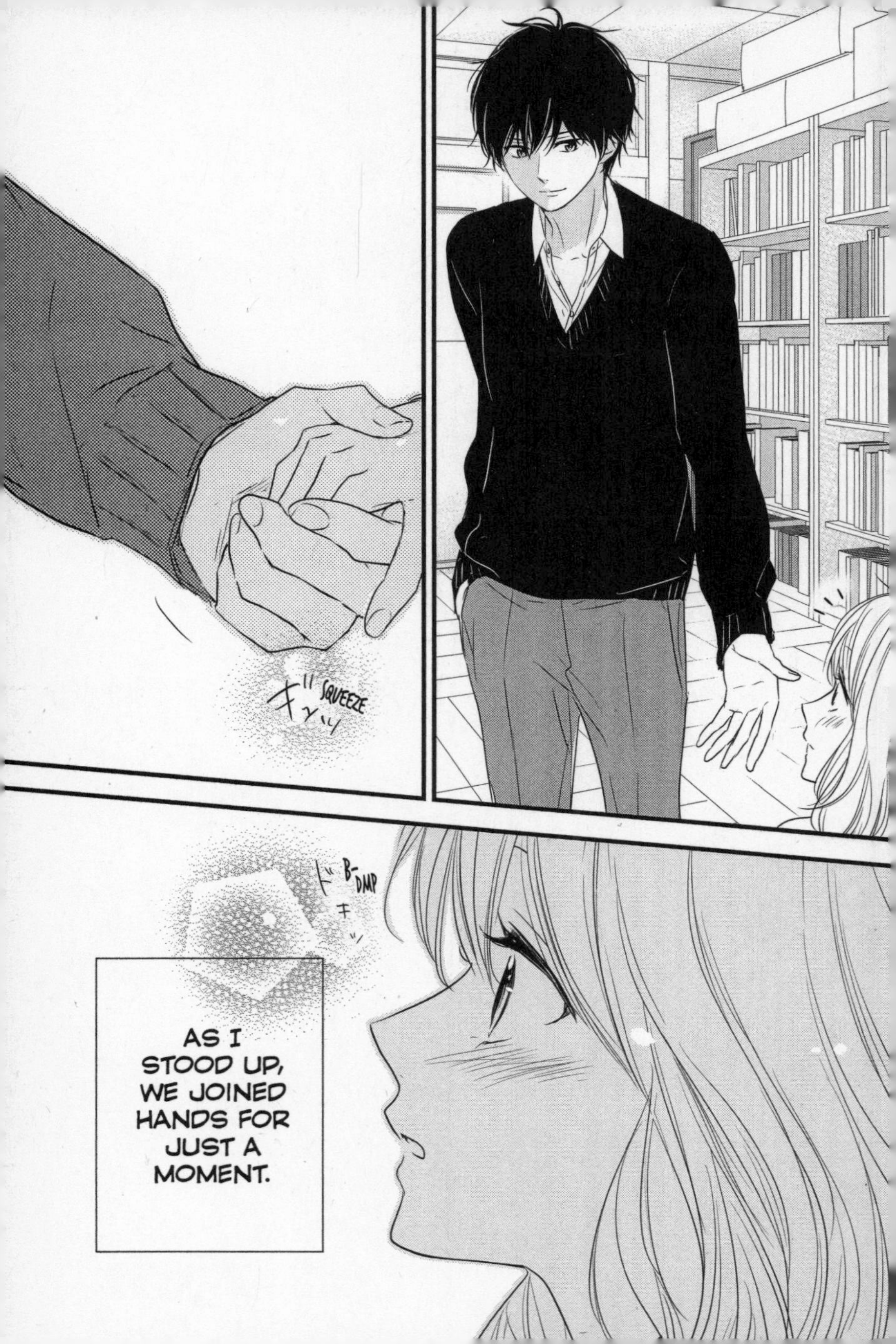
ギュッ SQUEEZE
ドキッ B-DMP
AS I STOOD UP, WE JOINED HANDS FOR JUST A MOMENT.

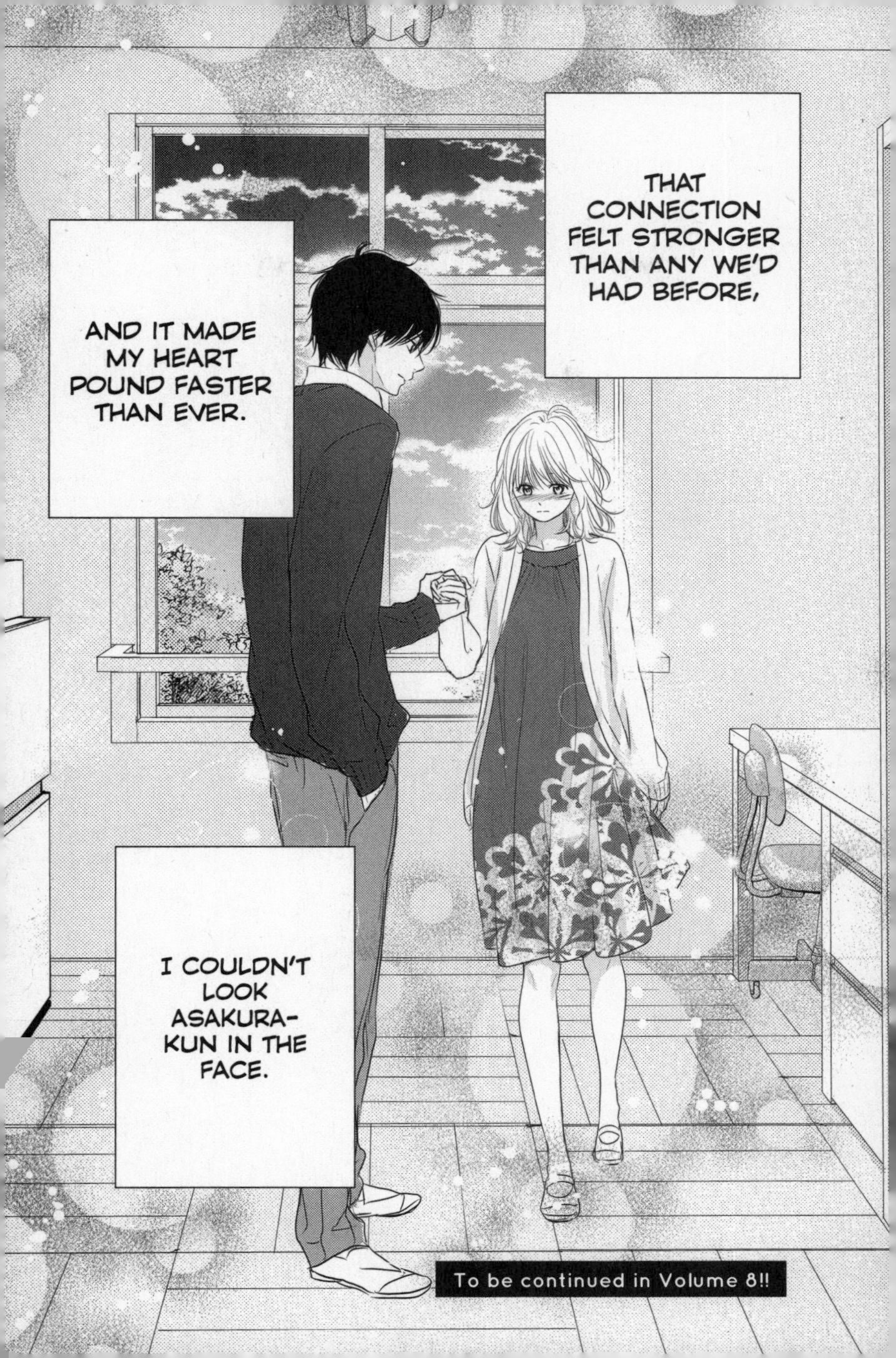
THAT CONNECTION FELT STRONGER THAN ANY WE'D HAD BEFORE,
AND IT MADE MY HEART POUND FASTER THAN EVER.
I COULDN'T LOOK ASAKURA-KUN IN THE FACE.
To be continued in Volume 8!!

Bonus Manga

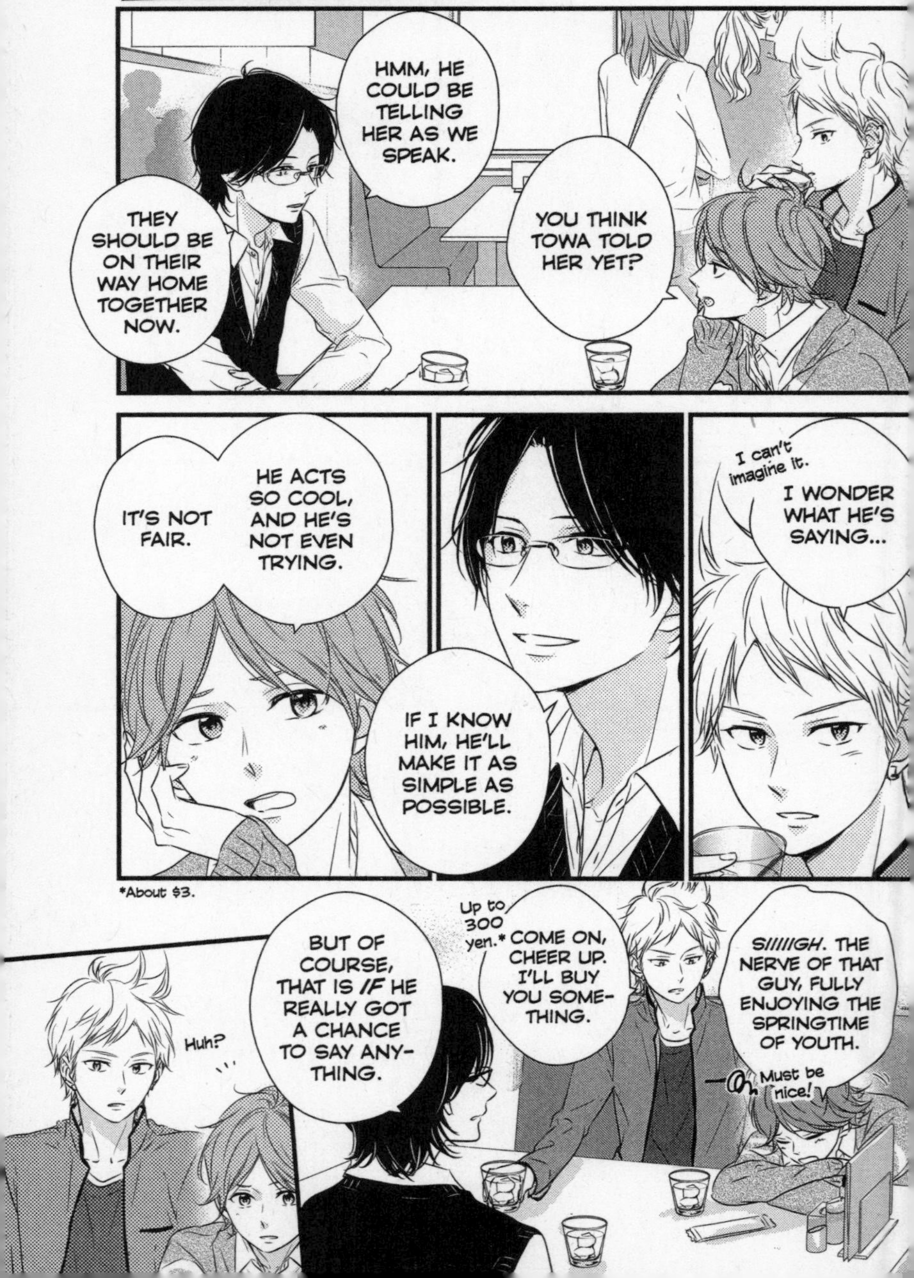
YOU THINK TOWA TOLD HER YET?
THEY SHOULD BE ON THEIR WAY HOME TOGETHER NOW.
HMM, HE COULD BE TELLING HER AS WE SPEAK.
I WONDER WHAT HE'S SAYING...
I can't imagine it.
IF I KNOW HIM, HE'LL MAKE IT AS SIMPLE AS POSSIBLE.
HE ACTS SO COOL, AND HE'S NOT EVEN TRYING.
IT'S NOT FAIR.
SIIIIGH. THE NERVE OF THAT GUY, FULLY ENJOYING THE SPRINGTIME OF YOUTH.
Must be nice!
COME ON, CHEER UP. I'LL BUY YOU SOME-THING.
Up to 300 yen.*
BUT OF COURSE, THAT IS *IF* HE REALLY GOT A CHANCE TO SAY ANY-THING.
Huh?

*About $3.

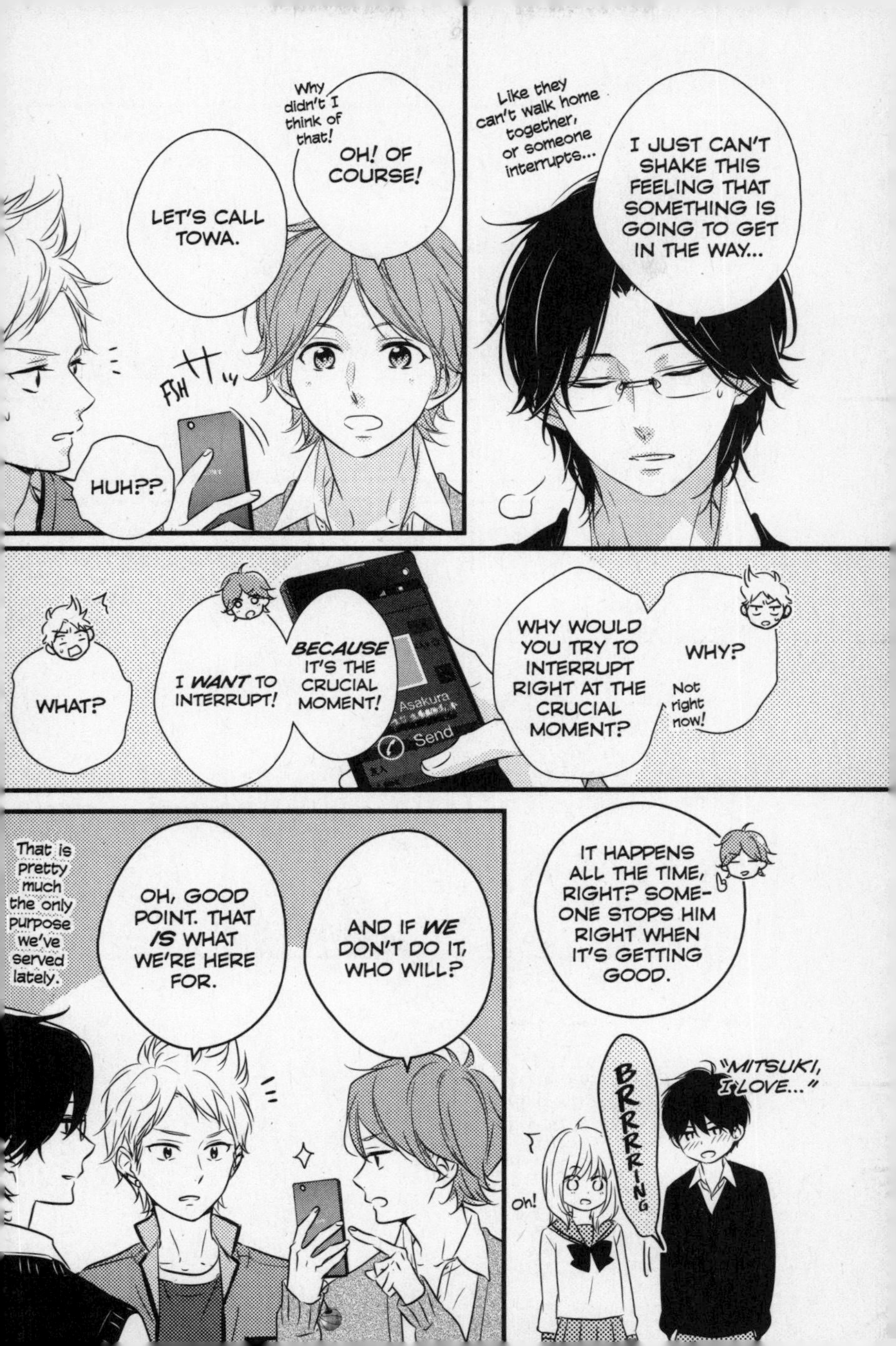
Like they can't walk home together, or someone interrupts...
I JUST CAN'T SHAKE THIS FEELING THAT SOMETHING IS GOING TO GET IN THE WAY...
Why didn't I think of that!
OH! OF COURSE!
LET'S CALL TOWA.
FSH
HUH??
WHY?
Not right now!
WHY WOULD YOU TRY TO INTERRUPT RIGHT AT THE CRUCIAL MOMENT?
Asakura
Send
BECAUSE IT'S THE CRUCIAL MOMENT!
I *WANT* TO INTERRUPT!
WHAT?
IT HAPPENS ALL THE TIME, RIGHT? SOME-ONE STOPS HIM RIGHT WHEN IT'S GETTING GOOD.
"MITSUKI, I LOVE..."
BRRRRING
Oh!
AND IF *WE* DON'T DO IT, WHO WILL?
OH, GOOD POINT. THAT *IS* WHAT WE'RE HERE FOR.
That is pretty much the only purpose we've served lately.

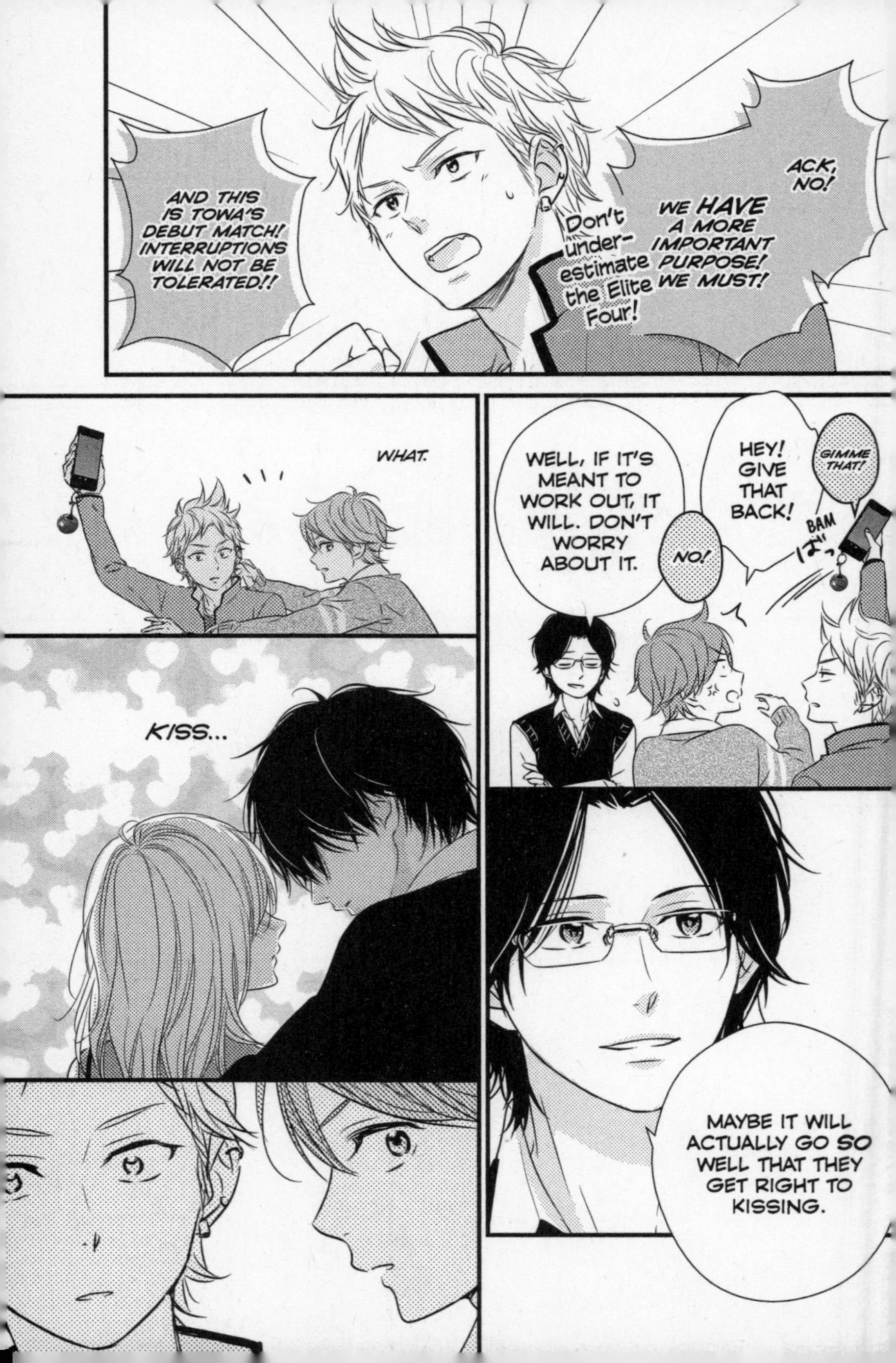

ACK, NO!
WE HAVE A MORE IMPORTANT PURPOSE! WE MUST!
Don't underestimate the Elite Four!
AND THIS IS TOWA'S DEBUT MATCH! INTERRUPTIONS WILL NOT BE TOLERATED!!
GIMME THAT!
BAM
ばっ
HEY! GIVE THAT BACK!
NO!
WELL, IF IT'S MEANT TO WORK OUT, IT WILL. DON'T WORRY ABOUT IT.
MAYBE IT WILL ACTUALLY GO SO WELL THAT THEY GET RIGHT TO KISSING.
WHAT.
KISS...

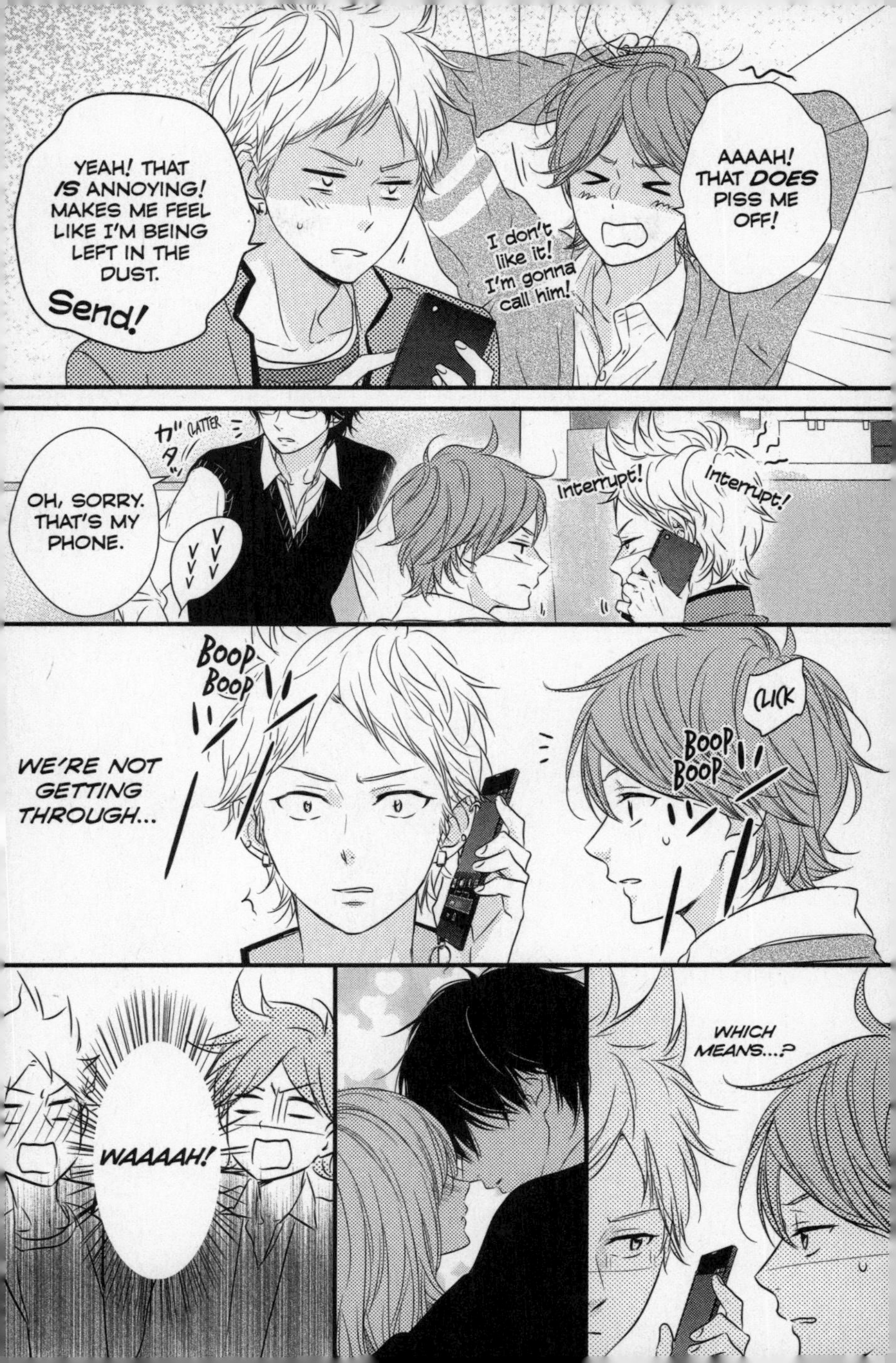
AAAAH! THAT DOES PISS ME OFF!
I don't like it! I'm gonna call him!
YEAH! THAT IS ANNOYING! MAKES ME FEEL LIKE I'M BEING LEFT IN THE DUST.
Send!
Interrupt!
Interrupt!
ガタ
CLATTER
OH, SORRY. THAT'S MY PHONE.
CLICK
BOOP BOOP
BOOP BOOP
WE'RE NOT GETTING THROUGH...
WHICH MEANS...?
WAAAAH!

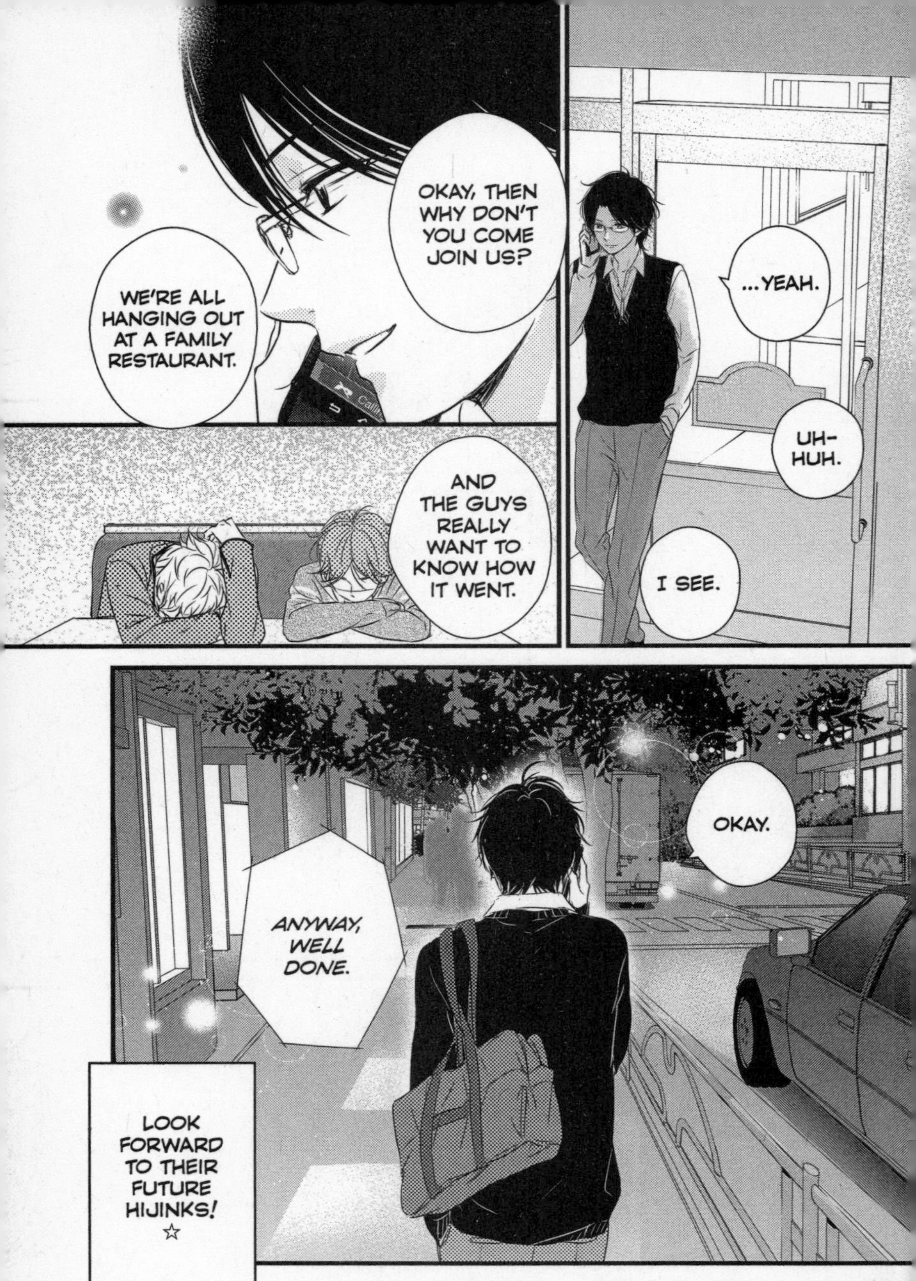
...YEAH.
UH-HUH.
I SEE.
OKAY, THEN WHY DON'T YOU COME JOIN US?
WE'RE ALL HANGING OUT AT A FAMILY RESTAURANT.
AND THE GUYS REALLY WANT TO KNOW HOW IT WENT.
OKAY.
ANYWAY, WELL DONE.
LOOK FORWARD TO THEIR FUTURE HIJINKS! ☆

Please check out Volume 8, too!

Because she borrowed a hoodie from Asakura-kun in Chapter 27

I MADE SURE TO WASH IT.
I USED MY FAVORITE FABRIC SOFTENER ♪
THANK YOU, ASAKURA-KUN.
OH, IT SMELLS NICE.
Eh heh heh ♪
I fell asleep!
GASP! IT WAS A DREAM?!
Asakura-kun's sweatshirt!
I HAVE TO BRING IN THE LAUNDRY!
HUH?! MOM! WHERE'S THE DRY LAUNDRY?!
The hoodie is gone!
I TOOK IT IN AGES AGO!
I'M OFF FOR MY JOG!
RIGHT HERE.

I'M HOME!
D...!
DAD...!
?
THAT'S ONĒ-CHAN'S FRIEND'S HOODIE...
WHAT.

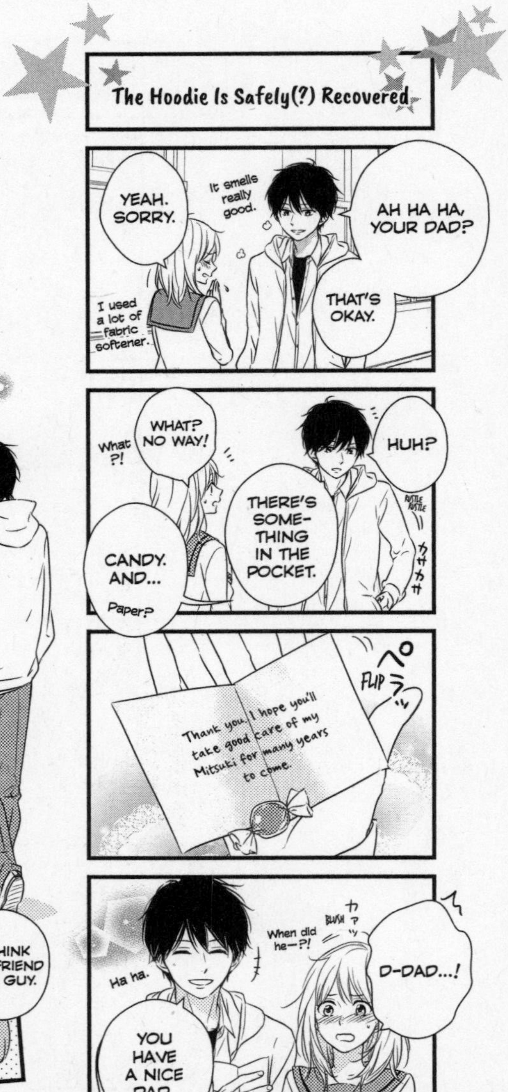
The Hoodie Is Safely(?) Recovered
AH HA HA, YOUR DAD?
It smells really good.
YEAH. SORRY.
THAT'S OKAY.
I used a lot of fabric softener.
HUH?
RUSTLE RUSTLE
カサカサ
WHAT? NO WAY!
What?!
THERE'S SOME-THING IN THE POCKET.
CANDY. AND...
Paper?
ペラッ
FLIP
Thank you. I hope you'll take good care of my Mitsuki for many years to come.
D-DAD...!
カァッ
BLUSH
When did he—?!
Ha ha.
YOU HAVE A NICE DAD.

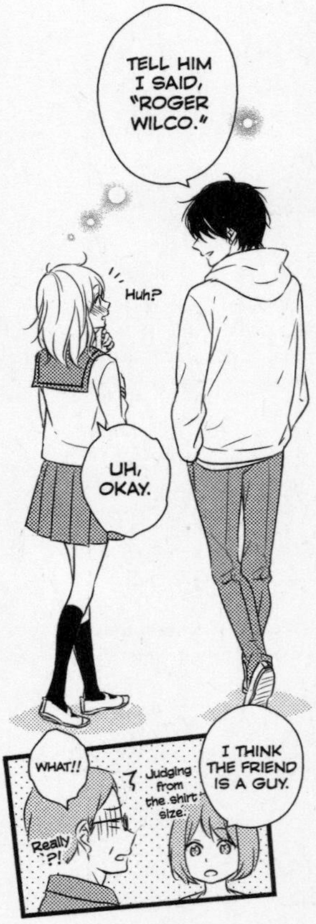
TELL HIM I SAID, "ROGER WILCO."
Huh?
UH, OKAY.
I THINK THE FRIEND IS A GUY.
Judging from the shirt size.
WHAT!!
Really?!

To be continued in Volume 8!!

Translation Notes

Ennichi party, page 50

An *ennichi*, or "related day," is a day that is related to a Buddhist or Shinto deity, sort of how saints are honored on certain days in Christian traditions. On these days, people often visit the Buddhist temple or Shinto shrine related to the deity whose day it is, where there will often be a celebratory festival. In that vein, this class is holding a festival within a school festival, including traditional festival games.

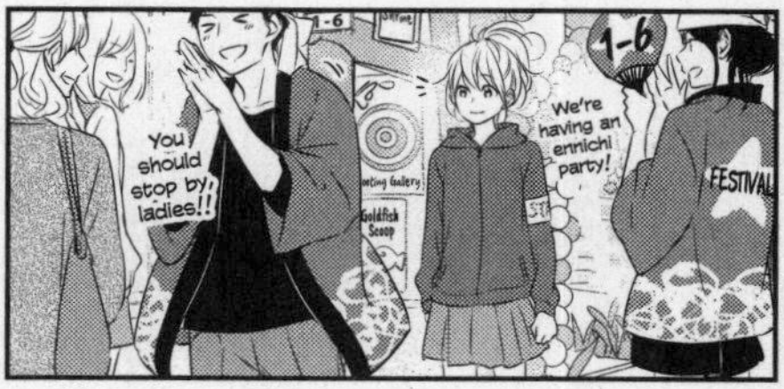
1-6
We're having an ennichi party!
FESTIVAL
Goldfish Scoop
You should stop by, ladies!!
1-6

New team tournament, page 71

Specifically, the tournament played with the new team. Now that the big summer tournaments are over, the third-years have retired from the team, and the *shinjinsen*, literally "new person contest," will be played by a team of only first- and second-years.

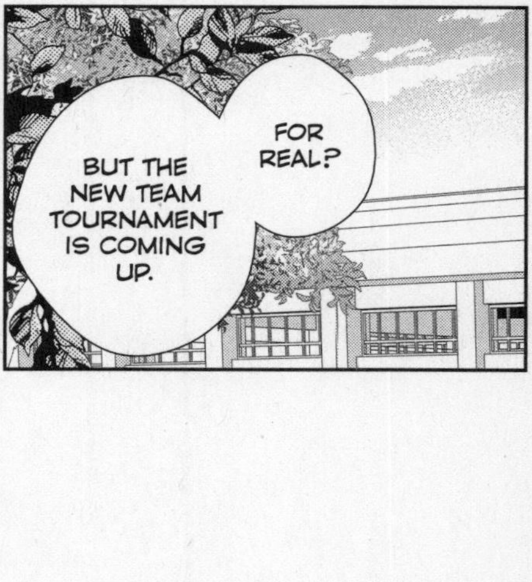
FOR REAL?
BUT THE NEW TEAM TOURNAMENT IS COMING UP.

Waiting for Spring

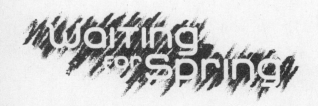

Aho-Girl
\'ahô,g rl\ *Japanese, noun.*
A clueless girl.
KC KODANSHA COMICS
Anime now available on Crunchyroll!
Fans of anarchic slice-of-life gag manga like *Azumanga Daioh* – these are the new laughs you've been waiting for!
Yoshiko Hanabatake is just your average teenage girl. She hangs out. She goes to school. She doesn't like studying. She's got the usual ambitions - win the lottery, play around all day, and never have any responsibilities. And she likes bananas. She really, really likes bananas. Okay, maybe she's not average. Maybe she's below average. Way below average. Fortunately, Yoshiko can rely on her old friend Akkun to keep her in line. Assuming he doesn't strangle her first.
AHO-GIRL
© Hiroyuki/Kodansha, Ltd. All rights reserved.

FAIRY TAIL S

For the members of Fairy Tail, a guild member's work is never done. While they may not always be away on missions, that doesn't mean our magic-wielding heroes can rest easy at home. What happens when a copycat thief begins to soil the good name of Fairy Tail, or when a seemingly unstoppable virus threatens the citizens of Magnolia? And when a bet after the Grand Magic Games goes sour, can Natsu, Lucy, Gray, and Erza turn the tables in their favor? Come see what a "day in the life" of the strongest guild in Fiore is like in nine brand new short stories!

KC
KODANSHA COMICS

A collection of *Fairy Tail* short stories drawn by original creator Hiro Mashima!

KC
KODANSHA
COMICS

In love, there are
no save points.

NOW AN ANIME!

ヲタクに恋は難しい

WOTAKOI:
LOVE IS HARD FOR OTAKU
by FUJITA

Narumi has had it rough: Every boyfriend she's had dumped her
once they found out she was an otaku, so she's gone to great
lengths to hide it. At her new job, she bumps into Hirotaka, her
childhood friend and fellow otaku. When Hirotaka almost gets
her secret outed at work, she comes up with a plan to keep him
quiet. But he comes up with a counter-proposal:
Why doesn't she just date him instead?

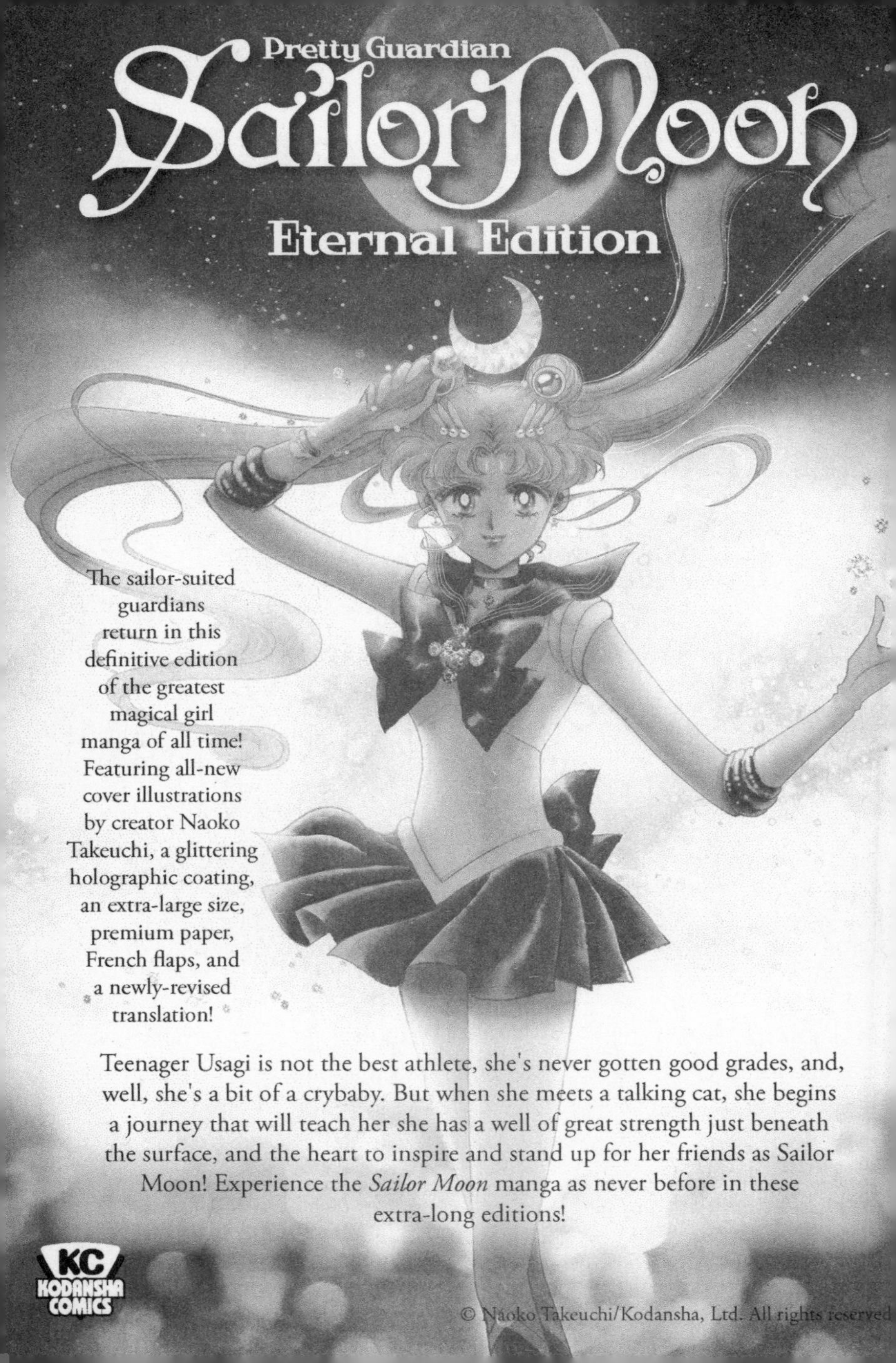
Pretty Guardian
Sailor Moon
Eternal Edition
The sailor-suited guardians return in this definitive edition of the greatest magical girl manga of all time! Featuring all-new cover illustrations by creator Naoko Takeuchi, a glittering holographic coating, an extra-large size, premium paper, French flaps, and a newly-revised translation!
Teenager Usagi is not the best athlete, she's never gotten good grades, and, well, she's a bit of a crybaby. But when she meets a talking cat, she begins a journey that will teach her she has a well of great strength just beneath the surface, and the heart to inspire and stand up for her friends as Sailor Moon! Experience the *Sailor Moon* manga as never before in these extra-long editions!
KC KODANSHA COMICS
© Naoko Takeuchi/Kodansha, Ltd. All rights reserved

A Kodansha Comics Trade Paperback Original
Waiting for Spring volume 7 copyright © 2017 Anashin
English translation copyright © 2018 Anashin

All rights reserved.

Published in the United States by Kodansha Comics, an imprint of Kodansha USA Publishing, LLC, New York.

Publication rights for this English edition arranged through Kodansha Ltd, Tokyo.

ISBN 978-1-63236-631-3

Printed in the United States of America.

www.kodanshacomics.com

9 8 7 6 5 4 3 2 1
Translation: Alethea and Athena Nibley
Lettering: Sara Linsley
Editing: Haruko Hashimoto
Kodansha Comics edition cover design by Phil Balsman